Can We Live Together?

For Simonetta

A book we have lived through together

Can We Live Together?

Equality and Difference

Alain Touraine

Translated by David Macey

Stanford University Press
Stanford, California

Stanford University Press
Stanford, California

This translation © Polity Press 2000

First published in France as *Pourrons-nous vivre
ensemble? Egaux et Differents*
© Librarie Arthème Fayard, 1997.

Originating publisher of English edition: Polity Press
in association with Blackwell Publishers Ltd.

First Published in the U.S.A. by Stanford University
Press, 2000

Published with the assistance of the French Ministry
of Culture.

Printed in Great Britain

Cloth ISBN 0–8047–4042–9
Paper ISBN 0–8047–4043–7

The Library of Congress Card Number. 99–69761

This book is printed on acid-free paper.

Contents

Translator's Note

Although every attempt has been made to avoid sexist usage in this translation, both the historical context and French usage mean that masculine forms are, on occasion, used here in their so-called 'universalist' sense. The French adjective *identitaire*, which is a neologism pertaining to the concept of 'identity politics', has been rendered quite literally as 'identitarian', partly to avoid cumbersome paraphrase and partly to retain the parallel with 'communitarian' (*communitaire*). For the sake of completeness, a number of references that do not feature in the original have been added to the bibliographical references.

DAVID MACEY

Acknowledgements

This book could not have been completed without Jacqueline Blayac, who produced the manuscript and whose intelligence and generosity were a constant source of help to me. It is a product of the collective work carried out at the Centre d'Analyse et d'Intervention Sociologiques, where Michel Wieviorka, François Dubet and all the research workers and their colla- borators constantly provide a stimulating working environment.

Like many of my earlier books, *Can We Live Together?* draws on the many seminars and lectures I have given, mainly in Latin America, Spain and Italy. My thanks are due to all those who were kind enough to help me develop my ideas, and especially to Manuel Antonion Garréton (Director of the University of Chile's Department of Sociology) and Ricardo Pozas Horcasitas (Director of the Institute for Sociological Research, UNAM, Mexico). This book is above all a product of the seminar I taught at the École des Hautes Études en Sciences Sociales between 1993 and 1996, which took the form of a dialogue with students from many different countries. I hope that my interlocutors will find in it a record of our exchanges.

Introduction

Like capital and commodities, information crosses frontiers. What was once far away comes closer, and the past becomes the present. Development no longer means the series of stages whereby a society emerges from underdevelopment, and modernity is no longer something that succeeds tradition. Everything merges into one; space and time have been compressed. In vast areas of the world, the social and cultural controls established by states, churches, families and schools are being relaxed, and the boundary between the normal and the pathological, the permitted and the forbidden, is becoming blurred. Don't we all live in a globalized world society that is invading on all sides the private and public lives of the majority? The answer to the question 'Can we live together?' seems at first sight to be simple, and formulated in the present tense: 'We already live together.' Billions of individuals watch the same television programmes, drink the same drinks, wear the same clothes, and even use the same language to communicate from one country to another. We are seeing the formation of a world public opinion that takes part in huge international meetings in Rio and Beijing and is worried, on all continents, about global warming, the effects of nuclear tests or the spread of AIDS.

Does this mean that we can say that we belong to the same society or the same culture? Certainly not. The defining characteristic of globalized elements, be they consumer goods, means of communication, technologies or financial flows, is that they have become detached from any particular social organization. Globalization means that technologies, instruments and messages are present everywhere, or in other words that they belong nowhere. They are not bound up with any one society or culture, as we can see from the ever-popular images that juxtapose petrol pumps and camels, Coca-Cola and villages in the Andes, jeans and royal palaces. The divorce between networks and collectivities, the indifference of the signs of modernity to the slow work of socialization that was once undertaken by families and schools – or in a word, the desocialization of mass culture – means that we live together only to the extent that we make the same gestures and use the same objects, but that we cannot communicate with one another except by exchanging the signs of modernity. Our culture is no longer in control of our social organization, and our social organization is no longer in control of technological and economic activity. Culture and the economy have become divorced from one another, as have the instrumental world and the symbolic world.

Our small societies are not gradually merging into one vast global society. The simultaneously political, territorial and cultural entities that we once called societies, civilizations or simply countries are breaking up before our very eyes. We can see the growing divorce between, on the one hand, the objective universe of the signs of globalization and, on the other hand, sets of values, cultural expressions and sites of memory which no longer make up societies, both because their instrumental activity has been taken away from them and globalized, and because they are becoming inward-looking and prioritize values rather than technologies, traditions rather than innovations.

At the end of the nineteenth century, when the industrialization of the Western world was in full flow, sociologists taught us that we were moving away from a community trapped in its overall identity, and towards a society whose functions were becoming differentiated and rationalized. But the evolution we are living through is almost the opposite of that process. What is emerging from the ruins of modern societies and their institutions is, on the one hand, global networks of production, consumption and communication and, on the other hand, a return to community. Once we saw the extension of the public and political space; that space is now breaking up under the contradictory effects of the trend towards privatization and the process of globalization.

It is true, in a sense, that we do live together at a planetary level, but it is also true that throughout the world there are more and more identity-based groupings and associations, sects, cults and nationalisms based on a common sense of belonging, and that they are becoming stronger. Societies are becoming communities once more as they closely unify a culture, politics and power within territories governed by religious, cultural, ethnic or political authorities that might be called charismatic, in that they derive their legitimacy not from the sovereignty of the people, economic efficiency or even military conquest, but from the gods, myths or traditions of a community. When we are all together, we have almost nothing in common, and when we do share beliefs and a history, we reject those who are different from us.

We can live together only if we lose our identity. Conversely, the return of communities brings with it a call for homogeneity, purity and unity. Communication gives way to a war between those who make sacrifices to different gods, who appeal to mutually alien or antagonistic traditions, and who in some cases even regard themselves as biologically different and superior to others. The eminently seductive idea of the global melting pot that will make us citizens of one world merits neither the enthusiasm nor the imprecations it often inspires. It is so far removed fom observable reality, even in the United States, as to be nothing more than the soft ideology of the promoters of global spectacles.

Those who speak of American or Western imperialism rather than of globalization are making the same mistake as the moralizing optimists. The dissociation of global networks and introverted communities is greater in American society than in most others. Whilst many global networks are based in Los Angeles, that urban zone is neither a city nor a society, but a series of ghettoes or communities which are foreign to one another and intersected by freeways. The same is true of New York, even though that city still displays the forms of urban life that past civilizations created on every continent, and especially in Europe. Because the imaginary conveyed by mass communications is increasingly American in origin, part of us is becoming Americanized. In the future, part of us might become Japanese or Brazilian, and that might happen more easily, in that these images are not transformed into models for behaviour or into motivations. When a message is transmitted by mass media and without social relays, it does little to modify behaviour. Those who live in the slums of Calcutta or remote villages in Bolivia's Altoplano have very little in common with the Hollywood films they watch. It is not the accelerated mutation of forms of behaviour that we should be looking at, but the growing fragmentation of the experience of individuals who belong simultaneously to several continents and several societies. The ego has lost its unity. It has become multiple.

How can we live together when our world is divided into at least two continents that are drifting further and further apart: a continent of communities that are defending themselves against individuals, ideas and customs that penetrate them from without, and a continent in which the corollary of globalization is a relaxation of controls on individual and collective behaviour?

Some will say that it has always been like this, and that all societies have always made a distinction between the street and the house, as they say in Brazil, or between public and private life. The classical idea of secularism both separated and reconciled a public space that had to be ruled by the law of the father and by reason and a private space where the authority of mothers, tradition and belief could still prevail. That complementarity, however, was based upon the limited extension of public life, the preservation of local ways of life, and a social hierarchy that made public life the preserve of higher categories. These have all disappeared. Mass culture is penetrating private space and occupying more and more of it. It has the side-effect of strengthening the political and social desire to defend a cultural identity, and the end result is a new communitarianism. The desocialization of mass culture does plunge us into globalization, but it also drives us to defend our identity by turning to primary groups for support and by re-privatizing part, and sometimes all, of public life. We therefore both take part in completely extroverted activities, and inscribe our lives within a community that forces us to obey its commandments. The sophisticated equilibrium we established between law and custom, reason and belief, is collapsing, as are our nation-states, which are being invaded by mass culture, on the one hand, and fragmented by the return of communities, on the other. Those of us who have long been accustomed to living in diversified, tolerant societies in which personal freedoms are safeguarded by the law are more attracted to mass society than to communities, which are always authoritarian. But communities are returning in force in our societies too, and those we euphemistically call 'minorities' are now beginning to assert their identity and loosen their ties with the rest of society.

We are caught in a dilemma. We can grant minorities and communities their full independence and simply ensure that everyone respects the rules of the game and the procedures that safeguard the peaceful coexistence of interests, opinions and beliefs. But if we do so, we automatically break off mutual communications, because we no longer recognize that we have anything in common except a refusal to prohibit the freedom of others and a common involvement in instrumental activities. The alternative is to believe that we do have common values – moral in the American view, political in the French – and therefore reject those who do not share them, especially if we give those values a universal import. Either we live together, and communicate only in impersonal terms and with technical signals, or we communicate only within communities that are all the more introverted in that they feel threatened by what they see as an alien mass culture. We lived with the same contradiction from the beginnings of large-scale industrialization in the late nineteenth century to the First World War. The dominance of finance capital and colonization led to the rise of communitarian nationalisms both in industrial countries like Germany, Japan and France and in dominated countries where anti-imperialist revolutions often led to totalitarian communitarianisms in the twentieth century.

Are we already reliving the history of the breakup of national societies, and will it benefit international markets, on the one hand, and aggressive nationalisms, on the other? This break between the instrumental world and the symbolic world, between technology and values, runs through the whole of our experience, from individual life to the world situation. We are at once here and everywhere, or in other words nowhere. The links that a local or national society once established through institutions, language and education, between our memory and our impersonal involvement in productive society, have been weakened. We have been left to manage two separate realms of experience, but we have no mediations or safeguards. We therefore all find it increasingly difficult to define our personalities, which have indeed suffered an irremediable loss of unity because they have ceased to be coherent sets of social roles. We often find this so difficult that we can no longer stand it, and try to escape from egos that have become too fragile or too fragmented by taking flight, destroying ourselves or plunging into an exhausting whirl of diversion.

What we once called politics, or the management of the affairs of the city or the nation, is, like the individual ego, in a state of decay. Governing a country today means primarily making its economic and social organization compatible with the demands of the international economic system. At the same time, social norms are becoming weaker, and institutions more modest, which leaves more room for private life and voluntary organizations. How can we go on speaking of citizenship and representative democracy at a time when our elected representatives look to the international market and voters to their private lives? The only things that now exist in the space between the two are increasingly conservative appeals to values and institutions that cannot keep pace with our practices.

The media play an increasingly important role in our lives, and television takes pride of place, because it establishes very direct links between our most intimate lived experience and reality at its most globalized, and between our emotions at seeing the sufferings or joys of a human being and the most advanced scientific and military technologies. That direct link eliminates the mediations between the individual and humanity, and, because the messages are decontextualized, it may play an active role in the general trend towards desocialization. The emotion that we all feel when we see images of war, sport or humanitarian action is not transformed into motivations, and does not make us take a stand. As viewers, we are no more involved when we watch the tragedies of the world than when we watch violence in the cinema or on television. Part of us is immersed in world culture, but, because there is no longer a public space where social norms could be formed and applied, another part of us either retreats into hedonism or looks for a sense of belonging that is more immediate. We live together, but we simultaneously merge with one another and remain apart, as in David Riesman's 'lonely crowd', and we become less and less capable of communicating. We are, on the one hand, world citizens who have neither responsibilities, rights nor duties and, on the other, defenders of a private space that has been flooded by waves of world culture. Both individuals and groups are therefore less and less defined by the social relations which until now defined the field of sociology, whose goal was to explain behaviour in terms of the social relations in which actors were involved.

Until very recently, we tried to understand a society by understanding its social relations of production, its conflicts and its negotiating methods; we spoke of domination, exploitation, reform or revolution. Now we speak only of globalization or exclusion, of growing social distances or, at the opposite extreme, of the concentration of capital or the ability to disseminate messages or forms of consumption. We were once accustomed to situating ourselves in relation to others in terms of social scales of skills, income, education or authority; we have replaced that vertical vision with a horizontal vision. We are either in the centre or on the periphery, inside or outside, in the light or in the darkness. This localization no longer makes reference to social relations of conflict, cooperation or compromise, and gives an astronomical image of social life, as though every individual and every group were a star or a galaxy defined by its position in the universe.

The daily experience of this growing dissociation of an objectified world from the space of subjectivity immediately suggests a number of responses which need to be mentioned, even though they do not provide an answer to the questions 'How can I communicate and live with other people? or 'How can we reconcile our differences with the unity of a collective life?'

The first and weakest response is to try to revive the social models of the past. It appeals to the collective consciousness and the general will, to citizenship and the law. But how can this halt the trend towards both globalization and privatization that is weakening the old forms of social and political life? When Americans talk in neo-Tocquevillean terms of moral values, or when the French speak in neo-republican terms of citizenship, they are rejecting rather than asserting something. They are therefore invoking ideologies which, although they were intended to be inclusive, result in the exclusion of those who do not subscribe to them.

The second answer is the direct antithesis of the first. It tells us that the rupture we seem to be deploring is not only something to be welcomed; we must speed it up and experience it as a liberation. If we are no longer defined by our social and historical situation, so much the better; there are no longer any limits to our creative imagination, and we can move freely across all continents and all centuries: we are postmoderns. Given that the dissociation of instrumentality and identity lies at the heart of our personal and collective experience, we are indeed postmoderns in some sense: first, because we have less and less faith in the historic vocation of a class or nation, or in the idea of progress or the end of history, and secondly, because, as an ecologist remarked in the course of one of my research projects, we no longer demand a better life tomorrow, but a different life today. Yet the attractions of the postmodern are restricted to domains relating to cultural expression. They fade as we come closer to social realities, because, if the decline of the political is accepted unreservedly, all that will be left to regulate collective life is the market. If we accept the removal of social controls on the economy, how can we prevent the strong from crushing the weak? How can we prevent the distance between centre and periphery from growing, as we can see happening before our very eyes in the most liberal societies? The postmodern may well be attractive when it results in the weakening of norms and allegiances, but singing the praises of the void leaves us defenceless against violence, segregation and racism, and prevents us from establishing communications with other individuals and other cultures.

A third answer has been formulated in an attempt to get beyond the intolerable contradiction between those who want only unity and those who seek only diversity, between those who speak only of 'us', even if it means excluding what they call minorities, and those who speak only of 'me' or 'that' and who, in the name of justice and fairness, refuse to intervene in social life or to undertake any action. This might be called the English answer, so closely does it correspond to a tradition that has long been illustrated by British politics. If we are to live together and still be different, let us respect a code of good conduct or the rules of the social game. This 'procedural' democracy is not content with formal rules; it guarantees respect for personal and collective freedoms, organizes the representation of interests, formalizes public debate and institutionalizes tolerance. This conception is related to the idea of constitutional patriotism, which has been put forward by Jürgen Habermas in Germany. Awareness of belonging to German society must no longer mean an awareness of being part of a community with a cultural and historic destiny, but an awareness of belonging to a political society which respects the principles of freedom, justice and tolerance that have been proclaimed and organized by the democratic Constitution.

As Habermas himself admits, this answer has both the advantages and the disadvantages of all minimalist solutions. It safeguards coexistence, but does not ensure communication. Even when it goes beyond mere tolerance and positively recognizes that every culture has universal aspirations and uses a particular experience to create and express universals, it leaves the problem of communication unresolved. It puts us in front of others, as though we were in front of a museum display case. We recognize the presence of cultures different from ours, their capacity for a discourse on the world, human beings and life, and the originality of these cultural creations demands our respect and enjoins us to understand them; but that does not allow us to communicate with them or, in other words, to live in the same society as them. It puts us on parallel lines and allows us to exchange cordial greetings, but it no more facilitates interaction than the fact of knowing that Chinese is a cultured language allows us to converse with the Chinese if we have not learned that language.

This answer therefore does little to ensure communication, just as the political democracy of the nineteenth century proved somewhat ineffective when it came to preventing the proletarianization and exploitation of workers, or the destruction and inferiorization of colonized cultures. Those who fall back on the first of the answers we have invoked are not wrong to remind moderate and tolerant liberals that we need common values and institutions if we are to be able to resist barbarism, totalitarianism, racism or the effects of a severe economic crisis.

As we end this brief examination of the answers that are usually put forward, how can we avoid the conclusion that their weakness stems from their failure to look for a social or institutional solution to the dissociation of the economy and cultures, given that the most direct effect of this great rift is the weakening of all social and political mediations? We can quite understand that many respond to this desocialization by calling for a resocialization or for a return to the spirit of citizenship, the nation or the Republic; but this is no more than a nostalgic homage to a past that has gone. The idea of the nation-society or of a constitutional nation-state was the great creation of our early modernity. In order to reconcile a triumphant rationalization and the individualism stimulated by the Reformation and the critique of political and religious institutions, the moderns of the seventeenth and eighteenth centuries forged the idea of a popular sovereignty which could combine individualism and rationalism by giving legal beings an absolute supremacy over social beings and by contrasting natural rights with positive rights. This idea found its highest expression in the American and French Declarations of the Rights of Man and the Citizen. Universalist individualism became the foundation of the political realm, defined as the realm of freedom and as the only realm capable of governing a social order which was still dominated by private interests, traditions, privileges and irrationalism. But it is the realm of the political that has gradually been destroyed by the growing autonomy of economic realities. As a result of economic globalization and the appearance of so many new industrial countries and technological revolutions, the economy escaped from its social framework, especially at the end of the nineteenth century and then after the Second World War and the subsequent period of national construction or reconstruction.

The institutional, political and juridical synthesis of rationalization and moral individualism survived as long as individuals took part in public life only as citizens and as long as their economic lives as producers or consumers were to a large extent still inscribed in a local society with its own customs and traditional forms of power. At that time, societies could be identified with the creation of a political realm. That is why revolutions served the sovereignty of the people, citizens and the nation. The individualist-universalist conception of right established an almost natural link between the universalism of reason and an individualism that went beyond the defence of personal interests. The emergence of industrial society replaced the citizen with the economic actor and, in more concrete terms, antagonistic classes. This led to the disappearance of any principle that could integrate science and consciousness, and industrial society seemed to its best thinkers to be dominated by the class struggle. From the end of the nineteenth century onwards, of course, an industrial democracy was established, first in Great Britain and Germany and then, much later, in France and the United States, but, despite its name, it did not establish the rule of the citizen. It established, rather, negotiated principles of justice that were designed to reconcile conflicting interests. These principles were fragile, as technological and economic revolutions made it necessary to restructure the work-force, and made it more difficult to reconcile productivity with the protection of jobs and working conditions. The European model of social welfare, which is not to be confused with economic and corporatist interventions on the part of the state, has been largely preserved in Western Europe, but it does not have the solidity of the institutional model born of the Dutch, English, American and French revolutions. It has been bypassed by the globalization of the economy, which is now beyond the control of what are still national political authorities. The result, in both Europe and wherever the European model has been introduced, has been the triumph of cultural nationalisms and identity politics that appeal to cultural beliefs and heritages and lead to a rejection of diversity and communication.

Over the last century, we have seen the emergence of political movements which identify the state with a national, racial, ethnic or religious heritage. As the economy and culture become dissociated, state and heritage merge as all possible cultural resources are mobilized on behalf of a state which defines itself as the defender of the community. This solution defines the totalitarian state. It came into being at the moment when a nation was no longer seen as the creation of the sovereignty of the people, but as the victim of a denationalized economy that has no home country. Hence the anti-capitalist reaction, which sometimes took the exacerbated form of a radical anti-Semitism that accused the Jews of betraying the fatherland in the name of an abstract universalism – the universalism of money, thought and deracinated art. This totalitarianism found its most aggressive expression in Nazism, but it also triumphed when Stalinist despotism began the forced construction of a homogeneous society and eliminated the bourgeoisie, intellectuals who 'defended its interests', and traitors 'in the service of foreign powers'.

In more recent years, this totalitarianism has reappeared both in the form of a mobilization of Islamic forces against foreign capitalism and the Great Satan and in the form of the radical nationalism which, in parts of the former Yugoslavia, is enforcing the ethnic cleansing that has transformed Serb (and sometimes Croatian) nationalism into an agency for the destruction of foreign elements. All the movements that we describe as fundamentalist – and they are variants on the totalitarian model – demonstrate the strength of the anti-liberal solution in the late twentieth century. They also show that it may take different forms in the twenty-first. Just as the period of imperialism was followed by the triumph of Leninist revolutions, we may see, in the post-globalization period, the re-emergence of totalitarian regimes or an alliance between economic liberalism and cultural nationalism in the new industrial countries. Whilst social struggles may lead to democratization, as in North Korea or Taiwan, this national liberalism may lead to increasingly totalitarian mobilizations in other countries.

The European social model can and must be defended against this threat, which it would be foolhardy to believe disappeared with the fall of Hitler and the breakup of the Soviet Union. Yet that model no longer has enough theoretical power, or enough power to mobilize. As for the American model, which juxtaposes a high level of techno-economic development and a high degree of social fragmentation, it is conceivable only in a society that is integrated by its awareness of being destined to lead the world. That awareness has been strengthened by the fall of its main enemy, by the economic difficulties confronting Japan since 1985 and by Europe's lack of political will.

Like historians, sociologists base their reflections on factual observation before they elaborate new concepts or reinterpret existing concepts. Before we formulate a conception of justice or freedom, we must therefore take stock of the fact that we are witnessing the decay of the image of a society built and managed by a political project, institutions and socializing agencies. Social democratic politics, the Welfare State and even the economic policies inspired by Keynes have produced remarkable concrete expressions of the triumph of political thought over social practice, but they are all in a state of decadence or decay.

The state, defined as the central agency for growth and justice, is under attack from the internationalization of the economy, on the one hand, and the fragmentation of cultural identities, on the other. A study of history may lead to a better *a posteriori* understanding of how political and juridical institutions have tried to reconcile freedom and equality and the way in which, in our democracies, every citizen feels that he or she can, in theory, take an active part in the search for the most rational and fairest solution. But night has already fallen on that republican ideal. The goal of sociological analysis must now be to discover what freedom, solidarity and equality might mean in a social situation in which the centre – the palace of the prince – is empty, and in which the throne room is full of draughts and has been invaded by bands of speculators and *paparazzi*.

Sociologists have to get up early and walk at dawn through the new landscape created by the upheavals of the night. They cannot apply to new realities interpretations that are so elaborate that it took long days of analysis and reflection to knock them into shape. Their primary role is to note discontinuities, to stop looking at the lights of the past and to look at the confusion of visible reality, and to formulate the most worrying of all questions: if institutions have lost their power to regulate and integrate, what power can now bring together and reconcile a transnational economy and infra-national identities? And, given that this power can no longer be directly institutional, how can it be used to reconstruct mechanisms that can regulate social life?

This book is an attempt to answer these questions. It must, however, begin, not by formulating an answer, but by recognizing the fact that the old answers have become inaudible or inapplicable, and that the institutions we hoped would establish order have often become agents of disorder, of inefficiency, injustice and paralysis.

Any effective answer to the dissociation of the economy and culture must introduce a principle that can bring about a new reconciliation between two worlds that have become divorced. We know that it cannot be an abstract principle, and that it can no longer be the principle that elevates natural law and citizenship above social and economic reality. Conversely, we also know that it is not immanent within economic reality. The market itself cannot provide a model for social regulation, because, whilst it allows the diversification of demands and the adaptation of production to those demands, brings down traditional barriers and authoritarian systems of social control, and allows, finally, collective bargaining and useful compromises, it also subordinates consumer demand to a very concentrated supply system. The model of the balanced competitive market is the direct antithesis of that of the republican state, but both are far removed from contemporary social realities. Both presuppose the existence of a stable political or economic order, whereas our reality is that of tumultuous change and innovation, and of companies and networks that increasingly anticipate demand, laws and collective movements.

That is the situation to which we are trying to find an answer. It is no longer a matter of overthrowing absolute power or of finding a counter-weight to capitalist power, but of finding a fixed point of reference in a changing world in which our experience is fragmented and in which the place that was once occupied by institutions has been taken over by the strategies of the great financial, technological and media organizations. The era of order is coming to an end; this is the beginning of the era of change. Change is now the central category in both personal experience and social organization. Ulrich Beck expresses this idea well when he speaks of a 'risk society' that is ruled by uncertainty and especially by risks with a low probability but major possible effects, such as a nuclear explosion, major changes in atmospheric conditions, or the spread of epidemics for which there is no known medical cure (Beck 1986). This vision does not prophesy unavoidable calamities, but it does make it impossible to have any long-term faith in institutional solutions. Even though no conception of personal and collective life can do without juridical safeguards, and therefore political decisions, we can no longer look to a political realm that is deemed superior to the social realm to find ways of resisting forces whose strategies impose uncontrolled changes on our experience of life.

Thinking about contemporary societies is dominated by the two main observations we have just formulated: the growing dissociation of the instrumental world and the symbolic world, and of the economy and cultures, and, secondly, the increasingly diffuse power, within a growing social and political void, of strategic actions whose goal is not to create a social order but to accelerate change and the movement or circulation of capital, commodities, services and information. For power no longer belongs to a prince who forces his arbitrary decisions on us, or even to a capitalist who exploits wage-earners; it belongs to strategic innovators or financiers who conquer markets rather than governing or administer-ing territories. What we are looking for must therefore be a force that can reintegrate the economy and culture, a force that can challenge the power of the strategists.

How are we to escape the worrying choice between an illusory global-ization which ignores cultural diversity and the disturbing reality of introverted communities? The answer appears to be that it is impossible to do so – as impossible as squaring the circle, as I was recently told by an eminent American anthropologist. The formula is provocative, and might seem discouraging. It is in fact injudicious. Reconciling cultural unity and cultural plurality is no more contradictory than reconciling the accumulation of investments with the mass distribution of the fruits of growth, or a unitary law with a diversity of opinions and interests. A modern society is defined by its historicity, or by its ability to produce and transform itself, and any modern society must both increase its historicity (and therefore concentrate resources and power) and expand its participatory mechanisms. We have been discussing the contradictions between freedom and equality, or between capitalism and social justice, for centuries; but in the course of those debates we did invent political democracy and then social democracy. Why should we abandon the attempt to reconcile universal reason and cultural identities, or the unity of the technological and commercial world with a diversity of cultures and personalities?

If we cannot find an acceptable solution to the problems we have raised, we have no option but to accept a world-wide civil war – and it will be an increasingly hot one – between those who control the international networks of technology, financial flows and information and all those individuals, groups, nations and communities who feel that this globalization is a threat to their identity. We must, however, take stock of the magnitude of the task we have to accomplish, as we shall find no compromise solution to the contradiction between unity and diversity.

Two ideas will guide us in our search for a solution. The first, which is the central theme of the first part of this book, is a direct corollary of the theme of the dissociation that leads to what I call 'demodernization'. It asserts that the only space in which instrumentality and identity, and the technological and the symbolic, can be reconciled is a personal life project, which implies a refusal to allow our experience to be reduced to a kaleidoscopic existence or a discontinuous set of responses to the stimuli of the social environment. Such a project is an attempt to prevent our personalities being rent apart and to mobilize an experience and a culture in our technological and economic activities in such a way that a series of lived situations becomes an individual life story and not an incoherent set of events. In a world of permanent and uncontrollable change, the individual attempt to transform lived experiences into the construction of the self as actor is the only stable point of reference. I call the individual's attempt to become an actor 'the Subject', which is not to be confused with experience as a whole or with some higher principle that guides individuals and gives them a vocation. The Subject has no content but its own production. It serves no cause, no values and no law other than its need and desire to resist its own dismemberment in a changing world in which there is no order or equilibrium.

The Subject is an assertion of freedom in the face of the power of both strategists and their apparatuses and communitarian dictators. Fighting on two fronts, the Subject resists all the ideologies that would make it conform to the order of the world or the order of the community. The answers to the questions we have posed are therefore indivisible. The appeal to the Subject is the only answer to the dissociation of the economy and culture, and it is the only possible source of social movements that can oppose the masters of economic change or communitarian dictators. Being an assertion of personal freedom, the Subject is also, and by the same criterion, a social movement.

The second part of this book is mainly devoted to how this non-social principle can be used to reconstruct social life. There are two stages to this task. First, the individual can be transformed into the Subject only if Others are recognized as Subjects striving, each in their own way, to reconcile a cultural memory and an instrumental project – that being the definition of a multi-cultural society, which is as far removed from the fragmentation of social life into communities as it is from a mass society that is unified by its technological or commercial logic and rejects inter-cultural communication. The idea of the Subject implies the idea of inter-cultural communication, but it is the combination of the two that provides an answer to the question we are asking: how can we live together in a society that is increasingly divided up into networks that instrumentalize us, and into communities that imprison us and prevent us from communicating with others?

The second stage in the reconstruction of personal and collective life is based upon the idea that the personal Subject, like communication between Subjects, requires institutional safeguards. This means that we have to replace the old idea of democracy, defined as participation in the general will, with the new idea of institutions that safeguard the freedom of the Subject and permit communication between Subjects. I describe this conception as 'the politics of the Subject', and I have tried to apply it to the important domain of education by describing what a school for the Subject might look like.

The primary meaning of this book resides, then, in the unity of the two parts that go to make it up. We can live together, or in other words reconcile the unity of society and a diversity of personalities and cultures, only if we make the idea of a personal Subject central to our thought and action. The dream of making all individuals obey the same universal laws of reason, religion or history has always turned into a nightmare and an instrument of domination; but the rejection of all principles of unity and the unqualified acceptance of differences leads to segregation or civil war. In order to escape this dilemma, this book paints a portrait of the Subject, defined both as a combination of a personal identity and a particular culture and as an involvement in a rationalized world, and therefore as the affirmation of the freedom and responsibility of that Subject. This is the only approach that allows us to explain how we can live together, equal and different.

I do not propose to describe here the transformations of our social life, the effects of the globalization of the economy and of new information technologies, or the deterioration of the socio-traditional environment. Before we can clearly perceive the spectacle that is unfolding before our eyes, we must make sure that we can see properly. We therefore have to check the quality of the instruments of knowledge that we use to perceive the world around us and ourselves. In the great industrial countries and the oldest nation-states, an attachment to a past that deserves admiration can be a source of resistance to the intellectual changes that have to take place. But if we give in to it, that resistance will soon throw the political debate into confusion and put more obstacles in the way of all forms of innovation. We must obviously not adapt passively to a mass culture and a mass society which mask the very real forces of domination that we must identify and fight, but the choice we have to make is not one between defending the order of the past and accepting the disorder of the present. We have to conceive and construct new forms of collective and personal life.

This book deals with ideas rather than facts, but what is at stake in it is as practical as it is theoretical. We have to understand that we are moving from one stage in modernity to another, and define the nature of the crisis we are living through. We have to be able to reconstruct our capacity to manage the mutations that are occurring and to define possible choices. We are not faced with a stark choice between never-ending progress and a labyrinth from which there is no escape.

There is more to history than the successes of those who have, both intellectually and practically, built a new world. History is also about the fall of societies which did not understand, permit and organize new forms of economic, political and cultural life. Past successes are no guarantee that a country, individual or institution can understand and master new forms of personal and collective life. As we stand on the threshold of the new century that began with the fall of the Berlin Wall, are we capable of understanding the world we have already entered?

PART I

The Production of the Self

1

Demodernization

We no longer believe in progress. We obviously go on wondering about what new technological products will change our way of life, and about when biology and medicine will conquer the diseases that strike down so many of us. But our hearts are no longer in it, even if we do go on defending ourselves against irrationalist currents that muddle up demonstrable truths with arbitrary assertions. It is not enough, however, to say that optimism has given way to pessimism, and that we are living through a new 'crisis in progress', to use the title of one of George Friedmann's first books; we are as uncertain about the risks we are running as we are about the victories we might hope for.

The crisis we are living through is more serious than a bout of fear or disenchantment. Modernity's strongest assertion was that we *are* what we *do*. We know from bitter experience that we are no longer what we do, and that we understand less and less about the way we are forced to behave by the economic, political or cultural apparatuses that organize our experience. Some of us fling ourselves into the flow of information and of the products of mass society; others try to reconstruct a community that can protect their identity by filtering the stimuli that come from mass production, consumption and communication. But the vast majority of us belong, and wish to belong, to both worlds.

We are dominated by mass culture, but we are also retreating into our private lives. When we go into hospital, we place our faith in medical knowledge, but we feel that we are ignored or mistreated by systems and individuals who certainly do not think that relating to their patients is a primary concern. If we are studying at school or university, we accept that qualifications are the best defence against unemployment, but we live in a youth culture that is alien to a decaying academic culture. When we go to work, we are grateful for having a job and often invest more and more of our knowledge and projects in our activity, but we also have the impression that the work we are doing counts for little in a world dominated by money, competition and technology, and where the key words 'flexibility', 'competitiveness' and 'reskilling' conceal so many broken lives. As we become increasingly involved in a world that is 'global' in terms of production, consumption and information, we also feel a need to find some stability in our private lives to ensure that we are not swept away by the messages of mass society, which are both seductive and impersonal.

The classical model

For a long time modern society tried to bring individuals into harmony with institutions, because it asserted the universal value of a rationalist conception of the world, society and the individual. That conception was so grandiose that we can well understand why some people are still so attached to it, even though it has been in decline for a long time (a hundred years now!). The corner-stone of that world-view was the idea of sovereignty of the people, and the project of building a society of free, rational citizens on the ruins of ancient regimes that were still ruled by tradition or the divine law. The central assertion of modern politics made man a citizen, and then a worker. The citizen is a free man because he is defined by the law that grants him the right to contribute to the general will; the worker too is a free man if he can win respect for the energy and skills of the producers, as opposed to the representatives of rents and profit. The rational organization of society must permit the free development of all needs; the individual and the collective must be in perfect harmony. They can be in harmony only if reason can dominate the passions, if there are harsh laws to punish profiteers, and if schools teach children to curb their instincts and vices, and to train themselves thanks to strict disciplines and a familiarity with the great works of the human mind.

Such were the complementary aspects of 'classical' thought. (I use the word in preference to 'modern' to describe the social philosophy which, from the beginnings of liberal political philosophy with Machiavelli, Hobbes and then Rousseau, saw the political realm as the site of reason's triumph and as the place where, thanks to the removal of all intermediary bodies, the individual could come into contact with the universal.) This Enlightenment philosophy, which lived on in the ideologies of progress, is so far removed from the dissociation of a social world governed by instrumental reason and individual life that it is hard to understand how such a reversal could have come about.

In fact, modernity did, from the very beginning, dissociate the world of natural laws from the world of the Subject – or extension from the soul, as Descartes puts it. Modernity was born of the collapse of the religious world-view, which was at once rationalist and finalist. God, it said, created a world governed by the natural laws discovered by science, but he also created man in his own image. Nature was sacred, because it was made by God, but human beings were still more sacred because they were both creators and creatures. They must therefore be regarded as being both marked by the Fall and as having a potential for grace which, whilst it was arbitrary, could also be manifested through good works. Modernity destroyed that religious model completely at the decisive moment when the Renaissance, and above all the Italian Renaissance, began to celebrate the beauties of the scientific realm and the absolutist state. A paradoxical denial of the existence of free will allowed the Lutheran Reformation, for its part, to assert the existence of an inner world. This was the world of grace, but it was also the world of faith, piety and, ultimately, ethics.

This dualism has a long history. It was inscribed in the Christianity that separated spiritual power from temporal power, or the power of the Pope from that of the Emperor. It was also inscribed in the tradition – and it was primarily a Franciscan tradition – of challenging the social order in the name of religion. The idea of natural law, which culminated in the American and French Declarations of Rights, asserted that the social order had to be founded upon not only the general will, but also a non-social principle, namely equality. This conception might be described as 'bourgeois'. For a very long time, it made it possible to regard the construction of industrial society and respect for personal freedoms as complementary. It was very different from the capitalist world-view – and this includes state capitalism – which gives boundless powers to a rationalizing society that is quick to repress anything that does not conform to the rational pursuit of self-interest.

Before modernity could develop, it required a principle of order and integration, as well as this individualism. In the earliest modern societies, that principle was supplied by the idea of society. Society was viewed as a constitutional state, or a set of institutions functioning in accordance with the principles of a universalist and individualist law. Every individual was seen as a rational being who was conscious of his rights and duties. The individual had to obey the laws that safeguarded his legitimate interests and his freedom in private life and at the same time ensured the solidity of society or the social body, whose health was preserved by the normal workings of its organs. In this secularized modern world, human society was no longer made in the image of the City of God: the general interest is the supreme law, and it cannot be divorced from its members' freedom to pursue their own interests. The law, on the one hand, and education, on the other, ensured that individuals and society lived in harmony. Institutionalization and socialization were the two basic mechanisms that ensured that society and the individual were mirror images of one another.

This institutional image of society lay at the heart of modern political culture. If the classical image of modernity is shaped by the interaction of three elements – rationalization, ethical individualism and institutional functionalism – the third element is the corner-stone of the system as I have defined modernity in terms of the growing dissociation of system and actor, and therefore in terms of the disappearance of any meta-social principle that can make them complement one another. Rather than forming an articulated whole, the market economy and the autonomy of private life (or consciousness) tend to contradict one another. All that holds them together is the modern idea of society, which is much more than a way of designating a social and political aggregate such as a nation, a city or a professional milieu. The modern idea of society asserts that individuals become truly human only when they take part in collective life and, as workers, but also as members of a family, help to ensure that society works properly. This is above all a political conception of society, and the human ideal it proposes is that of the citizen. It is therefore much closer to the Athenian or Roman model of the Freedom of the Ancients, as defined by Benjamin Constant, than to the Freedom of the Moderns, which, according to the same author, is individualist rather than participatory.

Their general will transforms individuals who were involved in the war of every man against every man that is characteristic of the state of nature into members of a society, and thus guarantees the freedom and happiness of all. The Americans and the French named the free society that was so constructed the nation or the republic. It ensured that reason could triumph over tradition, and equality between individuals over the inequalities that triumphed in every domain of civil society or in traditional communities. The universalism of reason and ethical individualism merged to form the idea of a society that was freely organized by the law. In so far as instrumental rationality and ethical individualism tend to drift apart and can be held together only by political institutions, this model of the social system can be represented as a triangle whose base has been broken:

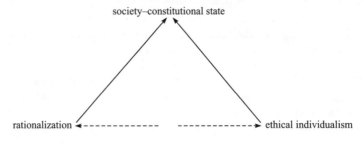

The model is transformed by the development of industrial society, but its nature does not change. Indeed, it takes on its most elaborate form with industrial democracy and the Welfare State. Personal well-being and the market economy are reconciled thanks to the intervention of the democratic state, which guarantees that the requirements of the economy coincide with social demands.

This model of society has always had weaknesses that threaten its survival, but before we go on to look at its decline and fall, we must recognize its exceptional strength: it gave the 'West' several centuries of self-sustaining development, and allowed it to dominate the world. It would be a mistake to reduce it to the caricatural image of a suffocating network of rules that forces individuals to play insincere roles in a social comedy, and reduces rationality to the worship of money. The word 'bourgeois' has come to have many negative connotations, but this bourgeois society was also the society of the revolutions of the seventeenth and eighteenth centuries. This was the society that finally recognized the importance of feelings in personal, family and public life. It was in this bourgeois, scientific, national and, in a word, secular society that we once lived. And it was to this model of society that we turned when we fought social injustices, arbitrary power, aggressive nationalism and a suffocating colonialism.

The fall of the classical model

Yet social institutions have never abolished the dissociation of private life from public life. Even during the age of Enlightenment, the market economy encouraged modes of behaviour that deviated from a morality based on feeling, piety and the idea of human rights. The idea of progress, which seemed to have triumphed in the nineteenth century, was undermined in more obvious ways by the rule of money, the rise of nationalisms, working-class and urban poverty, and the class struggle. It is true that the optimism of the nineteenth century was still in keeping with what was at stake in its social movements: capitalists and workers referred to the same movement in order to justify their demands and to condemn their adversaries, whom they defined as obstacles to progress. But as their struggles became more intense, the social adversaries' shared reference to progress, history and rationalization became less obvious.

It was mainly in the second half of the twentieth century that the social model came under increasing attack, and this coincided with the development of the social struggles of industrial society. Its decline can be explained primarily in terms of the growing autonomy of economic

forces, which increasingly escaped state-imposed regulations and prior-
ities. The Western world threw off the domination of the political in order
to allow the market to organize an economic life that was increasingly
differentiated from the other domains of social life. The entrepreneurial
spirit, capitalist profit and, according to Georg Simmel, money itself
destroyed the constructs, principles and values of the old social order.
Now that it was out of step with economic realities, the idea of society
could no longer reconcile economic or technological rationalization and
ethical individualism. Even in our own day, many people go on attempting to give the political realm a central role once more because they
believe it capable of imposing its principles and laws on economic activities, as well as on all the needs of private life and civil society. Their
attempts will, however, become increasingly artificial, and all social and
economic actors – dominant and dominated alike – will struggle, on the
contrary, to subordinate political power to their interests. Political economy has replaced constitutional law as the central principle of public life.
Countries like France and Spain, where the nature of the state and its
relations with the Church remained the central themes of political life, are
testimonies to the scale of the obstacles that delayed their entry into
industrial society.

The cultural pessimism that dominated the end of the nineteenth century in Paris and London as well as Vienna and Berlin was an expression
of the ruination of this modernity and the balance it had been able to
maintain between public life and private life. Within the space of a few
decades rational society's foundation myth had collapsed, together with
the harmony that once existed between individual and society. First
Nietzsche, then Freud, asserted that there was a contradiction between
the individual and the social order, and between pleasure and the law. The
rationalization of industrial society seemed to the greatest sociologists,
namely Durkheim and Weber, to be as fraught with danger as it was full
of hopes. The idea of the nation ceased to designate a collectivity of free
citizens, and came to mean the search for a collective and historical
identity. A society based on production was beginning to be transformed
into a consumer society.

We have long been unable to believe in the final triumph of a constitutional state that can maintain an even balance between the industrialization of the world and personal freedom, between the public space and
private life. The unity of reason and conscience has been shattered. The
twentieth century was dominated by the conflict between a Communist
totalitarianism based on faith in reason and a Fascist or nationalist
totalitarianism that aggressively defended a racial, national, ethnic or
religious identity. And ever since those monsters disappeared, our planet
has been dominated by the conflict between globalized markets and

exasperated national or cultural identities. The point is illustrated by the differences between two representations of the world.

According to Francis Fukuyama (1992), the Western model has triumphed throughout the world: now that the Communist model has collapsed, the interdependence of the market economy, parliamentary democracy and cultural tolerance provides the only social model to which we can refer. According to Samuel Huntington (1996), on the other hand, the world is dominated by cultural or religious wars, and they are more radical than the wars of old, which were wars between nations or classes. On the one hand, a unified economy with a unitary institutional framework; on the other, the fragmentation of cultural identities. It is impossible to choose between these interpretations, not only because they both jump to conclusions, but mainly because they both fail to see what is really happening. Two worlds are being dissociated: the world of technologies and markets and the world of cultures, the world of instrumental reason and that of collective meaning, that of signs and that of meanings. What lies at the heart of our experience at the end of the century is the dissociation of extension and soul, to use the old terminology, or the dissociation of the economy and cultures, of exchanges and identities.

I describe this dissociation as *demodernization*. Whereas 'modernization' meant using the idea of a national society to manage the duality of rational production and the Subject's inner freedom, demodernization is defined by the breaking of the links that bound together personal freedom and collective efficacy. The obvious image that comes to mind here is that of the decay of our cities. The idea of the city or, more accurately, the urban community was for a long time indissociable from that of citizenship and the division of labour. The city was the place of production, commerce and socialization; it was society's concrete name. It was possible to hope that in cities private life and public life could coexist in a state of mutual respect. But our passionate attachment to cities such as Paris, London, Amsterdam or Rome, which we have inherited from what is already a distant past, is sustained by the anxious awareness that our cities are falling into decay, and that only a few privileged enclaves will escape that fate.

I find the notion of postmodernism useful as a critical instrument that allows us to perceive the crisis and the end of the rationalist model of the Enlightenment. But I think it incapable of taking on board the implications of the divorce between the two halves of our existence that it records. The fact that culture no longer has anything to do with the economy, or that we have to get rid of evolutionism and historicism, is no defence against the threats I am describing. How can we prevent dehistoricized cultures from becoming introverted? When people are no more than globalized consumers, what can be done to preserve their capacity for political action? Postmodern thinkers are often aware of these limitations. They have done their work of criticism. We now have to deal with the more difficult problems posed by the analysis of a society dominated by the crisis in classical modernity. That is the society in which we now live, and it is not reducible to the anarchic atomization of interests, imaginaries and systems of signs.

That is why the idea of demodernization, rather than that of postmodernity, must be the starting-point for our analysis. Elements that were once associated have been dissociated, and the two worlds – the world of networks of exchanges and the world of lived cultural experiences – are drifting apart more rapidly than ever. It is as impossible to believe in a world that is unified by trade and respect for the rules that govern its workings as it is to accept a complete fragmentation of interests, or an absolute multi-culturalism that makes it impossible for closed communities to communicate with one another. But before we transcend this dissociation and this shattering of modernity, we have to recognize them as our central experience.

We also have to avoid taking a purely pessimistic view of demodernization. The collapse of the social and political mediations between economic activity and cultural experience both destroys or weakens repressive social controls and increases the danger of disorganization. We all know this, because we are both drawn to and frightened by the idea of living in the great metropolis, and rarely feel nostalgic for small towns, where social integration is based upon conformism rather than democratic debate. Living in an open society can feel like living in a jungle, but closed societies are like prisons. We should not pass any moral judgement on demodernization. The collapse of society, defined as a model of order and integration, does lead to a social crisis, but it also leaves the way open for the search for a new principle that can reconcile instrumental rationality and cultural identity. What we are calling the crisis of the old model of modernity is also the development of modernity itself, and it is defined by the growing dissociation of two worlds. I stress the crisis element purely in order to underline the passing away of the old principle of building a modern society, and the futility of trying to revive it at a time when there is a growing gulf between a globalized economy over which states have less and less control and private or communitarian identities which are turning in on themselves.

Liberal ideology

The idea of globalization does not simply mean that economic exchanges take place on a global scale: it means that we have to adopt a conception of social life quite different from the conception that dominated the post-war period. The new conception is dominated by the collapse and destruction of the social and political mediations that once bound together the economy and culture and ensured, in accordance with the classical model, that all elements in social life were highly integrated. The idea of an industrial society in which there was a close link between economic rationalization and political and administrative interventions has given way to a widening gap between the world of markets and that of civic life. The world of markets does not constitute a social system, but rather a field of strategic action in which actors strive to use an uncontrolled or even unknown environment. That is why it is more and more difficult to locate individuals on a scale of qualifications or even authority; they are defined, rather, by their position in a market or, in other words, by their ability to master change or, conversely, their tendency to fall victim to it. Change replaces order as the framework for analysis and social action, because the field of strategic action is a constantly changing set of possibilities, opportunities and risks. As a result, many people are afraid when they see the declining level of state intervention, the breakup of systems of safeguards, the unpredictability of their careers and retirement, the disappearance of the established rules of the game, and the integration of social or economic demands into the apparatus of the state.

The decline of what I have termed 'the mobilizing state' does indeed lead to the breakdown of what were once highly or excessively integrated social, political and administrative systems, and to their replacement by a dynamic that liberalizes trade and conditions of production; but this is also a process of desocialization and depoliticization which weakens political mediations and the mechanisms of social integration.

The triumph of the market economy does not in itself mean that we are moving from *dirigiste* societies to liberal societies, but simply that the economy is breaking free of the non-economic constraints that were once imposed upon it, regardless of whether or not we wish to establish new forms of social controls over economic activity.

Economic development is a combination of two contradictory but complementary trends: the removal of the non-economic constraints that strangle the economic system and the integration of economic activity into a wider political logic. At the end of the nineteenth century, we saw the formation of political and social movements that demanded social controls over what they saw as a wild and destructive economy. At the end of the twentieth, we are witnessing something very different. Everyone wants the economy to be liberalized, and we are seeing the decline of all forms of economic interventionism, from post-colonial nationalism to the national-popular regimes of Latin America or India, from communism in the East to the Welfare State in the West.

Production centres that are at once economic, social and political have less and less control over trade flows, which are becoming an end in themselves. The primary goal of financial exchanges is no longer the organization of exchanges of commodities and services. Available capital, such as that of pension funds or insurance companies, looks for the greatest possible financial returns. Finance capitalism is breaking free of industrial capitalism, and the power of the techno-structures is waning. In the same way, the international media create or amplify shifts in public opinion that have little to do with the social movements in which real groups involved in direct conflicts can at any moment calculate the gains and losses they can expect to make from collective action. Such media campaigns are all the more successful in that they mean that we do not have to think about the truly political meaning or effects of the things to which they are reacting. They relate to a global society in which there is no state, and to risks, threats or disasters that are unrelated to any social context or any concrete politics. It is as though the constantly expanding market for news necessarily divorced it from its social conditions of production or reduced it to the status of a commodity, as they used to say in the Marxist tradition, which had the great virtue of looking beyond the world of commodities and at the social relations of production. This globalized liberal ideology looks for support to economic leaders and above all to the mass media, rather than to active participation on the part of the people. It is therefore inscribed within the tradition of the liberalism of the last century, and this allows us to see the limits of its action: it has no understanding of the mechanisms of political decision making, which have by no means lost all their power, especially when they are in the hands of those states that are most heavily committed to the struggle for world hegemony, or those that are most subject to the pressures of cultural nationalisms. These limits, the indeterminacy of the goals, and the difficulty in controlling the social and political effects of media campaigns have not stopped them from creating a global public space which exists in the full glare of the media and which places considerable restrictions on political action, especially in countries that are deeply involved in the globalized economy without being in a position to play a dominant role in world politics.

Whilst it is essential to analyse the information society, the creation of global firms and the emergence of so many new industrialized countries, the idea of globalization also has to be seen as an ideology which masks relations of economic domination by generating the image of a world-wide economic community that is either self-regulating or immune to the interventions of political decision-making centres. This liberal-inspired ideology is so far removed from observable reality that it is simply not an acceptable description of a new and lasting societal type. And the

memory of the early years of the twentieth century should make us take a
critical view of it. At that time, the Western world was dominated by the
idea that the open economy and finance capital would conquer the world,
and that nationalisms and the defence of professional or regional interests
were rearguard actions. Yet, even at the very beginning of the twentieth
century, the Mexican Revolution, the Great War in Europe, the Soviet
Revolution and then the forceful reappearance of the idea of rationalization in Germany and the United States destroyed our faith in an all-
powerful liberalism, which perished in the Great Crash of 1929. One
wonders, then, whether the ideology purveyed by the theme of globalization will last any longer than the *belle époque*'s blind faith in the internationalization of capitalism.

Just as it would be dangerous to attempt to maintain the old social
controls over the economy because it would mean defending vested interests or privileges, so it would be dangerous to describe as 'free' an
economic system that is subject only to self-regulation, the judgements
of international rating companies, decisions taken in lawyers' offices in
New York or London, and a few concerted interventions on the part of
the central banks. Such an economy is in fact wild. It leads to growing
inequalities and greater social exclusion, and it will inevitably provoke
violent reactions, especially on the periphery of the world system, where
the worst effects of the growing dualization are being felt.

This critical analysis is not a repetition of the all too common argument
that the globalization of the economy, and therefore of part of culture,
directly serves the interests of the United States or the great international
banks. The global economy is itself the dominant force. It cannot be
called a ruling class, because it is not supported by a category of real
actors, but it does constitute the dominant pole in the asymmetrical and
unequal relationship between the globalized economy and the fragmented
cultures which defines the world society in which we are now living.

Nor does this analysis deny that technological innovation and the
globalization of trade can play a positive role. For over a century, attacks
on 'technology' and 'money' have constantly sustained authoritarian neo-
communitarian movements, beginning with the various forms of fascism
and then cultural nationalisms of all kinds. We must not surrender to an
anti-liberalism that might generate the monstrous quest for social and
cultural homogeneity. Our best defence against all national, ethnic or
religious fundamentalisms is an open economy. In an open economy,
economic, political and cultural powers merge to only a minimal extent.
Conversely, fear of neo-communitarianism must not lead us to accept the
liberal ideology of the financial and industrial managers of transnational
companies. If that ideology did triumph, the dominance of the global
economy's networks would be contested by a disparate but united and

numerically superior resistance front, with all its forces fighting in the name of the defence of identities ranging from French-style republicanism and the isolationism of America's moral majority and Asian cultural nationalism to the fascistic resistance movements of the threatened middle classes and religious, ethnic and national fundamentalisms. We cannot side with either globalization or identitarian and communitarian movements, and one of the constant concerns of this book will be to look, first at the level of ideas, for ways to rearticulate a controlled but open economy and respect for identities. But, having taken all these precautions against lapsing into the errors of those who reject industrial society, either in the name of anti-capitalism or in the name of the defence of vested interests or cultural traditions, it is important to stress that the desocialization and depoliticization of economic and financial networks are in themselves mechanisms of domination, and that they benefit those who own capital. By stating this, we can apply to the analysis of the modern world general analytic categories, and reveal that, as in other types of societies, relations of domination and social conflicts do exist within the information society. We can also reject the disturbing idea of a society that is defined only by the changes that occur within it, of a society which has thereby been reduced to markets and strategic action, and which has rid itself for all time of social conflicts and social actors. Our reliance on such analyses, which were elaborated mainly with reference to industrial society (which justifies the idea of a post-industrial society), must not, however, lead us to transpose analyses of industrial society to the information society, just as it was impossible, in industrial society, to content ourselves with using analyses formulated at the time of the formation of nation-states.

This position seems to me to be close to that of Ulrich Beck. Beck's main theme is this: 'The further the modernization of modern societies proceeds, the more the foundations of industrial society are dissolved, consumed, changed and threatened' (Beck, Giddens and Scott 1994: 176). More specifically, our industrial societies are being transformed into a different type of society. Or perhaps they are heading towards their own destruction, but without knowing it and without thinking about it. The old pilots (parties, unions) are becoming powerless. What we call 'the ecological crisis' is the self-endangerment of industrial society. It is possible that this crisis of our own making will provoke a reflexive attitude, or an attempt to understand and take control, but that will not necessarily be the case. Our society could just as easily fall apart or be struck by a disaster born of its own workings. This extreme distrust of modern society, this rejection of the Enlightenment utopia and of the dream of an increasingly rational and self-conscious society, might certainly lead to a postmodernist conception, but it can also lead us to stop placing

our hopes in industrial society. And doing so is essential if we are
to understand the dangers of the demodernization that threatens us.
Our societies need to be more reflexive if they are to avoid what
Beck calls their unintended or unseen reflexivity, or in other words
their capacity for exposing themselves to risks that may result in their
destruction.

Communitarian identity

The dissociation of the economy and cultures either reduces the actor to
the logic of the globalized economy, and thus leads to the triumph of the
global culture we have just been talking about, or leads to the reconstruction of non-social identities based upon cultural loyalties rather than
social roles. As it becomes more difficult in this globalized society to
define oneself as a citizen or a worker, it becomes more tempting to define
oneself in terms of a cultural community such as an ethnic group, a
religion or belief, a gender or a mode of behaviour. This return to community, which Tönnies was already predicting at the end of the nineteenth
century, has always been laden with contradictory meanings, and our
attitudes are so fundamentally ambivalent that it is impossible to choose
between them.

The creative aspect of these new identifications is that they free cultural
diversity from the iron cage of Enlightenment rationalism. As that theme
is present throughout this book, a very general statement is all that is
required here.

When the global culture becomes detached from social institutions,
those institutions become mere managerial tools. Political parties are
reduced to coalitions that are formed to take power, and businesses
become military forces involved in a globalized competition and committed to the struggle to increase productivity by mastering technologies
and taking the right strategic decisions. Actors cease to be social, become
introverted, and are defined in terms of what they are, and no longer in
terms of what they do. For a long time we defined modernity as the
triumph of achieved status over ascribed status. For us, a modern society
was one in which individuals were rewarded on the basis of their output
and their merits, and not on the basis of their birth, race, private beliefs or
gender. The reason why we are now seeing 'being' taking its revenge on
'doing', or God (as Gilles Keppel puts it), ethnicity, the nation and gender
taking their revenge, is that demodernization has destroyed individuals'
identification with their citizenship, their professions or even their standard of living. Globalization has deprived society of its role as the creator
of norms.

Making a functional contribution to society by being a good citizen, a good worker, or a good father, mother, son or daughter is no longer an adequate, or even acceptable, moral norm. Our analysis has to begin with this observable fact, just as the analysis of industrial society had to begin with the destruction of the local communities, associations and traditions that made up pre-industrial society. The widespread argument that there has been a divorce between a rationalized public life and a traditional private life has become untenable. Private life has been invaded by mass culture, and public institutions are being swept away by a flood of demands that no longer pertain to the creation of a rational order. At the same time, we are all becoming aware that we belong to a tradition, a memory or a being (defined primarily in biological terms), which is the only thing that can resist the globalization that has swamped or swept away social institutions. The destruction of the Enlightenment cultural model, which is sometimes said to be Eurocentric, is a cultural revolution, and it is taking place both in some new industrial countries, especially in Asia, in an Islamic world that is undergoing a development crisis, and in the United States.

America's best universities have been shaken by great intellectual battles, and there is nothing to be gained from failing to recognize their importance. Political correctness should be condemned only when it denies the very principle of inter-cultural communication. We have to destroy a representation of society and history that gives absolute priority to the idea of a rationalist society inhabited by rational citizens, and which has been freed from a cultural diversity bound up with the survival of local and particular traditions, beliefs and forms of organization. And we have to replace it with the idea of multiple and multi-directional changes, all of which mobilize the past in order to invent a future, and therefore both make use of a reference to what has become an instrumental rationality and recognize the existence of actors who are also defined by an individual and collective identity or heritage.

Suffice it to mention the most important cultural reversal. It concerns women. What is at stake here is not only the struggle for equality or freedom or, conversely, the search for the specificities of women's experience, as opposed to that of men; it is the assertion that human universality cannot be embodied in the figure of a Man, who was in fact an adult, educated and economically independent man. It must be embodied in the duality of a man and a woman who initiate, sometimes in different ways and sometimes in the same way, the same process of combining a particular being with a general rationality, either substantial or instrumental. This is neither a particular demand nor the action of a minority, and feminists like Gisèle Halimi are right when they angrily reject definitions that claim that women are a minority. The critique advanced by women does have a general value: it is aimed at destroying the identification of culture or modernity with one particular social actor – nation, civilization, class, gender, age-group, profession or level of education – because it traps other actors into the status of inferiors and dependants.

According to the classic Enlightenment conception of modernity, the image of modern society corresponded to that of modern Man. Today's global society no longer corresponds to any one human type or emblematic image: neither men nor women, neither young nor old, neither the inhabitants of New York or Paris, nor those of Rio or Calcutta. The destruction of social mediations results in a stark conflict between the globalization of the cultural field and an untranscendable multiplicity of social actors. The dark side of this multi-culturalism is the danger that every culture will be trapped into one particular experience that cannot be communicated. Such cultural fragmentation would lead to a world of sects and a rejection of all social norms. In most cases, positive discrimination or affirmative action, and the related policy of making quotas and subsidies available for particular categories, is a justifiable response to real inequalities, but it is dangerous to situate or judge individuals purely on the basis of their membership of a community. That would result in the triumph of a generalized racism, and the trial of O. J. Simpson in the United States is a disturbing example of what that could mean.

This becomes a major threat only when identities defined in a purely defensive manner, like the identities of victim groups, ask some authoritarian power to defend them, or allow it to do so. That power then uses the struggle against the Other to define and legitimate its policies, and rejects the universalist principles of the law. Just as a working class that is defined solely as a proletariat, and not as a body of wage-earning manual workers, or in terms of what it has lost and not in terms of its positive contribution, inevitably becomes a social resource for an authoritarian power, so a communitarian identity defined solely in terms of the discrimination it suffers can be activated only by authoritarian political leaders who mobilize it to serve their own purposes. Whilst it may seem to imply a return to ethnic or religious origins, a communitarian identity in fact becomes, for better or worse, a force for authoritarian-nationalist modernization, as we have seen in many countries. It took a moderate form in Bismarck's Germany and in Meiji Japan, but it increasingly takes authoritarian forms that evolve into totalitarianism rather than democracy.

Communitarianism transforms cultures into calls for political mobilization and the rejection of the Other. Cultures are debased in the same way as a mode of production is debased when it is reduced to being a market. We cannot naïvely accept this ideological reinterpretation of cultures, because a culture is neither a world-view, an ideology nor a holy book; it is a combination of techniques for using natural resources, modes of integrating individuals into a collectivity, and references to a conception of the Subject, which may be either religious or humanistic. It is not a body of beliefs and practices, and it can therefore be transformed when any one of its three major components is modified. Because it is not, in relative terms, highly integrated, and is therefore capable of change, a culture is increasingly weakened as technological change speeds up, as changing and diversified collectivities replace smaller collectivities with indirect social controls, and as secularization and what Max Weber calls 'worldly asceticism' become more widespread. Modernization has often been defined in terms of the growing autonomy of different realms of social life such as public and private life, the economy, politics and religion, science and ideologies. Modernization leads to the decay of communities, which are defined, in contrast, by a high degree of inter-dependence between technology, social integration, and religious or moral beliefs. Demodernization, on the other hand, gives birth to retrospective utopias: we dream of going back to a global order based upon religious beliefs or political institutions, which can put an end to the fragmentation of lived experience. This is an impossible dream, and it can result only in the fusion of a communitarian ideology and a modernizing project controlled by an authoritarian power. Such powers are often mistakenly described as fundamentalist, but they are not trying to go back to their origins; they mobilize a myth of origins to impose a nationalist and authoritarian conception of modernization. Given that they cannot revert to being the type of society their ideology demands, neo-communitarian policies and movements replace a lived cultural experience with an ideology which is usually imposed in authoritarian ways.

We are experiencing the debasement of two things: economic activity, which, now that it can no longer unify technologies, social relations of production and a market, has been reduced to being an internationalized market and cultural identities, which are being used to legitimize authoritarian powers. In both cases, we are witnessing the perversion of something: an economy reduced to a market and cultures used as ideologies. There is no longer any communication between, on the one hand, an economy that has been reduced to the circulation of capital and, on the other, cultures that have been transformed into manifestations of authoritarian policies. The truth of the matter – when it is not concealed by some authoritarian power – is that cultural loyalties, beliefs and modes of behaviour have emerged from the private space to which they were once confined. The militant feminists put it most forcefully when they said that the personal is political, and thus rejected all essentialism. In the nineteenth century, it was the economy that was political. Today, it is culture, and the most empassioned political debates are no longer about the nationalization or privatization of companies or banks, but about legislation on abortion, fertility treatment, the care of the dying, or even how private life should be portrayed on television or how schools should relate to children from different cultural backgrounds.

The world of instrumentality and the world of identities are not, however, like two armies facing each other across a no man's land where the bullets fly. Each is trying to use the other for its own ends, or at least to integrate it by controlling it. Neo-communitarian powers, for example, usually adopt policies of modernization. It is very easy to do this when the oil flows freely and creates a *rentier* economy that can easily tolerate the preservation of traditional forms of social and cultural organization. On the other hand, the reduction of sexuality to a form of consumption is one of the most pronounced and visible trends in liberal societies. Sexuality permeates mass culture in the form of a commercialized eroticism, or even pornography. In individualist societies, by contrast, sexuality is one of the central expressions of an identity that is no longer policed by general social and cultural norms. Its positive meaning explains the attention that is now given to homosexuality and especially gay culture; it is both ludic and erotic, and rejects traditional norms. In a culture dominated by instrumentalism and therefore by the relaxation of social and institutional controls, eroticism is the equivalent of the defence of a collective identity in societies that collectively resist globalized free trade. The so-called consumer society tries to control this eroticism by treating it like any other creditworthy demand, but eroticism refuses to be reduced to these logics, just as a culture or a religion refuses to be reduced to the ideology of a neo-communitarian regime. Commercialism tries to use all forms of identitarian behaviour in the same way that neo-communitarian powers use industrial technologies and financial circuits.

This rending apart of modernity, this divorce between the economy and cultures, does not provide a complete description of our collective experience at the end of the century. This is both because social policies do preserve many links between the two worlds as they drift apart and because there is considerable resistance on the part of privileged categories or categories with a state-guaranteed professional status. Indeed, in day-to-day life, that resistance seems to be more visible than tendencies that are so general that they cannot be dominant in all places and at all times.

The important thing is not to recall that the past, distant or recent, has not been abolished and that the rifts and discontinuities do not prevent continuities and particularities from surviving. The important thing is to recognize that we have been living in a new situation for at least twenty-five years. Whilst it is a mistake to believe that our nation-states are now powerless in the face of globalization, it is an even greater mistake to believe that the whole of our social, political and intellectual lives have not been transformed by the transition from the era of national reconstruction (1945–75) to the era of globalized markets and financial flows. And it is because we are living in a new type of society and leading a new international life that talk of postmodernity is dangerous.

The decline of institutions

Demodernization is defined by the dissociation of the economy from cultures and by the debasement of both. Their debasement is the direct result of demodernization. It began at the end of the nineteenth century with the formation, on an unprecedented scale, of an international financial and industrial economy which provoked the resistance of cultural and national identities in the central countries, and anti-colonial uprisings in the dependent countries. It was masked by the Second World War and the period of reconstruction that followed.

By revealing and speeding up the globalization of the economy, the collapse of the Soviet model accentuated a trend that had become visible from the end of the period of post-war reconstruction onwards. From the early 1970s, or in other words after the cultural rebellion of French and American students, the collapse of the international monetary system, and the alarm bells sounded by the first oil crisis, it became increasingly obvious that the rationalist-liberal model of modernization, which seemed to have taken on a new lease of life after the fall of Nazism and during the cold war, had been shattered. Its destruction did not coincide, however, with a flowering of intellectual creativity comparable with that of the late nineteenth century, mainly because the intellectuals, especially in France, were still under the spell of the Enlightenment model and a republican spirit dressed up as Marxist fundamentalism. When the Berlin Wall came down, it was no longer possible to ignore the brutal reality of what was happening around us, and we have no option but to kick aside the ill-conceived ideologies that promised the planet a happy ending and prophesied that all the peoples of the world would be reconciled in the model society perfected once and for all by the United States and its European ancestors.

These breaks do not occur solely at the international level; they affect all societies, all organized collective actors and even individuals. The fact that institutions, customs, beliefs and programmes still give a semblance of unity to fragmented personalities, fragmented societies and a fragmented world must not blind us to the obvious: our modernity is in shreds, and we cannot make light of its decomposition by claiming that we are moving into a postmodern era which supposedly has all the charms of critical individualism and is at the same time miraculously safe from identitarian and communitarian reactions.

Whilst demodernization means primarily that there is a rift between system and actor, its main – and complementary – aspects are de-institutionalization and desocialization. These strange words do not refer to hidden transformations that are hard to discover. On the contrary, they designate massive upheavals or mutations that affect the most important aspects of our social experience.

De-institutionalization is to be understood as meaning that codified norms safeguarded by legal mechanisms no longer exist, or, to put it more simply, that the judgements of normality that were once applied to institutionally governed forms of behaviour no longer apply. Some people complacently describe the societies we are now entering as 'tolerant'. That sounds nice, but the absence of norms in those societies allows different types of social organization and cultural behaviour to coexist in every domain, and that is at once liberating and a source of anxiety.

In this respect, the most illuminating example is that of the family. Louis Roussel summarizes its recent evolution when he speaks of an 'uncertain family'. Both the law and public morality make fewer and fewer normative judgements, and make no distinction between extended families, nuclear families, single-parent families, families that have been reconstituted, homosexual families, families based on marriage and families made up of couples living together. This is because we no longer define family situations in institutional terms, but in terms of communication between members of family units, or even in terms of the recognition of the personal rights and interests of all the individuals in a family. Our main expectations of the family are that it should shape both the personality of children and sexual and affective relations between adults. In so far as the position of women and fatherhood are concerned, the main effect of the crisis in the family has been to focus the debate on how individuals can become Subjects and live as Subjects. We are now more likely to speak of the effects of an absent family than those of a tyrannical family.

What applies to the family also applies to schools. Whilst some still feel a certain nostalgia for the culture of the school as institution, both it and the role once played by the 'master' who transmitted both knowledge and national or social norms are in an advanced state of decay, and have almost vanished. François Dubet and Danilo Martuccelli (1996) have forcefully demonstrated that, whilst this classical model is still powerful in primary schools, it is disappearing in secondary schools. In primary schools, the teacher–pupil relationship remains central, and children define themselves in relation to their teachers; in secondary schools, young people begin to reject academic culture. Secondary-school pupils are torn between two worlds: the world of work that lies ahead and that requires qualifications and the world of a youth culture that has developed freely in our schools, but which has so little in common with academic culture that it seems incomprehensible or aggressive to their teachers. The world of work and technologies is coming into conflict with the world of identity and community.

The decline of institutions does have some positive effects. It means that sociological analyses will have to look at actors rather than systems. At this stage of our analysis, it is only natural that we should take a negative view of the decline of institutions and see it as a form of demodernization, but I will be saying again and again that we are being arbitrary if we see it only as a symptom of crisis and decay. We should, rather, be speaking of a mutation, or even of the emergence of a new cultural and social landscape in which the Subject will take the central place that belonged to society in the old landscape. We should not, on the other hand, underestimate the importance of the phenomena of decay.

Given that we are living through an in-between period, we must be careful not to lose our sense of direction and must not ignore the possibility that the past might decay without our constructing a future. The turn of the century is not experiencing the cultural pessimism of the late nineteenth century, but it is experiencing a loss of direction. No debates are taking place, and there are no social and cultural conflicts. It is as though we could easily become schizophrenic, and live partly in the world of technologies and the market and partly in that of identity and community. The price we have to pay, of course, is a profound change in both our personalities and our social life, but we are not rebelling or drawing up projects for reforms or revolutions as a result. Throughout almost the whole of the nineteenth century, we dreamed of the future. We imagined it, loved it and desired it. It was inscribed on the banners we carried in our social struggles and in our cultural creations. Today, we cannot even define the mutation that is occurring as the birth of a future. There is no longer any 'principle of hope', to borrow a phrase from Ernst Bloch, and we have less and less in common with all those who believed, like Bloch, in the creative virtues of utopia. We face the difficult task of discovering just what society and what culture are emerging without referring to some supposed historical necessity or meaning of history.

The demodernization we are living through is defined by *desocialization* as well as by de-institutionalization. Once again, we have to be careful not to understand this notion in terms of the idea of decline or loss that it might seem to imply. It should allow us to orient ourselves as we search for the new relations, or even the new forms of integration, that we might be able to establish between the two worlds that are now drifting apart before our very eyes.

We once shaped our personalities by thinking about the social roles we assumed, or about the way the way others saw individuals playing their social roles. We could do so because all roles related to common forms of authority, norms and values. What German authors call the lifeworld (*Lebenswelt*) was strongly defined and socially organized. It was, it was assumed, by becoming a citizen, a worker, a father or a mother that an individual became a respectable person and entered the realm of universal rights. There was therefore no break between the lifeworld and the social system. The actor and the system shared the same perspective; the system had to be analysed as a set of mechanisms and rules, and the actor had to be analysed in terms of the internalized values and norms that determined how he behaved.

I use the term 'desocialization' to describe the disappearance of the social roles, norms and values that were once used to construct the lifeworld. Desocialization is a direct result of the de-institutionalization of the economy, politics and religion. Whereas a system of production was of necessity seen as a system of social relations of production, a market economy governed by international competitiveness, the proliferation of new technologies and the speculative movement of capital has become increasingly divorced from the social relations of production. Similarly, education can no longer transmit the behavioural norms (discipline, work, deferred gratification) imposed by a mode of production. Daniel Bell (1980) was the first to say that norms of production, norms of consumption and the norms of the political system are now dissociated, or even mutually contradictory.

Under these conditions, individuals are either reduced to being mosaics of behavioural patterns that are so diverse that they cannot generate any unitary personal principle, or seek that unity in a cultural heritage, a language, a memory, a religion or even a libido which is as impersonal as a culture, but which does supply a principle around which a personality can be built. Hence the central paradox of our society: at the very time when the economy is being globalized and transformed rapidly by new technologies, the personality is no longer being projected into the future, and is looking, on the contrary, to the past or to an ahistorical desire for support. The system and the actor no longer share the same perspective; they are diametrically opposed.

The explanation is that we have left productive society behind us, and that the actor has been desocialized. The economy is no longer a social system, but a flow or set of flows, and it is almost impossible to predict or control their jerky movements. In industrial society, it was possible to defend a certain balance between the world of the system and the lifeworld and to resist, as Jürgen Habermas does so vigorously, strategic action's invasion of the lifeworld. That vision presupposed, however, the existence of a solid link between the two worlds, and it was their social character that provided it: a social actor acted within a social system, but was at the same time motivated by a different action logic. We now live in a state of demodernization in which the break between actor and system is complete. And this means that we have to reason differently.

It would be as dangerous to defend the decayed lifeworld as it would be to defend a system of production that has been reduced to a market. It is futile and dangerous to choose one part of the ruins as opposed to another. Above all, we have to be wary of the idea that our societies are, like the industrial society of the past, highly integrated sets of economic, political and social actors. The most influential thinkers of the 1970s denounced this integration as suffocating and manipulative. We are now in a very different situation. Social systems are breaking down, the system and the actor have been divorced, and the beginning of the new century is already dominated by the hostile complementarity that has developed between the world market and cultural nationalisms or fundamentalisms, and between a globalized economy and fragmented cultures that are obsessed with defending their identity.

As a result, the idea of demodernization is impervious to the critiques that were made of industrial society. Those critiques were directed against the social organization, the appropriation of production and the distribution of wealth, but they did not (with some exceptions) challenge the idea of progress, which provided the basis for industrial society and which was as dear to socialists as it was to liberals. The break we are experiencing today is more serious. It is not only society that is under attack. Also under attack is culture and, above all, the previously unquestioned harmony between culture, society and personality, which were once regarded as three compenents or levels in the analysis of a single social aggregate. We are now seeing the disappearance or decay of the social mediations between the globalized economy and fragmented cultures. Is it possible to imagine a historical reality being more completely destroyed? Social thought is disappearing, and is being replaced by either the analysis of the global culture or the defence of identities, particularisms, beliefs and communities. Can there still be an organized conflict between forces that have become as totally alien to one another as the market and fundamentalist movements? Are we no longer in a situation in which social movements can fight over the social control of resources and in which the value of cultural models can be recognized by both adversaries? Is it not inevitable that violence should replace negotiation, just as contradiction is replacing conflict? Are we not now caught up in what Weber called the war between the gods?

This desocialization is also a depoliticization. The political order no longer constitutes or founds the social order. We still live under the rule of law, but we have already emerged from the era in which we believed that the law or a power supported by social movements could give birth to a new society and a new man. The crisis of the political takes an acute form in the contemporary world. The crisis of representativeness and trust worsened as parties came more and more to resemble political companies that mobilized resources, both legal and illegal, to produce elected representatives who would be 'bought' by voters if they saw them as defending their own interests. We can no longer regard such representatives as the agents of social creativity. This crisis is closely bound up with the crisis of the nation-state, which is so often said to be too small to deal with the big problems and too big to deal with the small ones.

The destruction of organized and self-regulating bodies such as civilizations, societies and political systems also has its effects on personal experience, as the unity of personal experience was once a mirror image of institutions: the image of the citizen or worker internalizing the norms and values of orderly societies and progressive societies. Our unitary civilization is decaying, and so too is our lived experience. Hence the decay of the ego, which was once shaped through the internalization of relations with others and, therefore, of the roles it was expected to play. The ego can no longer play its role as a psychological mediator between a global culture and psychical representations as diverse as the libido, the language we use and our adherence to the cultural beliefs that have been handed down to us. The lifeworld, which François Dubet (1995) refers to as experience, no longer has any unity, not because contemporary society is too complex and is changing too fast, but because its members are affected by centrifugal forces which draw them, on the one hand, towards instrumental action and the attractive symbols of globalization and a modernity which is increasingly defined by desocialization and, on the other hand, towards an 'archaic' membership of a community defined by the fusion of society, culture and personality. Being both hyper-modern and anti-modern, we are being swept along by demodernization, as is particularly obvious to those of us who hold that the model for the future will be supplied by societies and individuals who are more concerned with equilibrium and survival than with growth and change. The lifeworld can no longer impose its norms and values on strategic action, because it is no more than a shadow of its former self.

This cultural rupture is accompanied by a social rift. Latin American economists and sociologists long ago described the dualization which divides society into 'included' and 'excluded' or which, to use the title of my book on Latin America (Touraine 1988), divorces the world of speech, or in other words participation, from that of blood, or exclusion and repression. The same dualization has now spread throughout the world.

New York is both the centre of the world economy and a Third World city. Similarly, the Greater Paris area is traversed by the frontiers that divide the urban centres from the suburbs, and it is increasingly difficult to cross them. In all Western countries, and in the crisis-hit developing countries, the internal frontier is becoming more visible by the year. Talk of social problems or of problems relating to youth, unemployment, drugs, immigration and violence often heightens our awareness of the internal frontier. When they trace this frontier, the richer countries isolate minorities, but those minorities are as large as they are in poorer countries. In Latin America, the formal and informal sectors of the economy are of comparable size throughout the continent; in Western Europe, those who put their faith in the economic openness symbolized (in their view) by the Maastricht Treaty do not outnumber those who reject a treaty which seems to them to announce their own marginalization and the disappearance of the safeguards afforded by nation-states, which have allowed them to survive until now. Until quite recently, we thought that our society was made up of a vast middle class, which was in the majority, a ruling élite that was rapidly acquiring wealth by investing in the markets, and the excluded or the poor, who could not keep up in the marathon as the pace got faster and faster.

Part of that middle class now feels that it is being dragged downwards, and is turning against the excluded and trying to use them as scapegoats for its own insecurity. It no longer believes that the economic system can do anything to prevent social disintegration. Whilst one-third of the population looks forward with confidence to the open market, another third is demanding state protection, and 'the state' is falling back on authoritarian solutions in its attempts to displace the threat hanging over them on to those who are even more threatened with exclusion.

Our social welfare institutions are powerful, and can still do a lot to attenuate the threat of exclusion, but the fact that they are partially successful cannot conceal the gravity of the situation, and the remedies they offer are inadequate. In the European Union, it is estimated that about half of the men and women who are capable of working do not have real jobs; statisticians arrive at this figure by totalling the official figures for those who are seeking work and in receipt of benefits, the number of students who have delayed their entry into a world of work in which there is now little job security, the number of people who have taken early retirement, and of those (mainly women) who, when they reach the age of forty-five or fifty, give up trying to find work. It is no exaggeration to say that, whilst a small minority is living in extreme poverty, and whilst a much larger minority is actively being excluded by other categories, between one-third and one-half of the population of the countries of Western Europe feels threatened by social disintegration and social exclusion. Some of those who are threatened with exclusion escape that fate by bringing great pressure to bear on the state, but the pressures they bring to bear – usually successfully – have the effect of increasing the threat to the most vulnerable, namely the unemployed, young people without jobs, immigrants and those who live in underprivileged areas or neighbourhoods. In the United States, Great Britain and France, we are seeing the development of an underclass, or a new category of poor people. It is as though the price that has to be paid for the salvation of the majority is the damnation of an increasingly large minority. In this context, it is vital not to see the cultural divide and the social rift, or demodernization and the dualization of society, as separate phenomena. How can we fail to be aware of the failure of policies of using economic growth and social redistribution to promote social integration, when the social gulf between rich and poor is growing both on a world scale and within many national societies? How can we accept the optimism of the competitive and the protected who refuse to see that, further down the social scale, society is disintegrating and that violence and exclusion are on the increase?

Modernity in crisis; modernity transformed

The present situation may come to resemble the situation that character-ized the darkest period of both capitalist and Communist industrializa-tion: open conflict between money and workers and the reduction of public life to the courts' defence of the powerful, the intervention of a policeman-state and the admonitions of philanthropists. Our social welfare system is under threat. What is worse, we are staring into a disturbing political void, and it cannot be filled by appeals from the humanitarian organizations that have taken on the role of philanthropists now that our social integration policies are in ruins. We are trapped between the calculations of the financiers and the fatwas of the ayatollahs. All eyes are turned on the United States, but that country is both the main centre for world markets and an increasingly fragmented collection of communities, conflicting opinions and ghettoes.

This deliberately schematic overview calls for two responses, and they will be the main themes of this book. The first is that trying to go back to the past is futile. Many people, however, are trying to revive the image of a society based upon shared values that can be transformed into juridical and social norms and in which there is room for both technological and economic activities. They dream of a society which is integrated by courts that punish deviancy and schools that socialize new members of the collectivity. This image, which was elaborated and then piously handed down by so-called classical sociology, is out of step with observable reality. Today's sociology usually shows us systems without actors and actors without systems, because there is almost never any relationship of reciprocity between institutionalized norms and socialized actors. Sociologists, like everyone else, must get used to the idea that society is a thing of the past, assuming that we understand the term to mean a principle that can regulate behaviour. We no longer live in a world of institutions, but in a world of markets, communities and individuals. The very word 'society', which was the corner-stone of classical sociology, is becoming meaningless as its rules fall out of step with our practices. We have to stop trying to found social life on the famous cultural consensus, the religious morality of the United States, the French Republic's principles of individualistic universalism, and the principle that we are all equal in the eyes of the law. Whilst these ideologies are a testimony to how difficult we would all find it to live in a world completely divided into two by the realm of the market and the realm of communities, they cannot help us to face up to the future.

We now have to go back to the beginning. It was the strength of the constitutional nation-state that made rationalization and ethical individualism the twin pillars of modernity. That was the great strength of the Republic and the Nation, of the truly political order that took priority over society as a whole, just as reason or the meaning of history took priority over individual interests. That was the strength of the state, in the sense in which the French use that word to describe an executive power that merges into an administration, a nation that identifies with its history, republican institutions, territory and landscapes. For a long time, social problems arose within a national framework, and economic development itself was defined as the combination, within the territory of a state, of productive investments and social and political redistributive mechanisms.

The problems I am trying to define here would not arise, or would require only limited reforms, if the framework of the nation-state were still capable of integrating and reconciling the conflicting tendencies within the economy, society and culture. The effects of the crisis in the democratic nation-state are being felt mainly in Great Britain and France, which were its main inventors, but they are also spreading to all the industrialized countries. The crisis is affecting both the United States and those regions that experienced the triumph of anti-colonial nationalisms and that are now being torn apart by the violent clash between economic liberalism and cultural, ethnic or religious fundamentalism.

In France, both the Left and the Right, being equally republican, tried for a long time to subordinate the life of the French to the *grandeur* of the state, even though it was becoming more and more difficult to define what that meant. The French believed that all they had to do to alleviate the effects of both the globalization of the economy and cultural fragmentation was to appeal to everyone to rally round a unitary state. They were as suspicious of cultural diversity as they were of economic competitiveness, and they marginalized both the thought and the action of women, which were becoming increasingly important in many other countries. That period seems to be over. The 1995 presidential campaign was dominated by the convincingly realistic themes of *la fracture sociale* ('the social fracture') or *la faille sociale* ('the social fault-line'), which was threatening a large minority of the country's inhabitants with exclusion, and the breaking of the social bond. This shift in public opinion and in the thinking of political leaders is such an important element in the current situation that it cannot be omitted here, as I would not be raising the problem of demodernization or worrying so much about it were I not convinced that the way it is dealt with will to a large extent determine the future of the society in which I live.

Demodernization is merely the other side of modernization. Modernization could occur so long as the divorce between nature and the Subject went hand in hand with a combination of economic growth and ethical individualism within the framework of a nation-state which was itself based upon the complementary relationship between a diversified local life and a national life that was at once restricted and organized in accordance with strict rules. It turned into demodernization at the point at which society came to have less control of itself, and especially when the success of the constitutional monarchy, and then of the republican nation-state, social democracy and the Welfare State, gave way to the great rift that divorced the globalized economy from identities which were ceasing to be social and becoming, or reverting to being, cultural. The globalization of economic activities destroyed the social and cultural controls that once governed them. Stimulated or used by the labour movement and campaigns for social reform, political institutions tried on several occasions to regain the control they had lost. They built an industrial democracy, and then social democracy and the Welfare State. These were so many syntheses of economic modernization and social integration, and they are not to be confused with new figures of modernity. On the contrary, they helped to hasten the decay of modernity by reducing ethical individuals to their social roles or social utility. Whilst the tension between rationalization and ethical individualism was the source of both modernity's strength and its weakness, we now heard the triumphal argument that economic progress and social progress complemented one another. The mood was close to the optimism of the ideologies of progress. Because they were suspicious of this progressive moralism, the intellectuals withdrew and, following the example of Jean-Paul Sartre, came to associate the defence of freedom of conscience with the insurmountable problems of a society based upon profits and power. The Welfare State was a social success, but it meant giving economic leaders intellectual and institutional control over the whole of society – hence the force of the critical reaction against that control initiated by the Critical Theory of the Frankfurt philosophers and, in France, by Michel Foucault and the researchers of the Centre d'Études, de Recherche et de Formation Institutionnelles. The collapse of this social democracy from the 1970s onwards certainly posed a serious threat of social regression, but it was a more limited phenomenon than demodernization, in that it was merely a synthesis of economic growth and social integration, and not of ethical individualism and rationalization. What might be called the social-democratic spirit was an effective response to the damage done by capitalist industrialization, but it was no more than a late and limited form of the idea of the nation, whose invention had been the founding achievement of the English, American and French revolutions.

The tragic thing about this retreat on the part of social-democratic regimes is that it leaves a yawning gap between a globalized economy, which has been transformed by information technologies, and a personal morality which is increasingly dominated by the importance it accords to sexuality and intimacy, as well as by the search for an identity. The Welfare State could conceal the gap, but it could not fill it.

This great rift is a threat to modernity. Worse still, it makes it quite impossible to fall back on institutional conceptions of modern society. The current crisis in demodernization therefore has two meanings. On the one hand, it poses such a threat to modernity that it has provoked the formation of a postmodernist current which refuses to recognize the existence of any link between the two halves, now separated, of modern life. On the other hand, it forces us to look for a non-institutional principle for the reconstruction of modernity, because we can no longer hope to revive the political Subject of the classical period (to say nothing of the religious Subject), and because believing that we can reconcile rationalization and progress is out of the question. In short, we no longer believe in the anthropomorphic god known as progress.

Demodernization is the result of the crisis affecting (and perhaps destroying) a mode of managing the two worlds whose separation defines modernity. Acknowledging that this is the case does not mean that it is impossible to find a new way of reconciling instrumental rationalization and ethical individualism. Indeed, the search for such a solution is this book's *raison d'être*. To put it more simply, the breakup of national-political society does not have to be seen in purely negative terms. The desocialization of mass culture does not just create a deracinated world. Like industrialization and urbanization before it, it encourages production rather than reproduction, and innovation rather than the heritage of the past; it tears down the barriers erected by time and distance. Information technologies are having a decisive effect here. They are wresting us out of our spatial and temporal framework. They are replacing seriality with simultaneity, evolution with diversity, and distance with proximity. In more general terms, the desocialization I have been describing means that we can do less and less to predict how we will behave on the basis of our understanding of our economic or professional situation. We complain (not unreasonably) that television decontextualizes events, which should be placed in a historical context if they are to be understood, and transforms them into human situations which provoke the elementary reactions of sympathy or antipathy. Yet it is also thanks to the media that we cease to be social beings whose roles are defined by established social norms. At a deeper level still, social definitions of sexual identity (gender) are becoming blurred. Sexuality circulates freely, and may or may not involve feelings, dialogue or love. We are discovering ourselves to be individuals whose morality consists not in any reference to a model, but in the preservation or enrichment of our individuality in the midst of a whirlwind of events and information.

We shall not rediscover the *terra firma* of a social order built upon solid institutions and harsh methods of socialization. We are living in a period of permanent change, which is destroying institutions as though they were so many sandbanks and blurring social reference points and norms, as well as what we once called 'community values'. All the swimmer can do is to build a raft and hope to survive.

The remedy for demodernization is not nostalgia for a social order or community that has gone; it is the acceptance that the old synthesis known as *Homo politicus* has been destroyed, and that we need to discover how to construct a new modernity. The foundation for that modernity can no longer be the law; we have to look for it in every individual's desire to combine, in his or her personal life, an involvement in the technological (and economic) world and the mobilization of a cultural (and personal) identity that is always out of step with instrumental rationality. It is thanks to the crisis of demodernization that we shall discover the need to appeal to the personal Subject.

Condemning or extolling the information society is as unacceptable as expecting industrial society to produce miracles or catastrophes. We have to reject these simplistic evolutionary visions, and recall that a modern society can exist only if we respect the divorce between human subjectivity and the outside world. On the other hand, we must also find some way to reconcile them or make them compatible. If the two horses drawing the carriage pull in opposite directions, it will inevitably topple over and be wrecked. Rather than prophesying, at the end of the millennium, an era of troubles or a new period of technological victories, we should be asking ourselves how a new synthesis can enable us to leave demodernization behind and to live new forms of modernity.

Backs to the wall

We are faced with an enigma: can we reconcile liberalism and community, the market and cultural identity? Can we live together, at the same time both equal and different? The young *Beurs* (the French-born children of North African immigrants) who took part in the March for Equality used to chant 'Let's live together with our differences'. Yes, but how? Can we avoid having to choose between two equally destructive solutions: living together and setting aside our differences or living apart in homogeneous communities which communicate only through the market or through violence?

I recall the *Beur* movement of 1983 because the hopes of that time are so far removed from the revolts and clashes of today that we have to stop putting too much faith in institutions and public opinion. We now hear fewer and fewer calls for the excluded or the marginal to be integrated into a society which is itself in decay and which makes certain categories bear the weight of exclusion and poverty. The distance between 'Let's live together' and 'with our differences' is growing all the time. Some of us want to concentrate on keeping the 'together', and others 'the differences'. I would like to demonstrate that we can and must reconcile the two or, in other words, that we can give democracy a new face. We must both recognize pluralism and maintain the universalist rule of law. But the search for a new democracy means that we have to call into question a lot of ideas, and a lot of our analytic and intellectual equipment.

How, first of all, can we abandon the idea of society? Sometimes the word is almost meaningless. We speak of 'British society' in order to study certain aspects – mostly institutional – of a state, namely the United Kingdom. The word 'society', as I have said, once had a very strong meaning. It meant a normative principle. The common good, the general interest or the national interest were so many figures of the principle we used to define good and evil, the normal and the pathological, inclusion and exclusion. It replaced the sanctity of tradition. I say again that, no matter whether it takes the form of communitarianism, a moral and legal consensus or the republicanism that appeals to the law, this sociologism is no longer anything more than an ideology that promotes exclusion rather than integration. It is an assertion of superiority, rather than an attempt to reduce social distances. But I immediately add that the reduction of social life to a market where globalized currents meet and to identitarian islands would produce a violent storm zone. A collectivity that is not to some extent self-regulating (and therefore normative) is inconceivable, as is a collectivity that does not have some political conception of what it is. All democracies are based on the belief that collective action can promote personal freedoms. That, however, is no reason for not thinking about the nature of a democracy that could promote the interests of human Subjects, individual or collective, who are not only, or not even primarily, citizens.

Our modernity based society on politics, and laws on government by the people and for the people. Political philosophy was the earliest form of sociology. Sociology acquired an identity of its own only when the definition of the social by the political and the juridical was inverted by the industrial revolution, the rise of nationalisms, of consumerism or working-class struggles, and by the recognition of sexuality. All these mutations made it impossible to identify modern man with a citizen defined by his respect for the laws he helped to draw up. Nor can we rely on the state for support. It counts for relatively little against world markets, except when it mobilizes a highly dangerous cultural nationalism. As we come to the end of this first chapter, let us quickly try to find a solution to the two problems we have noted. The world of the economy, markets and technologies is becoming divorced from the world of collective and individual identities. Once they are separated, both these worlds are debased. At the same time, the social and political mediations that once bound them together are vanishing.

We will have come a long way if we can agree that this is how we should define our problem. We must reconcile the unity of instrumental reason, realistic calculations and the power of the mass media with a diversity of cultural identities. We have to reconcile the market and communities. Our objective is very different from the central objective we set ourselves for more than a century: reconciling the concentration of investments with the redistribution of the fruits of growth, or in other words transforming the class struggle into a policy for economic and social development. And our objective is still further removed from the conflict, which dominated the earlier period, between the formation of a central state and the defence of the interests and freedoms of citizens. We first learned to think our history in political terms, and then to interpret it in the light of the economy and social relations of production. We now have to analyse and construct it in cultural terms. The conflict is no longer between a king and a people, or capitalists and workers, but between globalized information and communitarian identities that are defined in cultural rather than economic or social terms.

This leads us to the preliminary conclusion that the history of all modern societies has been dominated by basic conflicts between the accumulation of the means to transform social, political or cultural life, and the defence of the freedom of those actors and social groups who are most deeply implicated in the relationship between the concentration of means of action, and the free and responsible involvement of people who do not want to be mere resources in the hands of the leading players. It also leads to a second conclusion. We urgently need to revise the notions we have so constantly been using for the last 200 years: classes and social movements, nation, democracy, State, identity and education. Above all, we must abandon visions of history presided over by some meta-social principle such as God, reason, history or the totality, defined in the Hegelian–Marxist sense in which Lukács used that term. The meaning of a collective action was once defined on the basis of whether it was or was not in contradiction with the higher principle of the workings and evolution of society. Personal and collective actions could therefore be evaluated only on the basis of their role: did they help to disarticulate or rearticulate a shattered experience? Our analysis of social life can no longer be governed by a goal that looks at social actors from the outside – such as growth, the acquisition of wealth or rationalization. It must be governed by the desire to reconstitute the social and political field by finding some form of communication between the world of instrumentality and that of identities.

These questions are, by their very nature, disturbing. Our starting-point is pessimistic. That is why this book is so different from the much more optimistic analysis I gave at the end of the 1980s when I was writing *Critique of Modernity*, first published in French in 1992. At that time, I wanted to put the idea of modernity back on its own two feet, and I was critical of those who had reduced it to rationalization by following in the tradition of the philosophers of progress, the positivists, the liberals and the revolutionaries. I contrasted the bourgeois and then working-class (and feminist) defence of freedom with the rationalizing model which submitted everything to some image, either capitalist or socialist, of a triumphant and transparent reason. I thought that the historical experience of modern and democratic countries had taught us that it was possible to appeal at the same time to human rights and the sovereignty of the people, to freedom and equality. And a century of successful social reforms seemed to me to have demonstrated that economic modernization and social justice were, assuming the existence of a democratic culture and democratic political institutions, compatible rather than contradictory. The collapse of that optimism, which has since been exacerbated by both the almost complete destruction of every form of developmentalist and mobilizing state and the triumph of globalization, has forced me to extend my earlier analysis. We have lived through some very rapid mutations at the turn of the century.

Whereas some saw the ending of the cold war as the beginning of a trend that would lead to one world based on one model, I saw it as the beginning of a split much deeper than that between the social classes of industrial society. That is why the question whch this book is trying to answer is not about the future, the evolution or the meaning of history, or about the forms and effects of a mode of production, but about the conditions of existence of social life, of living together, and about communication between individuals or collectivities.

I no longer think that the political order can itself integrate such obviously contradictory tendencies, but I cannot reconcile myself to there being no communication with the Other. This contradiction calls for an urgent response; otherwise we will quickly be submerged by aggressive cultural nationalisms, or reduced to being mere consumers of cultural models constructed by markets. As I have already said, I regard a complete divorce between system and actors, or total demodernization, as impossible or dangerous. A society that has been reduced to a network of motorways through mutually hostile or alien ghettoes would see the outbreak of tribal wars, segregation and racism. And I have also said on every page of this chapter that it appears to me that the optimism of the Enlightenment and progress has been exhausted and now has perverse effects. I therefore cannot preach a blind differentialism.

It is time to get down to work. It is time to look for an answer to the riddle: How can we live together with our differences? How can we articulate the success of instrumental reason with an increasingly radical defence of personal and collective identities?

2

The Subject

If I am not for myself, who will be for me?
And even if I think of myself, what am I?
And if not now, when?

'Song of the Gedalists', cited in Primo Levi, *If Not Now, When?*, inspired by a saying of Rabbi Hillel in *The Maxims of the Fathers*, I. 13

Death of the ego

After a century of totalitarianism and authoritarianism, we are so distrustful of social religions and political mobilizations that we can no longer attempt to build a bridge between the two continents that are drifting apart by appealing to any figure of the Subject that is defined as the servant of God, reason or history. The image of the militant, like that of the crusader, arouses suspicion rather than admiration. We are even abandoning the idea of the ego because we have discovered that its unity was never anything more than the projection on to the individual of the unity and authority of the social system, or of a prince who had been transformed into a father and internalized in the shape of ethical norms. Socialization once allowed the reality principle to triumph, imposed the law of order on the disorder of desires, and replaced the war of every man against every man with the peace established by Leviathan or the general will. And it is precisely that social and civic religion that is breaking down, together with the educational supports that were once supplied at school and at home by the schoolmaster and his syllabus and the father and his structuring authority.

This may lead to the fragmentation of cultural experience. Studies of young people show that, outside the increasingly small number of families that teach the next generation to accept social responsibilities and to develop their personal autonomy, the education of the young is increasingly chaotic. Most young people experience, either alone or in primary groups, combinations or sequences of all sorts of things that cannot be integrated, rather as though every individual were home to several personalities. They live several different temporalities – that of school, that of their peer groups and that of sexuality – and they usually do so without any principle that allows them to integrate their various experiences. The idea of a gradual submission to the norms of social life, or those of the world of work and the family, is fading. The classic complementarity between the imposition of norms and the conquest of individuality, or the idea that it is by internalizing norms or even constraints that individuals become conscious of their own freedom (to the extent that it can be defined only with reference to limits and prohibitions), is becoming so blurred as to be invisible. Some would like to revive the idea of citizenship, and argue that individuals become free by identifying with a community of free citizens. Yet, whilst those who worry about the desocialization of youth or the difficulty of integrating immigrants have been inspired to write fine words by this civil ethics, it provides no solution to the real problems with which we are faced. In a society which tends to be organized around consumption, the personality has no integrative principle. Socialization was once based upon the acquisition of closely associated images of time and space; we are increasingly denied socially defined time and space. Television brings distant things very close, and the idea of history, which has always meant the history of a nation or territorial collectivity, is, as Pierre Nora has shown, being replaced by that of either an individual or a collective memory. What we initially perceived as a crisis in the family or our schools, and therefore in education and socialization, is also a crisis in the shaping of individual personalities. Social norms and individual or collective identities used to complement one another, but this is no longer the case. Similarly, the decline of Taylorism or, in other words, of the rationalization of production is inseparable from the decline of the working class, which was once defined by the fact that it was dominated by the masters of rationalization. As a result of the breakup of both society and the personality, many people say that the principles of both conflict and identity are disappearing, and that our society is beginning to look like a department store or an airport, rather than a factory or a system of juridical norms.

Mass society is the most direct threat to the Subject. In this society, individuals avoid making any reference to themselves. They are creatures of desire who have completely abandoned the reality principle in their quest for an instinctual or, in other words, impersonal liberation. By contrast with the authoritarian regimes which, like Stalinism, called for a new man, or which, like the legend over the gate to Auschwitz I, proclaimed that work would make us free, many have pursued the critique of power and its hold over individuals so far as to preach an unrestricted polymorphous sexuality that heeds no prohibitions and requires no justification. If we take that position, which may still have an emancipatory effect when it represents an aesthetic stance, how can we avoid falling into the trap of reducing the Other to the status of a mere object of pleasure? How can we prevent the strong from imposing their power on the weak: adults on children, men on women and Europeans on the colonized? If that happens, the very social relations we are trying to escape will appear in their most pathological form, and the richest consumers will have a monopoly on meaning.

In today's world, the consumer society which manipulates us and the pursuit of pleasure that traps us within our passions are as great a threat to the Subject as obedience to the law of God or society was in the past.

An escape from two things

We do, however, have to accept that we are witnessing the breakup of the dominant social and psychological model we began to construct at the end of the nineteenth century, and which made the thought, literature and art of the twentieth century so powerful. The destruction of the ego which, in the name of society, its needs and its conventions, once imposed its law upon the body, its drives and its violence, has done as much to transform our lives as the destruction of the principles of the social order itself. As cultural identities rose up in rebellion against Eurocentric universalism, sexuality and death began to escape the controls imposed on psychic life by internalized norms. The eroticism of the Batailles and the Bacons has destroyed the social order, just as the return of ethnic and religious identities has destroyed Western man's claims to be able to identify his history and his interests with universalism. Now that financial and communication networks are becoming divorced from human experience, it is very tempting to leave the Subject and its appeal to universalism to die, and to give a free rein to both cultural differences and the impersonality of desire and violence.

Before we begin to try to reconnect the two worlds which are both drifting further apart and being debased, we have to realize that both the ego and social rationality have been destroyed. We are living in the ruins of Marxism–Leninism, which tried to equate the social and national demand with the rational laws of historical development. And we are also living in the ruins of the bourgeois society, whose good education and great principles were powerless to prevent the triumph of violence and persecution. Were it not for the death of society and the ego, both the quest for the Subject and the defence of the Subject would be meaningless. We have to accept that the threat of demodernization is the central thing in our lives. We have to abandon the positive principles of reconstruction, and the appeals to Man, Order and Peace bequeathed to us by the past.

Our real point of reference is not hope, but the pain of being torn apart. Because the world of objectivation and its technologies has been so debased as to be no more than a market, whilst the world of cultural identities is locked into the communitarian obsession, the individual who exists inside us all is suffering the agony of being torn apart, of feeling that his or her lifeworld is as decayed as the institutional realm or even the representation of the world itself. We no longer know who we are. For a long time, the repressive weight of prohibitions and the law was the main pathological factor. We are now experiencing a very different pathology: the impossibility of formulating an 'I', because it is either drowning in a mass culture or being confined within authoritarian communities.

This experience of being personally torn apart, of the loss of identity that we resist by giving such importance to self-esteem, self-development and, in a word, to autonomy, does not encourage us to try to overcome social contradictions, but it does encourage us to heal the sufferings of individuals who have been torn asunder because they can no longer call upon either a divine creator, a self-organized nature or a rational society. Individual suffering is the primary force that allows us to resist the sundering of the demodernized world. The suffering is all the greater in that poverty, insecurity and social rejection make communication between the two worlds more difficult; but the cultural rift is obvious to anyone who does not identify completely with either the world of success or the world of tradition. The tearing apart of identity I am talking about here is not a pathological condition seen only in extreme cases; it affects us all. The way in which we experience it will determine how much room for manoeuvre we have.

We will be unable to reconstruct our experience unless we free ourselves in two ways. We have to resist the debasement of both the disssociated halves of our existence. It is easier to describe how we can free ourselves from communities. This is a matter of freeing a culture from a community, and therefore from the social and political framework in which it has become trapped. In the Western world, Christian society was broken up in the name of Christianity itself, and this led to the internalization of faith at the time of the Catholic and Protestant reformations. Similarly, in the Islamic world, Islam is being invoked as the best defence against political neo-communitarianism. The same process can be observed whenever a culture becomes the captive of communitarian controls, because, far from being a figure of the Subject, the community with which an individual identifies binds that individual to a law, customs, representations and transitional forms of power and social organization. They become sacred, and thus conceal the distance that lies between any Subject and social reality. It is because there is a distance between the two that, rather than simply legitimizing it, the Subject can be a defence against social reality.

We can no longer contrast the lifeworld (*Lebenswelt*) with the strategic action of instrumental rationality. The Subject comes into being only by rejecting both instrumentality and identity, because identity is no more than a debased and introverted lived experience that is in a state of decay. Not only our contemporary demodernization, but modernity itself, results in the breakup of lived experience, of the premodern harmonies that once existed between individuals, society and the world. Both demodernization and modernity invalidate the constructs of a functionalist sociology whose central principle was the harmony between institutions and motivations, between system and actor. The personal Subject can come into being only if it is freed from communities which are too concrete and too holistic, and which impose an identity that is based upon duties rather than rights, and on membership of a community rather than freedom.

The main difficulty resides not in analysing the form of the reconstruction of actors, but in defining the forces that result in their reconstruction and that resist the coexistence of pure consumerism and the communitarian spirit. The young unemployed Algerians who use the black market of the cities to gain access to Western-style consumer goods also take part in Islamicist demonstrations. As a result, their personalities are fragmented, and they are dependent upon both mass culture and neo-communitarian political leaders. What can be done to make them reject such contradictory behaviour in favour of positive demands that are both social and cultural?

It is difficult to answer this question, as it is very tempting to introduce the *deus ex machina* of a need for self-assertion, a need to participate or even to protest, but that would trap us in a tautology. The Subject is not a 'soul' that is present within the body or the mind of individuals. The Subject is an individual's quest for the conditions that will allow him to become the actor of his own history. And that quest is motivated by the pain of being torn apart, and by the loss of identity and individuation. It is not a question of the individual enlisting in the service of some great cause, but primarily of the demand for the right to have an individual existence. That demand can be formulated only at the point where the rift is felt most keenly. There are two very different situations in which the

individual cannot make such a demand: exclusion, which leaves no solution but communitarian defence, and massification, which does in fact
integrate the individual into a hierarchical social order because mass
culture, which is in a sense a misnomer, abounds in signs indicating the
social level which an individual has reached or wishes to reach.

*The Subject is the individual's desire to be an actor. Subjectivation is the
desire for individuation*, and individuation can come about only if there is
an adequate interface between the world of instrumentality and that of
identity. If that interface does not exist, it is difficult not to both lapse into
a mimetic involvement in the instrumental world and retreat into a community, even though the two things are contradictory. This usually happens in times of difficult cultural or social change, or when individuals are
excluded from both the country they have left and a host country which
refuses to integrate newcomers.

Freeing the Subject from the power of markets and empires, on the one
hand, and the confinement of communities, on the other, is the necessary
pre-condition for the establishment of Subject-to-Subject communications, or for what Apel (1990) calls 'an ideal community of communication'. This is also the pre-condition for the transformation of the
principles of justice, solidarity and mutual responsibility, which facilitate
communication and argumentation, into actions that either break down
communitarian hierarchies or restrict their power. It should be added that
this ideal community of communication is indeed no more than an ideal,
and that it is therefore always embodied in a real social setting, such as
institutions that have interests of their own. Those interests can generate
either bureaucracy or élitism, or even the search for a consensus. International assemblies or debating circles are also ideal communities of
communication, but they have little impact on either the stormy ocean
of markets and technologies or the fortified islets occupied by communities. Apel's analysis of the internal pre-conditions for communication
tells us little about how these public spaces are constructed, and still less
about their ability to impose transparency, peace and dialogue on the
economic forces and communities that resist them.

Only a personal Subject can do both these things, and the virtues of a
personal Subject are not the virtues required by the ethics of discussion.
The first is individual courage (to denounce powers), and the second is the
power of collective action (to safeguard the rights of individuals, and thus
allow the Subject to survive). Ethics is not reducible to establishing the
pre-conditions for a discussion in the Academy, and it is far from certain
that power, clans, ignorance and hostility do not interfere with communication there, as they do elsewhere. Apel argues that, in so far as they are
autonomous legislators who can impose duties upon themselves, the
authority of human beings has to be related to the foundational act

whereby they freely acknowlege the norms of the argumentative discourse that effectively makes them rational beings.

The Subject is not merely a form of Reason. The Subject exists only if it can calculate and use technology. It must also use memory and solidarity, and above all it must fight in the hope that it can inscribe its personal freedom in social battles and cultural liberations. The Subject is a form of Reason, but it is also freedom, liberation and rejection, and that is more important. There is very little room left for discussion and democracy. What room was left for them in a Peru caught between the violence of Sendero Luminoso and the authoritarian neo-liberalism of Fujimori, between the vast informal economy and the drug cartels?

How are those vast areas of the world that are ruled by hunger and violence to interpret the reduction of ethics and politics to reason? They inevitably see it as the utopia of a continent which was dominant for so long that it has forgotten how it too resorted – and resorts – to force and exploitation. The idea of the Subject does not grow in over-protected greenhouses; it is a wild flower.

Subjectivation

No recourse to a higher principle of meaning and no act performed in the name of a law – be it that of God, the people or reason – will transform a disoriented world that has been torn apart and divided into two universes that do not communicate with one another into a social field where actors can both co-operate and come into conflict. That transformation can be brought about by a demand on the part of an individual who will no longer tolerate being divided into two or being subject to a twofold dependency. Such an individual is not simply trying to reconstruct his individuality as such, or to recover his unity and his awareness of that unity. The reconstruction of the individual can come about only if that individual can recognize and assert himself as a Subject, as a creator of meaning and change, as well as of social relations and political institutions. The individual cannot sew together the divided halves of his existence, but the Subject does manifest its presence within individuals. The individual is the Subject's starting-point, but it is no longer a Subject that can illuminate the social field with a supernatural light that shines from on high.

An individual who is defined solely as an individual responds to the appeal of the market, or of belonging to a community; subjectivation, on the other hand, is a will to individuation, and it begins with the rearticulation of instrumentality and identity. Individuation begins when individuals are once more defined by what they do, by what they value and by the social relations in which they are involved. Individuation frees the individual from market and community alike, and in doing so brings the individual back into the field of production and culture, whereas the market and the community are the mutually estranged forms of a modernity that has degenerated into demodernization. Given that demodernization is our most powerful and most threatening experience, it is the resistance of the individual, the individual's desire to be an actor, and the individual's attempts at subjectivation or, in other words, to re-articulate an instrumentality redefined as production and a community redefined as a culture that allow a Subject to appear. This Subject's position is not above society, but it can use the consciousness of individuals to reappropriate the whole of society. The will to individuation, or the desire for individuation, is not to be confused with a quest for difference at all costs. Such a quest would be self-defeating. It would mean either identifying with a community or being seduced by commercial or political marketing. Individuation requires the individual to assert himself as an actor who can orient and transform social life. This process of subjectivation can begin only when individuals resist their dismemberment and their loss of identity. This is the novel feature of a situation dominated by demodernization: subjectivation no longer takes the form of the defence of the rights of workers or citizens; it is initially manifested at the level of individual lived experience, of the anxiety that is born of one of the increasingly contradictory experiences to which I have referred so often. Schoolchildren and students are torn between a youth culture and the need to obtain the qualifications they will require to enter the world of work; hospital patients expect to be cured by medical science and technology, but they also find that being in the social environment of a hospital can be a painful experience in personal terms. Neither solitary mediation nor passive suffering is enough to construct individuation; the individual must also recognize himself as Subject.

Although it is less intent upon describing subjective experience, the analysis put forward here is similar to analyses that stress the individual's 'capacity to keep a particular narrative going', as Anthony Giddens puts it (1991: 54), to retain a sense of biographical identity whilst living through a series of very different situations, and to struggle against the effects of the split consciousness that R. D. Laing (1965) explores. Its ambitions are, however, more sociological, and, rather than confronting the consciousness of the I with a multiplicity of different situations and experiences, it sets it in the midst of tendencies that threaten it because they are contradictory. If we wish to discover the pre-conditions for inter-cultural communication and democracy, the idea of the Subject is indispensable, and in this context it takes on a political significance.

Sexuality and happiness

This construction demands a struggle on two fronts, or what I have described as an escape from two things. This allows us to avoid any confusion between the I and an ego which, whilst it believes itself to be free and released from all constraints, is largely a reflection of the powers, hierarchies and preferences that dominate society and penetrate individuals through and through. Individuation cannot, however, be reduced to a rejection and a critique. Individuation is also a positive experience: the lived experience of the reconciliation of the world of the economy and the world of culture. Sexuality and loving relationships are the most obvious examples of their reconciliation. We feel the shattering of lived experience here too. On the one hand, eroticism is becoming more autonomous; Georges Bataille regards eroticism as a manifestation of the sacred to the extent that sexuality is never completely separable from reproduction (even though it is never reducible to reproduction). It therefore plunges the individual back into the flow of life, which exists beyond consciousness and culture. On the other hand, we are surrounded by a world of mass consumption, and we see its models in the media. The world of eroticism is drifting further and further away from the world of cultural, social or political taste. The loving relationship is the one thing that can reduce the gulf between them by giving a central role to the relationship with the Other, regardless of the Other's sex. Eroticism, or shared tastes and a recognition of the Other as Subject, can therefore be reconciled within the unity of a loving relationship, defined as a desire that is directed towards the Other and the Other's desire. The Other, in the meantime, is also a combination of eroticism, shared tastes and a recognition of the Other as Subject. Love is not reducible to either a form of consumption or the 'divine' eroticism that is its opposite; it reminds the individual of what he or she is, and of his or her free creativity, pleasure and happiness.

It is difficult to conceive of how the Subject can be constructed outside a loving relationship. Whilst such a relationship is not reducible to a libidinal drive, it is a search for happiness through pleasure. I speak of happiness in this context because the word designates a form of self-realization that is an end in itself, and not something that is mobilized in the service of a cause. The experience of happiness is the experience of feeling at ease with oneself, both in the events of life and in the human and material environment, and it becomes all the more intense as the twin pressures of demodernization increase.

The idea of happiness developed together with modernity itself, but it was only when all the other meta-social guarantors of the social order had been exhausted, and when our attitudes to both the nation and growth became more ambivalent, that we gave pride of place to the idea of happiness. The opposite of happiness – unhappiness – is just as important. We no longer need an analysis of exploitation or foreign domination to feel the unhappiness of those who have lost their lives as a result of violence, a natural disaster, a personal tragedy, illness or repression. There is no real distinction here between natural and social causes. When the thread of life is snapped or cut, the cause is less important that the effect. Life no longer means simply a biological existence. It is a network of projects, exchanges and affections. When we look at them, we all recognize our own faces and hear our own voices. No one is unaware of the fact that unhappiness often results from social or political causes, or that happiness presupposes an end to dependency and exploitation. But we can no longer forget that the ultimate goal is the happiness of all, and not the construction of a new society and a new man.

The ethics of duty is a thing of the past. It is being replaced, not by an ethics of intentionality and duty analogous to that of the great religions, but by the pursuit of happiness. There is no happiness without pleasure, and the Subject is manifested only in the individual, even though it is not reducible to the individual, simply because happiness is not something that is given. It is something that is acquired and won in a battle with forces that constantly seek to destroy it. Both joy and sadness are manifestations of the construction of the Subject and its pursuit of happiness. This is more obvious in the case of joy, as collective joy is the joy of a liberating and generous action, just as personal joy is the joy of discovery and projects. The emphasis I am placing on the Subject's struggle against its twin adversaries must not trap our analysis in an overly Jansenist or angst-ridden vision. Collective action, like a personal adventure, creates a space for freedom, inventiveness and imagination; the denunciation of the forces of death sustains our *joie de vivre*. It is not simply because they are a response to media pressure that so many social movements are famous for their songs and theatricals, just as they were once famous for their literary expressions. Festivals and theatres are spaces that encourage and sustain the hope of liberation.

Yet the Subject is also shaped by sadness. After the sufferings and failures the self has experienced, illness and the proximity of death remind it of what it is. The men and women who give the dying palliative care, who establish both verbal and non-verbal communications with them, help them to feel that they have been recognized as Subjects, and sometimes even that they are happier now than they were for most of their lives because they feel that they are loved for their attempts to behave as dignified and free beings at the moment when death is carrying them away.

The construction of the Subject never results in the organization of a fully protected psychological, social and cultural space. We never really escape from commodities and communities; the space of freedom is constantly being invaded, and the Subject is constituted as much through what it rejects as through what it asserts. The Subject is never its own master; nor is it the master of its environment. It always forms alliances with the devil against the powers that be, with the eroticism that overturns social codes, and with its own superhuman or divine self-image. Those who have reduced human beings to what they do trap them into being dependent on technology, businesses and states. The Subject has to outwit the categories of social practice; far from being the architect of an ideal city, the Subject cobbles together fragile and limited combinations of instrumental action and cultural identity by taking things from both the world of commodities and the space of communities.

It is this weakness of the Subject as it battles endlessly with the forces that threaten it that prevents me from agreeing completely with Luc Ferry's forceful attempt to show that the humanization of the divine, the disenchantment of the world and the decline of religion have resulted in the deification of man, and have produced new transcendental values that are imposed on us just as forcefully as the old, albeit in a different way: 'Transcendence is still an appeal to an order of signification which, although it has its roots in human beings, none the less refers to a radical exteriority' (Ferry 1996: 127). 'Modernity', he concludes, 'has led to the humanization of transcendence and therefore not the eradication of the traditional figures of the sacred, but rather their displacement' (Ferry 1996: 128). When I look at modernity, which has been freed from all copies of religious thought, I see neither sanctity nor sacrifice, as the latter involves, as Luc Ferry rightly notes, a recognition of the sacred. The appeal to one's own dignity and the dignity of the Other does not establish a world of values, but merely a world of protests and indignation. And sacrifice is replaced by solidarity, as it is the weakness of the Subject that gives it the strength to fight that which threatens it. This idea has already been expressed, in a Christian context, by Simone Weil and, in a very different context, by Jean-Paul Sartre. We have to create spaces for freedom, intervene in the world of evil in order to save lives, and not reconstruct an ideal society. The idea of value cannot be divorced from the idea of norms, authority and social organization, which are logically associated with one another in the sociology of Talcott Parsons, and which must all be called into question. Whilst I agree with Luc Ferry that we have to demonstrate the limitations of the reductionist explanations of human behaviour put forward by biology and sociobiology, I by no means recognize the radical exteriority he evokes, because the Subject is primarily a refusal, a self-awareness and a recognition of the Other as

Subject that is not based on any external principle or any world-view, be it humanitarian or ecological.

The idea of the Subject has its roots in lived experience. It is constantly present as a force or, conversely, as an absence when we feel ourselves to be depersonalized, unloved and misunderstood. We must not, however, contrast the subjective experience of the Subject with collective manifestations of the assertion and defence of the Subject's rights; it is the link between personal experience and collective action that gives the Subject the best chance of surviving the attacks of its powerful adversaries.

How can we create happiness and the Subject? How can the individual (or the group) create the autonomous space that allows the Subject to recognize itself as such? By fusing the two worlds of instrumentality and identity, which tend so often to drift apart. Each world prevents the other from being debased. The openness of the market and the demands of technology are the best defences against the confines of communitarianism, which inevitably makes both ends and means irrational, and which cannot use the available technological and economic resources properly. Similarly, how can we resist the heteronomy of mass culture, or the prioritization of the most commodified demands, unless we rely on a communitarian identity or the power of the libido? Nothing could be more arbitrary, or even more dangerous, than denouncing only one of the forces of demodernization. Those who denounce strategic action and market pressures, and those who regard technology as the devil incarnate, have no option but to extol the integrative power of a community, people, race or sect. Similarly, those who denounce only the communitarian spirit or the extreme multi-culturalism of political correctness tend to equate individual life with an acceptance of whatever the market has to offer. Demodernization makes obvious what modernization taught us: there can be no positive response – individual or collective – unless it is a combination of contrary demands. Such a combination can never lead to the synthesis or transcendence that is so dear to dialectical thought, as it is a product of the constant effort which individuals make to recompose themselves and to transform themselves into Subjects by escaping both the openness of markets and the confines of a community.

Subjectivation means constructing the Subject in the course of the pursuit of a happiness that can be born only of the recomposition of an autonomous personal experience. The Subject cannot and will not choose between a ubiquitous globalization and identity. This work of articulation is always under threat, and it is never complete. Its only evaluative criteria are the happiness it creates or the unhappiness it wards off or survives.

If it wishes to preserve its own unity, social organization must be based upon this ethics of the Subject. In the absence of this constant reminder of who we are, social organization will be torn apart by the power of markets and the demands of the community. If this happens, both individual and collective experience will be dominated by the violence of the now intolerable contradictions between the centrifugal forces that are irreparably destroying the integrative forces created by modern bourgeois society. Being founded on the personal will to happiness, the Subject is the one power that can initiate a dialogue between the tendencies that are dismembering both personal experience and social life, and promote their mutual understanding.

The weakness of the Subject

This *weak* image of the Subject is to be contrasted with both the image of an individual who is capable of making free rational choices and that of a member of a community (a nation-state, a *polis*, a religious, ethnic or linguistic group or whatever else it might be) who feels responsible for the common good and the preservation of the moral and institutional principles on which that community is based. Even when it is defined as citizenship, the communitarian spirit presupposes that everyone takes part in social life, and therefore that they share common values. The growing autonomy of economic life has put an end to this situation, by isolating individuals and merging groups and individuals from different cultures, by assigning a growing importance to relations of power and dependency, and by extending zones of marginality and anomie.

In a world where inequality is growing, and where poverty, unemployment and job insecurity are spreading, the very different image of an individual who, guided only by self-interest or pleasure, makes free choices and ignores all influences, especially state intervention, provokes reactions of indignation. Rightly so: it is only because real inequalities exist that equal opportunities are an ideal.

Self-assertion is creative because it involves a rejection of two things, or an estrangement from two things. It takes its most extreme form when it is most desperate, when it is reduced to being an exemplary protest against a totalitarian power that combines the might of a technocratic and bureaucratic organization with an obsession with communitarian homogeneity. The *dissident* is the very personification of this refusal, and his strength of conviction is all the greater in that he supports no ideology and no party, and denounces the intolerable and the scandalous. Even when he is reduced to silence, the active presence and sufferings of the dissident do not supply a remedy. They reveal what was hidden. The dissident names those who would like to remain anonymous and takes risks, like the demonstrator in the white shirt who risked his life by standing in the way of the tanks as they entered Tiananmen Square.

This protest, or this act of witness, has no need of hope, explanations or projects. It is an individual act, and it is precisely because it is neither representative nor organized that it has a universal value. What this refusal reveals is the positive existence of an individual who says 'no', the irreducible character of what, from this point onwards, has to be termed the Subject, or in other words an actor defined by the will and the ability to act, rather than by what the market has to offer or by what a communitarian power orders him to do. This interpretation of refusal in exceptional cirumstances must, of course, be complemented by an analysis of how the Subject asserts its presence in less extreme situations, especially when the two orders of constraint that weigh it down have been dissociated.

In an integrated society, loneliness and the feeling of having been rejected are the worst forms of suffering; in our divided culture, the collapse of the Subject and the loss of subjectivation are the worst forms of suffering. The work of subjectivation can end in failure because it has been undone (or not done in the first place) or because, when there is nothing to filter the contradictory effects of the market and communities or drives, the individual sinks into depression.

The space that lies between these contrasting figures of pure will-power and complete powerlessness is the place where we witness the formation of a Subject that uses culture and work to combat communities and mass culture.

What, then, is the Subject, given that it is not the ego and that it does not speak in the name of any god? It is little more than the need for individuation – which implies, as we shall see, that this need is recognized in others as well as in ourselves. This need is its own foundation. It does not seek any external legitimation, and can therefore be defined as a right. It experiences everything that threatens its existence as an injustice, or even as evil. Good and evil are no longer defined with reference to social utility or duty, but in terms of the individual's self-presence or self-absence, in terms of the recognition or denial of the individual's right to live an individual life, to be different from others, and above all to be truly self-consistent, despite the diversity of his experiences and situations. The Subject is therefore the principle that allow us all to relate to ourselves and to others.

Many give primordial importance to communications. I think, on the contrary, that the relationship with the self determines relations with others. This is a non-social principle which determines social relations. It means that, now that the long period in which we tried to explain the social solely in terms of the social is over, we can once more recognize that the social is based upon the non-social, and is defined only by the role it gives, or refuses to give, to the non-social principle known as the Subject.

I know that the idea of the Subject has moralistic connotations, and I understand Michel Foucault's hostility to the theme of subjectivation. All the more so, perhaps, in that in cultural terms I belong to a country with a Catholic tradition, and in that, whilst I do recognize a culture of modernity in the self-control we see in Dutch portraits, it also makes me somewhat afraid and makes me long for the liberating sensuality of Flemish or Venetian painting. We have, however, little in common with that triumphant bourgeoisie; our mastery of time and space faded as our identity ceased to be defined by the acquisition of social roles. We no longer live in one of those societies where the controlling gaze was everywhere. For us, that image evokes a totalitarian society, and we find it threatening, even though it is far away, and even though we are safe from it. Our society, on the other hand, is becoming more and more confused; there are whole areas of life in which behavioural norms no longer exist. Our society usually puts us in a position of marginality rather than one of belonging, of change rather than identity, and of ambivalence rather than clearly positive or negative convictions. Those who – and I am one of their number – stress the need for self-consciousness certainly do not believe that personalities and social roles coincide, since they take their inspiration from Freud, who, more so than anyone else, shattered that illusion by showing that the world of desire was in conflict with the world of the law.

It is true that moralizing tendencies do exist. They were given a free rein in the nineteenth century, when attempts were made to use the principles of religion to instil morality into the working class. A critique of such campaigns and of conservative calls for self-control, which were in reality designed to enforce social norms, is certainly needed; but we also have to remember that this is no substitute for the self-assertion of the Subject, for its efforts to achieve its own liberation or to construct itself through culture and labour.

That is why Michel Foucault's criticisms seem to me to apply to a type of society that is increasingly far removed from ours. We are, that is, suffering from fragmentation and decay, rather than excessive integration or manipulation. Foucault's criticisms are, however, a useful reminder that it is vital not to confuse the idea of the Subject with that of a social individual who, like a good citizen and worker, is aware of his rights and duties. The Subject is suffering rather than triumph, and desire rather than ownership. Anthony Giddens (1991: 67) rightly makes a distinction between a guilt axis, which is concerned with the violation of social codes or taboos, and a shame axis, which is concerned with the overall tissue of self-identity. A homeless person begging outside the Métro writes 'I am ashamed, but I am hungry' on a piece of cardboard. As Vincent de Gaulejac (1996) remarks, guilt is on the decline, and the feeling of shame is becoming more common.

In our societies, where social and cultural controls have been relaxed, the most direct threat to the Subject is the opposite of that denounced by Foucault. Because we are afraid of a normative and moralizing consciousness, we are quite content with the 'modern' image that presents the Subject as a constant experience of the diversity of lived experiences and as a mere quest for what Gabriella Turnaturi (1994) calls consistency, or the assertion that a constantly changing amalgam does have its unity. Consistency means, above all, a refusal to allow ourselves to be mutilated in any way. Turnaturi illustrates this definition by contrasting the modern figure of Pierre Bezukhov with that of Prince Andrei, the main characters in *War and Peace*, and by citing the letter to Lou Andreas-Salomé in which Rilke expresses his desire to be a river that is no longer confined between its banks and spreads out to become a whole delta. Baudelaire provides the first and best description of this self-presence, and it does have great aesthetic power. It establishes a *persona*, and Turnaturi is right to prefer the theme of consistency to those of coherence and authenticity, which reintroduce values, norms and principles. But if the unity of the persona is no more than the unity of a particular experience, how can we avoid the conclusion that its complexity and fragility are meaningful only when they are situated in relation to a social position, or, in a word, that their unity is that of a *habitus*, to borrow a phrase from Norbert Elias and Pierre Bourdieu, and that this takes us back to a very objectivist analysis that is far removed from the idea of the Subject?

If we wish to develop a sociology of the Subject, it is not enough to stress that the ego is weak and that it is constantly being reshaped. That is why I emphasize that the Subject and its self-consciousness are based upon two things. The first is the struggle against the logic of the market and the logic of the community, and that struggle implies that the Subject's behaviour is governed by firm and constant principles. The second, which complements the first in a positive sense, is the will to individuation that tries to answer the question *Ubi consistam?* (to cite Gabrielle Turnaturi). This question can be answered only if the actor's environment is so controlled that he can integrate memories of the past, contemporary experiences and future projects into a life experience with which he can identify and which he can use to create a personal time and space. This gives the theme of the Subject a much greater dramatic power and, above all, a more visible social and political content than the image of an ego in search of a 'mobile centre of gravity' (Turnaturi 1994: 127).

It is for similar reasons that I reject the idea that it is only through communication with the Other that a relationship with the self can be constituted. Social debate is not reducible to communication. Demands for freedom and identity do not have a directly universalist content, and they are subject to constraints that are largely external and beyond our control; they are bids for emancipation, and it is only later that they become proposals for a better organization of society. The quest for justice is not a cognitive activity. It is best defined as a search for the collective pre-conditions for personal freedom, or in other words the ability to reconcile instrumental rationality and a personal and cultural identity within a personal experience. In order to arrive at the idea of the just society, we therefore have to go through three different stages. The first is the open conflict between the demand for freedom and the power of systems, and the second is the debate that defines the institutional pre-conditions for the respect and encouragement of the freedom of all. When we reach the final stage, we can establish in general terms what we mean by fairness and, in more concrete terms, the pre-conditions for social integration and sustainable change. It therefore seems to me that the approach I am outlining here anticipates that of Jürgen Habermas, who has greatly influenced John Rawls. As we move from one stage to the next, the analysis moves from the personal Subject to communication between Subjects, and then to institutions. It transforms the affective and rational call for the freedom of the Subject into an increasingly cognitive analysis of the rules that allow society to function. If we invert this order, we inevitably deny that institutions have a lived content, and we therefore divorce institutions from modes of behaviour, because we define the former in abstract universal terms and the latter in concrete particularist terms.

Beyond the political Subject

These analyses deliberately keep their distance from both philosophies of history and religious world-views. Our century has seen so many totalitarian or authoritarian powers establishing themselves in the name of meta-social principles, trying to establish an order against which there can be no appeal, and calling for a general mobilization against evil, that we are also very suspicious of all eschatologies. It is true that there is a mystical anarchism that rebels against the absolute power that has been established in its name, but that revolt is too desperate and too late to produce any positive effects. Those who thought that the revolt of the poor, the exploited or dependent peoples could be the light of the world created closed communities living under authoritarian rule, like the utopian cities of the seventeenth and eighteenth centuries or the more recent forms of millenarianism that inspired Canudos and many other sects and communities, especially in Brazil and the Congo. They supported emancipatory powers that wielded the sword as well as propaganda. We have learned to distrust all hope and, to refer to the theological virtues once more, we prefer charity and compassion to hope and its arrogant pride.

It will be objected that, for a long time, I too spoke of the historical Subject rather than the Subject when I discussed social movements, but that objection is based upon a misrepresentation of my analyses of the labour movement and of what I call 'new social movements'. I have never described working-class consciousness as a force that could negate the contradictions of capitalism and found a rational society that would be both creative and free. On the contrary, I defined working-class consciousness as the defender of a working-class autonomy that had been invaded by industrial rationalization – capitalist or Communist. That conception was based on the surveys I had carried out, and they showed that this class consciousness was strongest in the skilled categories that were being attacked by scientific management. Outside those categories, working-class consciousness was restricted to either a corporatist defence of a position within the labour market or an increasingly political, and therefore dependent, struggle against a productivism that was generating new forms of exclusion. Many analysts thought that this final stage of industrial evolution heralded a movement that would be more radical and more revolutionary than ever before; from the early 1960s onwards, I was predicting the decline of working-class consciousness and, therefore, of trade unionism. In 1968, I subsequently tried to demonstrate that the student movement of May was characterized by the contradiction between new cultural protests and an ideological discourse inherited from revolutionary socialism which was out of step with the new demands and their associated utopias.

It is difficult to free the idea of the Subject from the great traditions of thought and action that have given it its historical forms, but they have little in common with the forms we have to elaborate today, even though there is, at a more general level, a certain intellectual kinship between the two. Thanks to a series of successive mutations, the idea of the Subject descended from the heaven of ideas to the field of the political, and then to social relations in the work-place, and it is finally coming to grips with lived experience. The universalist image of a human Subject defined in law, and therefore divorced from any particular experience, and of a Subject which was neither man nor woman, master nor slave, was replaced first by the idea that the Subject could take the historical form of a republican state or an enlightened despot, and then by the idea of a particular class with a universal emancipatory mission. In each case, the appeal to the Subject founded an absolute power. As the Subject became more concrete and more involved in social realities and social relations, the power that spoke in its name became more totalitarian and, as Michel Foucault has demonstrated, penetrated every cell of social life. Modern history is the history of two contradictory but complementary tendencies: the increasingly obvious emergence of the personal Subject and the growing dominance of a moralizing and normative power. When it spoke in the name of man and the rights of man, political action identified with the establishment of citizenship, but also with the Terror. The defence of workers' rights gave birth to the dream of a fair and egalitarian society, but also to forms of political servitude disguised as social liberation.

For a long time, political or social leaders, including intellectuals, regarded themselves as the guardians of higher values, and felt that they had a responsibility to defend an exploited, alienated or colonized people that had no voice. Those days have gone, for better and for worse. For worse, because when we say that the people has spoken, we usually do so in order to justify a dominant ideology and a dominant power. For better, because individuals now evaluate the action of leaders by the standard of their own demands. Those demands go far beyond their material interests, and thus introduce the idea of the Subject, and of the freedom to use personal experience. Social movements call less and less for the creation of a society or a new social order, and more and more for the defence of personal freedom, security and dignity.

In all my studies of social movements, I have stressed that they are not based on ethical principles alone, but also on a social principle. They do not bear within them an image of a fair society, as elaborated by a philosophy of history. They demand a justice that has more in common with the declaration of the rights of man than a constitution or a political programme. Working-class consciousness was based upon a call for freedom and happiness which went beyond the historicist or economic critique that saw capitalism as diverting the productive forces into capitalist profit. A social movement is always a moral protest; it rises above society in order to judge it or condemn it, and it does not stand in its midst so as to manage it or steer it in the direction demanded by Reason or History. That is why I have always stressed the contradiction that we can observe in all social movements between a core of protests and an interpretative discourse. The central orientation of the labour movement (working-class consciousness), in particular, was opposed to the socialist discourse which interpreted it, and to which it was usually subordinated. Similarly, the students of Berkeley and Nanterre were opposed to the revolutionary or workerist discourses to which so many of them none the less rallied, despite, in the case of Nanterre, the opposition of Daniel Cohn-Bendit, who always refused to have anything to do with those hyper-Leninist discourses. In similar fashion, we have seen how women's demands have been modelled on either a republican-style, egalitarian discourse or a socialist-style, revolutionary discourse, even though both were quite alien to the inspiration behind a movement which gained public popularity only when it freed itself from such modernist and revolutionary justifications.

From the French and American Declarations of the late eighteenth century to our own day, the divorce between political programmes and social movements has grown as political forces become more managerial and more concerned with economic constraints, and as social movements penetrate more deeply into our culture and personalities.

Having stressed that the Subject does not have an ideal model for society, we must also rediscover the personal Subject that exists within the historical Subject, or even within the religious Subject. The religious Subject is at the heart of visions of society and the world. Religious phenomena have usually been analysed as instruments for communitarian integration and for the transmission of the tradition whose origins gives the community its foundation myth; they thus appear to sanctify the social. No one would dream of rejecting this truly sociological interpretation, but it should not be allowed to monopolize our understanding of religious phenomena. We must also look at another aspect of religious conduits: the non-social, and in many cases anti-social, reference to a divine will that either rewards or punishes society and individuals and to the purity of intentions or morals. Although Max Weber speaks of the transition from other-worldly to worldly asceticism, and although the latter is clearly associated with the formation of the modern Subject, all forms of asceticism (including contemplative and mystical detachment) have to be seen as an appeal to a Subject which has yet to be humanized, but which cannot be identified with a community.

We can apply the same approach to social movements that support what I call a 'historical Subject'. Whilst some of these movements do refer to the image of an ideal or historically necessary society, many of them appeal to freedom and justice – and especially equality. The appeal to God, reason or history may lead to the sanctification of society; it may also desanctify society by criticizing it or demanding that it conform to principles which cannot be reduced to rules for the organization of social life.

Rather than stressing the singularity of the contemporary situation, giving pride of place to the idea of the Subject should lead us to look for the different or successive figures of the Subject in all societies that have a certain level of historicity, or in other words the ability to produce and transform themselves. In all such societies, the Subject has two contradictory faces. In proto-modern society, it was incarnated in the nation-state, which it sanctified, but also in the rights of man, which placed limitations on social power. In industrial society, it once more sanctified the social order by dreaming of the perfect socialist society, but the Subject's voice could also be heard in the labour movement's call for workers' liberation and justice. At each stage, and in each type of society, the Subject is alienated in the myth of a sanctified order, but it is also a principle of revolt which breaks with the order established by a power.

We therefore have to reject the conventional image of modernity. Far from representing the triumph of instrumental rationality and rational choices, modernity increasingly gives a direct importance to the idea of the Subject, which provides the only possible link between economic and administrative rationalization and the ethical consciousness. For a long time, it was moral and juridical philosophy that established the link between these two aspects of modernity. That social link is now too weak to hold together a globalized economy and actors who are obsessed with their social identity and especially their cultural identity. The idea of the Subject, defined as above, thus becomes essential. As a society becomes more modern, it is increasingly the case that it is at the level of the actors themselves, and not at the level of institutions or universalist principles, that an attempt is made to reconstruct or rearticulate the social and political field, so as to prevent it from becoming completely fragmented or from disappearing. Although it has often been claimed that organizational rationality is both modern society's sole foundation and the one source of its legitimacy, it seems to me that the most obvious characteristic of modernity is the weakening of the social field. Social membership of a community conferred both the right to use its technologies and the right to have recourse to a representation of the Subject. As modernity progresses, both technology and representations of the Subject become more independent. Community membership becomes less important, and the system of norms and values that gave it its integrative power becomes weaker and vanishes. The stark conflict between instrumentality and identity is all that remains. It is not only that society does not become an all-powerful system: it is incapable of producing and reproducing itself, and is in fact dependent on the Subject's ability to transcend the decay of the social.

We resist these ideas because we are still influenced by the representation that sees society as a coherent whole made up of interdependent parts and claims that it is its own end. This representation takes two main forms: one stresses the pre-conditions for the integration of society or its ability to adapt to change, and the other sees social organization as the implementation of power and domination. What we have to recognize is that, on the contrary, in modern societies the self-regulating social system is divorced from the cultural models that give them their historicity. These models are not a reflection of society. Nor do they serve to strengthen a social power. They must be understood as the forms in which the Subject is appearing or, in other words, being secularized. The models are increasingly divorced from both the social organization and its reproductive mechanisms. The Reformation of the sixteenth century did not take the same course as the Renaissance; at a later stage, the ethical individualism of the bourgeoisie came into conflict with the spirit of capitalism. If we read Jacques Le Goff, we find that St Louis, who gave the religious, feudal and monarchical model of society its most coherent form, was also familiar with a form of piety that was not organized around sacraments, rites, prayers and crusades. Le Goff calls it an internalized piety, or a piety of consciousness. This internalization of faith, and this eminently Franciscan moralization of religion, can be seen as constructing an ethical model which, because of its extreme character and even its archaism, had little to do with the requirements of the royal function and ecclesiastical control. As at the time of the Reformation, there is, albeit in a more limited and more fully controlled way, a growing distance between the 'inner man' and the management of the natural world that characterizes modernity.

Over the past century, the divorce between culture and society has accelerated as the idea that there was a correspondence between system and actor became less tenable. That is why ethical categories now have much more importance than social categories: ethical categories alone make it possible to rearticulate cultural orientations that have been freed from communitarian constraints and productive activities that are irreducible to jobs that provide access to mass consumption. This reversal has been hastened by our societies' growing ability to either transform themselves or destroy themselves. It is so easy for us to put our collective survival at risk that we can no longer believe in the omnipotence of rationalizing models, as we did from the sixteenth to the nineteenth century. The image of social life bequeathed to us by 'classical' sociology seems to us to be far removed from the observable reality and from the consciousness of our actors. Where can we see systems of values being transformed into social norms, and social norms into forms or authority, statuses and roles? Who, apart from a few ideologues, believes in the gradual unification of a world that has been completely commodified? Those who do observe social reality are searching for the dangerous passage between the two oceans that share the greater part of the world between them: the world of communitarian identities and the world of the globalized economy. What passage can there be, other than every individual's demand that he should be an actor in his own story, a being in search of happiness, and a citizen who seeks, for his own freedom and that of others, the protection of the law?

A Subject without consciousness

For a long time, the idea of the Subject was closely associated with the idea of a higher principle of intelligibility and order. It is because they had in mind these religious, philosophical and political conceptions of the Subject that so many thinkers have, over the last century, demanded the death of the Subject. My point of departure is the same; but in my view, the demise of philosophies of the Subject gives birth to the idea of the personal Subject. That idea could take shape only when all conceptions of a world order had collapsed. Systems of thought which subordinated social actors to the laws of nature, a divine message or a political project prevented the personal will to freedom from being divorced from the forces that are struggling for a return to the order of things and against what they condemn as collective or personal deviations. It is the completion of modernization, or in other words the ruin of all systems of order, that allows the Subject to find its legitimacy within itself and prevents it from entering the service of some supposedly higher law.

Once it has been liberated in this way, the Subject must seek its own figures in the systems in which they are trapped without ever being fully integrated into them. It must also assert its freedom, and recognize that it is not a principle that establishes a religious, political or social order. The Subject is nothing more than its assertion of its own freedom in the face of all social orders, which, for their part, become increasingly constraining, manipulative and repressive, and which threaten it.

The subject tries to escape these constraints and threats, to escape both the blandishments of the market and the orders of the community. It is defined by this twofold struggle, which it wages with the help of its labour and culture. Its goal is its own freedom; it strives to extend the space it liberates by removing these external determinants, but this is not a space for saints and sages. The Subject's self-consciousness helps it to escape external influences, but does not reveal a basic code of values and norms. The Subject has no content except the *bricolage* through which it attempts to reconcile its labour, or in other words its involvement with the world of technologies and markets, with its culture, or the force that constitutes its identity by giving its experience a meaning.

If the Subject is transformed into self-consciousness, it sees only the self-images that others reflect back to it, and the opinions and tastes that correspond to its position within the social organization and within relations of power and authority. In any society or culture, the Subject is a force for liberation. It can be defined only in negative terms, and it is only by recognizing the Other as a Subject, only by following the juridical and political rules that teach it self-respect and respect for the Other as

Subject, that it acquires a content. The Subject can exist only if it frees itself from both its self-consciousness and the forces that it perceives as external but which in fact permeate it through and through. It bears witness to freedom, but not as a moralist, still less as a moralizer and a defender of the dominant norms and values.

This, I repeat, is why I see the *dissident* as the exemplary figure of the Subject. The dissident bears witness, even without any hope of being heard, against the powers that take away his freedom. The Subject is speech, and its act of witness is a public one, even if no one can hear it or see it. Our cultural history abounds in appeals to a demand that is above the law: Antigone's sacrifice, the Sermon on the Mount, the Declaration of the Rights of Man, and the acts of the resisters and dissidents who have fought inhuman regimes.

It is not inconceivable that there are also individuals who have achieved a high degree of subjectivation, and who are therefore capable of sublime actions, but who are still trapped in a false self-consciousness. I use the word 'sublime' because of the use that was made of it during the early phase of industrialization, and which has been analysed so well by Alain Cottereau: those workers who were recognized as 'sublimes' were both militant revolutionary workers and heavy drinkers or delinquents. The combination of the two, which was so frequent and so charged with meaning in religious stories, social movements and popular imagery, is indeed important. It is a reminder that subjectivation too is a way of deviating from the functional modes of behaviour required by the social order.

Subjectivation would not have the power to transform and subvert society if it did not break with the mechanisms of cultural reproduction and social control. That is why the Subject is always in some way eccentric to itself; or, rather, that is why each one of us is exceptional and unique to the extent that we bear within us some element of the Subject.

In liberal societies, where regulation works mainly through the market, and therefore at least partly through demand, subjectivation can take place without encountering any insurmountable obstacles. In such societies, the main threat to subjectivation is the reduction of the I to an ego, to a certain psychological well-being, or to the illusion that private life can be sustained and protected from crises in public life. This ethics of labour, honesty and duty is by no means to be despised, but it is alarmingly fragile: the barriers that protect it will be broken down by the first storm to hit public life. Subjectivation, by contrast, thrives only in times of trouble, suffering and hope. What I call 'the Subject' has nothing in common with what is known as subjective life, as it is open, exposed to the pressures, seductions and threats of systems which seek to destroy those who oppose them in the name of their freedom and individuation.

The Subject is exposed to every danger, and it could not survive if it were not.

The weakness of the Subject is the most obvious difference between it and those figures of the Subject that were both protected and alienated by a meta-social guarantor of the social order, such as God, reason or history. Those figures once dominated history and inspired charismatic heroes; in a world defined by its historicity, they no longer exist. It is when human action seems to be most powerful, or in hyper-industrial societies, that the Subject appears to be at its weakest. It is swamped and crushed by both instrumentalism and communitarianism, but for the first time it also becomes the principle that directly guides its own actions.

Defence of the Subject

There is a great continuity between the ethical conscience that subordinates the individual to duties and the political consciousness that leads to sacrifices in the name of a collective or transcendental cause. And how can we escape both these realms of duty without succumbing to a pure individualism which is increasingly invaded by mass consumption or, at the opposite extreme, driven by impersonal desires?

We now have to go back to our starting-point. In hyper-modern societies, the individual is constantly subjected to centrifugal forces: on the one hand, the market; on the other, the community. The contradiction between the two often tears the individual apart. The individual becomes either a consumer or a believer. The earliest and most important manifestation of the Subject is our refusal to be torn apart in this way, our desire for individuality, or in other words our recognition of ourselves in every form of behaviour and every social relationship. In several regions of Latin America, for example, ethnic groups are struggling both for economic survival and for the recognition of their cultures. Sometimes they proclaim their will to defend their communities, but usually they melt into the lower strata of urban society in order to find work, resources and educational opportunities for their children. But there are also cases of groups attempting to reconcile the defence of their cultural identity with a greater involvement in the economic and political system. At this point, they become capable of collective action, and may even become social movements. Such groups are consciously trying to find an answer to a question I have been asking in a very general form: how can we reconcile a culture and the economy? Doing so presupposes that we open up the community and reconstruct a system of production and a system of historical action that is not confined to the market. But opening up or transcending a community through work and using a culture to transcend the market presuppose the intervention of some collective action. The Subject cannot possibly be constructed unless it can refer to some such collective action. *That is why the central point in my argument is the link between the idea of the Subject and the idea of a social movement.*

This idea contains two assertions. The first is that the Subject is will, resistance and struggle, and not an immediate experience of the self; the second is that no social movement is possible without the Subject's will to liberation. A collective action defined as an agent of historical progress, the defence of a community or a belief, or simply as the power to destroy traditional barriers and customs cannot become a social movement, and quickly becomes an agent of oppression in the service of a power. The Subject is neither a self-contemplative individual nor an ideal self-image that an individual paints in private: the Subject is action and work. That is why it never coincides with individual experience. Could we speak of the will to individuation if the reflexive consciousness were enough to ensure the existence and freedom of the individual? The idea of the Subject has nothing to do with Montaigne's sceptical freedom. It is closer to Pascal's angst. Above all, the Subject is present whenever and wherever a collective action constructs a simultaneously social, political and ethical space for the production of an individual and collective experience.

The very idea of the Subject is a clear indication of the priority which these analyses give to the individual. They ignore neither the individual's loyalties, his situation nor all the things that influence him, and define the individual as an actor who can modify his environment. It is the actor-Subject who must have the last word, not the meta-social guarantors of the social order.

The social actor supports the Subject in its interpersonal relations, its social relations, and in political institutions as well as forms of collective action. But if we wish to discover the Subject, neither institutions nor interpersonal communication can be our starting-point. We must start with the lived experience of the Subject. We must stop, once and for all, defining the Subject in terms of the presence within an individual of a universal principle – Truth, Beauty, Goodness – to which the individual supposedly aspires. The Subject is nothing but the resistance, will and happiness of an individual who is defending and asserting his or her individuality against the laws of the market and the laws of the community. The Subject acts and manifests itself below, and not above, in individuation not in identification.

The ethic we inherited from the earlier forms of modern society was both personal and social. It was, as Zygmunt Bauman (1993) has said, based upon universal principles and solid foundations because it defined the rules we had to follow in order to perform our social duties properly. Our ethics, by contrast, tends to become detached from those social roles, and this makes us ambivalent about socially defined choices. We are less rationalistic, prone to be caught up in insurmountable contradictions and suspicious of universalist precepts. Although the word 'ethics' once designated practical rules for life that were derived from moral precepts, it now has little to do with either social frameworks or moral ideas and precepts. In our experience, ethics reminds the Subject of its own existence. What we mean when we speak of an ethical orientation towards others is that we are looking for the Subject within them, just as we are looking for it in ourselves. The field of ethics therefore centres not on our interaction with others, but on the way we relate to ourselves. Our relationship with ourselves is the most direct determinant of how we relate to others – as we can see so clearly in our most interpersonal and most intimate relations. The 'we', or the reference to the group or the institution, is losing ground to the way we relate to ourselves through our relations with others, and above all to the happiness, pleasure or sadness we experience in those relationships.

When ethics is oriented towards practice, social ethics and norms of socialization become less important. This new orientation is a continuation of the work of all those thinkers who have asserted that there is a principle of humanity that exists over and beyond social and cultural differences. From monotheism to the Declarations of the Rights of Man and contemporary humanism, there is a constant tendency to divorce social or biological beings from the Subject that has given us the right and duty to resist oppression and the intolerable. What has to be called 'humanism' has nothing in common with appeals to natural entities, such as nations, races, the proletariat or colonized nations, that have been converted into voluntaristic principles for action, or that have been transformed into figures of the human condition because of the exploitation that they have suffered.

This absolute separation can be maintained only if the appeal to a universalist consciousness avoids the temptation to base society on reason or to create a scientific or transparent society, as that would in fact generate a kind of domination or despotism based upon something other than the superiority of a race or a class. That is why, ever since the time of Bartolomé de Las Casas, the proclamation that humanity is one has always gone hand in hand with the recognition of cultural pluralism, and even of the right to cultural differences. It is as though the most demanding monotheism could not do without a certain polytheism so as to prevent a people, a church or certain customs being mistaken for God. What I call 'the Subject' cannot exist in the absence of the assertion of the freedom of an individual situated in social relations, relations of domination, and a cultural and technological environment.

Those who proclaimed the death of the Subject – and, as Alain Finkielkraut (1984, 1996) reminds us, they chose the worst possible moment to do so, as they were speaking in the aftermath of the massacres and exterminations perpetrated by the totalitarian regimes – were not wrong to denounce the naïve identification of freedom with property and of universalism with colonialism. They did, however, make the serious error of both rejecting the presence of the Subject and refusing to recognize social and cultural diversity. They put to death an abstract humanism from which they could not emancipate themselves; they proved themselves as incapable of denouncing totalitarianism as of understanding the great task of reconciling humanism and cultural diversity that both Montaigne and the Spanish theologians had begun. Let us stop waging false battles which are all the more exalted in that the enemy is an imaginary enemy who has no real forces, and devote ourselves to the essential and difficult struggle against the dominance of the market and neo-communitarianism. That battle can be waged only in the name of a Subject that is at once a universalist consciousness of freedom and a will to existence. The Subject combines experience and memory within a particular life trajectory.

The I and the Other

The Subject is centred on the individual, and the individual's will to autonomy and freedom is an essential part of its formation. The Subject is, at the most profound level, therefore very different from a social actor, as a social actor is defined in relation to another actor, which presupposes the definition of roles, statuses, forms of organization and authority, and therefore norms. From a purely liberal point of view, it is easy to stress the freedom of the Subject, to define the institutional pre-conditions that safeguard that freedom, and to formulate a declaration of the rights of the Subject and the human subject. It is, it would seem, difficult to define social relations without displacing the centre of the analysis from the actor to the system, or without contradicting everything we have said so far.

This is a real contradiction, and it is indeed impossible to reconcile an appeal to the freedom of the Subject with an ethics of duty or a functionalist analysis of society. The contradiction would be insurmountable if the Subject were defined as an appeal to desire, as opposed to rationalization, to consumption as opposed to production, or to identity as opposed to participation. Such a complete break, which leads either to extreme hedonism or radical multi-culturalism, obviously prevents us from asking the question posed by this book: how can we live together? How can we reconcile freedom, or identity, with involvement in social life? The notion of the Subject was introduced, not to defend the lifeworld against strategic action, but to struggle against the reduction of social life to the status of a market and, at the same time, to prevent the lifeworld being replaced by a closed community. The Subject refuses to reduce social organization to a market, or identity to community. It is because it is impossible to accept the complete dissociation of the market and communities that I constructed the idea of the Subject, and it in its turn makes possible the idea of the social actor.

We must, however, define in more concrete terms the social relations in which the Subject is involved. The Subject can relate only to another Subject who is also inspired by a will to double engagement and self-construction. The actor relates to another actor, not as a similar or radically different being, but as another being who is making the same attempt to reconcile involvement in the instrumentalized world with a personal and collective experience. This relationship with the Other is based upon sympathy, or even empathy, and upon an understanding of an Other who is partly different and partly involved in the same instrumental world. There is no common feeling of belonging here; nor is there the discovery of something completely different, as there was at the time of the discovery of America. The boundaries between same and different, civilization and savagery, here and elsewhere, have become blurred. The Subject is always to some extent alien to the situation in which it finds itself, as it is defined not only by its belonging but also by its resistance and estrangement.

Relations between Subjects are therefore not ordinary social relations. The principle on which they are based is not membership of the same culture and society, but the joint effort to constitute themselves as Subjects. Without this recognition of the Other, the transition from Subject to social actor would be impossible. The understanding of the Other establishes a relationship which is of a different order to professional or economic relations, and it is also the relationship existing between people who belong to the same cultural community. It gives rise to a counter-society, to the beginnings of a political society which is no longer a community of citizens, but a voluntary association of social actors who resist all the impersonal logics of power. This is an amicable relationship which respects distance but which also creates communications, and which does not entail the complicity implied by membership of a community. It demands respect. The Other is seen as an equal, even though the relationship is not inscribed within a greater whole encompassing both the I and the Other.

We tried to recognize the Other as the bearer of a universal at the time when we regarded ourselves as being oriented towards the universal. But the world of the Enlightenment, which we inherited from the religious world, has fallen into decay, and it is now impossible to base communication with the Other on the principles of a triumphant modernity. Both modernity itself and, in still more brutal fashion, our recent demodernization have made the idea of civilization null and void.

From Subject to actor

It is the sufferings of a tormented individual and relations between Subjects that allow the desire to be a Subject to be transformed into the ability to be a social actor. The Subject no longer comes into being, as it did in the classical model, by taking on social roles or winning rights or the ability to become involved. The Subject constructs itself by forcing an instrumentalized, commodified and technological society to accept organizational principles and limits that conform to its desire for freedom and its will to create forms of social life conducive to its self-affirmation and its recognition of the Other as Subject.

Hence the new importance of the idea of human rights, and hence our return to the right to resist oppression. Hobbes, Locke and Rousseau all speak of that right, and contrast it with the idea of the rights of the citizen, which emphasizes civic duties rather than individual freedom.

Moral convictions must place restrictions on the duties of citizens. It must be recognized that conscientious objectors have the right not to bear arms, but also that doctors and nurses (but not hospitals in receipt of public funding) have the right to refuse to carry out abortions, even if we approve of the law that legalizes abortion. I agree with Pope John Paul II when he calls for religious convictions to be respected, and asserts that the law does not have the right to infringe upon them. We must oppose all attempts to make secularism the principle of social ethics. To do so would result in, at best, conformism and, at worst, repression. Democracy is based both on the recognition of basic rights which place restrictions on all social powers and on the solidarity that allows all individuals to assert that they are social Subjects.

To sum up: the identity of the Subject can be constructed only thanks to the complementary relationship that exists between three forces: the personal desire to safeguard the unity of a personality that is torn between the instrumental world and the communitarian world; the collective and personal struggle against all the powers that transform a culture into a community and labour into a commodity; and the recognition, both interpersonal and institutional, of the Other as Subject. The Subject is not constituted within an immediate self-to-self relationship, in the most individual experience, in personal pleasure or in social success. It exists only in the battle against the forces of the market or a community. It never constructs an ideal city or a higher type of individual. It creates and protects a clearing that is constantly being invaded. Rather than participating, it protects; rather than making prophecies, it defends itself. It is true that it cannot be a creature of rejection and struggle alone. It is at once an assertion, happiness and success. But it is not the architect of an ideal order: it is a force for liberation.

Nothing could be further removed from the idea of the Subject than paeans to an individual who is free of all ties, who acts in accordance with his whims, who seeks his pleasures and zaps from one television channel to another. We do, however, require that image, as well as the complementary image of social exclusion and the destruction of personal identity, if we are to free ourselves from all social ethics – to say nothing of communitarian temptations – and if we are to discover how the idea of the Subject can inspire collective action and orient laws and organizational systems. It cannot, that is, be divorced from the idea of a social movement.

From one book to another

The major difference between the final section of my *Critique of Modernity*, first published in 1992, and what I am now writing is that, in that book, I took an optimistic view and tried to arrive at a richer and more balanced notion of modernity by defining it in terms of both ethical individualism and the rise of instrumental rationality. I therefore attached equal importance to the theme of subjectivation and to that of rationalization. I still maintain that my analysis was correct, but I would now add that during the first stage of modernity, or before the development of industrial society, rationalization and ethical individualism could be reconciled only within the concrete framework of the republican nation-state and of a conception of human beings as citizens who freely submitted to the laws that protected their freedom and organized the rational pursuit of the collective interest.

Rationalization, ethical individualism and the community of citizens are the three terms that together shaped the architecture of modernity, and hence classical sociological thought. It was the collapse of that republican conception of the nation that triggered demodernization and the breakup of the classical model. Bypassed by the nation-community, on the one hand, and the internationalization of trade, on the other, the nation of citizens has been weakened. This has led to a crisis in political mediation, as there is no longer anything to establish a link between the globalized economy and introverted communities. As a result of the collapse of modern society, the two forces that the nation-state held together and made compatible have been divorced and debased, as productive society has been transformed into a market society and as self-identity has become trapped in a communitarian identity. The notion of the Subject has become as debased as that of rationalization, so much so that the twentieth century was dominated by totalitarian powers which legitimized their absolute power by claiming to be creating a new man in a new society. The process has been well analysed by Louis Althusser. This explains why the thinkers of his generation waged war on the idea of the Subject, which, in their view, served to justify all forms of moral order. They therefore adopted Nietzsche's radical criticisms of moralization.

This debasement of both the nation-state and self-identity, or the demodernization that has led to de-institutionalization and desocialization, was the starting-point for this book. That is why the idea of the Subject does not appear in the same context as in *Critique of Modernity*. I now locate the Subject midway between the world of instrumentality and that of identity. It is now the only force that can prevent them from drifting apart and being debased, by acting as a principle for the reconstruction of social experience. This is why I insist on distancing myself from all personalist visions of the Subject. I am describing an *empty* Subject which has no content other than its attempt to reconstruct the unity of labour and culture as it resists the pressures of both the market and communities. The difference between the two books is that the Subject has now become a more tragic figure; at the same time, it acquires a more central role, because it is no longer defined as one aspect of modernity. In a world that is decaying so rapidly and in which regression is speeding up, the Subject is modernity's sole defender. The opening up of markets, brutal proletarianization and the defensive actions of local communities were all side-effects of the first great liberal shock to hit the modern world, which at that time effectively meant Western Europe. A century and a half later, we are experiencing a second shock. But the democratic nation-state has been weakened in the meantime. The link between society and culture has been broken, and the messages distributed by the media have led to the proletarianization of culture All that remains is the conflict between arrogant markets and aggressive communities. In a world torn apart by what have become civil wars, we no longer encounter the triumphant Subject of the Declaration of the Rights of Man; we encounter a Subject that is fighting for survival. It is the only force that can resist the complete and definitive break between the world of markets and the world of communities. It is a fragile force, and it is at the mercy of both mass culture and communitarian authoritarianism. And yet it is the focus for the world-wide attempt to construct personal life and social life.

The two faces of individualism

Am I making it sufficiently clear that the idea of the Subject is a deliberate move away from the all too common theme of the transition from forms of wisdom based upon the renunciation of the world to an ethics of efficiency and social utility? The modern world is supposedly character-ized by the fact that everyone tries to be a good citizen and a good worker, and even to be tolerant, whereas the old world subordinated the indi-vidual to the natural order of the world, to divine commands or the human mastery of desire. Louis Dumont (1983: 33–67) has demonstrated to remarkable effect that, on the contrary, the idea of renouncing the world or of unworldly individualism was present throughout the trans-ition from the early Christianity of Gelasius I to the Pope's appeal to Pepin, which gave rise to the idea of a Christian kingdom, and to the coronation of Charlemagne in AD 800. Calvinism represents its final triumph. The negative corollary of individualism was the identification of the individual with his good works, and therefore with the social order. That idea is more clearly presented in the writings of Calvin than in the great works written by Luther in 1520. According to Calvin, the state is a sanctifying institution (a *Heiligungsanstalt*, according to Troeltsch). Rousseau and his revolutionary successors made the same point in even more forceful terms, and thus gave rise to the widespread view that modernity itself can be defined as a transition from other-worldly indi-vidualism to worldly individualism.

The idea of the Subject takes us in a different direction. It seeks, in every society, a principle that allows us to appeal against the order of things. In traditional societies, such as India, that order is a natural order. In the modern world, it is an artificial order constructed by collective action, technology and the law. The Indian renouncer, or the renouncers of certain Christian traditions, do not withdraw from the world; they find their inspiration in an unworldly principle, but use it to act on the world through their words, teachings and example. Similarly, the appeal to human rights in the modern world is not a withdrawal into a universalism that is marginal to the active life and social organization; it is primarily a constitutional principle that is above the law. It allows us to construct a social life that is not reducible to the instrumental or utilitarian organiza-tion of collective life. To put it in still more concrete terms, any appeal to a figure of the Subject implies a critique of order. It asserts that there is a dark side to individualism, and that desire (which is the source of the passions) and, above all, the worship of money and power destroy order.

Enhancing everyone's freedom to live an individualized and meaningful life will not in itself release us from both social norms and individual desires (which are largely socially determined). We can do so only by appealing to reason against tradition, conformism and everything else that influences us. And we cannot do it alone. We have to do it in social life and through conflicts, but also by building fair institutions, or in other words institutions that safeguard this attempt at subjectivation.

Although the transition from traditional society to modern society might be described as the triumph of an artificial order over a natural order, we find, then, the same basic elements in all societies: a reference to an order, the appeal to a subject that exists outside the social order, and a critique of an order that is powerless against the disorder of self-interest and desire. Hence the need for an intervention on the part of a figure of the Subject. That is the one principle that allows us to construct an order which is neither natural nor artificial, but ethical.

There are two contradictory tendencies within any religious or ethical conviction. On the one hand, the *sanctification* of the social gives powers, institutions and the social organization the irrefutable power of a transcendental principle, irrespective of whether it creates a society that conforms to a divine revelation or a rational society which can be identified with progress. On the other hand, there is an appeal to the non-social basis of the social order, or to what I call 'the divine'. In religious cultures, this takes the form of faith. It may also take the very different form of a reference to an ethical being whose criterion for evaluating its own situations and behaviour is its ability to find in them the unity and continuity of a life project. This will to individuation corresponds to what I call 'the Subject'. Louis Dumont's definition of the individual in modern societies appears to me to confuse the two meanings of ethical individualism: 'an autonomous, ethical individual who is therefore essentially non-social, who represents our supreme values and whom we encounter primarily in our modern ideology of man and society' (Dumont 1983: 35). Alain Renaut's critique of Louis Dumont starts out by making the same point: 'According to Dumont, who sees individualism simply as the opposite of holism, the collapse of traditional values simply results in the triumph of the individual, and he overlooks the question of just what makes individualism possible ... the humanist valorization of man as Subject. *Individualism might be situated midway between holism and individualism; and the Subject, midway between the whole and the individual*' (Renaut 1989: 80, emphasis in the original). But Alain Renaut takes a different line from me by stressing the opposition, which is not mentioned by Dumont, between the independence and autonomy of the Subject and by opting for a Rousseauist conception of autonomy. In other words, he makes autonomy synonymous with a voluntary submission to the laws created by the general will. Because I find a complete and unthinking submission to the law, and therefore power, disturbing, I, by contrast, defend the independence of the Subject, but do so in a way that does not take me back to modern individualism, as defined by Dumont. Yet I do rely on that same author when I introduce my point of view, because in *Homo hierarchicus* Dumont attaches great importance to the figure of the renouncer, or the *sannyasi*, and that figure represents a form of other-worldly individualism. The distinction between social and non-social definitions of the individual seems to me to be even more important than that between the holistic societies of old and modern individualistic societies. Both types of society are Janus-faced, because there is no fundamental difference between an individual who is trapped in the roles imposed on him by the community and an individual whose actions are determined by his social situation and the highly effective blandishments of the market. At the same time, there is a similarity between the renouncer and the modern individual who appeals to the universal rights of man, and in particular the dissident or the resister who risks his life by challenging a social order which, in his view, is an affront to human dignity.

The pride of modernity was based on the sanctification of a world created by human action and by the scientific and technological creations of human beings. And for a long time, the idea of modernity was associated with this triumph of human action. This conception of modernity is increasingly contested, not least because the triumph has turned into a catastrophe and a threat to both civilization and the human race. The work of criticism must go hand in hand with a more positive approach. We must be able to have recourse to some principle that can limit social power, or even to a non-social basis for the social. That principle is precisely what I call 'the Subject'. The forms of the Subject that we project beyond the world, or into the transcendental realm, can be found in religions. Modernity makes the Subject more self-present, more reflexive and more capable of intervening in all human practices. Ultimately, there is very little difference between those who identify the freedom of the Subject with free trade or with an abundance of consumer goods and those who, both in the past and the present, describe the dissolution of the Subject into a homogeneous community as freedom. They all claim to be defending individual freedom and happiness, but in fact subordinate the members of a society to the logic of a system, and therefore to the material and ideological interests of those who dominate and rule that system. No matter whether they take the form of a stoic or religious acceptance of the natural world order or the apparently antithetical form of complete faith in the conquests of science and technology, all these appeals to nature are in direct conflict with the idea of the Subject. This becomes more obvious, in our day, if we contrast the laws of life with women's will to control their reproductive function, or the laws of the economy with individual and collective experience. The idea of the Subject has more in common with a certain aspect of religious thought than with utilitarianism, as it is based on a refusal to make the actor conform to the system or to reduce actors to social roles.

Some readers may conclude from all this that I have broken completely with the idea of modernity, and that I have rallied to an ethical conception which no longer believes that the conquests of reason and technologies can liberate human beings. I completely reject that conclusion. My refusal to identify the freedom of the Subject with technological and economic progress by no means implies a complete rejection of a historical vision of the human condition. On the contrary, I defend that vision against all forms of postmodernism. On the one hand, the Subject resists social norms in all situations. On the other, in both traditional and modern societies, the Subject becomes self-conscious, ceases to project itself onto a divine figure, or onto a community with its myths and heroes, and asserts itself in increasingly direct ways, or in other words, in ways that are less and less social or cosmological. These are complementary, not contradictory statements. It is in that sense that I share Louis Dumont's definition of our societies.

This answer allows us to arrive at a better understanding of the sociological approach as a whole. It analyses how the Subject, and its relations with both systems of power and individual desires, is transformed by the growing historicity of societies, or their growing ability to transform themselves.

Neither God nor man

The idea of the Subject is defined by its refusal to do two things, and those two things reveal that it is part of two very different traditions. It refuses to identify human beings with their works and social roles, and this book voices its refusal to do so in no uncertain terms. The triumph of the rationalization, technologies and strategies which buoyed the hopes of so many combatants as they marched towards their liberation has caused resisters, dissidents and minorities pain, because they were crushed by a totalitarian order. It has caused others pain by giving them no choice but to zap between the advertisements produced by the market. Their freedom has been reduced to the freedom to do whatever is in the interests of the powerful.

Science can no longer be used to legitimize power, be it aristocratic power or people's power. The trail of suffering left by the twentieth century is more visible than the zones of well-being that have illuminated it from time to time. As the new century begins, we must therefore make a comparison between sociological analysis and religious thought (which is always a meditation on suffering). In accordance with the teachings of both Buddha and the Gospel, the idea of the Subject divorces lived experience and consciousness from social belonging. Buddhism uses the image of a chariot to symbolize both physical and spiritual life. If it is drawn by horses, or the senses, it will go astray; if it is drawn by the soul or the real self (*atman*), it will reach its destination. This extreme religious stance can also be seen in the Christian calls to break our material and ethical ties: 'If any man will come after me, let him deny himself' (Matthew 16: 24), and 'I live; yet not I, but Christ liveth in me' (Galatians 2: 20). These calls reveal the nature of the second refusal implicit in the idea of the Subject. The other-worldly religious self is eternal, whereas the Subject exists in the world. It came into the world in the form of reason, defined both as the principle of the world-order and as intentionality, but the divorce between the two worlds is now complete. The external world can now be grasped by science, but the world of consciousness is far from the rationalized and instrumentalized world.

The idea of the Subject is anti-religious in the sense that it contrasts the splendour of being with its own 'lightness'. Its lightness does not allow it to walk on water like Buddha or Jesus, but it does prevent it from being crushed by the weight of markets or communities. A form of being that exists beyond consciousness has been replaced by a consciousness or reflexivity. It inherits the Cartesian *cogito*, but it is now bound up with action and the constant effort to rediscover the actor in the midst of his works and his own alienation.

The Subject is both post-religious and anti-religious, both rationalist and anti-rationalizing. It rejects religion because it belongs to modernity; but it also rejects all forms of positivism, both sociological and juridical, because there is an unbridgeable gap between utility and value. The Subject does not stand midway between religious thought and a utilitarian or positivist belief in progress. It is not ambivalent, and it does not alternate between loving and rejecting first progress and then the religious vision. It is self-centred, which means that the two worlds in which it is situated must be reconciled to some extent, but it also actively struggles against both worlds. The Subject is neither an eternal being nor the humanity that is set free by progress. It is neither God nor man.

3

Social Movements

The central conflict

Whereas most political ideologies assert that political action alone can give a general import to demands, which are always particular, the idea of a social movement seeks to demonstrate the existence, within every societal type, of a central conflict. It was a central conflict that set nation against prince, and then workers against employers. Does such a conflict exist today?

Many people answer this question in the negative, and turn to the study of particular demands and political crises. I am defending the opposite view: yes, a central conflict does exist in our post-industrial society – or the programmed society, the information society or whatever else we wish to call it. To be more specific, there is a central actor, and a conflict over an issue of central importance. The title of this book indicates the nature of what is at stake: can we live together, or will we allow ourselves to become trapped in our differences, or to be reduced to the status of passive consumers of a mass culture produced by a globalized economy? To put it a different way: will we become Subjects, or will we be torn, as the whole of social life tends to be torn, between the world of instrumentality and the world of identity? The central conflict in our society is being waged, according to my analysis, by a Subject struggling against the triumph of the market and technologies, on the one hand, and communitarian authoritarian powers, on the other. This cultural conflict seems to me to be as central to our society as economic conflict was to industrial society, and as political conflict was to the first centuries of our modernity.

Before I clarify and discuss this assertion, a word of warning is necessary. If we call any type of collective action a social movement, it is neither necessary nor even possible to theorize it – no more than doctors can theorize spots or fever as general types of disease, since very different pathologies can generate such symptoms. Those who think they are making an analysis by describing anything that disturbs the social organization as a social movement are saying nothing. The notion of a social movement is useful only if it allows us to demonstrate the existence of a very particular type of social action: a type of social action that allows a social category – and it is always a particular category – to challenge a form of social domination that is at once particular and general. It does so in the name of general values or social orientations which it shares with its adversary, and it does so in an attempt to deny the adversary's legitimacy. If we invert the formula, we can also recognize the existence of movements supported by dominant categories and directed against popular categories, which are regarded as obstacles to social integration or economic progress. But in both cases, the social movement is much more than an interest group or a tool for bringing political pressure to bear; it challenges the modality of the social use of resources and cultural models. It is in order to avoid any confusion between this type of collective action and all the rest, which many are too quick to call 'social movements', that I will speak here of 'societal movements', in order to make clear that they challenge society's general orientations.

Does this definition correspond to contemporary realities? Do societal movements exist in our type of society?

When we read that our society is constantly changing, that the economy has become divorced from social life, and that social actors are retreating into private life or communities, we seem to be ruling out the very idea of a central conflict, and therefore of a central societal movement. Does not that idea imply a society in which there is a close association between the economy and social relations and forms of political power? Does it not refer to structural conflicts, and are we not now talking, rather, of inequality of opportunity in a time of change and even exclusion? And is not the word 'exclusion' the opposite of 'exploitation', just as 'globalization' is the opposite of 'ruling class'? In a word, is not the idea of a social movement associated with a productive class society, or a society with orders and estates – in the sense in which we used to speak of the 'Third Estate' – whereas we are now conscious of living in a globalized market rather than an industrial or pre-industrial society?

These objections come to mind so naturally that we have to begin by looking at how societal movements and conflicts can be included in our representation of our society. That representation appears to be dominated by the juxtaposition of the economy and a number of cultures, and by the absence of the political mediations and social systems that allow societal movements to emerge. Those who identify societal movements

with the combination of class struggle, national consciousness and historical optimism that was conceived and constructed by the revolutionary
ideology of the industrial era are in danger of applying to contemporary
society a conception of societal movements that actually corresponded to
a very different historical situation. In the present chapter, we will constantly move, therefore, between an analysis of contemporary actors and
conflicts and a much more general consideration of the nature of societal
movements.

My justification for speaking here of societal movements is that my
analysis began with the dissociation of the economic world from the
cultural world. That break leads to the debasement of both worlds, and
threatens the unity of personal identity. An actor who has been unsettled
in this way tries to safeguard or reconstruct his capacity for action and the
unity of his experience. Conflict is therefore present throughout this
analysis. The Subject can be constituted only through the struggle against
the logic of markets, on the one hand, and communitarian power, on the
other.

This brief reminder also brings out the main differences between this
conception and those associated with the societal movements of earlier
periods.

The first and most obvious difference is that the old binary oppositions
(king/nation, bourgeoisie/people, capitalists/workers) have been replaced
by the image of a Subject struggling on two fronts because the dissociation of the economic from the cultural is now the central fact. This
difference masks a second, more important, difference. In the past, the
popular actor was seen as the agent of a positive logic. Being identified
with a community, labour, energy or the people, the actor was moving
with the flow of history, and was in conflict with dominant actors who
were defending particular interests, privileges or profits. The victory of
that popular actor would mean that society had been reconciled with
itself, that contradictions would be overcome, and that equality, fraternity
and justice would triumph. The greater the sufferings of the dominated,
the greater the need for revolutionary violence in order to ensure the
triumph of popular unity. Such is the message of all revolutions, from
the French Convention to the Mexican Revolution (whose ideology and
hopes were painted by Diego Rivera in his great frescoes on the walls of
the Ministry for National Education), and then the Cuban Revolution
and the Chinese Cultural Revolution.

This revolutionary conception of social movements ascribes a very
determinate role to the people. Although the people is expected to rise
up against an intolerable domination and exploitation, it is the intellectual
and political élite alone who can interpret the meaning of history, subordinate social practices to reason, and bring about progress. The more

underdeveloped the country, or in other words the weaker the forces of self-sustaining modernization, the more dictatorial the power of the leading élites who speak in the name of the divided people, and the greater the likelihood that they will serve a party, a class, an ethnic group or a supreme leader. The social movement will therefore always be subordinated to an action and a consciousness that comes to it from outside. The labour movement itself was usually under the leadership of a political party.

These social movements were at least inspired by the will to overcome the contradictions between master and slave, by creating a collective Subject defined in either religious, communitarian, political or class terms. A social movement is never reducible to the defence of the interests of the dominated. Its ambition is always to abolish a relationship of domination, to bring about the triumph of a principle of equality, or to create a new society which breaks with the old forms of production, management and hierarchy. This conception, which has set history ablaze on more than one occasion, has now disintegrated and is in a state of decay. In developing societies, the gulf between popular uprisings and the exercise of power is constantly widening, and the role of popular movements has been reduced to the promotion of new élites. The revolutionary situation in Tsarist Russia led, for instance, to the Bolsheviks' *putsch* (the road to it had been paved by the breakdown of the old order, the rebellion of sections of the army and navy, and the overthrow of the regime in February), but the victorious party immediately imposed its dictatorship, dissolved the Duma and eliminated the workers' opposition.

Elsewhere, and especially in the industrialized countries, we have seen the development of partial conflicts without revolutionary ambitions, and of interest groups which cannot be regarded as societal movements because they do not have any image of the liberated Subject. Now a purely conflictual vision of society will inevitably be transformed into an ultra-liberal conception which reduces society to a market and social actors to competitors. That is why we are seeing the world-wide fragmentation of collective action and the development of what Ulrich Beck calls 'sub-politics'. Within this heteroclite collection of demands, protests and obstructive actions, we can, however, distinguish between three very different categories of initiative. The first concerns the defence of vested interests. They are defended against technocrats or financiers, and sometimes against the legitimate or inevitable appearance of newcomers or new forms of economic activity. These demands can be judged in different ways, depending on one's opinion of what they are fighting, but they are in themselves no more than defensive actions, and are incapable of giving their fight a general meaning. The second category is more consciously political, in that it is a matter of re-establishing or enhancing a political decision-making capability by resisting forces that claim to be, and are often seen as, natural or even rational. One such force is the famous globalization, which its enemies usually refrain from analysing so as to make it seem more frightening. The final category does imply an appeal to the Subject, defined both as freedom and culture. We hear that call in, for instance, both women's movements and movements concerned with minorities.

In the past, social movements were the embodiment of a project for a radical reconstruction of society and a figure of the Subject. The project was often more important than the figure of the Subject. Marxists called it the 'totality', the end of the prehistory of humanity or communism. The modern world's first revolutionary explosions were attempts to create a society of equal and pure individuals who would be free from both poverty and the domination of masters. Like the revolutionary movements of seventeenth- and eighteenth-century Europe, from the English Levellers to the French Montagnard Convention, they were often millenarian or messianic, and attempted to establish an absolute and egalitarian people's power and to abolish privileges. No societal movement can now surrender to the charms of such a powerful utopia; collective action must directly serve a new figure of the Subject. In societies that are fully supported and constantly transformed by their historicity, or by their ability to produce and change themselves, the Subject can no longer commit itself to, or be alienated in, an order, a community or a political power. The sole objective is to create the Subject through the struggle against the powers that dominate the worlds of instrumentality and identity; there is no longer any principle that can found the new order that can abolish history by bringing it to an end or going back to its beginnings.

This reversal of perspective disconcerts all those who are still trying to use popular movements to build political parties, and especially neo-communitarian powers. In the most highly industrialized societies, societal movements now have to take the form of collective actions that directly assert and defend both equality and the rights and freedom of the Subject. In that sense, we can say that societal movements have become ethical movements, whereas in the past they were religious, political or economic movements.

Contemporary societal movements are not the servants of any model of the perfect society or, therefore, any political party, whereas at the time of the great revolutions that founded political modernity, societal movements were subordinate to, and almost marginalized by, political action, as François Furet (1995) has demonstrated in his critique of Albert Mathiez and Georges Lefebvre's account of the French Revolution.

The weakness and failure of what, in the mid-1970s, I called the 'new social movements' stemmed from the fact that, although they were the bearers of new social and cultural projects, they were prepared to accept the authority of a political ideology and a political strategy. And the weakness of that ideology and strategy, which in France were represented mainly by Marxist-inspired active minorities, did not prevent them from smothering the novel aspects of those new societal movements, which rapidly split into a radical wing which defended the priority of political action and a wing that was more concerned with social and cultural innovation, but degenerated into either reformism or a narrow communitarianism.

Those who wish to revive the old priority of political action rightly speak of the defence of the Republic rather than of social movements, and of the nation rather than cultural diversity. Their conceptions have always resulted in the subordination of societal movements to a power and a political ideology. In asserting that there is a very close link between Subject and societal movement, I am trying, by contrast, to understand the conflicts that run through our society. Our society no more believes in political transcendence than it believes in religious transcendence, and its conflicts cannot be limited, therefore, by either the religion of reason or the cult of the nation. As we have said, the only societal movements that are possible today are movements that defend the personal Subject against the power of markets and the power of communitarian and nationalist powers. But this statement requires immediate qualification, as it might trap us in the epic conception of a 'conscious and organized' movement, or of a crusade for values or ethical reform, whereas the Subject is neither a consciousness, a concrete actor nor a personality.

If the Subject is an attempt to break free from two things and a struggle that never triumphs, a societal movement can be no more than an attempt to combine the struggle against enemies who pose a constant threat with the defence of social and cultural rights. As that goal is never really achieved, the movement is always fragmentary and full of contradictions. Far from being a prophetic figure, a societal movement is a changing set of debates, tensions and internal rifts; it is torn between grass-roots opinion and the political projects of its leaders. And it is the orators and writers on the fringes of the movement, who are quickly rejected if they attempt to occupy the centre, who state the meaning of the collective action and say what makes it a movement. That, if Jean-François Lyotard is to be believed, was the role played by Byron, Petőfi and Hugo, and even Lawrence and Malraux.

In a societal movement, self-consciousness, aesthetic recreation, political strategy and grass-roots solidarity combine, complement one another and come into conflict, but no doctrinal or political message is formulated by any one of its component elements. That is why the growing autonomy of societal movements is the source of their political weakness and their organizational fragility.

Subject and social movement

We now have to undertake an internal analysis of societal movements. I have said that they are a combination of a truly social conflict and a cultural project which is always defined with reference to a Subject. The Subject has appeared in a religious or political form, and in the form of a class and a nation; here, I will be constantly defending the idea that, in our type of society, the Subject can only appear 'as such', or in the form of a personal Subject. But in all societies, the Subject is revealed by the presence of ethical values that come into conflict with the social order. A societal movement defends a social modality of the use of ethical values, and comes into conflict with the modality that its adversary is trying to defend and enforce. Ethical references and an awareness of a conflict with a social adversary are both aspects of a societal movement, and they are inseparable. This ethical reference is not to be confused with the discourse of demands, as that discourse attempts to modify a cost–benefit ratio, whereas the ethical discourse of a societal movement speaks of freedom, life projects and a respect for basic rights that cannot be reduced to material or political gains.

It is because we have become accustomed to representing societal movements as forms of mobilization in the service of great causes that we now have to emphasize the goal of subjectivation. Subjectivation always presupposes that we to some extent distance ourselves from the social and political goals of a collective action. If we trap ourselves into an ethics of responsibility, we leave an unbounded and uncontrolled space for the war between the gods, to use the terminology of Max Weber, who was one of the first to show the dangers inherent in a rationality that has become purely instrumental and unleashes an irrational, non-negotiable and unargued appeal to convictions and their meta-social foundations. The idea of a Subject, like the related idea of a social movement, attempts, by contrast, to re-establish a link between the kingdom of means and the kingdom of ends, between instrumental rationality and beliefs, and between market and community. Whilst the kingdom of ends has been divorced from that of means, just as the rights of man have been divorced from practical politics, the idea of the Subject is both safeguarded by, and trapped in, a world of principles which is almost always crushed by the world of power, just as the idea of the rights of man was crushed by the Jacobin interpretation of the sovereignty of the people, and just as the revolutionary working-class movement was crushed by the post-revolutionary dictatorships. As the appeal to the Subject becomes more concrete, or in other words is grasped in terms of its social situation, its cultural heritage and the history of its personality, so it leaves the realm of principles, enters the public space, and becomes involved in political debate and collective action. But the Subject is certainly not identified with an interest group, a class or a nation, for that could lead only to new forms of absolute communitarian power. On the contrary, and like the modern idea of democracy, it combines the safeguarding of personal freedoms with involvement in collective decision making.

Those who are involved in a societal movement wish to put an end to the intolerable by taking part in a collective action, but they also always make a distinction between their convictions and their action. The supply of protests and hopes is inexhaustible, and the action of a societal movement is always incomplete. It is this combination of commitment and abstention from commitment, of a struggle against external threats and reminders that the actor is a unitary individual, that defines a collective action undertaken in the name of the Subject.

There are two aspects to any societal movement: one is utopian, and the other is ideological. At the utopian level, the actor identifies with the rights of the Subject; at the ideological level, the actor concentrates on the struggle against a social adversary. The theme of class struggle is ideological, as it stresses social conflict rather than the fact that shared values are at stake. The American and French student movements of 1964 and 1968, on the other hand, were so influenced by utopianism that they defined their adversaries in very vague terms, and this allowed certain ideological groups to interpret them as new 'fronts' that could advance the struggle of the working class. That is why the student movements turned to violence in an attempt to arouse the alienated masses. Now, whilst a societal movement is always asymmetrical to some extent, it cannot exist in the absence of either of these two elements.

In our type of society, both adversaries speak of individual freedom. It is individual freedom that defines the field of their conflict. We have, then, a conflict between two conceptions of individualism. One defends the multiplicity of choice that mass consumerism and mass communication offer the vast majority of individuals, and regards the market as a liberating force which is destroying the regulatory power of a state, belief or established social hierarchy. The other argues against this conception in the name of a collective Subject entrusted with a cultural heritage. One side talks of freedom of choice; the other, of identity and lived experience. Both conceptions have a common concern with the defence of the individual, but they come into conflict. That conflict may transform them into societal movements, as the most obvious difference between them and a demand or a reaction to a political crisis is that societal movements have a clear definition of their adversary. Just as a political crisis brings social groups into conflict with institutions, laws and decision-making systems, and just as a demand is centred on the actor himself and on his needs and social utility, so a societal movement is sustained by a conflictual dialogue. The labour movement was opposed by the action of capitalists, anti-colonial movements by colonizers, feminist movements by male domination, and student movements by an educational system.

The close link between social movement and Subject might suggest that we should be speaking of *civil society*, but political philosophy finds it easier to handle that notion than does contemporary sociology. We must also bear in mind that, for thirty years, the expression 'civil society' has been used to designate a set of social actors that fought both capitalist domination and the authoritarian state in very different ways, which Jean Cohen and Andrew Arato (1992) have described with great precision. The idea of civil society is indispensable, however. Civil society is the place where collective actions are initiated to free social actors and to combat the workings of an economy dominated by profit and the political will to dominance. In their struggle against both systems of power, all figures of the Subject strive to create an autonomous intermediary space. All contemporary theorists of civil society, and especially Claus Offe, deal with this theme; but it must be complemented by the idea that the central goal of civil society's actors is their own autonomy. In the struggle against absolute monarchies, it was the economic actors, or the bourgeois, who defended civil society. In a society dominated by the market economy, movements to defend cultural rights are civil society's best representatives; in totalitarian societies, total social movements like Solidarity in Poland are its best representatives, because they challenge a total power in order to liberate an actor who is at once national, democratic and working-class. If we have to speak of civil society today, it is because we have to assert that, from now onwards, the Subject speaks for itself. It can do no other, because it is encircled by both the economic world of the market and technologies and communitarian ideologies embodied in states or political parties.

Because the demands it puts forward are ethical and cultural, rather than economic, this civil society can act only if it liaises with political forces, but those forces are not to be confused with the parties or coalitions that manage national politics. Civil society can then construct a set of mediations which are at once social and political, and which exist midway between political programmes and social situations. The NGOs of the underdeveloped countries are the most obvious example; whilst they are opinion-led movements or even social movements, they are also elements of the political system – and they are sometimes accused of being

an integral part of it. The link between social demands and protests and
forces with political influence is established at the local level, rather than
the professional level, and this makes local political and social life increasingly independent of the national level. Cohen and Arato are right to
make the participation of citizens in public life part of their definition of
civil society (1992: 19). But civil society decays when social demands are
subordinated to a political programme. There is no contradiction between
saying that, in civil society, social demands and political influences coexist, and saying that the new societal movements are more directly concerned with the defence of the Subject than were those of the past. The
two statements are in fact complementary. Conversely, the strongest
social movements of the past were subordinated to political agents,
because they were wedded to national or class ideologies. The 'weakness'
of new societal movements and of civil society is simply a corollary of
their independence. The 'new social movements' of the 1970s were rapidly
exhausted, because they remained pre- or para-political movements. The
women's movement, by contrast, did not become a political force, and
therefore penetrated more and more deeply into personal modes of behaviour, family relationships, and conceptions of law and education.

Societal movements and revolt

A societal movement is indeed made up of a combination of an ethical call
and an explicitly social conflict, or in other words a conflict between one
socially defined actor and another. The heritage of the last two centuries,
which forms what Eric Hobsbawm (1962) calls the age of revolution,
has, however, partly masked the general nature of societal movements,
because the dominated social actor appealed to meta-social principles in
the struggle against the master. Because the actor appealed to meta-social
principles such as freedom, the nation or progress, he rejected the adversary completely and regarded it as an obstacle to the realization of those
principles or the laws of history. Such was the definition of revolutionary
action. For a long time, we had a combination of societal movements and
revolutionary breaks, just as, for a very long time, we once had societal
movements combined with the defence of a community or faith. That, as
it happens, is why the expression 'societal movement' has been adopted
only recently, and at the suggestion of sociologists; previously, we preferred to speak of 'social movements', and used that term as a generic
description of both social protests and political action. The labour movement was the central societal movement in industrial society, but all too
often it became confused with the socialist idea, which was sustained by a
belief in progress and reason. No matter whether it was reformist or

revolutionary, the socialist idea was a political force rather than a social actor. We still find it somewhat difficult to free ourselves from the historicist ideologies which for so long gave social struggles an importance which they would not otherwise have had. I am by no means suggesting that we should remove the reference to values from the definition of societal movements; I am suggesting that we have to recognize that those values can now be based no more on historical or natural laws than on a revealed religious message, and that they have finally become a direct assertion of the rights of the Subject.

This is why societal movements are very different from revolts against suffering, poverty or slavery. Societal movements have positive objectives; revolts are defined by what they reject and not by a social, political or cultural objective. Revolts are centred upon both the sufferings of a population and the rejection of a state of affairs that is defined in global terms and cannot be improved to any great extent. Such were the revolts staged by serfs who had been crushed by feudal lords, prisoners who had been reduced to slavery, peoples who had been destroyed by foreign domination, and the victims of totalitarian regimes. Revolts necessarily become fragmented and take on contradictory meanings, but they are always extreme. What is more, those who are oppressed cannot liberate themselves by relying on their own force. It was not the deported who destroyed the camps, and it was not the slaves who overthrew slavery. Only political freedom, and above all the opening up of economic exchanges and the substitution of the power of money for personal domination, could transform victims into free, exploited workers, or even into citizens. In extreme cases, poverty makes liberation almost impossible. When the system of domination is shaken, revolts break out, but they either remain episodic or are manipulated by demagogues, who use them to build up their despotic power and who soon use it against the rebels. And when the crisis in the old system becomes generalized, a revolutionary *putsch*, carried out in the name of the downtrodden people, but not by the people or the organizations it has founded, puts a post-revolutionary ruling élite in power. When, finally, the mobilization is more direct and on a mass scale, the popular revolt itself may become authoritarian, and turn against foreigners or minorities. Emancipatory action does not promote the cause of freedom in any of these examples.

Even when there is a historical connection between the two, there is a profound difference between the forms of action and thought known, respectively, as a revolt and a societal movement. Those involved in revolts believe in the implacable logic of domination, in the contradictions of the system, in social revolts and in the need for truly political action if they are to be meaningful; societal movements assert the existence of actors who can overthrow a social domination and use cultural orientations against their adversaries, even though they both subscribe to those orientations. Such movements combine consciousness and action, conflict and utopia, and assert their own priority over political action. France is a statist country rather than a society, a country of politics rather than social action, and of revolutions rather than democracy, and it has until now constantly shown a preference for the most political conception of political change. That conception associates popular revolts and popular suffering with truly political action, marginalizes social movements' attempts to organize autonomously, and gives only a limited role to direct action syndicalism or those whom Hobsbawm calls 'primitive rebels'. Hobsbawm too believes that only the political party can transcend their primitivism. And the organic intellectuals of the revolutionary parties mercilessly attack all those they generically refer to as petty bourgeois, humanists, liberals or social traitors, and anyone else who believes in the possible existence of societal movements that can transform the political field itself.

Whilst any societal movement is obviously inspired by a project and wants to get results, there is within it, even as it negotiates, a permanent core of protest. And if I opt for societal movements rather than revolt, it is because, although I recognize the centrality of the societal movement, I do not deny the existence of rejectionism. By contrast, those who assign central importance to such rejectionism persist in making the radical critique of the idea of the Subject which dominated the thinking of the 1970s and which was associated with the image of a society completely dominated by the logic of power and the reproduction of inequalities. This current of thought was powerful, but it failed to see that the historical conjuncture was changing, and that the globalization of the economy was weakening the controls imposed by the state that disciplines and punishes. When one lives in a country that has been transformed by industrial democracy, the Welfare State, mass consumption and neo-corporatism, it is particularly dangerous to prophesy the immobility of the social order and to believe that the only way out for the dominated is a hopeless revolt or a flight into the hills. Indeed, in such a country it is impossible to see in social struggles only the endless revolt of the wretched of the earth, who in fact do have the ability to exert considerable pressure and influence. It is equally wrong not to see the presence of societal movements in struggles to defend an identity or a community. Such struggles can obviously be transformed into manifestations of an intolerant populism that is obsessed with the quest for purity or homogeneity, but they can also be an expression of democratic aspirations, as we have seen in South Africa, and as we see in the Zapatista movement in Mexico's Chiapas and in other Indian movements in Latin America. And we cannot really condemn the lower-caste and untouchable groups in India for taking political action without running the risk of justifying nationalist campaigns that promote the interests of higher castes. Not all social struggles will develop into societal movements, but we always have to look for the presence of a societal movement, or in other words for a cultural project combined with a social conflict, in social struggles.

Cultural movements and the defence of identity

It was the development of industrial society that forced us to recognize the existence of class actors, and therefore to abandon the view that popular struggles were indirect agents of modernization in favour of a truly sociological approach to societal movements. I have just recalled the general principles of that approach. This recognition did, however, meet with resistance on the part of the ideologues and politicians who wanted to make the labour movement a mere tool for the extension of political democracy. It was the moment when the labour movement had to be defined as a collective struggle over the social management of industrialization that gave birth to the idea of a social movement which could be at once modernist and particularist, emancipatory and defensive.

The same was true, slightly later, of the anti-colonialist and anti-imperialist movements and of the women's movements. All defended a particular experience and, at the same time, appealed to the universalist principles of freedom and equality. There was therefore a growing distance between the progressive, republican or even socialist forces, which increasingly inscribed themselves in the field of a modernity defined in universalist terms, and societal movements which called increasingly for the recognition of a concrete historical actor and of that actor's rights, interests and culture. The new societal movements were as different from those of industrial society as 'life politics' is different from 'emancipatory politics' (Giddens 1991: 215). Whereas an emancipatory politics is defined primarily by the obstacles or contradictions it seeks to overcome, the main goal of a life politics is to enhance the capacity for action and freedom of choice. It seeks to change life rather than to transform society.

The difference between the end of the century and the early years of the century, which saw the rise of the labour movement, is that in the early part of the century there still seemed to be a link between intellectual and political progressivism and working-class action. Working-class action soon became a victim of that confusion. The apparent complementarity of the social actor and the political agent was shattered, together with Marxism–Leninism, which was the principal ideological mediator in the alliance, but which died in the convulsions of the Chinese Cultural Revolution and with the transformation of the Cuban guerrilla army into a dictatorship. The independence of social movements was proclaimed in May 1968. At the same time, the dangers inherent in their independence (counter-cultural exhaustion and sectarianism) were also clearly recognized. This hard-won independence gave societal movements their full importance at a time when the politicians and organic intellectuals were hypocritically lamenting their disappearance.

Political action and social action therefore have to be defined in different terms. Norberto Bobbio (1994) has defined the Left as the defender of equality, and the Right in terms of its rejection of equality. I define societal movements in different terms, as they usually appeal to a meta-social principle. It may be religious, political, societal or cultural, but it always has an ethical basis or a conception of human beings which imposes limits on all forms of power.

Societal movements 'from below', which must not be described as 'popular' (because the idea of the people is nothing more than the state in disguise), also defend social and cultural diversity. They therefore also defend fairness, which presupposes pluralism and difference, whereas the call for equality often results in a policy of homogenization and the rejection of differences in the name of the universal character of the law.

If, however, a societal movement is characterized by the fact that a category of actors comes into conflict with an adversary over how society's ability to act upon itself should be managed, the movements we have seen developing since the 1960s cannot, with some exceptions, be described as societal movements. They are, rather, *cultural movements*. I understand that term to mean collective actions that strive to defend or transform a figure of the Subject. These movements are riven with social conflicts between the defenders of what might be termed 'cultural liberalization' and the men and women who assert the specific rights of a cultural actor. They are centred on the assertion of cultural rights, rather than on a conflict with an adversary, who may be defined only in vague terms. In historical terms, the most important cultural movements have been religious movements; in our world, which is a product of industrial society, the most important are the women's movement and political ecology, but what we term the 'defence of minorities' (which may be either ethnic, national, ethical or religious) often develops into a cultural movement.

That these movements mobilize categories that are not socially defined is further confirmation that desocialization is one of the characteristics of our era of demodernization. The categories mobilized in collective actions are defined less and less by their activities, and more and more by their origins or loyalties. Whereas our societies were once vertical, they are becoming horizontal. Diversity is replacing hierarchy. This is for both better and worse, because the answer to the demand for equality may be segregation: equal, yes, but separate.

The women who are struggling for their liberation want to abolish the discrimination and social inequality that victimizes them, but they speak as women. Similarly, national liberation movements, which always have a living relationship with the past, often come into conflict with class movements, which fear that nationalist demands will play into the hands of a national bourgeoisie which is prepared to reach an accommodation with the old sovereign. These movements resist the social organization, and especially its leaders, by asserting an experience that cannot be reduced to a social status or social roles. This often puts such movements in a contradictory position which exhausts them. Even in its higher forms, political ecology, for instance, can evolve into an anti-humanist naturalism – hence Hans Jonas's (1979) call for a 'principle of responsibility'. Karl Otto Apel (1990) rightly remarks that this implies a utopian view of responsibility which desperately overburdens the individual on whom it is incumbent. It results in an understandable but dangerous awareness of being powerless in the face of the new problems posed by collective responsibility for the results of collective activities.

Similarly, the weakness of feminists who define all their actions in political terms or in terms of the struggle that has to be waged against a system of domination is their refusal to see that women's personalities, self-expression, affective life and action can all take very different forms.

This transcendence of the social can lead to neo-communitarianism, and may allow loyalties and heritages to triumph over freedoms and choice. The only way to avoid that happening is to recognize that the new issues and the new actors are figures of a Subject which is at once rational and defined by cultural identifications. That is why the theme of diversity has become so central to the definition and defence of democracy. Social identity was for a long time defined by the match between an individual's position within a social system and their pattern of behaviour. And it is that match, which sociology has often used to define itself, that is disappearing. As what I call 'demodernization' gets under way, its demise leads, not to the disappearance of social actors and movements, but to their profound transformation: they are no longer defined with reference to society, but with reference to the Subject. For 200 years, the ruling ideas tried to convince us that we were social beings, and sometimes even that we were rational economic agents, but we now find that what we used to call 'society' is being de-institutionalized, and either bypassed or cut in two by networks and markets. At the same time, the actor discovers his individuality and the history of his personality through his drives, parental relations and mechanisms of identification. Squeezed between a globalized world and private experience, the social

definition of situations and actions loses all content. The societal movements of old degenerate into interest groups or corporatism, and we
rightly speak of the end of the ideologies that once led social actors into
political battle.

The reconstruction of what might be called 'self-identity' will not come
about through an identification with an economic, natural or religious
world order, but through the recognition that elements that once combined to form an integrated experience have become dissociated. The new
cultural movements refuse to identify with any one social category; they
appeal to the Subject itself, and to the Subject's dignity, self-respect and
ability to reconcile its instrumental roles and its individuality. This presupposes a recognition of everyone's psychological and cultural specificity, as well as of their creative capacity, regardless of whether it is based
upon reason or some more direct assertion of their creativity. Identity is
not constituted through an identification with a world order, a social
group, a cultural tradition or even individuality itself. Identity is, on the
contrary, shaped through disidentification and thanks to the reminder
that the self does exist. As I have said elsewhere, Freud's notion of
secondary narcissism may be one of its expressions.

These contemporary cultural movements can be studied by using the
same categories that we use to study any other movement, and religious
movements in particular. I have described religious movements as having
a twofold orientation; on the one hand, they based the freedom of the
Subject on a meta-social principle and, on the other, they absorbed the
Subject into the natural logic of a higher order – hence the internal
struggles within religious worlds, and in more concrete terms churches,
between those who appeal in mystical or eschatological terms to faith and
charity and those who want to spread or enforce forms of morality and
rites that demonstrate the sacred's hold over both personal and social life.
Within the Catholic world, there is a very obvious difference between
those who turn to the figure of Christ and those whose piety is addressed
mainly to the Virgin and the saints, in the belief that they are agents who
can instil a religious morality. The same difference can be observed,
sometimes in even more dramatic form, in the Reformed Churches,
which have, sometimes simultaneously, appealed to faith and either
founded theocracies, like Calvin, or supported princes, as in the case of
the Lutherans. The contradiction between the two aspects of religion
probably takes on its most extreme form in Islam, where we have an
identification of the religious message with the social order, on the one
hand, and mystical Sufism, on the other.

There are two aspects to the national idea too. On the one hand, we
have the idea of citizenship, which is based upon the sovereignty of the
people. Its most admirable expression was the French Revolution of 1789,

which inspired German thinkers from Kant to Fichte and the young Hegel. On the other hand, we have the idea of the nation-state, which sanctifies the state in the name of the nation, and which has fuelled both authoritarian regimes and international wars.

The same duality and the same internal conflicts can be observed in our industrial society's two main cultural movements. The women's movement leads to the discovery that women are Subjects, and that the Subject is therefore gendered and can no longer be described as Man. The Subject is both man and woman, and they are separate but equal. In the name of its struggle against male domination, the women's movement seeks, however, to eradicate 'gender', or social roles identified with a sex, in the name of a future society and the reign of an equality that will erase natural differences and give unto each in accordance with their talent or, more concretely, their social utility. This liberal and utilitarian conception contradicts identity-based demands.

As Luc Ferry (1992) has underlined, the contradiction between the two orientations is more extreme still in the case of ecology. Deep ecology goes so far as to found an anti-humanist cult of nature which can feed into certain authoritarian ideologies, but can also reconcile itself to a capitalist globalization that seeks to remove political and social controls over the economy. The defence of cultural diversity and of endangered species of plants and animals (and, more generally, the call for responsibility on the part of societies, which have to make development something we can live with) is, in the meantime, based upon an extended and uneasy conception of human freedom, as well as on the right to life and to freedom of cultural expression.

The internal conflicts characteristic of cultural movements are also social conflicts to the extent that all manifestations of the sanctification of the social order, no matter whether it is sanctified in the name of a god, reason, history or nature, tend to be ideologically recuperated by the ruling élite, where recourse to a figure of the Subject, externalized or not, is associated with social protest and is often sustained by messianic movements. Movements of this kind, to which Henri Desroche (1973) has devoted the greater part of his work, are at once social and religious. The social and political struggles waged by a cultural movement sometimes even appear to be the most real things about them. This is (at least apparently) the case with organized women's movements, which usually break up or become weaker when they succeed in having certain laws repealed (or passed), and then regroup when a social or juridical reaction appears to pose a threat to those reforms, as in the United States. This interpretation, however, is a serious distortion of reality. Cultural movements are affirmative, and not just protest movements. They represent an attempt at subjectivation, and they are emancipatory movements, even when they are inspired by a pessimistic image of humanity, as is usually the case with reformist religious movements.

New historical movements

It is true that these new societal and cultural movements rarely take an organized form. They are now less visible than what I call 'historical movements', which challenge not the masters of a stable social order, but the élites who control change. The world is in fact living through a liberal shock whose effects are much more far-reaching than the industrial revolution that caused an upheaval in parts of nineteenth-century Europe. Throughout the world, various modes of bringing the economy under social and political control are breaking down, exploding or being destroyed. This does not mark a transition from industrial society to post-industrial society, but the transformation of societies mobilized by voluntaristic states into societies that are regulated by the international market. The most obvious development is not the formation of a new mode of production, but the triumph, or at least the provisional triumph, of a new mode of development. The market is destroying the old systems of social controls over the economy or forcing them to undergo profound transformations. An upheaval of this kind results in the formation not of social movements but, rather, of historical movements that lead to conflict between the people and the élites, or between those who undergo change and those who organize it.

We must differentiate between three situations. Where the new liberal model triumphs, historical protest movements are reduced to marginality. This radicalizes them, but reduces their influence. When the new forces that impose social controls on change allow some state intervention, negotiations and compromises between the past and the future are possible. The third situation is defined by the existence of very strong resistance to the new liberal model and the continued existence of a mobilizing, managerial and redistributive state: an open conflict with the central sectors of the economy is then inevitable. Within the Western world, the United States, Great Britain and, in the period following the fall of the Berlin Wall, Russia, Poland and Hungary have conformed to the first model. Germany, Sweden and to some extent Italy and the Czech Republic are good examples of the second situation, as is Brazil; whereas Chile and Argentina have chosen the first model. France is an example of the third type; since at least 1986, its political and social life has been dominated by chronic conflicts, their main actors being public sector wage-earners. The great French conflict of November–December 1995 was, despite the corporatist demands and the political crisis it revealed, a historical movement inspired by the wage-earners' distrust of the élites who were forcing through a liberal policy that threatened to destroy the safeguards, status and social welfare systems which they had won in the previous period. That movement was therefore, in part, a historical movement. That was its central meaning, even though its most highly organized actors were always more interested in a more defensive, demand-based action. It was made stronger by the authoritarian methods used by the French government – the same methods used, with comparable effect, by the Berlusconi government in Italy. This serves as a reminder that a collective action usually means several things at the same time.

Historical movements challenge an élite rather than a ruling class, and because they appeal to the people to resist the state, they have a greater mobilizing power, but not the purity of social movements which clearly express their own nature, that of their adversary and that of the disputed issues that led to the conflict. A historical movement is therefore more unstable than a societal movement, because it often tends to become a tool in the hands of a political counter-élite or, conversely, a way of defending certain vested interests. Independent historical movements, however, are beginning to take shape at the international level, in response to the globalization of the economy. Great ecological campaigns challenge not only the policies of one country or one firm, but a whole mode of development. In poor countries, many NGOs have gone beyond their strictly humanitarian remit, and are pointing the finger at the authoritarian or corrupt forms of political organization and the organization of the world economy that have brought about the poverty they are supposed to be relieving. They have large numbers of militant social and political leaders, and are already playing a role comparable to that played by European and American trade-unionism during the industrialization of those countries.

The difficult formation of societal movements

Cultural movements and historical movements often come into conflict. The latter strengthen the state, appeal to tradition, and impose homogeneity. The former bypass the national or communitarian level in two ways. The demands made by political ecology and by humanitarian movements go beyond the national-communitarian level, whereas demands for the protection of minorities, the recognition of women's rights and, more generally, the defence of personal rights are made at the sub-national level. This contradiction is much greater than the contradiction within the labour movement, which divided the political militants from those who became trade-unionists primarily because they were convinced that the emancipation of the proletariat would be brought about by the workers themselves.

The important thing today is to recognize that cultural movements and historical movements are more conspicuous than societal movements. It is impossible to think of any movement that is identified both by the adversary it is fighting and by its reference to the values of the information society, which I have also described as the programmed society, or by its claim to be defending that society. Because no adversary has been identified, hostility to the globalized society, which is immune to any social and political constraints, goes hand in hand with a direct appeal to the Subject, and it is an ethical rather than a social appeal. Economic power itself seems to be based upon the circulation of commodities and information rather than the social relations of production. This negative conclusion is not satisfactory, however. It is based upon the assertion that society can never be anything more than a flow of permanent changes, and that there can therefore be no more social order, and no centre of power. The direct implication is that societal movements are now impossible – and many are tempted to agree with that statement, which echoes what the most liberal analysts are saying. But whilst it is true that we are living through a period dominated by a mode of development rather than a mode of production (which can also be described as a system of historic action), there are no grounds for saying that this mode of development is so powerful that it can destroy all structural elements, or that change and market strategies are all that remain.

Societal movements exist, or can come into existence, wherever the logic of technologies and markets come into conflict with the logic of the Subject. Such situations are common, and have a powerful subjective effect in our societies. Medical technologies and the organization of hospitals may infringe upon the freedom and dignity of the Subject; pupils resist curricula which do not transmit knowledge; we resist television programmes which appear to be concerned only with commercial success. All these situations are clearly defined by the presence of an adversary, and we can find in them an embryonic societal movement. Even if we are aware of the accelerated development of new technologies, it tends to be the opening up of the economy and the effects of liberal policies on employment, social welfare and wages that mobilize our attention and reactions. Similarly, we spent much of the nineteenth century talking about capitalist accumulation, proletarianization and political repression before learning, in the second half of that century and above all in the twentieth, to look at how rationalization affects industrial relations. That is why, in the early stages of industrial society, political problems were, as they are today, more conspicuous than the truly social problems that call into question the relations and forms of production.

On the other side of the planet, or in independent or excluded countries or categories, we also find that societal movements are dominated, or are even being destroyed, by neo-communitarian policies that sacrifice all freedoms to a general mobilization against an external enemy. Yet it is essential to see that liberation movements do exist there, as well as in the central countries. They may well be based on a cultural identity, but they are waging an economic and social struggle, and do want to win rights. The women who are fighting for their freedom in Algeria and those who lead most of the collective actions that are taking shape in Latin America's *poblaciones*, *favelas* and *ranchitos* are indeed social and cultural actors whose action is designed to create a democratic space. In South Africa, the victorious action of the ANC under the leadership of Nelson Mandela has to be interpreted in the same way.

The most conspicuous collective actions emerge initially from a challenge to the economic and political forces that are trying to impose the logic of globalization, and therefore to disperse social actors and cultures into flows of mass production, consumption and communications that reach the four corners of the globe. But not all forms of resistance to globalization are potential societal movements. Many are content to defend vested interests, legitimate and otherwise; others become trapped in an aggressive and authoritarian communitarianism. By contrast, the new historical movements are fighting to give Subjects the right to reconcile their cultural identity with a greater involvement in the professional, economic and political life of the world.

Is there any logic which determines whether or not a cultural movement develops into a historical movement which will then become a societal movement? It is tempting to conclude that the 1960s and the 1970s were, despite the ideological agitation bequeathed them by an earlier period's societal movement, dominated by cultural movements and to say that, when all countries followed the example of the United States and Great Britain and began to make the great transition to liberalism, most of the emerging movements were historical. They were, that is, a combination of defensive movements that resisted globalization and all those forces that were resisting the new mode of economic development.

This sequence is not, however, apparent in all countries; it corresponds, rather, to the process of the formation of social movements in the central countries. In the peripheral economies, or in countries with authoritarian regimes, the divorce between the three categories of social movements (societal, historical and cultural) is much less pronounced and often non-existent, especially when transformations take the form of sudden crises and mutations. For the moment, we can accept the hypothesis that there is, at least in the case of industrialized countries, a sequence of phases, each dominated by one type of movement. We can therefore conclude that, over the coming decades, we will see the emergence and growth of the societal movements we saw at the end of the great period of post-war industrialization. They have been rediscovered by cultural movements and, especially in the last decade, by historical movements fighting the liberal mode of development. New societal movements, which were unable to develop, and still less able to influence political action, during the 1970s and the 1980s, should reappear. The crisis in our schools and the current inability of medicine to treat serious illnesses such as cancer and AIDS are already giving rise to public debates over the relationship between young people and education, or between curing the illness and caring for the patient, as the English put it.

The relative weakness of these new societal movements, and above all their organizational weakness, must not obscure the fact that they are making a stronger and more direct appeal to the Subject than any earlier movement. In the most central domains of post-industrial society (health, education and information), we are seeing the emergence of protests, debates and proposals that are designed to defend the Subject against a technocratic and commodified logic. We can also see public opinion debating the question of multi-culturalism and expressing a wish for the recognition of the diversity of cultures that are to be found in our societies. Cultural, social and political problems are therefore merging into one another, and we find ourselves confronted with the central problem, which also defines the field of this book: how are we to reconcile a diversity of cultures with the idea of the Subject, which is at once universalist and individualist? We can do so only by criticizing and combating the neo-communitarian powers that are emerging, especially in the Muslim world, just as, in France and other European countries, we waged a long battle against the idea of a Christian civilization and a Christian society, and at the same time insisted that Christianity played an essential role in the formation of the Subject and the assertion of the freedom of the Subject. In Western countries, we have to struggle against the identification of our particular histories and institutions with universal values, as that has always served to justify systems of domination, and colonial domination in particular.

Communitarian power, and the power of technologies and commodities, can be fought only in the name of the defence of the Subject. This principle of action no longer implies any reference to a theory of history or society, but simply a reference to a conception of human freedom. That is why ethical themes and social themes are now more closely associated than they were in the past. They are closely associated because the Subject can come into being only through a combination of instrumental action and the assertion of identity, and the combination of the two can only be forged in the heat of the twofold struggle against financial powers and communitarian powers.

The complete integration of an ethical issue (and not merely a social or historical issue) and a twofold social and political struggle is centred on the personal Subject to such an extent that it cannot be brought about at the top of society by parties and governments. It can be brought about only at the base, or at the point closest to personal experience. The labour movement itself was, in organizational terms, 'weaker' than the parties that won civil rights for all; it replaced elected members with delegates, and gave the base greater control over its representatives. This trend continues in our post-industrial society, where associations are taking the place of the unions and parties that preceded them. Public life is becoming less and less formal; actions are also becoming more discontinuous and diffuse. This gives the media a growing importance, even though intellectuals often denounce them in summary terms. Currents of opinion shaped, amplified and also distorted by the media now often pose more basic problems than the parties and unions. And the parties and unions are so aware that this is the case that they deliberately hold back. They no longer try to lead, but simply try to influence movements which are no longer economically motivated but ethically motivated too.

The formation of new societal movements meets with great resistance throughout the world. Intellectuals and politicians are reluctant to recognize either their nature or their importance. Throughout the world, leaders and ideologues are on the look-out for survivals of revolutionary action. But it has been a long time since popular movements took revolutionary action to overthrow a social domination, as happened with the Bolivian peasant movement before and during the revolution of 1952, or with the Sandinistas' attack on Somoza's power. It is rulers, military leaders and prophets who have been cut off from the world revolution who now talk of revolution, some to mobilize and discipline their regiments, others out of a spirit of sacrifice and in the hope that their adventurism will inspire others to follow their example. Peoples, popular classes and subject nations or minorities no longer speak the language of revolution. It makes no difference; some people are still nostalgic for historical epics and cherish the loyalty of old soldiers. The generations born after the conquests of social democracy or after the Third Worldist revolutions are, for their part, reluctant to recognize the spaces where the new societal movements are taking shape. This is because the militants have become *apparatchiks* or ideologues, or, more simply, because it is difficult to admit that history is made up of discontinuities rather than continuities, and because it is impossible for new societal movements to be created without breaking with those whose historical role has been played out.

However that may be, we have to reject the idea, which is far too widespread at the moment, that the world is being thrown into upheaval by economic and technological revolutions, and that we can only react defensively and on a private, individual or communitarian basis. We also have to reject the confused ecumenism that muddles up modernity and tradition, rationality and affectivity, and then claims to speak in the name of an integral vision of our lived experience. We are not being swept away by a flood we cannot control, and we do not simply have to try to survive as best we can. There are fixed points of reference, both in analysis and in action. Collective actions that carry the seeds of a societal movement are proof of that. Everything points to the clear distinction between consciousness and movement, peace and war, or freedom and instrumentality. And our analysis has to respond to these demands, by according a central importance to the production of the Subject and by showing that this objective is central to social movements (be they cultural, historical or societal), which are not reducible to attempts to protect old interests and old ways of life.

When change accelerates and when the old social and political mediations collapse, the first reaction of many people is to try to reconstruct them or even to look to a more distant past to defend themselves against a threatening future. Because we are not in control of the changes that are going on, we assume that they are both hateful and inevitable, and we swing from boundless optimism to an equally boundless pessimism. It is high time that we got over this state of shock. Are our present social and political reactions the harbingers of an analytic renaissance? We already regard as unacceptable the extreme liberal discourses that reduce society to a set of markets, and personal and collective decisions to rational choices. On all sides, we are trying to escape from the great liberal transition that all countries have embarked upon, and which no country has rejected. We are worried by the dualization of our societies; the crisis in our political institutions and political forces looks dangerous; the absence of personal and collective projects seems to portend a decadence whose disastrous effects will soon become irreversible. We do need to reconstruct society and politics, but we also need new analyses that can reveal where power lies and where new social movements (cultural, historical or societal) will emerge. We need to know what is at stake in political life, and who the new actors will be.

I began by making the idea of the Subject central to the analysis; I am now demonstrating that, far from being marginal to social realities and collective action, the idea of the Subject is the principle that defines the action of the new social movements. In the second part of this book, we will take up the theme of the reconstruction and definition of the multi-cultural society whose necessity is inscribed in the very definition of the Subject and in our analysis of the new social movements. But before going any further, we must pay greater attention to the threats that hang over both the Subject and the new societal movements.

Social anti-movements

Societal movements can, like historical and cultural movements, degenerate into social anti-movements. This occurs when a social actor identifies completely with an issue such as progress, and therefore rejects the adversary as an enemy, a traitor or a mere obstacle that has to be eliminated. This destroys the very definition of a societal movement – a conflict between actors over the social management of a cultural issue which is never completely reducible to the self-interest of one party or the other. When this happens, an action which once challenged the general orientations of society degenerates into a sect or an authoritarian mobilization.

The contemporary world is being invaded by social anti-movements, particularly when the defence of identity becomes divorced from the control of production and turns in upon itself and becomes the assertion of a cultural or historical difference. Whereas in industrial society, the labour movement was associated with a progressive, industrialist ideology, many of today's movements proclaim themselves to be anti-modern and to be defending communitarian or national values against economic transformations and their social consequences. We have seen the emergence of numerous defensive actions, ranging from American-style radical multi-culturalism to sects of all kinds and even politico-religious fundamentalisms. They challenge the dominance of the instrumental world, but they speak in the name of a communitarian tradition and do not defend the freedom of the Subject. Sometimes, these communitarian movements fall back on the defence of a threatened autonomy; sometimes, by contrast, they resort to violence in order to fight the forces that threaten them or oppose their independence. Social anti-movements are always dominated by a political power, be it that of the guru of a sect or that of a political avant-garde which mobilizes cultural resources in its struggle for power. What makes them totally different from societal movements is that they identify with a concrete historical being, a social group, an ethnic group or a religious community and never appeal to the notion of the Subject and the universalism it implies.

The new, worrying factor is that social anti-movements are no longer, as Michel Wieviorka puts it, distorted or inverted social movements; they appear before the social movements, and are so powerful that it is difficult for social movements to emerge. This is a direct result of the dissociation of the economy from culture that defined demodernization. Whilst the networks of what some call the 'noolithic age', or in other words the information age, are taking shape, collectivities are being cut off from social relations that have been destroyed by the new technologies, and are falling back on their identity, often under the sway of authoritarian powers. Social closure is the defining characteristic of social anti-movements.

For a long time we were convinced that the forces of progress would always defeat the forces of conservatism or reaction, and we reduced those forces to the negative role of obstacles to technological or economic modernization. The situation has now been inverted. The increasingly powerful assertion and defence of cultural, political or national identities is a world-wide phenomenon, because technological progress no longer leads to social and cultural transformations; there is no direct link between the two, as there was in the past. As technological progress becomes more abstract, it tends to create a virtual world, and the real world seems to recede into identities and communities which are not traditional, but which have been reinterpreted and transformed into forces that can resist technologies and the new economic organization.

This situation is so obvious that some readers may wonder why I am speaking of social anti-movements, and not simply of the defence of identity. The explanation is that it is no longer a matter of defending traditions in the way that fundamentalist movements, regimes or sects defend them. It is in fact regrettable that the word 'fundamentalist', which is borrowed from the history of Protestantism, should have been used to designate neo-communitarian political forces which are in no sense traditionalist. Anti-movements are characterized by their struggle against technological and economic imperialism, and, rather than defending the Subject, they trap themselves into reconstructing an identity. The content of such fundamentalisms is political rather than cultural or religious. The use of a policy of ethnic cleansing to create a Greater Serbia cannot be reduced to the expression of a Serbian nationalism which has traditionally been opposed to Croatian or Bosnian-Muslim nationalism. At the international level, the response to this nationalist fundamentalism was a shift in public opinion. Public opinion is too weak to become a political force, but it has fought the horrors of ethnic cleansing in the name of the cultural freedom of all and of real democracy. More recently, we have also seen the emergence of the Serbian democratic movement. Here, as in other cases, it was the anti-movement which appeared first and took power; the social movement was formed in opposition to it, and it might be said that it initially appeared as a form of resistance to the social anti-movement and did not directly defend a political and social expression of freedom.

Many people explain the strength of these nationalisms in terms of resistance on the part of age-old cultures which are being threatened or crushed by what they see as a foreign or hostile state or empire. But Ernest Gellner (1983) is right when he argues that these national traditions are a reinterpretation, in modern terms, of very different ethnic realities. Age-old hostility between the Croats, Serbs and Islamized Croats of Bosnia does not explain the violence of the clashes that have taken place in the former Yugoslavia. In Bosnia, it was Milosevic's decision to oppose all attempts to build a democracy, and therefore to recognize ethnic plurality, that triggered the war of conquest. The decision came from the top, and was motivated by a political will reinforced by an ideological mobilization. This encouraged Croat nationalism, and even strengthened Muslim nationalism in Bosnia at the expense of the multi-cultural and multi-ethnic conception of which Sarajevo became the martyred symbol. The clash of nationalisms was an effect of the Yugoslav crisis, not its cause.

Similarly, in Algeria, it was the failure of the FLN government at both the political and the economic level that led the military itself to adopt a policy of Islamization and, more specifically, to introduce a new Family Code. Islamic fundamentalism fed on the political failure of the nationalists, the frustration of the population and especially the frustration of the deracinated young people of the towns. Their anger was directed against a Western producer-consumer society that was at once so close and so inaccessible. Because political and social conflicts could not take an organized form, the protests degenerated into violent cultural anti-movements. What we are seeing is not so much a return to religion as the political and social failure of modernization. It is that failure which is leading to a crisis that makes it impossible to build a democracy or to mobilize a communitarian, cultural and religious identity against what have been defined as external obstacles. It is when internal conflicts become impossible that the struggle to the death against foreigners is proclaimed.

Social anti-movements are appearing in the democratic countries too. They appeal to a national tradition which is being threatened by an invasion of foreign populations or foreign customs. In Western Europe and the United States, the rejection of immigrants and the defence of 'national preference' may not seem to be capable of destroying democratic institutions, but they do take the form of an obsession with identity that rejects modernity. Modernity is seen as something stateless or foreign-dominated, and this ideology is similar to the ideology that gave birth to the anti-Semitic nationalisms of the nineteenth century.

What is new about this ideology is that it is a response to new cultural movements which no longer appeal to nature or energy. They are direct assertions of cultures or social groups defined by a cultural identity rather than a professional or economic identity. Such is the new figure of racism, and it too is a social anti-movement. It is no longer biologically based, but culturally based (the non-assimilable customs and beliefs of the Other), and it relies less on the theme of inferiority than that of difference. The 'clash of cultures' theme is more important than that of relations of production and colonial domination – so much so that the colonial scorn for the Arab which led many *pieds noirs* to support the anti-Arab racism of the National Front in France does not really explain the increased vote for Le Pen, whose most popular theme is national preference and the rejection of foreigners. Le Pen has no desire to dominate Arabs or to proclaim their natural inferiority. The Other, and particularly the Arab, is rejected, therefore, because he is a strong figure who asserts cultural values in a way that we cannot. We are being invaded by foreigners, says the racist, but not just in the way that rats or mould invade a poor neglected house. The foreigners are a communitarian group, an ethnic presence, a religious affirmation. They are all strong, and we resent them because they are aggressive. There is as much envy as hatred in today's racism, and there is also an element of self-hatred on the part of those who feel weak and impotent. Contemporary racism turns the Other into an anti-Subject, in order to express the misery and shame of no longer being a Subject.

Michel Wieviorka rightly stresses that the racism we are seeing today is so different from that of the late nineteenth and early twentieth centuries that we should give it another name. One can take the view, however, that it is more important to stress the analogy between the two mechanisms of rejection rather than their different content, as naturalistic references were as widespread in nineteenth-century society as discourses about cultural differences in the twentieth. Rejection of the Other is not the same as the marginal acceptance of foreigners or hostility towards an enemy. It means excluding someone who is resented because he or she negates a society's principal cultural model. This is a feature common to both racism in the strict sense and cultural xenophobia. The racism of cultural difference plays the same role in our culture that the racism of natural inferiority played in the culture of industrial society. The racist is all the more ready to see the adversary as a community, or in other words a collectivity that is at once social, cultural and political, to the extent that he himself lives in a society in which these different dimensions are highly differentiated. That is why the colonized are the object of a limited racism, as the racist continues to use the people he rejects, whilst contemporary racism wants a complete break and the expulsion of the Other.

The strength of a far-right racist party in France can probably also be explained in terms of the gravity of the crisis of the nation-state in a country that has experienced it in more tragic terms than other European countries. All those who prioritize political and national objectives over collective social movements are on the side of the social anti-movements. In France and elsewhere, Bonapartism was not a despotism, but a social anti-movement which used the language of revolution and citizenship. Jacobinism itself, which has so often been analysed as a social movement, was the most general expression of the 'political illusion' for which Marx rightly criticized the French, and it prevented the formation of a powerful labour movement and a social democracy.

We must develop a radical intellectual critique of the revolutionary ideologies and actions which have always, from the Terror to Leninism and, at the opposite extreme, fascism, led to the essentially totalitarian regimes that have been the main social anti-movements of the twentieth century. The main point is that it is impossible to divorce the formation of societal actors, and therefore societal movements, from the political mediations that are such a central and indispensable element in democracy. The three themes of the Subject, social movements and democracy are just as inseparable as the antithetical combination of historical necessity, revolutionary action and totalitarianism, which leads to the hell of violence, not to the creative and emancipatory paradise of social movements.

Societal movements of all kinds have democratic aspirations. They try to give a voice to those who have no voice, and to allow them to take part in the shaping of political and economic decisions; whereas revolutionary actions always dream of social, political, ethnic or cultural cleansing, of a unified and transparent society, of the creation of a new man and of the elimination of everything else that stands in the way of unanimity. And guaranteeing the popularity of totalitarian power rapidly becomes unanimity's sole function. A societal movement is no more a struggle to the death than it is a mere campaign for reforms.

The presence of a societal movement is not bound up with a revolutionary situation whose objective gravity can be diagnosed by an economist or a political scientist, or with the power of an ideological discourse or a political leadership. A societal movement is bound up with the actor's ability to elaborate a praxis, or in other words to become committed to a social conflict and, at the same time, to become the defender of societal values which cannot be reduced to the actor's self-interest, and which therefore cannot lead to the annihilation of the adversary. An actor who defines his adversary in non-social terms or as an absolute evil may well believe that he is strengthening his movement by demonstrating its radical nature, but he is in fact taking the dangerous road that leads to social anti-movements.

When the uprising of May 1968 was over, the intellectuals tried to impose a workerist class struggle on a student-youth movement which was above all a cultural movement and whose effects were felt in almost every domain of social practice. The intellectuals imposed upon the intellectual and academic world a post- and hyper-Leninist leftist radic-alism which stifled intellectual life and which, in certain countries, had the more tragic effect of ushering in the 'years of lead', when a French-style ideological violence was overtaken by Italian- and, to a lesser extent, American- and German-style political violence. During the 1995 strike in France, the presence of leftist intellectuals was still tangible but more limited, because the movement was devoid of revolutionary impulses and could be interpreted as a combination of the defence of vested interests, a political crisis and a virtual historical movement.

It would be a caricature to reduce social movements to the most ideological forms of action. Such forms of action usually have very little to do with praxis. When they are closely related to praxis, it means that the movement has degenerated into an anti-movement with authoritarian or totalitarian tendencies. All absolute forms of ideological mobilization, and every identification of a social actor with a god, reason, history or the nation, result in the destruction of social movements, because ideologies which think themselves radical replace plurality with the One, conflict with homogeneity, and protests with manipulated participation. Revolu-tionary, populist or fundamentalist leaders and intellectuals are agents who actively destroy social movements.

How can we not be intellectually preoccupied with this theme at the end of a century which has seen a proliferation of neo-communitarian move-ments, and when the most powerful of them are calling for a theocratic society? It is ludicrous, however, to contrast these anti-movements, which are at once societal, cultural and historical, with the image of a society ruled by purely individualist and universalist rules. It is ludicrous because the entire history of human rights is the history of the necessary trans-ition, which is sometimes successful and sometimes a tragic failure, from the defence of human beings who were not defined by any concrete social situation, or by unequal relations of power and property, to the defence of human beings who are enduring a concrete social, political or cultural domination. The transition ends in failure when, rather than constructing a social, political and cultural democracy, the dominated group builds a fortress or a fighting force in order to destroy a social order which is deemed completely evil and imposes an absolute political power which leaves no room for social demands, intellectual protests or political debate. The labour movement led, on the one hand, to industrial democracy and social democracy and, on the other, to Bolshevism and Maoism. Today, we are seeing two different responses to the globalization of the economy: the emergence of a cultural democracy which recognizes the rights of minorities and the emergence of anti-movements which are giving birth to sects in the democratic countries and new grass-roots totalitarian movements which may be either nationalistic, ethnic or religious.

Social movements in a non-democratic situation

The reader might object that, whilst this analysis explains what is happening in the developed countries, or in other words in those countries where modernization is self-sustaining, it may not be applicable where democracy does not exist, or where a state, be it national or foreign, or an oligarchy which is more concerned with speculation and absolute power than economic rationality, imposes its absolute power and adds exclusion to exploitation.

Are not social movements impossible when the dominant mode of development is either statist or, on the contrary, controlled by foreign capitalists? In the former case, do not social movements degenerate or even become so perverted as to be authoritarian agents of the social control of a people that has been reduced to being a mass to be mobilized; and in the second, do they not fragment into a multiplicity of pressure groups whose demands merely exacerbate social inequalities? Can social movements exist in non-democratic situations? The idea of the Subject provides an answer to this question. Given that the Subject is always a manifestation of the struggle against both the market and the community, it makes its presence felt in the form of opposition and liberation, not only in the world of the market but also, and with equal force, in the communitarian world. Like the Subject itself, social movements can manifest their presence within modes of development or even forms of social power that are incompatible with their conditions of existence.

In historical terms, the most important examples are those social movements which have taken shape in authoritarian societies dominated by a despotic power, a national oligarchy or a foreign colonizer. They are forced to combine the defence of the dominated and democratic demands with a truly revolutionary action designed to destroy a power which resorts to authoritarian or dictatorial methods in the economic realm or the political realm. This does not make them any different from the movements that took shape in democratic countries. For example, there was always an element of violence in the labour movement; it was a response to the violence of the employers or the government. The strategy of a social movement and its leaders must be to combine rejectionism with democratic action, to combine the logic of the struggle against powers with that of the defence of freedoms. Their attempts to do so often end in failure; trade-unionism, for example, become a non-autonomous instrument in the hands of a new political power. In other cases, the defence of freedom is reduced to meaning the defence of relatively privileged categories. But, numerous and serious as they may be, these failures must not prevent us from recognizing the presence of a movement (which may be either societal, historical or cultural) in an action that may lead to non-democratic solutions. It is true that the Algerian national movement put a military dictatorship in power for a long time, and that it finally opened fire on the people in the streets of Algiers in order to repress protests. This does not mean that the Algerian movement was not an anti-colonial national liberation movement. And the horrors of the Terror in no way detract from the days of May and June 1789 which laid the foundations of democracy in France. There is no such thing as a purely democratic social movement, or a revolutionary crisis without a democratic content. International opinion was right to support the Iranian and Afghan liberation movements, even though, even more so in Afghanistan than Iran, they gave birth to anti-democratic movements which destroyed the very idea of a social movement.

The same conclusion applies to the labour movement. It has been transformed into a number of pressure groups and even into the corporatist movements that defend the interests of one social category within the state apparatus. The limited nature of their strategic objectives does not mean that a social movement cannot emerge from within such movements, or that it cannot transcend them. Limited demands have often given rise to movements that have challenged the basis of the social order.

The sociologist has to look for the presence of social movements behind the extreme ideologies that conceal them. In Algeria and other countries, notably Egypt, there are political groups that are using Islam to take power and to construct an Iranian-style society which will be fundamentally anti-modern. But in order to survive, they use the techniques of modernity. This does not mean, however, that we can forget that Islamist movements also express the feelings of a deracinated population, and especially of unemployed youth. We must not, in other words, forget that there are elements of historical movements in political actions whose objective is clearly to establish an authoritarian regime. Those who contrast the virtues of secularism with the dangers of policies which mobilize religious beliefs are right up to a point, but they are mistaken when they refuse to see that many social movements derive their strength from the culture and society they are defending precisely because they think it is living under the threat of death. We can no longer regard the Vendée uprising as a mere counter-revolutionary movement.

Similarly, the public sector strike in France in December 1995 cannot be reduced to the defence of corporatist interests or privileges. It was also an expression of a popular rejection of an economic policy which subordinated the whole of public life to the reduction of the state deficit. Reducing the deficit was seen as a necessary pre-condition for joining the single currency, which would, it was assumed, automatically bring prosperity and full employment.

Conclusion

The theme of societal movements is a challenge to both liberal thought and the call for revolution. Neither liberals nor revolutionaries believe that social actors have the ability to produce their history through their cultural orientations and social conflicts.

The idea of a societal movement, by contrast, combines the appeal to the Subject with the struggle against a social adversary. Just as the call for freedom suddenly inspired the Third Estate to rise up against the king and privilege, and just as the appeal for social justice found its incarnation in the workers' struggle against exploitation at work, we now see the Subject fighting both exclusion and the loss of identity. The idea of a social movement, more than anything else, teaches us that globalization does not just mean the continued expansion and integration of world trade, and that it is not an international division of labour, but a system of power which both includes and excludes, which does as much to destroy cultures as it does to create new forms of consumption. As in Marx's day, we must therefore uncover the social relations of domination that are concealed behind the domination of commodities.

Of course, social movements have come up against major obstacles in all ages. Poverty creates obstacles, as do the search for individual solutions and the hope of being promoted within the system. These obstacles have never been, and are not, insurmountable. No situation is, in reality, completely conducive to societal movements, and industrial society was no more conducive to them than any other. What has changed is the nature of the forms of behaviour that are associated with societal movements, and which try to dominate them. Appeals to the people, the nation or a church have often transformed popular movements into social anti-movements, and the revolutionary idea has transformed societal movements into totalitarian regimes. Today, it is the obsession with identity that is undermining societal movements by transforming their adversaries into foreigners and replacing the ideal of emancipation with the fanatical quest for homogeneity and purity.

My insistence on making the idea of the Subject central to my analysis is designed to release societal movements of all kinds from the political instruments and ideological apparatuses that mask them and prevent us from seeing that any movement of this kind is an appeal to the freedom of the Subject. The Subject does not exist in the social void of political freedom, but, on the contrary, within social relations of domination, ownership and power. A societal movement is therefore both a struggle against power and a struggle for a vision of society.

These ideas meet with the objection that our societies have become so complex and are changing so fast that they inevitably experience a multiplicity of tensions and particular conflicts, or that their experience is limited to a combination of resistance to change, various pressures and equally various assertions of identity. Proto-modern societies, by contrast, could be thrown into turmoil by mass movements in which popular beliefs and ideological prophecies are combined with military mobilizations. But the weakness and contradictions of this image soon become obvious. In such societies, the strength of collective mobilizations has always gone hand in hand with the weakness of societal movements which were dependent upon the action of their religious or political leaders. Throughout modernization, we have seen the independence of societal movements growing as they define their own roles. Truly social actors can emerge. The labour movement was an early societal movement that could commandeer the action of political parties even though the latter often became the masters of social forces, when they should have been their servants. The characteristic feature of our post- and anti-totalitarian period is the huge effort that has been made to free social, cultural and even historical movements from the controls that the power élites attempt to place on them. This does not fragment or limit political actions, but it does depoliticize and demilitarize them. They then become more and more directly oriented towards the assertion and defence of basic civil, social and cultural rights.

For societal movements not to make progress in our societies, those societies would have to be completely decadent. Only social anti-movements would exist, as was so often the case in the Europe of the nineteenth century. We would have to look elsewhere to find societies capable of using their social conflicts to create their future. This vision is over-pessimistic: the reason why Western societies sometimes seem incapable of generating new societal movements is that the old order within them is already in a state of decay, and that the field of new problems has not yet had time to take shape.

The importance of social movements relates to their place in social life. They do not exist at either the centre or the summit of society; their presence or absence determines almost all forms of social action. They are best defined by the link they establish between certain cultural orientations and a social conflict in which demands are being put forward, and which has political aspects as well as societal aspects. If a societal movement does not take shape, all these elements become divorced from one another, and as they drift apart, they are transformed and degenerate. When, on the one hand, cultural orientations become divorced from social and political conflicts, they become 'moralistic'. They become principles that define who belongs and who is excluded, as well as mechanisms of cultural control and norms that determine social conformity. When, on the other hand, political conflicts become divorced from societal movements, they are reduced to struggles for power and hasten a dissociation of state and society which becomes increasingly pathological as a result of mass production, mass consumption and mass communications. When, finally, demands are left to themselves, they tend to increase inequalities, because it is the most powerful and most influential categories, which have the most vested interests to defend, that are in the best position to press demands. We thus have a combination of limited pressure groups, a tendency to reject categories that are defined as minorities, deviants, or social and cultural foreigners, and a communitarian populism which condemns leaders and intellectuals in the name of an indeterminate people. It seems at first sight that each of these aspects of social or political life should be studied in its own right; but that rapidly proves impossible, because no collective action is a purely rational defence of self-interest or a pure assertion of communitarian values. All collective actions contain traces of a social movement which is either absent or has decomposed. The movement does not yet exist, but we have to accept the hypothesis of its existence if we are to understand those modes of behaviour which either reject it, show us what it may become, or animate it.

We are all the more in need of such a hypothesis, in that we live in a shattered society which has no self-consciousness, which is unclear as to what is at stake in historical change and as to who the actors are, and in which discourses and ideologies either lag behind practices or lend them a spurious radicalism. Our societies are in danger of becoming meaningless, because they are dominated by the dissociation of practices from consciousness, acts from discourses. In other eras, we suffered from an excess of societal movements, which became tools in the hands of governments or official ideologies. Today, on the contrary, the centre of society is empty. It is strewn with the debris of old battles and old discourses which have become commodities to be bought second hand by power merchants, ideology merchants or even collectors. That is why the idea of a societal movement has to be defended: because it gives a meaning to all the apparently contradictory patterns of behaviour that have been born of the demise or decay of old societal movements.

4

Early, Mid- and Late Modernities

The three ages of modernity

(1) For a long time, modern societies believed that their main objective was to use the law and education to promote social integration. The purpose of social integration was to strengthen society itself, which thus became sacred, and to ensure that political powers and social hierarchies were preserved and handed on. The first objective was central: institutions had to create links between, or even harmonize, the divergent tendencies that defined modernity: the rationalization of the world and ethical individualism. Reason had to control the school curriculum, laws and the progress of knowledge. This idea was so powerful that I have often described as 'classical' the figure of modernity which triumphed with the revolutions that created nation-states, first in the Netherlands and England, then in France and the United States, in Spanish- and Portuguese-speaking Latin America and, later, in Central Europe and other parts of the world, notably Egypt and Turkey. This sociocentrism, however, was overtaken and then overthrown by the growing autonomy of economic activity and, more specifically, of capitalism. It was reduced to being no more than an ideological response on the part of the middle classes, which were threatened by the power and profits of entrepreneurs, on the one hand, and the poverty and demands of the workers, on the other. This ideology inspired increasingly conservative attempts to moralize collective and individual life.

(2) The centrifugal forces that created both wealth and poverty, innovation and exploitation, gained the upper hand as the industrial revolution and finance capitalism began to spread from Great Britain to the rest of

the world, from the nineteenth century onwards. This period saw the beginnings of the dissociation of the international economy from the nation-state, and it led to the destruction of the nation-society in which the world of instrumental rationality and that of cultural identities coexisted in harmony.

Yet no modern society can exist without a principle of unity, or in other words without a principle that integrates the two contrasting faces of modernity. Whereas early modernity believed in the order that reason introduced into the apparent chaos of the world, the diversity of interests and the disorder of the passions, industrial society focused both its thought and its organization on the idea of development, which it preferred to call 'progress'. In its most ambitious form, the idea of progress was a creation of the eighteenth century, and was best expressed by Condorcet at the height of the French Revolution. It replaced order with movement, and made it the principle for the construction of both collective and personal life. Until the inter-war period of the mid-twentieth century, and then again with the collapse of Hitler's empire and more recently with liberation theology, it was possible to hope that a satisfactory order would emerge at the end of a historical process marked by conflicts and contradictions. This, it was hoped, would be both a natural order that transcended the social order and an order of abundance in which all would receive in accordance with their needs. This conception in fact took such contradictory forms that they became mutually destructive. Pure capitalism, said Schumpeter, was incapable of building a society and winning the support of the majority; a merciless proletarian struggle would, for its part, inevitably lead to a warlike, authoritarian and repressive society.

As the two armies clashed, the idea of development therefore took the form of the assertion that either industrial democracy or a new enlightened despotism could, at every moment of modernization, establish a link between economic efficiency and social integration. During the quarter-century that followed the defeat of Nazism, many attempts were made to promote development, both in the oldest industrialized societies, which had been rocked by the great crisis and the upheavals caused by the Second World War; in those countries that were winning their independence, in Latin America or India, which were creating so-called national-popular regimes; and in those countries that had been absorbed, willingly or otherwise, into the Communist world. Between 1945 and 1975, it was possible to believe that the time had come for a great synthesis of order and development, and that the turbulence of economic take-off would lead to controlled, self-sustaining growth. Some economists rediscovered the importance of human capital; others saw state intervention in response to social demands as the best means of initiating an anti-cyclical action that would put an end to the infernal spiral of crises. We believed, if not in progress – whose reputation had been tarnished by all the wars and totalitarianisms – at least in development, defined as an interaction between economic growth and greater social participation, under the leadership of a political power that could both integrate and strengthen the nation. All conceptions of development were closely associated with the national idea, whilst the conflicting conceptions of class struggle – capitalist and Communist alike – rejected the idea of both development and the nation in the name of a pure economism that postponed the reconstruction of social life until the end of history, even though no one was too sure how social life would survive the competition, the monopolies, the civil war and the violence.

(3) The last quarter of the twentieth century saw the collapse of the voluntaristic union between industrialization and the nation. Ever since the collapse of the Bretton Woods institutions and the oil crises of the 1970s put an end to the apparent world order which provided the framework for national policies of development, we have been heading – and, truth to tell, we have been staggering rather than running – towards a complete divorce and a complete separation between an internationalized or globalized market and the nationalisms that defend threatened identities or use authoritarian methods to mobilize a country's material and cultural resources and make it internationally competitive. The idea of order that governed early modernity is now so remote that it has taken on repressive connotations. The alliance between economic modernization and social justice is breaking down throughout the world. Ideologies of progress are in decay. Social democracy or labourism is now exhausted in Western-type countries, both in Europe and in the great countries of the Commonwealth, all of which are at a loss as to how to reconcile international competitiveness with the preservation of the Welfare State or the guarantees that have been won by certain categories. At the international level, the most significant development is the collapse of the regimes and ideologies created by Lenin and Mao Zedong, which combined industrializing rationalization with the mobilization of national forces. The spirit of Bandung is also in a state of decay. Nationalism has become populist or fundamentalist, whilst the pressure brought to bear by the international markets, the World Bank and the IMF has transformed Asian and Latin American developmentalism into economic liberalism. The crisis in socialist thought, especially in Europe, and its almost total demise in the rest of the world signal the end of a model which was so powerful and so creative that outcrops of nostalgia for it can still be found amongst leftists and reformists alike. This is especially true in France, where, more so than anywhere else, the state became the dominant economic modernizer and

social reformer, and restricted the action of a capitalism which did not play the principal role during the phase of post-war reconstruction.

The concrete image of a world torn between the economy and politics, the market and the state, and exchanges and identity, has been replaced by the more abstract image of a divorce between a reason that has become instrumental, or the reason of strategic action, and the symbolic world of cultures. Reason is no longer both a means and an end; more so than ever before, there is a conflict between the ethics of conviction and the ethics of responsibility. As Max Weber predicted, our experience is dominated by the divorce between technological rationalization and the war between the gods, which now takes the form of personal moral conflicts, and sometimes that of mass crusades. We have entered a third period of low or late modernity (*Spätkapitalismus*). The question we have to ask, and which this book is trying to answer, is this: how can we build societies, now that we are living through the third stage of modernity? What principle can reconcile the rationalization of the world and personal freedom, science and conscience? What principle can replace the social order and economic development, which have both lost their power to integrate?

Many people identified modernity with the project of constructing a vision of a rational world, a rational society and rational individuals. Might it not be more accurate to describe the long period of the Enlightenment as 'early modernity'? It did not break with late premodernity, in that it wanted to preserve the union between nature and culture, natural phenomena and the higher meaning of human experience that characterized religious thought. The idea of nature often replaced that of God, but there was very little difference between the two, and nature was often seen in anthropomorphic terms.

The idea of progress tried for a long time to preserve the ideal of a rational order within a changing society: that order would be established when reason triumphed at the end of history. Such was the dominant idea during the central period of modernity, which is usually described as 'industrial society' and which, in order to put it in a wider historical perspective, I prefer to call 'mid-modernity'.

How can we believe in the alliance between might and justice after the world wars, the totalitarian regimes and their death camps? The image of the social world as chaos, disorder or a jungle is becoming increasingly widespread. Both the growth of international trade and the fast pace of technological innovation appear to be producing inequalities and more crises, rather than providing greater security and ensuring wider participation. Can we escape the chaos, the latent international civil war and the decay of nation-societies? If we are to avoid what I call 'demodernization' and define the societies of late modernity, we need a principle that can integrate two worlds that have become alien to one another, or that can at least make them compatible. The societies of late modernity are faced with an extreme divorce between an economy that has been globalized – or in other words desocialized – and individual and collective cultural identities, between an extroverted economy and introverted modes of behaviour. The principle we need cannot be something that shines on collective and personal life in the way that the sun of reason once shone on early modernity. This period requires a weak integrative principle, and it is therefore best described as 'late modernity' rather than 'hyper-modernity'. We have defined this principle as the Subject. We now have to explore the nature of those societies in which it is the Subject, and not an institutional order or the evolution of progress, that ensures the unity of social life.

The characteristic feature of our late modernity is the disappearance of all objectivist conceptions of social life. When a society reaches a very high level of historicity, its every aspect appears to be the product of an action and, therefore, of the ability to act. Marx was the principal creator of modern thought to the extent that he discovered, behind commodities and the apparent order of things, the real order of social domination. For more than 100 years, critical social thought explored and denounced the ubiquity of power, and Michel Foucault declared that there are no limits to power, and that social reality is nothing more than the discourse of power. Society's almost boundless ability to use knowledge, investments and ethical models to act on itself is not reducible to the wielding of absolute power by ruling élites or classes. It is increasingly necessary to define social life as the product of interventions. Anthony Giddens has provided the clearest account of this representation of modernity, which he describes as 'late modernity'. It is organized around three major themes.

The first is the spatio-temporal disembedding of social phenomena, which have been caught up in one or another form of globalization. The instantaneous world-wide circulation of capital and information is its most obvious manifestation. The second theme, which is inspired by the thought of Ulrich Beck, is that certainties have been replaced by doubts, and the reproduction of an order by risk. This gives an increasingly great importance to trust, an idea which is central to Alain Peyrefitte's (1995) analysis of the early modernization of the West, and the Protestant West in particular. The third theme is reflexivity, or our societies' growing ability to transform their practices, thanks to the self-knowledge they have acquired. In the very specific but essential domain of epistemological models and their effects, the idea of reflexivity takes us back to the more general theme of historicity, which is, in my view, of central importance. Giddens's analyses help us to define the societies of late modernity as 'intervention societies', which have replaced the development societies of mid-modernity and the ordered societies of early modernity before them.

I long ago defined the emerging post-industrial society as the pro-grammed society (Touraine 1971). I use that expression again here, because it clearly demonstrates that the most modern societal type is the result of decisions, policies and programmes, and not of natural equi-libria. The modern notion of the Subject is so far removed from its premodern figures that we cannot understand its emergence if we fail to see that it is the only possible answer to the all-pervasive power of those who are controlling a process of change that is so complete and so rapid that there is no room within it for what we believed to be the natural order of things. There is no more 'reality'. There are only the products of the scientific imagination, the political will and the search for profit. The complete objectivation of power goes hand in hand with an equally complete subjectivization of resistance to power.

It is therefore only at the moment when we leave industrial society that we enter fully into the most advanced form of modernity. The distinguish-ing feature of industrial society was that its social organization was inseparable from its methods of rationalization, that there was a link between the technical and social divisions of labour. In that sense, Georges Friedmann, Serge Malet and I were not entirely wrong when, in our different ways, we analysed that society, working-class conscious-ness and especially the labour movement mainly in terms of technology and its effects on the world of work.

Anyone who tries to analyse the societies of the early twenty-first century in the same way that we analysed the industrial societies of the last two centuries is, however, making a methodological error. The idea of a post-industrial society is acceptable only if it posits a complete break with the idea of industrial society. Before we define the new interventions that must replace the interventions that sought to promote order or development, we have to take stock of the rift in modern societies. Early modernity was based upon the central role of the constitutional nation-state, which reconciled capitalist rationalization with bourgeois individu-alism. It subordinated a social, multiple and diverse reality to a unitary politics and a unitary law. That construct is collapsing, and there is no longer anything to hold together economic activity and personal and collective identity. This weakening of institutions and of socialization does have emancipatory effects. Our societies are more innovative because they allow, or even safeguard, the development of internal areas of uncertainty, playgrounds, and free zones where science, technology, art and commerce are free to develop and innovate. Our personal lives are less and less regulated by norms, rites and hierarchies. But we cannot simply sing the praises of great metropolitan centres like Paris, London,

Vienna, Berlin, New York or Los Angeles, where so many elements of our civilization were created by a mixture of avant-gardism and social marginality. Creative marginality often comes to mean exclusion and ghettoes. The relaxation of shared norms and values works to the advantage of the strongest, and increases social inequalities. In extreme cases, the public space and even the political system disappear, because they have been invaded by a dictatorship, an ideology or the chaos of private interests acting outside the law.

An intervention society organizes and protects a space that can mediate between divorced and conflicting worlds. But it can do so only if society sets itself the primary goal of enhancing its own ability to intervene by increasing not only its reflexivity, but also its internal communications, debates and decision-making mechanisms. Its model must be based, that is, on neither order nor progress, but on the freedom and creativity of the personal Subject, defined as an agent who can reconcile instrumental action with the defence of an identity. When, I repeat, the two are separated, both degenerate: one into a desocialized financial economy, the other into an authoritarian communitarianism. The founding principle of the societies of late modernity is no longer triumphant, unlike that of societies of order or development. It is weak, fragile and unstable. It has to work every day to repair the torn social fabric. The ambition of the political Subject of early modernity was to become Moses or Solon, and the political Subject of mid-modernity identified with Prometheus. The Subject of late modernity no longer has a model in the strict sense of the term; like a do-it-yourself enthusiast, it uses whatever comes to hand to create its own space of freedom. Early modernity was organized around the central principle of order; mid-modernity was dominated by the tensions between progress and the social conflicts that gave progress a historical form. Late modernity is dominated neither by unity nor by duality, but by the simultaneously central and weak position of a Subject that lives between the conflicting worlds of markets and communities.

Reading Hannah Arendt

Demodernization is so fraught with danger that many thinkers, politicians and ordinary citizens are tempted to turn to an ever more distant past to discover principles of action which have been destroyed in a contemporary world dominated by production and consumption and, at a deeper level, by the inversion of the hierarchy of the forms of the active life described by Hannah Arendt in *The Human Condition* (1958), which is the second great work she published after *The Origins of Totalitarianism*

(1951). Action has been displaced by work (*Homo faber*), and work by labour as the *Animal laborans* comes to be dominated by the needs of production and consumption. Arendt defines the principal characteristics of the modern world as irreversibility and unpredictability. We are, she says, involved in a technical world which can develop only in an unpredictable way and which involves us in a sequence of events over which we have no control. What decadence, if we compare this world with the Greek *polis*, where action and speech created meaning, allowed every individual to show off his talent, and granted immortal fame to those who succeeded in distinguishing themselves in the *polis*. In those days, the space of freedom was more important than the space of necessity. It is true that if we identify with the models and discourses of one particular era, we necessarily conclude that others are inferior, but we still have to pay very close attention to Hannah Arendt's critical thinking in a period when there is so much enthusiastic talk of the emancipatory benefits of new technologies and globalization.

Despite our obvious differences, there are similarities between certain aspects of Hannah Arendt's thought and the argument I am putting forward here. The most obvious is a refusal to reduce human experience to the domain of needs, which, being socially determined, cannot provide the basis for freedom. The economism of the liberals and Marx, who was directly inspired by them, does not provide an answer to the problems of ethics and politics; the reduction of society to networks and markets certainly cannot do so. What is more important still is that Hannah Arendt shows that, in every age, we find a combination of an orientation towards the world and an orientation towards the self, defined both as an individual and as a social being, or in other words as a figure of the Subject.

Arendt's starting-point is the contemplative life and the representation of the world. She then turns to the figure of the citizen who expresses his personal qualities on the political stage. According to Arendt, the citizen embodies the highest form of the *vita activa*. It is true that she does not describe political action in terms of what we call 'action', but in terms of representation, discourse and deliberation. The defining characteristic of the actor is that he is neither reflexive nor conscious of his individuality – a notion that was foreign to the Greeks (Arendt 1958: 181). Yet we are dealing here with a conception of the Subject, and not simply of the citizen. 'The root of the ancient estimation is the conviction that man *qua* man, each individual in his unique distinctness, appears and confirms himself in speech and action, and that these activities, despite their material futility, possess an enduring quality of their own because they create their own remembrance' (Arendt 1958: 207–8). Arendt finds a form of self-realization in a civilization which appears to subordinate the individual to the *polis*. This allows us to arrive at a better understanding of the lasting attractions of the model that defines political man as the creator of meaning and remembrance. For my own part, I am trying to explain the decline of that model; I do, however, accept that it is still very close to us, in that the classical concept of education, from the Jesuits to the classical *lycée* and *Gymnasium* of France and Germany, is still inspired by the civic conception of education in which the examples of heroes, eloquence and feats of heroism are of central importance.

When scientific and technical creation, rather than political life, becomes central, the figure of the individual that appears is the worker and fabricator who is in pursuit of happiness and pleasure, even though he is suffering. The pain and exploitation of labour is the pre-condition for emancipation and well-being. Hannah Arendt understands that it is at this moment that the image of the world and that of the actor correspond most closely; both are the result of productive labour and historicity. Bentham's utilitarianism and his attempt to quantify ethical notions does not provide an adequate interpretation of this, and Arendt is unsparing in her criticisms. Distrustful of socialisms which are a debased form of political action, she none the less extols the virtues of the independent labour movement and especially workers' councils, always remaining loyal to them and celebrating their reappearance in Hungary and Czechoslovakia.

Perhaps we should extend this historical reconstruction to our own period. Arendt sees the triumph of *Animal laborans*, who loses all sense of duration because he is fully involved in his role as a producer and consumer. She also sees the disastrous domination of the political by the social (1951: 68–73), or in other words necessity, and, what is more serious still, the invasion of thought by the human sciences, which reduce action to its social determinants. The evolution she describes, however, can be interpreted in a different way. It is when the world becomes life and action, and when it appears that it had no reality until we discovered technologies, that a new figure of the Subject appears to oppose the constructs of instrumental reason. This figure is far removed from the citizen of the *polis* who acted out his role on the civic stage. This is a weak figure, and it is no longer heroic. This figure of the Subject is reflexively and critically self-conscious, because it cannot and will not be defined by the roles the *polis* wants it to play.

The man to whom Hannah Arendt looks is, in the tradition of Aristotle and St Thomas, primarily a social being defined by the networks of interaction that make up the greater part of his political life. And it appears to me that Karl Otto Apel's ethics of discussion and Jürgen Habermas's communicative action also look to this social being, or to this creature of relationships and communications. One can also take the opposite view and say that, as modernity progresses, the human actor becomes less social. The human actor was not social in industrial society, in which social life was based on production, and was so dependent on production that politics seemed to be determined by economic interests. The actor is even less social in late modernity; when he does not retreat into private life or a community, the actor is constructed as a Subject, or in other words attempts to re-create in his life and personal experience a unity that no longer exists in social life.

Hannah Arendt seems to be arguing along similar lines when she invokes two ethical attitudes: the forgiveness that can resist irreversibility and the power of promise which can help to prevent irresponsibility. The idea of forgiveness, which derives primarily from the Gospels, is too closely bound up with the appeal to the father – 'Forgive them for they know not what they do' – to retain its full force in a secularized world. I therefore prefer to speak of the solidarity that recognizes the Other as Subject in all circumstances, and of the indignation we feel when anything threatens the Subject. Like Arendt, I prefer to speak of the promise (or trust) that provides the only foundations for social life. The first of these three virtues asserts that the Subject is present in all individuals. The second fights the Subject's enemies, and the third lays the foundations for a free social life. Whatever virtues we evoke, the important thing is that the construction of social life begins with a moral commitment that resists the demands of instrumentality.

My main disagreement with Arendt centres on the assertion of the absolute superiority of political life over all other aspects of social life and her extreme distrust of all forms of individualism and especially private life. She chooses the freedom of the Ancients, as opposed to the freedom of the Moderns. It is more important still to understand that she constantly sought (and with such passion) a principle of freedom that can resist the reproduction of order.

I would add that her anti-modernism is the best answer to postmodernism. Would she be as worried as she is if it had actually become impossible to define the society we are entering, even by contrasting it with the founding modernity of the Greeks or of the century of Galileo and Descartes? The observation that action has degenerated into work, and then labour, outlines a philosophy of regressive evolution that is very dubious, in terms of both the overall interpretation and the imperious nature of each of the logics it reconstitutes. This exaggerated evolutionism does, nevertheless, open up more perspectives and debates than the facile idea that the contemporary world cannot be defined, or that it can be defined only in terms of what it no longer is. Some postmodern thinkers, such as Jean-François Lyotard, do share Hannah Arendt's desire for a critical analysis that can protect them from the illusion of living in a directionless world in which there is no dominant force. Phenomena such as the transformations of scientific thought, the explosion of information technologies and the internationalization of the economy do, however, have as great a structural effect as the industrial revolution or the Greek *polis*.

On the wrong track

If the interventions of the Subject do not curb it, the decay of culture, personalities and politics will lead to the decadence of societies (which will have no principle of unity) and to a crisis of the personality (which will become incapable of making personal choices and formulating personal projects). If we wish to avoid the decadence that leads to chaos and dependency, and if we no longer wish to resort to authoritarian solutions, our only option is to reconstruct social life, political action and education around the idea of the Subject, which can create a new kind of mediation between the world of instrumentality and the world of identities.

Our first reaction to this rift, which affects individual personalities as much as it does society, is to turn to the past, to surrender to nostalgia for a world united by shared values and laws that are in keeping with the rational pursuit of self-interest. But attempts to do so are derisory, as are all exercises in nostalgia. Those principles of unity are no longer powerful enough to bring about the integration of centrifugal forces.

This is the first conclusion to be drawn from the general analyses made in our first three chapters. The appeal to universalist principles such as reason or progress increasingly serves to defend particular interests which consider themselves to be the sole guardians of universalism. It was in the name of the rights of man that we refused to recognize the rights of women. Colonialism has been justified in the name of the Republic. We have refused to recognize cultural differences so as not to undermine citizenship. That such reactionary currents should develop is inevitable, but we have to recognize them for what they are, and not confuse them with current trends within modern societies. In France in particular, the resurgence of the republican theme has been quickly transformed into a defensive nationalism. It poses a major threat to the democratic spirit, which implies the recognition of a plurality of cultures and forms of social organization, as well as of interests and opinions.

A second, and very different, solution has greater and broader attractions. The will of an authoritarian political power can, it is claimed, be used to reconcile economic liberalism and cultural universalism. This voluntarism, which is both modernizing and identitarian, is a common response to the rift in the modern world. It is mobilizing a growing number of new industrial countries, from the emerging economies of Malaysia and Indonesia to those of Morocco, Tunisia and Libya. This nationalism or modernizing communitarianism is, in political terms, much more important than anti-modernist fundamentalism, even though the latter does have more influence on immigrants. Most Islamists, not least the Muslim Brotherhood, are modernizers who want to mobilize the cultural resources of their countries so as to resist foreign domination and reconcile economic openness with their cultural identity. The impact of internationalized finance capitalism is so great that countries which do not withdraw into their cultures have to impose an authoritarian power on their societies if they are to remain in control of an economic development that is both very liberal and very emancipatory.

The third answer, which I reject, suggests, by contrast, that we should accept accelerated cultural change because it increases our freedom of choice. Why not accept, they ask, what I am rejecting? Why describe autonomy, change and complexity as crisis, dissociation and fragmentation? Why evoke only the communitarianism, when the invasion of the public world by private life is a quest for pleasure and happiness as well as an assertion of sectarianism? Rather than submitting to the discipline of reason and programmes, why not indulge in the pleasures of the senses in this changing and chaotic world, as Gilles Lipotevsky (1983, 1987, 1992) and Michel Maffesoli urge us to do? This critique seems to me to be both unattractive and far removed from the reality of divided societies, dissociated personalities, and the clash between fundamentalisms and financial networks. One can certainly have one's doubts about politics, and even about our ability to understand the world, but it seems to me to be impossible to content ourselves with a social life that has become a vacuum and a thought that has become a silence. The suggestion that we should go back to immediate experience, on the other hand, does ring true when it helps us to recover a public space that has long been either deserted or taken over by market traders and creators who can no longer find of their own accord a way to communicate with a public which has been abandoned to forms of cultural consumerism that do not meet its expectations. It is easy to recognize the pursuit of pleasure, play and above all the aesthetic construction of the self, ambiguous as it may be, as diluted, indirect and sometimes deceptive forms of the Subject itself, but in most cases they are real forms of the Subject. The image of the Subject that I have described is both harsher and more tragic. Whilst our ability to elaborate or construct it depends upon our ability to initiate collective action, we should not forget the existence of the elementary forms of the demand for subjectivation.

The ethical basis of social life

Defining the societies of late modernity as intervention societies brings us back to the first question asked by sociology: what makes social life possible?

The usual answer is that the transition from chaos and violence to order and peace presupposes rules and laws, and therefore the ability to formulate and apply those rules and laws. This answer, however, can take very different forms, and we therefore have to describe briefly the three main ones. In its most demanding form, which was very influential in early modernity, the answer is that the social order is based upon an acceptance of shared values or even, some would say, a shared destiny. The second answer appeals to the more abstract principle of collective utility, which provides a criterion for the evaluation of modes of behaviour and the reconciliation of conflicting interests. The third is the most limited and formal answer: it reduces laws to the rules of a game, or to constitutional principles and procedures.

When they are going through a period of rapid change and define themselves in terms of their future rather than their past, modern societies move, after what might be described as an intermediary institutionalist phase, from the first answer to the third. This third answer is characteristic of liberal thought, which seeks to do all it can to reduce the weight of principles and rules on the grounds that they can all too easily be transformed into power, and possibly arbitrary power. Liberal thought pleads the case for a society without norms or universal principles, or for a society based on common law rather than Roman law. The strongest conception of integration, which is invoked by traditionalist societies, had the opposite disadvantages. It gave priority to the same, but did leave a place, albeit limited and controlled, for the Other, or for foreigners. What the liberal conception lacks is a principle of unity that can facilitate communication between different actors. This is why we see so many individuals fleeing into communities, which ensure a high level of communication but also enforce a homogeneity that is potentially intolerant and authoritarian.

It seems to me impossible to choose between the *liberals* and the *communitarians*. Liberals invoke a universalism that is so far removed from real social relations that it is in fact reduced to being a procedural democracy which guarantees respect for difference and tolerance, but provides no principle for social integration and inter-cultural communication. Communitarians stress the shared values that provide the foundations for collective life, but they can escape the communitarian logic that privileges homogeneity over diversity only by falling back on the idea of tolerance, and are therefore in much the same position as the liberals. Neither of these solutions allows us to reconcile unity and diversity, or integration and identity. Neither can explain how inter-cultural communication is possible, or how we can live together with our differences. The only conceivable solution is to resort to a principle of mediation which does not exist on the same level as either the universalist principle or the appeal to social or cultural communities. This is the least social and the least collective of all principles: the individual action that allows everyone to reconcile, within their personal lives – which thus become truly individual – instrumental action and cultural loyalties, as well as a personality that has been shaped through the management of the libido and family relationships. A multi-communitarian society is impossible, but inter-cultural communication does become possible if society recognizes and safeguards every individual's attempt to become a Subject, and if it encourages every individual in their attempt to succeed, in their own way, in reconciling instrumentality and identity. This presupposes that such a society both refuses to identify with a universalism by erasing all social and cultural loyalties so as to promote citizenship and refuses to define itself in terms of shared origins or a shared destiny.

It is because both the liberal response and the communitarian response are unacceptable or inadequate that I introduce the idea of the Subject and that of social movements. At this stage in our investigation, the idea of the Subject is the more important of the two. There can be no communication unless those who are communicating have a common unitary principle. And only the attempt to reconcile instrumental action and identity can supply that principle. That is the definition of the Subject. The only universal principle is this effort, this work of individuation, and it is, it seems to me, the central element in the self-consciousness and reflexive action which Anthony Giddens rightly regards as the central elements in modernity. The idea of the Subject corresponds to the highest level of historicity. Both society and actors reach this level of historicity when their objective is to become capable of acting upon themselves, to be the actors in their own history, not simply consumers or targets for advertising, propaganda or influences. Now I cannot recognize my own desire to be an actor without recognizing that others also have the right to be actors in their own lives. This idea is not far removed from the recognition of a natural right or an ethical law. The American and French proclamations of immortal principles must lead, through struggles for social and cultural rights, to the recognition that every actor, collective or individual, has the right to assert and defend himself as such, or in other words as an actor who is capable of being involved in the technological world and, at the same time, of recognizing and reinterpreting his identity.

This is not simply a matter of desire, work or will; it is also a matter of struggle and emancipation, since the actor is not simply a desire to be a Subject. The actor is primarily the pain of not being a Subject, of desubjectivation, and of being divided and fragmented. It is this that gives the construction of the Subject the tragic power of a social movement. Neither our common involvement in the technological world nor the diversity of our cultural identities allow us to live together. What does allow us to live together is the kinship between our attempts to make the two domains of our experience meet, to discover and defend a unity which is not that of an ego, but that of an I or a Subject.

Solidarity and communication

Nothing could be more difficult than abandoning the idea that society is based upon its own functional requirements, or upon integration, order and change. We have finally come to accept that our societies, which are constantly being transformed by projects for the future, are no longer systems for the transmission of a material and cultural heritage, or at least that the reproduction of the past loses much of its importance in a changing world. But we are still heavily influenced by the idea that social life must discipline and repress passions and violence, instil respect for order and property, transmit the older generation's knowledge and norms to the next generation, ensure that we are equal in the eyes of a law that applies to all, and impose a rational-legal authority. We are, in other words, convinced that society must behave like a rational being. We have to abandon much of this representation because consumption, information and production have been internationalized, whilst identities have been fragmented.

This leaves us with the alternative image of social life. Bequeathed to us by mid-modernity, it is the image of a productive society governed by technological rationality and the class struggle, by accumulation and conflicts over the distribution of the fruits of growth, by urban concentration and by hierarchies in the work-place. This image of industrial society, which is common to both the defenders of capitalism and the supporters of socialism, is based, like the earlier images, on the idea that the system comes first and that, if we can understand its inverted logic, we will understand change.

We are now faced with the task of understanding a society in which change seems to be the primary factor, and in which there seem to be no limits to change. Accelerated technological change, together with the globalization of production, consumption and communications, has finally convinced us that nothing is settled any more. Social life is no

longer constructed around any central principle. Social utility, rationalization and even the class struggle are things of the past. If change is
everything, how can there be norms, laws, or a social definition of good
and evil? Do we have to accept the extreme liberal conception, which
seeks to do everything possible to prevent society from intervening in its
own affairs, and thus traps the state into playing the role of a policeman?
This is a very short-sighted answer, as it sees only the bright side of the
world. It fails to see the dark side. Political and cultural fundamentalisms
and sects are proliferating. Personalities that have been torn apart by
instrumentality, and communities and individuality, are decaying and
being imprisoned in all kinds of ways. The contrast between the bright
side and the dark side is so great that there is no neutral ground between
the two. It is impossible for the Subject to act, because it is being crushed
between the markets, on the one hand, and communitarian powers, on the
other. What is more, this blind liberalism does nothing to restrict either
the accumulation of wealth or the growth of social inequalities. As the
pace gets faster and faster, more and more people are being injured in the
race or are being forced to drop out.

The lesson to be learned from the critique of the rationalism of early
modernity put forward by the economic thought of the industrial age is
that the social order and the formation of norms can no longer be based
upon a positive principle. But what today's liberal critique cannot recognize is the need to safeguard the Subject, the freedom of the Subject, and
communication between Subjects and cultures. This is not a matter of
'freedom from' but very much a matter of 'freedom to', even though it is
far removed from any idea of people power. It is a matter of safeguarding
the non-social principle (the freedom of the Subject) on which social
organization must be based. It is obvious that the primary objective of
the laws and rules that govern the workings of society is no longer the
general interest, the common good or social utility. They must actively
serve the cause of the freedom of the Subject, which would be crushed by
both instrumental rationality and the obsession with identity, were it not
protected by the law, norms, the spirit of institutions and recourse to
juridical institutions.

Placing restrictions on both the dominant powers – namely markets
and communities – has to be our starting-point. This is a way of asserting
the universalism of the Subject, defined as the right of all human beings to
give their existence a meaning. That right makes a duty of solidarity
incumbent upon us all. Solidarity is not a means of promoting social
integration and civil peace, but a means of giving everyone the autonomy
and security without which they cannot construct themselves as Subjects.
In this context, the expression 'equality of opportunity' must be understood in the strongest of senses, whereas it usually masks the acceptance

of real inequalities; it must make it possible for all to escape social determinisms and to act in accordance with a project, which may be personal or which may also develop into a collective action or even a social movement. Solidarity is the antithesis of welfare, which keeps people in a state of dependency and weakens their ability to act. Solidarity is based upon the recognition that everyone has the right to act in accordance with their values and projects.

It is more difficult, it would seem, to impose limits on the communitarian spirit and its obsession with homogeneity and purity. In the contemporary world, however, doing so is the most urgent of tasks, given the dramatic spread of communitarianism and its rejection of diversity. If solidarity is the first principle on which a free society is based, the will to communicate is the second. Communication implies a recognition of the Other, of diversity and of plurality – or in other words, a recognition that everyone has the right to reconcile, in their own way, instrumentality and identity, and reason and culture. Everyone, that is, has the right to play a part in reconstructing a dissociated society that has inherited from Western proto-modernization an artificial divorce between reason and nature or affectivity.

How, then, are we to reconcile the recognition of differences and the assertion of the universalist principle that all human beings are equal? In three ways. First, we have to recognize diversity, and therefore reject all homogenization and all denials of difference. Secondly, the recognition of differences must be compatible with the independent instrumental activities of the cultures in which they exist. And finally, both cultural identity and instrumentality must recognize, in every society, a reference to the Subject, or in other words to basic human rights. This is not a matter of saying that human beings are rational or that they were created by God, but of asserting, irrespective of whether or not we subscribe to such beliefs, that every human being is, and must be recognized as being, free to become an individual by reconciling in their own way a culture and an instrumental activity, without being reduced to either. This position is a challenge to anything that requires human beings to obey a higher law which prescribes more duties than rights. Scientific thought certainly has emancipatory effects, but it cannot establish either personal freedom or cultural diversity. Religious thought subordinates human freedoms to the one truth in even stricter terms, as Pope John Paul II reminded us when, in restating that principle, he consciously condemned the humanism that informs the argument I am putting forward here.

Neither the personal Subject nor democratic society can exist without a combination of these three elements. Communication between individuals can take place only if each recognizes the Other as a Subject, or in other words as a being who freely combines a cultural identity and instrumentality as he or she constructs an experience of individuated life that cannot be reduced to principles or general and universal rules.

The idea of the Subject breaks with both communitarianism and abstract universalism. A social order that promotes the freedom of the Subject must be based upon the twin principles of solidarity and diversity. The combination of the two defines a communicative society, which must be seen as an institutional field for the defence of the Subject and intercultural communication.

The safeguarding of the Subject is the only acceptable normative principle. So far as the rest of the law is concerned, it is enough to recognize the utility of measures that safeguard people and property from fire, theft and crime. We should not lend the slightest moral justification to protective measures such as the imprisonment of delinquents, as it is absurd to say that they are paying their debt to society or that attempts are being made to rehabilitate them. Rehabilitation is one of the important goals of a politics of solidarity, but everyone knows that prison is no preparation for rehabilitation, and that in most cases it actually makes it more difficult. Similarly, the treatment and prevention of all forms of drug addiction, and especially the use of hard drugs, does come within the remit of a politics of solidarity, but there is no obvious connection between a rehabilitation policy and the criminalization of drug use.

These few lines obviously do not pretend to exhaust such vast subjects. They merely indicate that these social problems must be examined in the light of a different conception of the law and norms. Such profound transformations obviously lead to similar mutations in the social mechanisms that shape norms. We once wanted those norms to be established by law, and we wanted laws to be drawn up by parliament and the government, with help or assistance from experts. We later encouraged contracts, and especially collective bargaining at work. Nowadays, norms tend increasingly to emerge from public debates. The problems of bioethics certainly require legal intervention. The law, however, should intervene as late as possible and as little as possible, as it is important that the acceptability or otherwise of certain measures should be decided by public opinion or the media. This gives an important role to the makers of public opinion, including scientists, spokespersons from the churches and the voluntary sector, and also individuals with a wide personal experience of life.

Social norms are becoming less and less formalized. The need to adapt them to different and complex situations makes casuistry and jurisprudence increasingly important, whilst the law intervenes less directly and only with reference to the principles invoked above. The domain of the law is becoming divorced from that of principles. The primary function of the law is to prevent people from failing to do their duty or perform their functions, and it does less and less to establish ethical norms. It prevents accountants from stealing, and demands that children receive adequate care; it does little to define what the family should be or to instil respect for one particular form of authority in the work-place. It can help to prevent AIDS by making condoms available, but it does not intervene in the sexual life of individuals, and especially not in that of the young. Working conditions and industrial relations have been transformed by the pressures brought to bear by the unions and by collective bargaining; whether or not a given mode of fertility treatment is acceptable will be determined primarily by public opinion itself. The law makes fewer and fewer interventions in the domain of morals, and what is conventionally termed 'normality' is becoming more ill-defined by the year; but more attention is being paid to the defence of what are judged to be basic rights and a new morality based upon respect for the human personality.

We have to stop hiding behind the law, and hold open public debates to find out what, after discussion and reflection, an informed public opinion regards as acceptable when it comes to the criminalization of this or that mode of behaviour, or the degree of trust to be placed in one or another way of preventing or punishing certain ways of behaving. Whilst it may well be a supreme court or a *conseil constitutionnel* which ensures that the basic freedoms written into the Constitution are not infringed, it is public opinion, as reflected in the media, which will determine what is, and what is not, an attack on personal freedoms. Public opinion supported feminist demands. Public opinion, as reflected in the media, also rejected the suggestion, put forward by certain politicians on the far right, that homo-sexuals were to blame for the spread of AIDS; public opinion put com-passion before the defence of good morals. Public opinion often reacts without being fully informed, but, despite the criticisms put forward by many experts, we do find one constant: the defence of a social ethics based upon the freedom of the Subject.

Public opinion does not intervene in the name of the general interest, or in order to protect society from threats and dangers; it passes moral judgements and looks for guilty parties. In France, this was obvious in the 'contaminated blood' affair, and in many other cases that did not claim any victims. Jurists may well worry about the implications of this return to the idea of guilt, but it is very much part of a civilization whose main principle of integration is no longer institutional, but ethical.

The superficial idea that modernization and secularization inevitably lead to the triumph of instrumental action, pragmatism or even rational choices has to be combated more actively than ever before. Whilst social thought and social ethics, civic religion and the themes of patriotic sacri-fice are losing their old importance, they are not giving way to hedonistic individualism. On the contrary, they are being replaced by a figure of the

Subject which brings about its own individuation and freely organizes its personal life – and this conception cannot be reduced to an ill-defined individualism, because the defence of the Subject is inseparable from social and political choices that promote solidarity and inter-cultural communication.

We are building a society which is without norms or order, but not without principles. Although some people still look to the past and to ideological traditions for the means to resist the power of the dominant economic interests, we have to look to the ethics of subjectivation to find a solid basis for a new, extended democracy. We shall not find the means to struggle against absolute power and inequality in the élitism of the American Federalists, the English Whigs or France's Tocqueville. We will find it by putting our trust in a public opinion that has a conception of human rights and extends it to include social and cultural rights.

Can we once more speak of development?

To represent the Subject as an agent for the reconciliation of instrumental action and a cultural identity is in keeping with our experience of modernization.

The destruction of the political and social controls that ensure the reproduction of a society rather than its transformation has always played a major role in the history of Western modernization. Modern society is, as Alain Peyrefitte (1995) puts it, a divergent society. The mobility of the factors of production, the constant displacement of centres of economic production, the openness of markets, economic pragmatism and the taste for innovation are all so many elements that strengthen this critical component in development. But, as Alain Peyrefitte again notes, the presence of a community, of a strong social or national entity, or of a society based upon trust, is equally important. The two components of development are complementary, and it is within this turbulent space that there appears the central figure of the innovator, the explorer, the entrepreneur or the maker of scientific discoveries. This is a concrete figure of a Subject that can reconcile instrumental rationality and a cultural identity. There is no contradiction between an integrated micro world and an open macro space. They do not destroy one another, provided that something appears to mediate between them. The mediators must be actors who produce transformations and create meanings. We therefore have to recognize that, whilst we do live in modernity, we do not have to choose between the unity imposed by a community and unbridled competition, or between the empire of markets and fundamentalist and nationalist kingdoms. We merely have to live with the complementarity between an open world (or even a shattered world) and a Subject that is struggling to give meaning to its experience of both individual and collective life. No general principle, no rationalization and no religious belief can lead to development, for nothing could be more antithetical to modernity than the absolute triumph of a central principle of order. We therefore have to abandon the idea that modernity's ideal is the creation of a rational society in which every citizen and every institution contribute to the smooth workings of a social system run by a constitutional state, and which can satisfy the enlightened self-interest of all.

This critique of the economistic conception and the sociocentric inspiration of 'classical' modernity calls into question recent ideas about development, which has long been identified with the modernization of the economy.

In industrial society, development was reduced to meaning the effects of growth on the rising standard of living conditions, and the forms of social and cultural life were analysed only in so far as they were factors that promoted or slowed down growth. The time has come to invert the relative roles ascribed to growth, culture and social organization, and to propose a new analysis of development in our late modern societies.

The UN and UNESCO have played an important role here. For a long time, the idea of development was eclipsed by, or contrasted with, the theme of dependency, but we are now seeing the appearance of the idea of human development, and it introduces a radically new definition of modernity. The new definition was supplied by the *Reports on Human Development* published by the United Nations Development Programme between 1990 and 1996. Whilst these reports speak of the right to life, knowledge and adequate resources, they also attach a particular importance to political freedom, creativity and personal dignity. This reversal of perspective with respect to the idea of modernization has a lot in common with my attempts to replace the idea of society with that of the Subject.

From this point of view, development has to be defined as something that enhances the majority's freedom of choice, or, more specifically and as Amartya Sen put it in testimony to the World Commission on Culture and Development, the process that enhances the effective freedom to pursue those activities that individuals have cause to value. Whereas modernization was once seen as necessarily eradicating particularisms in favour of science and technological efficiency, we now see development as something that enhances our ability to manage change in the light of our lived cultural orientations. Whereas the Western ideal was once to use the new to create the new, we now want to use the old to create the new by reinterpreting and reactivating the cultures we have inherited. We are no longer satisfied with talk of a natural right to freedom and equality that is restricted to the order of law and citizenship; having ensured that our social rights are respected, we now want to guarantee that our cultural rights, which we also describe as our subjective rights, are also respected. I find the expression 'subjective rights' appealing, because it reminds me of the idea of subjectivation, or of the construction of a Subject on the basis of a lived experience that reunites the 'inner man' of culture and the 'outside world' of technologies and markets. This conception should distance us from all forms of sociologism and from the unacceptable claim that it is only through socialization that individuals come into being.

Development no more leads to the emergence of one generalized human type than it leads to a pure flow of change. It leads to the increasingly divergent personal life-trajectories that allow all of us to reconcile a personal and cultural identity with an openness to the world of technologies and commodities. We therefore have to put an end to the conflict between universalism and particularisms.

This reversal of perspective leads to a new conception of social and political action. We once used the term 'progressive' to describe not only the triumph of reason and science, but also the triumph of industrial rationalization and the power of the administrative state. In Europe, and elsewhere, we once placed our trust in the revolutionary elimination of the cultural and social obstacles that stood in the way of progress. But we abandoned that idea long ago, because its greatness could no longer mask its tragic effects. It implies, that is, the idea of an absolute rational power.

After the First World War, modern European thought precipitated the collapse of modernist utopias that had already begun in the late nineteenth century. The Frankfurt school was a startling manifestation of the rejection of both capitalism and Bolshevism. But the force of that critique was blunted in a society where mass consumerism was increasing, where security was becoming a central value for the majority, and where trade was trying to meet every demand, even those demands that were once condemned by both the law and public opinion. The critical thought that could make its voice heard in a society characterized by poverty, repression and inherited inequalities gets a poor reception in a society where the largest categories are no longer at the bottom, but half-way up a social pyramid which has been transformed into a cylinder, and which is already beginning once more to look like an inverted pyramid.

Rather than endlessly prolonging the demolition of the optimistic Enlightenment model or denouncing the limitations of the Welfare State, should we not be trying to identify the new principle that will enable us to build a modern society? And, living as we do in a world of apparatuses and markets, on the one hand, and the madness of ethnic cleansing, on the other, what could that principle be, if not the defence of the individual's will to be an actor, or in other words to assert himself as a Subject? There can be no purely critical thought and action. Given that we no longer believe in the perfect society and its New Man, let us believe in the freedom of the personal Subject, and let us defend the social conditions that allow that freedom to exist and develop. This sociology of the Subject has nothing to fear from the criticisms of either those who still take a purely critical stance or those who still defend the idea of a society that is integrated around either universalist values or particular traditions. Even though the political forces it requires do not yet exist, this sociology is already powerful, because it alone can explain the nature of the new social movements, trends within public opinion, and the way more and more people see their lives. And because it contributes to the major inversion that takes us from a sociology and a politics of the social system to a politics of action, defined as the production of a meaningful personal life, it is our only defence against a demodernization which is not only tearing society apart, but dividing us and destroying our identity as Subjects.

All this takes us a long way from the self-confidence of the rational Subject of early modernity, which was both confident that it could dominate nature and its own passions and convinced of the need to destroy traditions, beliefs and affections. Having survived the wars waged on it by both an optimistic market and totalitarian dictatorships, the newly emergent Subject is a recourse, not a sovereign. It is a force that can contain and limit all powers, but not a principle that legitimizes a new moralistic power. The Subject is on the defensive.

In no sense does this appeal to the Subject mean that we can no longer have an overall historical representation of our society. On the contrary, the defining feature of the type of society in which we now live is that historicity is speeding up or, in other words, that society is becoming more and more able to act upon itself. This is particularly true of the nature of the relations of domination that characterize it and of the social movements that challenge that domination. The historical title I have given this chapter implies the idea that modernity evolves and is transformed, and it is important to recognize the stages of modernity. It is also important to demonstrate at the same time that not all its stages have generated a historicist or evolutionist self-representation. Early modernity was dominated by the formation of nation-states, and thought in terms of a juridical order and social peace; it was the mid-modernity of industrial society that thought in terms of stages of economic development, or the stages of the realization of Spirit. And our late modernity is primarily worried about its survival and the risks it is running. It aspires to being neither a society of order nor a society of progress, but a communications-based society, and it is therefore more afraid of intolerance than of poverty or illegality. The idea of the Subject now becomes central to the analysis, but this has nothing to do with the individual who is concerned with his self-interest or pleasure. On the contrary, it is an expression of the desire, both collective and personal, for historical action and the desire to reunify a lived experience that has been torn apart by the conflict between economic flows and cultural roots.

The transition from industrial society to the programmed society in which we now spend most of our lives has radicalized our image of modernity. Our era is more modern than previous eras, because it has eliminated all the higher principles that once integrated human experience and brought actor and system into harmony. It has severed the link with naturalistic visions of society, philosophies of history and all forms of sociocentrism. It rejects both the illusions of sociologies of hope and ideologies of order. Its ambition is to build a society based upon the freedom of the personal Subject, and not a common good or a general interest, which are no more than disguised forms of power.

The development of modernity is not linear, however. As we move from one era of modernity to another, the locus of the central social debate is displaced. Early modernity was interested primarily in politics. The French Revolution was organized not around economic categories or social classes, but around political categories such as the nation and citizenship. It was in the industrial society of mid-modernity that economic categories became the most important of all and that political behaviour came to be seen as a reflection of economic interests. Over the last twenty-five years, we have seen these notions fall into decline. Whilst political ideologies are becoming exhausted, or inspire fear because totalitarian regimes made so much use of them, economic debates are becoming professionalized to such an extent that there seems to be very little difference between the management of the state and that of a private business; both have to adapt to globalized competition and accelerated technological change. Conversely, it is the problems of private life that stimulate the most important public debates. The theme of the Subject, which is the basis for ethical demands, has replaced that of classes, just as the theme of classes once replaced that of the nation.

Our analysis has to follow those developments within the collective consciousness and in social thought that have established connections between notions as abstract as that of the Subject and public opinion's growing sensitivity to the rights of individuals. Whilst its primary concern is with the rights of women and children, it is also concerned with the rights of minorities and the excluded. We are thus rediscovering the ability to orient ourselves in the historical space in which we live, rather than being torn between a conservative attachment to traditions and the equally unthinking assertion that we have to adapt to global changes over which we have no control. The ambition of this book is precisely to help us to understand our personal and collective behaviour by constructing an analytic grid appropriate to the late modern society we have been living in ever since we emerged from industrial society.

In order to pursue this goal, we have to abandon all images of a continuous process of modernization that expands through both time and space, accelerates, sweeps away obstacles, and creates, if not a homogeneous world society, at least generalized systems of trade that weaken or marginalize particularisms. We have to reject the idea that modernization means the triumph of trade over reproduction, and the replacement of ideological and political systems of control by purely economic regulatory agencies. We have to reject interpretations which establish a close connection between modernization and universalization or globalization. Such interpretations have become very widespread, especially since the end of the cold war and the collapse of the capitalism–socialism dichotomy, the East–West dichotomy, or even the North–South dichotomy, which have dominated so many ideologies and policies.

Any interpretation of social life in terms of objective, technological, demographic or economic evolution is dangerous, because it reduces social life to a clash between future and past, modernization and tradition, and outside and inside.

At a time when the life of societies seems to be being reduced to their involvement in world markets and their competitiveness, I believe that it is indispensable to stress the destructive effects of such a restrictive conception, which leads to an inevitable backlash: the explosion of nationalist, ethnic or religious fundamentalisms. Reducing the economic and social management of every city, country or region to opening it up to the globalized market is unacceptable. Rediscovering political thought and political action is a matter of urgency.

The end of social man

The change that occurs as we move from industrial society to the society in which we are already living, or from mid- to late modernity, is as momentous as the changes that occurred when we moved from the period of the construction of modern states – from the fifteenth to the mid-nineteenth century – to the industrial society which triumphed from the early eighteenth century until the great upheavals in world economic life in the 1970s. Given that the objective of this book is not to analyse the new forms of social organization and cultural life that characterize our era, but to define the transformations needed in social thought and in the grid we use to analyse new realities, the sociologist's most important task is to recognize that the idea of 'social man' is now exhausted and almost non-existent.

I understand 'social man' to mean a representation of human beings which identifies them with their involvement in a collective activity and the life of a society. This conception of human beings appears to be the logical, and therefore desirable, outcome of secularization and rationalization. If human beings are what they do, and no longer what they are; if social authority is rational and legal, and no longer traditional or charismatic; and if the domination of nature replaces the reproduction of values, norms and forms of social domination, then individuals become individuals only because they have been socialized. The ideas of institutions and socialization were the twin pillars on which social thought was based from the classical period (when individuals appeared to be wild, violent and driven by boundless desires until they were educated and taught to obey laws) to the industrial period (which extolled the worker rather than the individual). The human beings known as *Homo politicus* and *Homo economicus* were perceived as social beings, and wished to be social beings. And modernity has often been defined as the moment when the gates of heaven closed behind humanity and when human beings had to live in the midst of phenomena, armed only with their reason, their technologies and their laws as they attempted to establish some order. Religious patterns of behaviour were defined as pre- or proto-modern, because they subordinated man to the will of God and therefore to a finalist vision of both nature and humanity.

Although we are still sensitive to the emancipatory appeal of work and revolution, and although we live in close proximity to emergent or resurgent societies that subordinate every aspect of their intellectual or collective life to the divine law, we have to sever the links that still bind us to that conception of society. We no longer believe that modernity dissolves the link between the spiritual and the social to such an extent as to identify the social with instrumental rationality. After a century dominated by crises, totalitarianisms, world wars and the reign of commodities, we want above all to reconstruct and protect human freedom from all the social powers that threaten it. In our struggle against all these forms of social domination, we are trying to forge a new alliance between private life and the law. Rejecting the ethics of responsibility, we once more give pride of place to the ethics of conviction whenever we speak of the rights of man or of the Subject, of the intolerable, of exclusion or of violence. All these things, negative and positive, and regardless of personal interest or the common good, urge all of us to fight for the freedom for all to create their individual lives.

This reversal of perspective is indispensable, and even a matter of urgency, because practices are already far ahead of theories and institutions. Whilst many intellectual discourses are still repeating that a return to full employment will put an end to social violence, day by day we hear young people singing, dancing and acting out their burning desire for individuation through sexuality, but also through words, riots and even flirting with death. Whilst schools try to adapt to the needs of the economy, schoolchildren and students want to give meaning to their lives. Whilst the political and religious authorities worry about the fall in population, women are, in a growing number of countries, enforcing their right to decide how they live their lives and how many children they have. We live in a world that is being driven by women's movements, the crises in our cities and schools, the cries of dissidents and humanitarian campaigns. It is both absurd and ineffective to respond with a discourse on social man or the principles of ethics.

The usual objection to this position is the claim that, although I use the words 'subjectivation' and 'freedom', I am in fact defending an extreme form of individualism which may suit the wealthy middle classes of the rich countries but ignores the forces of domination and repression that are crushing the greater part of humanity, from the workers of the industrial countries to the inhabitants of the Third World, who are ruled by both international markets and local dictators.

My answer to this objection is to point out that, throughout the preceding pages, I have stressed that the Subject must wage a twofold struggle if it is to survive and create a space of freedom for itself. It must struggle against authoritarian communitarian powers, on the one hand, and the domination of markets, on the other. And whilst I refuse to identify the Subject with a collective being such as a nation, class or church, I also denounce the illusions of those who reduce the freedom of the Subject to meaning freedom of consumer choice. Let me elaborate on my initial answer by adding that the dominance of markets and that of communitarian dictatorships are two aspects of a single phenomenon: namely the attempts that are being made to destroy the Subject by systems, policies and economies whose logic always leads them to seek more power and to become more and more independent of any intervention, any controls and any subjectivity.

To turn to the communitarian threat, I am saying that whereas communitarian powers try to establish a unitary link between one belief and one god, or one law and one community, modernity must break that unitary link. In that sense, it is synonymous with secularism and personal freedom. And that is true the world over. I denounce with equal fervour the globalization of information technologies and the development of international trade, and try to imagine a self-regulating economic system that has been freed from all political, social or ethical controls.

Is it not surprising that a sociologist should so forcefully reject the definition of modern man as a political and social being? That conception was in fact typical of early modernity. When sociology was established as a discipline in its own right, and gained academic recognition at the end of the nineteenth century, it certainly did not accept that early conception, which had more to do with political philosophy. On the contrary, it was critical of it. This was particularly true of Max Weber, who could not have been further removed from positivism, and who placed such emphasis on the separation and complementarity between rationalization and the war between the gods. For his part, Émile Durkheim's research into social integration and solidarity was based on an awareness that modernity was a crisis. Of all the founding fathers of sociology, Georg Simmel was the most individualistic and the least influenced by sociocentrism. Whilst it is true that sociologism, and especially utilitarianism, did see the interest of society, which it regarded as an organism, as the criterion that defined good and evil, sociological analysis was much more dominated by an awareness of the non-correspondence between system and actor. Were that not the case, the sociologists' central theme of social change would be incomprehensible. Marxist critiques of the social organization challenged the logic of profit and power in the name of needs and rationality. Similarly, the influence of psychoanalysis was apparent in the awareness of the contradiction between desire and the law. Is it surprising, then, that, having thought for so long about the conflicts between labour and capital, we should react so badly to critics who contrast an unfettered economy with desocialized identities or communities? The absence (or the decay) of society has become the central theme in contemporary sociology.

Even in early modernity, we did not in fact succeed in finding a satisfactory answer to the question of social integration, assuming we accept that the universalism of reason was a principle of domination and exclusion, rather than of integration. It was in the name of reason that the world was divided between superior beings who were endowed with reason by their education, work and wisdom, and inferior beings who were incapable of resisting their passions, beliefs and traditions. We will be even less successful if we allow ourselves to be trapped in our respective ethnic, religious or cultural nationalisms. Absolute differences create horizontal obstacles to communication, just as reason constructed vertical obstacles.

Tolerance does not offer a way out of this double impasse. The rich find it easier to be tolerant than the poor, but tolerance is never completely divorced from segregation, as the search for tolerance is acceptable only when it goes hand in hand with the rejection of the intolerable. Tolerance does not guarantee communication; nor does it allow the minority to become a majority and to decide in its turn what is tolerable and what must not be tolerated.

Interpersonal and inter-cultural communication are possible only if we cease to define ourselves in terms of our possession of a particular identity, or by referring to a reason that is so abstract as to make it inseparable from a ruling class made up of property-owners or citizens. They presuppose that the contradiction between a domineering universalism and an intolerant particularism can be transcended by having recourse to something that is neither general nor particular, but unique: the individuation of every personal and collective existence. And that experience is the product of the attempt to unite the two halves of human existence: namely instrumentality and cultural and psychological identity. Their divorce leads to demodernization.

We communicate only by recognizing in others the attempt to reconcile and integrate instrumental action and expressive behaviour that we all make in order to be individuals, or only if we recognize their will to subjectivation. No matter whether we call it 'solidarity' or 'fraternity', this recognition sees in every individual an attempt to reconcile difference and similarity.

This is obviously not the most direct way to analyse the pre-conditions for intra-cultural communication. It follows a winding path and examines the idea of the Subject, and then the relationship with the self, before looking at relations with others. But the fact of demodernization does mean that we have to find our way through the world of objectivity. Our ability to do so can no longer be guaranteed by institutions or trust in the laws of history. It can be guaranteed only by the idea of the Subject. And the Subject can be defined as moving between two worlds.

PART II

Living Together

5

Multi-cultural Society

Those who subordinate society to some higher organizational principle try to show how it affects the details of social organization and individual consciousnesses. As we begin the second part of this book, we find ourselves faced with almost the opposite problem. In the previous chapters we looked at social life not from above but from below, not in the light of a universal principle or a divine message, but in the light of the personal will to individuation that leads us to reconcile our individual personalities and our cultural heritage with our involvement in the world of technologies, the economy and the management of collective life, so as to construct our experience of our personal lives. Given that my starting-point is what some people wrongly regard as an extreme individualist position, how can I get back to the problem of social life, its organization and its institutions?

The answer to this question, obviously, is that the Subject is not to be confused with the individual, and that it is not a constantly changing aggregate of individual states of mind or social determinants. The Subject is an attempt, always under threat and never completed, to defend an actor who is being torn apart by the contradictory pressures of his instrumental life and his cultural identities. The starting-point for our analysis is neither the individual nor the ego; it is demodernization and the growing dislocation of modern societies. Rather than working backwards from the individual to society, our task is to explain why the appeal to the Subject is now the only possible answer to our initial question.

At a time when the continent of markets is drifting further and further away from that of cultural identities and when we are being encouraged to live in both a globalized economy and communities obsessed with purity, only the idea of the Subject can create not only a field of personal action but, above all, a space for public freedom. We will succeed in living together only if we recognize that our common task is to reconcile instrumental action and cultural identity and only if, therefore, we can construct ourselves as Subjects. We can live together only if the primary objective of our laws, institutions and forms of social organization is to safeguard our demand to live as the Subjects of our own experience. Without that central mediating principle, it is as impossible to reconcile the two sides of our experience as it is to square the circle.

There is no discontinuity between the idea of the Subject and the idea of multi-cultural society or, more specifically, of inter-cultural communication. We cannot live together with our differences unless we recognize one another as Subjects. I will attempt to demonstrate that democracy must be defined as the politics of the Subject, as the regime that grants the greatest possible number the greatest possible opportunity to succeed in individuating themselves, or in living as Subjects. This takes us far away from the old image of direct democracy, which was viewed as an expression of the general will, and further still away from the identification of the nation with the state, which has so often been proclaimed in France and other countries.

These analyses should allow us to formulate proposals for the two institutional domains where the most important norms are elaborated and applied: the law and education. The former domain is still beyond my reach, and I hope that jurists will show me the way and allow me to complete this essential task. I will, on the other hand, be putting forward proposals for the domain of education, which has, astonishingly enough, been overlooked. The projects that have been drawn up are no more than attempts to adapt education to what is obscurely described as the needs of the economy. The four chapters that make up Part II, therefore, all have the same objective: to wage a constant struggle on two fronts. This is a struggle against, on the one hand, communitarian ideologies and politics and, on the other hand, the neo-liberal ideology that dissolves real societies into globalized markets and networks. The stance I am adopting is not purely critical; my goal is also to make the personal Subject, its resistance, its hopes and its failures, central to both analysis and action, rather than the needs, functions and consciousness of society.

The limits of tolerance

Authoritarian powers seek to bring about the cultural unification of society so as to impose absolute controls on individuals and groups whose interests, opinions and beliefs are always divergent. The more these powers identify with one central unifying principle, be it reason, nation, race or religion, the quicker their societies' descent into the hell of total-itarianism. There have, however, been attempts to bring about cultural homogenization in more gentle ways, or without relying upon the coercive power of the state. The gentlest methods have been inspired by the conviction that the light of reason must dispel the mists of superstition. They place their trust in education and the beneficial effects of science, rather than in authoritarian rationalization. Midway between the despot-isms that think they are enlightened and this secular rationalism, we have the industrial rationalization that identified the progress of reason with the need to give management more control over workers, who were assumed to be both naturally lazy and creatures of habit. It was this conviction that led F. W. Taylor to use both the carrot and the stick to make the working class accept what he saw as the scientific organization of labour, and it subjected the workers to the domination of the captains of industry.

When it comes to attempting to use religious beliefs and practices to unite populations, there are also major differences between those who rely upon preaching and setting an example (and they pose as little threat as the rationalists who believe in the beneficial effects of education) and those who impose a religion by force of arms. The latter are as repressive as the apostles of the dictatorship of reason. People like Diderot are potentially just as dangerous, but pose little practical threat. They wish to bring about the unification of the world by destroying artificial moral-ities and laws, or by bringing about the triumph of nature. They are dangerous, because a society based upon the natural ethics that Diderot wanted so much would be as hierarchical as an animal society. It would, for instance, be a society in which, as Diderot himself says in the *Supplé-ment au voyage de Bougainville* (first published in 1772), women's subordination to men would be natural, because nature has made men stronger and more violent. Rousseau was sternly critical of this extreme naturalism and utilitarianism.

There are those who say: let us divorce public life from private life, respect the same laws, and allow everyone to act in accordance with their own beliefs and opinions. Why, they ask themselves, should we worry ourselves about an ill-defined multi-culturalism that can only lead to inter-communal clashes, and therefore to the strengthening of author-itarian or totalitarian states, when we can practise the well-tempered multi-culturalism that we call tolerance and secularism. Given that we have the good fortune to live in Great Britain, France or the United States, why, they ask, should countries that have long been integrated nations take the risks that have plunged Lebanon, the former Yugoslavia and even India into bloody conflicts? For a long time, the isolation of local life protected cultural diversity from the ambitions of centralizing powers whose capacity to intervene was indeed very limited; as a result of greater national integration, the growth of a more powerful administration and the beginnings of industrial mobilization, the democratic spirit then took the form of laws to safeguard cultural pluralism. It is true that, in France and in other countries, the clash between clericalism and secularism was violent, but in retrospect the violence seems more ideological than real. Today, those who turn secularism into a militant anti-clericalism are few in number and have little influence, and almost all of us expect secularism to encourage a peaceful coexistence and even good relations between a Christian culture and a rationalist culture. We also expect it to ensure respect for minority religions, beliefs, opinions and ways of life in countries where the influence of religious or ideological practices and beliefs is on the wane. Is there not an obvious parallel between the end of wars of religion and the decline of class struggles, which have been replaced by a growing awareness that investment, growth and standards of living are interdependent?

I have chosen to begin by outlining the moderate view because I write in a part of the world where cultural tolerance and even cultural relativism are constantly gaining ground. This perspectivism, which effectively denies that the theme of multi-culturalism has any importance, cannot, however, supply a long-term solution.

In many countries, some of them very close to us, bloody conflicts between cultures, religions, nationalities or ethnic groups are raging, and although there is often an element of truly political ambition or conflict, the cultural dimension also has a tragic importance. What is more, protests in the name of the cultural identities and rights of ethnic, social or moral minorities are being voiced in the richest, most peaceful and most democratic countries too. It was not the spirit of tolerance that brought about the decline of class struggles; they declined, rather, because the nation-society triumphed and became the principal mode of social organization. In certain countries, including France, there was a brief period in which the prevailing idea was that national integration alone, not mere tolerance, could transcend both the capitalist model of industrialization and localized cultural identities. The nation appeared to be the political form of modern society, which was both complex and changing. This society would see both the demise of particular local, ethnic or religious loyalties and the triumph of a rationality that could be translated into administrative rules, communication systems and educational programmes.

This national-democratic model made it possible, thanks to public freedoms, to reconcile a pluralism of interests and opinions with political unity. It brought about the triumph of secularism. The corollary was that, because it acted in the name of progress and the law, it often imposed the same rules and forms of life on all. Everything that could be labelled archaic, marginal or 'minority' was banned, repressed and labelled inferior. This process of integration now seems to have been less violent in the oldest nation-states, but that is because it took place over a long period of time. But, more so than anywhere else, it also went hand in hand with a violent rejection of cultural diversity. Gérard Noiriel (1988) has shown how, under the Third Republic, French thought, and especially sociological and historical studies, concealed the reality of immigration whereas many studies carried out in the United States noted its importance. When more studies of ethnic, national or regional minorities appeared, we discovered the extent to which cultures and societies had been destroyed, and not only by the wars that gave birth to the nation-states. When, for example, post-war Canada introduced legislation that provided for a census of the Inuit population and compulsory schooling for Inuit children, a society was transformed into a population of welfare-dependants in little more than a generation. The price that had to be paid for an improvement in their material living standards was a loss of personal and collective identity. The situation in many Indian reservations in the United States is more tragic still, particularly in the Sioux reservations, where social and personal disintegration has led to a very high suicide rate.

The imposition of a supposedly progressive and scientific model has not only led to the destruction of ethnic groups; it has plunged various minorities into marginality. Because they have been stigmatized as a result, we have been slow to analyse their situation in scientific terms. France, for instance, has been slow to recognize the disabled, and still does little to give them the help they should be receiving or to recognize their potential. The recognition of minorities, which is now rightly regarded as one of the main issues in a democracy, is still a long way off. The reason why I do not mention the emancipation of women in this context is that it is wrong to regard women as a minority, and that their action and the changes it has brought about in our social representations are of such central importance that they have to be examined in their own right.

The republican synthesis and the formation of the national-democratic Subject were powerful creations. They opened up a political space and guaranteed political freedom. Yet they also imposed powerful social and cultural constraints which cannot be seen as temporary restrictions on freedom. The destruction of both cultural diversity and authoritarian rationalization was regarded as a pre-condition for the triumph of political universalism. The fact that this model is now exhausted means that we take too kindly a view of it, and forget just how powerful it was. Whilst it is true that the violence of communitarian regimes has dominated the twentieth century and that, especially since 1968, more and more has been done to show how minorities have been excluded, we have to be as critical of the negation of cultural identities in liberal-democratic societies as we are of ethnic, national or religious fundamentalisms. And we have to be especially critical of liberal-democratic countries which closely identify the freedom of the people with the omnipotence of the republican (or imperial) state.

This ideal model of the nation-society, with its qualities and its flaws, is, then, in decline (which is why we now talk of multi-culturalism). Its decline has come about both because it has at times degenerated into an aggressive nationalism in order to defend itself against the globalization of the economy, and because particular identities have proved better at resisting globalization than a model which tried to retain control over both economic modernization and collective identities. And it is indeed the decline of this model that has given rise to the theme, the problems and even the contradictions of a· multi-culturalism which has nothing to do with the demands of local or minority societies and cultures living in empires or states that are still premodern and poorly integrated.

Our continued attachment to freedom of opinion and cultural tolerance does not provide an adequate response to the problems created by the decline of this model of national society. I have already said that this model was a figure of modernity, and even of the Subject, as the democratic nation aspired to being a political Subject that could reconcile, in a particular way, the unity of reason and the diversity of interests. Just as eulogies of tolerance provide an effective response to old conflicts which are in fact becoming meaningless, so our forced march into modernity exacerbates, decade by decade, the contradiction between instrumental rationality and the warring gods, and the open conflict between world markets and cultural and social identities. A country like France, which is so attached to the tradition of the liberal nation-state, is torn between its need to open up to a globalized market and culture and a desire to defend a political identity which tends at times to make it retreat into an essentialist conception of itself. It is no longer possible to believe that political institutions are strong enough to master and reconcile economic forces, the mechanisms of the personality and cultural loyalties, even though (or especially because) we are still convinced of the absolute need for democratic political institutions if we are to protect and encourage the personal Subject and its desire to reconcile instrumental rationality and cultural identity within a personal life history.

Communitarianism

The weakening and sometimes even the collapse of the liberal nation-state is both the cause and the effect of the disjunction between the economy and cultures, and it has led to the rise of both communitarianism and transnational economic forces. Communitarian ideology demands a complete harmony, within a given territory, between a form of social organization, cultural practices and a political power; it seeks to create a total society. It is pointless to invoke the classic dichotomy of community and society, which was first elaborated by Tönnies and then reinterpreted by Louis Dumont (1983) as a dichotomy between holistic and individualistic societies. 'Traditional' societies are now almost unknown. We can, on the other hand, speak of communitarization (*Vergemeinschaftung*) when a cultural movement, or more usually a political force, creates, in voluntaristic fashion, a community by eliminating those who belong to a different culture or society or do not recognize the power of the ruling élite.

The world-wide influence of the English language means that the word 'community' is now used in a very weak sense to designate local collectivities, neighbourhoods, religious or ethnic groups, or even groups defined by their customs or tastes, provided that they have a certain internal organization and, what is more important, the ability to make representations to the authorities. My concern here, however, is not so much with communitarian organizations as with communitarianist regimes which give the defence of a collective identity a political or military strength and a social cohesion that usually takes the form of a rejection of everything that is foreign.

Attempts to establish homogeneous communities whose purity is guaranteed by strict political controls and by the elimination of what are seen as deviant minorities have always led to bloodshed, as they did when the Nazis exterminated what they saw as inferior races, and as they did when the Serb government implemented its policy of ethnic cleansing after the breakup of the former Yugoslavia. It is, they say, as natural for a nation to want have its own language, customs and educational system as it is for it to want to live in its own territory and under a government that corresponds to the will of the people. Yet, whilst this is a legitimate demand, the use of force to homogenize and cleanse a diversified population destroys the very idea of citizenship. The only response to such cultural nationalisms, whatever their strength and intensity, is the separation of culture, society and power. The breakup of communitarian unity is an indispensable pre-condition for modernity, and national societies or social groups that attempt to re-create a communitarianist model are doomed to economic failure, social repression and the destruction of the very culture in whose name communitarian power speaks. A people has the right to fight for its national independence, and will fight all the harder when it does so in the name of a cultural, linguistic and historical identity. But when building national sovereignty leads to the rejection of minorities and 'national preference', it will soon end in disaster, because the community is no longer anything more than a tool in the hands of an absolute power or a communitarianist or nationalist dictatorship which will destroy both the culture and the economy, and replace the national consciousness with the rejection of foreigners.

Nothing could be further removed from multi-culturalism than the fragmentation of the world into cultural, national or regional spaces that are foreign to one another. Their obsession with an ideal homogeneity and purity suffocates them. What is worse, the unity of a culture is replaced by that of a communitarianist or nationalist dictatorship. Institutions are replaced by a command structure and a little red book or a little green book which has to be studied and quoted at every possible opportunity.

Am I using the pretext of a sociological analysis to plead the case for the type of political regime that dominates the richest countries? No. I think, on the contrary, that it is the lack of any correspondence between involvement in the world economy and social and national integration that has destructive effects. This is as true of countries that have come under the domination of communitarianist states as it is of those that are applying the political model of the fully extroverted economy. It is the failure of so many modernizing nationalisms that has resulted in the victory of hyper-liberal regimes, just as it was the failure of liberal democracies that led to the victory of authoritarian regimes. I by no means identify with the pluralist democracies of the West and reject all communitarianist authoritarian regimes; I regard both 'globalizing' economic liberalism and political communitarianism as serious, even deadly, threats to democracy, because they are two aspects of the same demodernization. Cultural nationalism would not be as powerful as it is, had it not been seen as a response to globalization.

Far from living under the universalist illusion that rationalization can unite the world, we are experiencing the dissociation (and fusion) of mass culture and the obsession with identity. This shows that, in their extreme forms (a world society or, conversely, a multiplicity of cultural worlds that are divorced from one another and communicate only through the market), both mono-culturalism and multi-culturalism are either ideological assertions or political campaigns, rather than social and cultural realities.

Since the relationship between globalization and cultural nationalism is one of mutual hostility, the first stage of our analysis must therefore be to recognize that there is an emancipatory dimension to multi-culturalist demands.

We are perfectly prepared to accept that this is the case in so far as we long ago abandoned the idea that the word 'people' refers simultaneously to all the victims of domination, the political majority and the guardian of rationality. The change of definition occurred during industrialization. Whereas socialism kept alive the spirit of the philosophy of the Enlightenment and progress, the labour movement defended working-class autonomy against a rationalization which claimed to be the agent of universalism, but which actually served the interests of the ruling class or the ruling political élite. Now that power is invading economic life and then cultural life, threatened cultures are reasserting their specificity or superiority. There is a conflict between a world society and local cultures; the defenders of the local (which includes planet earth) are resisting the industrializing and communicative pride of the financial centres that produce and distribute mass culture.

The offensive against the cultural domination of the world by a capitalism that has spread beyond the economic domain began with Frantz Fanon's early broadsides, which were popularized by Jean-Paul Sartre and transposed to the East by Chariati. Even though there is always the danger that it will degenerate into an aggressive communitarianism, we have to understand this offensive. For its part, the labour movement may well have led to the dictatorship of the proletariat and to the authoritarian regimes that were its self-proclaimed leaders, but it has often extended the field of democracy by stimulating the creation of industrial democracy. We have come to the parting of the ways in the cultural realm too. We have to choose between a cultural democracy which recognizes cultural pluralism (and minority rights) and a communitarian fundamentalism which identifies one power with one society and one culture.

Culture must not be confused with community. Being open to exchanges and change, no modern society has a truly unitary culture, and cultures are constructs which are constantly being transformed as they reinterpret new experiences. Attempts to find an essence or a national soul are therefore artificial, as is the attempt to reduce a culture to a code of behaviour. What is more important, the idea of a communitarian culture implies the existence of an absolute power that can impose juridical norms, respect for the rules of collective life and an educational system. Communitarianist ideology is, by its very nature, political, not cultural.

In the modern world, no religious culture is in itself communitarian, as every religion implies a non-social, or even an anti-social and anti-political, call to imitate a divine model handed down by God, the Son of God or his Prophet. Olivier Roy (1992) makes this point when he contrasts the fundamentalism of the ulemas, and particularly the pietism of the Tabligh, with political Islamism. The latter is political rather than religious, especially when it takes an extreme form. Farhad Khosrokhavar points out that Khomeini was acclaimed as a politician before 1979, and even during the brief period between the revolution and the outbreak of the war with Iraq. Olivier Roy has shown that Islamic Third-Worldism is spreading more rapidly amongst urban and educated categories than Marxism–Leninism, which seems, paradoxically enough, to have put down stronger roots in the rural world. This is why Roy's proposed category of neo-fundamentalism is scarcely convincing. One can certainly understand that, in countries with a high rate of emigration, the reference to an abstract *Umma* should have replaced the religious nationalism that dominates Muslim countries. But, as Olivier Roy himself points out, the nature of what he calls neo-fundamentalism is, especially in Great Britain but also in France, the same as that of political Islamism. It feeds on a rejection of the dominant society, on the perceived contradiction between the desire to be part of a technological and commodified civilization and the experience of a failure that feels like a rejection. Militant political Islamism exists everywhere, in both the dependent countries and the dominant ones. It is different from fundamentalism in the true sense of the word. Being based on an ethical conception, the latter is not unknown in the modern world either. Within the Islamic world, it is above all the difference between ethical and political fundamentalism that is creating divisions similar to the divisions that led to the schism in Christendom and to the rise of both social struggles and ethical individualism in the West.

To conclude, let us recall that multi-culturalism does not mean the endless fragmentation of cultural space, and that it is not a world-wide cultural melting pot. It is an attempt to reconcile the diversity of cultural experiences with the mass production and distribution of cultural goods.

Definitions

Making a critique of the communitarianism which is now invading the whole world is a more urgent task than dreaming of a rational society. The dream of the rational society led to equally tragic disasters, but it has been dissolved into the shimmering diversity of the consumer society. It is, however, still more important to critique something common to both conceptions: the idea that society must have a cultural unity, and that it can be created by reason, religion or ethnicity. Above all, we have to reject the ever-widening divorce between the unity of the market and the fragmentation of communities. This book asks the question 'How can we live together?', or in other words, 'How can we reconcile equality and diversity?' In my view, we can only do so thanks to a combination of political democracy and cultural diversity. Both are based upon the freedom of the Subject.

No multi-cultural society is possible unless we can turn to a universalist principle that allows socially and culturally different individuals and groups to communicate with one another. But neither is a multi-cultural society possible if that universalist principle defines one conception of social organization and personal life that is judged to be both normal and better than others. The call for the freedom to build a personal life is the only universalist principle that does not impose one form of social organization and cultural practices. It is not reducible to *laissez-faire* economics or to pure tolerance, first because it demands respect for the freedom of all individuals and therefore a rejection of exclusion, and secondly because it demands that any reference to a cultural identity be legitimized in terms of the freedom and equality of all, and not by an appeal to a social order, a tradition or the requirements of public order.

The defenders of radical multi-culturalism attack this conception in the name of a relativism that cannot be transcended. They say that my conception is an expression of the most extreme Western liberalism, and that it is both alien and unacceptable to all those who define themselves in terms of their membership of a cultural community that is both dominated and under threat. This criticism is very confused. I accept the criticism to the extent that it defends cultures that have been dominated or destroyed in the name of a progress that is, either naïvely or cynically, identified with the interest of the ruling classes or countries, but I find it unacceptable when it preaches a radical cultural relativism. This position is so artificial that it inevitably transforms the defence of independence into an instrument that strengthens an authoritarian power, just as the justifiable critique of the monopoly held by the international news agencies quickly proved to further the interests of authoritarian leaders who wanted to control all news about their countries. The same deviations in fact occurred in the heart of industrial society when some working-class militants took it upon themselves to promote proletarian culture at the expense of bourgeois culture. Their attempts to do so had little practical effect, but they did subsequently serve to justify the dictatorship of the proletariat, which soon set about destroying all independent working-class action.

These debates have recently taken an important political turn. Can we speak of the universal rights of human beings, or do we have to recognize that even the idea of human rights takes very different forms in different civilizations? At this point, we have to accept UNESCO's proposals. We do have to be critical of the identification of human rights with certain forms of social organization, and especially with economic liberalism, but it is more important still to assert that all individuals have a right to freedom and equality, and that there are therefore limits that cannot be transgressed by any government or any code of law. Those limits relate both to cultural rights such as the rights of women and to political rights such as freedom of expression and choice. This position is threatened both by those who would reduce society to the status of a market and by those who want to transform it into a community.

The conception I am defending here cannot be identified with the dominant practices of the rich countries, which define human beings both in terms of what they do and in terms of the social and cultural environment that has shaped their personalities. It belongs within the tradition of all those social movements which, from the working-class movement to national-liberation movements and the women's movement, have extended the original conception of civil rights, which was victoriously defended by the revolutionaries of the early centuries of modernity, to include the idea of social and cultural rights. And it recognizes that the greatest threat – totalitarianism – can be defined as a quest for cultural homogeneity, cultural orthodoxy or ethnic purity, and, therefore, as a recommunitarianization of society. But it also takes the view that a mass society regulated only by the market poses an equally serious threat to the existence of the Subject, because it either destroys cultural diversity or reduces it to the status of a spectacle. It asserts that both the defence of social and cultural plurality in liberal countries and the re-evaluation of the role of technology and new modes of communication in countries threatened by communitarianism are steps towards the creation of multicultural societies.

We must actively resist cultural colonization and the imposition of one dominant way of life on the whole world, but we also have to realize that there is now no such thing as cultural isolation. A crude dichotomy between dominated cultures and a dominant culture is always an expression of an authoritarian policy which, ultimately, cares little for tradition – hence the failure of the attempts that have been made by Indianists to establish a political movement to defend native cultures in various regions of Andean America. It is, on the other hand, essential that the Indian populations should be able to manage their cultural and economic interests within the framework of democratic institutions.

Anything that drives society and communities, or the globalized economy and isolated cultures, further apart has negative effects, and leads to the destruction of cultures, to social violence and to authoritarian adventures. We have to struggle at every level against the fracturing of the world, of national societies and of personal life. To do so, we must reconcile unity and diversity, exchange and identity, present and past. We must do so in different but complementary ways in every part of the world, in rich and poor countries alike.

If we refuse to take this path and become trapped in an extreme cultural relativism, we shall begin to want to divorce cultures from one another because they are defined by their particularisms. And we shall therefore build homogeneous societies. We can no more accept a multi-communitarianism that leads to discrimination and violence than we can accept a social rationalization that results in those who deviate from the dominant model being treated as inferiors.

Such are the principles that define the idea of a multi-cultural society. It is now as important as the ideas of popular sovereignty and the fair society, which we discovered in the early stages of our modernity, were and still are. This conception is a powerful challenge to both the idea of a multi-communitarian society and the idea of a homogeneous society, irrespective of whether the homogeneity in question is the product of uniform rules, the market economy or the preservation of a tradition. It calls for technological and economic norms to be divorced from various cultural values, but it also asserts that these separate orders can be reconciled and bound together only by having recourse to the *non-social* idea of the freedom of the personal Subject, and therefore the idea that all social, political, economic and cultural powers must be limited by respect for what we regard as basic human rights. Both the rule of commodities and the obsession with identity are threats to this idea. That is why a multi-cultural society cannot be a fragmented society, but must, on the contrary, be a society that is, in juridical and institutional terms, a strong society.

Inter-cultural communication is possible only if the Subject has already succeeded in escaping from its community. The Other can be recognized as such only if it is understood, accepted and loved as a Subject, or as an attempt to reconcile, within the unity of a life and a life project, an instrumental action and a cultural identity that must always be released from historically determined forms of social organization.

The recognition of the Other is possible only if everyone asserts their right to be a Subject. The corollary of this is that the Subject cannot assert itself as such unless it recognizes the Other and overcomes the fear of the Other that leads to the Other's exclusion. 'Our greatest fear', remarks Peter Brook, 'is our fear of opening ourselves up to the Other, and that fear paves the way for the far right and terrorism' (*Le Monde*, 14 September 1996).

I cite a man of the theatre because the theatre is the best place to see the Subject on display. Writing novels was once the natural way to describe characters whose individuality was inscribed in a socially and politically defined historical situation. An actor on the stage is as uncommitted to his role as a character in a novel is committed to his. And the attractive thing about cinema at its best is that it combines the two situations by putting theatrical figures, who are as uncommitted to their social roles as the characters in a western, in novelistic situations. Inter-cultural communication is not, however, reducible to interpersonal relations, or to the communication that takes place in the theatre. As Peter Brook puts it, 'With our spectators, it is possible to create a little series of models of what human relations might be if we were devoid of all fear.' Inter-cultural communication makes it possible to construct general forms of social and cultural life.

The position I have just outlined is not easy to accept. Some use political arguments against it. They say that certain cultures are so different that they cannot merge with or even understand one another; they must be kept apart in different territories or placed within a clearly defined relationship of domination-subordination, as was the case with the colonial system. This holistic conception is the form that is now taken by racism. It implies that wars between cultures and religions, or the organized segregation of minority cultures, are inevitable or even desirable. This position is so out of keeping with our individualistic culture, and is under such direct attack from the world-wide distribution of forms of production, consumption and communication involving people from very different cultures, that it is important and dangerous only when it becomes a defensive ideology for populations who feel that their social position or cultural identity is under threat.

The liberal-individualist critique, which takes precisely the opposite view, is much more important. Its most powerful exponent is Louis Dumont: 'If the advocates of difference are asking for both equality and for their difference to be recognized, they are asking the impossible' (Dumont 1983: 260). He adds in even more explicit terms that difference is always associated with inequality.

I disagree with this statement, because I define the Subject not in universalist, and therefore non-social, terms (as a creature of God, as someone made in God's image, as the possessor of a natural right, or as a citizen of a *polis* based upon a social contract and therefore the rule of law), but in terms of a combination of rational activity and a cultural and personal identity. Democratic society is based upon the attempt to reconcile the two, and not upon conformity to the universal principles of scientific knowledge, which are also mysteriously defined as the principles of moral or aesthetic judgement. The Subject exists at the point where general and particular principles of behaviour meet. This is where I disagree most strongly with Louis Dumont's conception of individualism. Dumont associates individualism with universalism because (I would say

'even though') universalism eliminates particular social and cultural loyalties. Because it has been brutally rejected, particularism then contests
abstract universalism in the name of a concrete, or even an excessively
concrete, differentialism. Its implications are as dangerous as, and even
more tragically destructive than, those of universalist individualism.
Empirical individuals are unequal. Some are stronger, and others (who
may be the same individuals) have a greater capacity for rational thought
or better memories. This is a problem for science, not for ethics or
sociology. The world of ethics is not, however, the world of the categorical imperative or of values. It is the world in which the Subject is
constructed and safeguarded. This is why difference and inequality are
not simply contradictory; the two are inseparable. A society in which
differences are not recognized would be a dictatorship which imposed
norms on its members, a sort of Taylorism extended to the whole of social
life, or even an exercise in ethnic cleansing. Conversely, a society in which
there was no equality would take us back to the hierarchical order of
holistic societies. We destroyed that order at the beginning of our political
modernity, and we have no wish to reconstruct it.

We obviously reject societies which, like the *ancien régime*, are based on
a hierarchy of 'orders', because the development of economic activities
automatically replaces reproductive societies with productive societies,
and estates (*Stände*) with social classes and interest groups. On the other
hand, there is no clear link between the growth of equality and the appeal
to the rule of reason that is so often presented as the theoretical expression
of that practical development. On the contrary, we might say that the
growth of equality provides modern foundations for an inequality which,
no longer being legitimized by tradition, is justified in terms of efficiency
and collective utility.

The republican idea was for a long time associated with the existence,
and even the strengthening, of the social barriers that were needed to keep
apart the élite of rational beings and the masses who could not enter the
realm of reason and whose lives were dominated by their needs, passions
and traditional beliefs. In England, the United States and France, the
theoreticians and leaders of the young democracies of the eighteenth and
early nineteenth centuries were obsessively afraid of the plebs, and were
therefore in favour of a limited democracy which took account of the
unequal distribution of talents. Does it have to be pointed out that
the introduction of 'universal' suffrage in France in 1848 still excluded
women from civil political life, or that Great Britain, that classic home of
democratic society, extended universal manhood suffrage to unskilled
workers only in 1884–5, and that it remains a country in which class
differences are strongly marked? In France, the rationalism of the bourgeoisie was mobilized against the workers' movement as well as against

clericalism. Those who talked of nothing but the equality of citizens in the eyes of the law claimed to be shocked by the suggestion that they should not be defending the rights of all human beings, but only the rights of certain professional categories such as bakers, miners, sailors, or even women and children; they are even more shocked when the most disadvantaged are given differential and preferential treatment. The call for equal civil rights has more than once helped to fuel opposition to social rights, just as it now fuels the refusal to recognize cultural rights. Democracy was originally reduced to meaning the rights of a minority of enlightened citizens, but it was extended when particular categories were granted social or cultural rights, or in other words when relations between equality and difference came to be both recognized and organized. Rather than contrasting equality and difference, we therefore have to recognize that we must reconcile the two if democracy is to develop. It is true, however, that they can be reconciled in very different ways. I will define three of those ways. The relationship or dialogue between them outlines all the ways in which a multi-cultural society can be built.

The meeting of cultures

The first answer seems to be the most direct evocation of the multi-culturalist theme and its connotations. It defines multi-culturalism as a *meeting of cultures*. It asserts the existence of highly structured cultural entities whose identity, specificity and internal logic must be respected, but argues that whilst they are different, they are not totally alien to one another. This is the conception of the anthropologists, who are anxious to struggle against the ethnocentrism that has so often led their societies to destroy, ignore or mutilate the cultures of the societies they dominate or once dominated. Claude Lévi-Strauss argues that defending the diversity of cultures facilitates only limited communication; this protects them from the major threat that one culture, which claims to be the only universalist culture, will gain a hegemony over others (Lévi-Strauss 1952, 1985). What is more, he bases the recognition of differences between cultures on a rejection of all humanism and of any appeal to a universal human Subject. This rejection of humanism is the logical outcome of his structuralist research on the workings of systems of exchange and cultural creations, which is inspired by the discoveries of linguistics. Subjectivities do not communicate. What is more, they are changeable and have little coherence. We will not discover the general laws that govern the workings of the human mind and the systems that shape societies by studying subjectivities, or any other form of consciousness.

At the political level, the recognition of cultural diversity leads to the protection of minority cultures such as the Indian cultures of Amazonia or other parts of the American continent. These are being destroyed, either because their territories are being invaded, because the people are being exterminated, or because the reservations that are being created are hastening the destruction of societies and individuals alike. Within the European world, this conception finds its most concrete application in Great Britain, particularly in that country's immigration policy. Like the policy of indirect rule that was used in India and elsewhere, this policy sets great store by the autonomous organization of immigrant communities. It reduces membership of society to a recognition of the political authorities and constitutional rules that guarantee respect for basic freedoms. This leaves a lot of room for autonomous social and cultural organizations, and therefore a plurality of cultures. The rules under which they operate are, for the most part, no more than a restatement of the Kantian principle of giving everyone complete freedom provided that it does not threaten the freedom of others.

The same conception gives museums an increasing importance in our societies, the views of those who believe that a modern society must eradicate the past and look only to the future notwithstanding. The beginnings of the industrial revolution of the eighteenth century gave rise to the fashion for ruins. The same period saw the birth of archaeology and even the creation of the model of classical Greece. Similarly, our era likes to bring cultural works from different cultures together in museums. The evocation and glorification of national antiquities has largely given way to a desire to communicate with distant worlds, to recognize that they are different, and, at the same time, to find in them common themes and fears or, at the opposite extreme, elements of modernity, such as the emergence of monotheism in the Egyptian culture of the period of Akhenaton and Nefertiti. André Malraux celebrated art's ability to do this.

These examples, which are deliberately chosen from very different areas of social life, show that the quest for inter-cultural communication is a pronounced feature of our society. This intellectual quest is not, however, such an obvious feature of its social practices. This is mainly because, in societies dominated by forms of economic, social and administrative organization that integrate culturally different groups and individuals, we can no longer observe the autonomous cultures studied by anthropologists. Jean-François Bayart (1996) is not wrong to condemn the way identities are arbitrarily constructed by ideologies which are either external to the society in question or are used by ruling groups as instruments of power. In complex societies which are not ruled by communitarianist and authoritarian powers, the situation is characterized by the application of the principle of secularism. This notion implies the lowest level of recognition of cultural diversity, because its underlying logic implies tolerating a diversity of beliefs and customs in the hope that all sections of the population will be gradually and irreversibly assimilated into the universalism of reason and citizenship. This logic is very far removed from the position of Claude Lévi-Strauss and all those who defend cultural diversity. Although this logic appears to be tolerant, it has always resulted in the destruction of local or minority cultures, just as it has stubbornly preserved a hierarchical relationship between men, who are in charge of public life, and women, who are confined to private life.

The fact that there is a hierarchical dimension to all social relations is a further factor in the eradication of differences and the decline in inter-cultural communication in complex modern societies. No matter whether we talk of employers and wage-earners, rich and poor, adults and children, or the literate and the illiterate, we are referring in all cases to an unequal distribution of wealth, power or influence. Is it possible to speak in purely cultural terms of the Turks in Germany, the Algerians or Moroccans in France, or the Jamaicans in Great Britain? The very high level of unemployment affecting the children of immigrants makes it difficult to integrate them into society, and that is an obstacle to the meeting of cultures. And how can cultures meet in a mass society, when almost all the individuals who make it up are involved in production and consumption, but still cling to a collective or personal cultural identity? The recognition of cultural diversity that began with the celebration of tolerance derived its power from the struggle against despotism. The most powerful demonstration of this is Montesquieu's *Persian Letters* (first published in 1721). His initial idea (that we only really understand the culture of others) does not lead to an absolute relativism that would offend his rationalism, but to a critique of the despotism that imposes one type of society and culture. Both freedom and the critique of absolute power begin with tolerance. Many of our contemporaries have reached the same conclusion, and it is critical rather than constructive, either because they worry about the claim that one culture or society has a monopoly on universalism, or because, like Tzvetan Todorov (1981), they have had personal experience of social and cultural diversity, and have seen how the French intellectuals amongst whom they live proclaim their universalist convictions, but do not apply them in either their lives or their books.

The spirit of tolerance, which was so powerful when it was fighting hegemonic ambitions, does not have any real answer to the question raised by relations between the particular and the universal. Or rather, it has a natural tendency to emphasize the recognition of differences, and therefore to observe societies from the outside, like Montesquieu, rather than to live within them, as the legislator or the sociologist must do.

The similarity between cultural experiences

An article by Michael Walzer provides a good account of a second conception of multi-culturalism: 'We respect different expressions of the rule to the extent that we recognize them as a reiteration of the moral effort we ourselves made on similar occasions but in different historical cicumstances and under the influence of different beliefs about the world' (1992: 132). This is what Walzer calls a 'reiterative universalism', and he contrasts it with the domineering law that seeks to impose its authority on all. The origins of this distinction go back to Kant. Whereas scientific judgement is a determinant judgement which moves from the universal to the particular, the judgement of taste, or aesthetic judgement, is a reflective judgement which goes from the particular to the universal. Because I think that there is in my particular experience something that transcends it, I think that others experience the same feelings as I do, albeit on the basis of different experiences; if I am to respect the nature of my own experience, I am obliged to postulate the existence of a shared conception of truth or beauty. But, as Pierre Hassner (1992) rightly points out, in Walzer's conception and, more generally in the transition from particular experiences to the universal, it is the diversity that is real, whilst the point at which particular experiences converge is so distant and so far removed from particular situations and constraints that it tends to mean little more than the Kantian principle of treating others as ends and not as means. This is not, then, a matter of dialogue or communication, but rather of the recognition of the Other. That recognition is indeed essential, as it protects the Other and either leaves intact or restores his or her dignity, but it does not allow experience to be integrated into a whole in which we can all recognize ourselves. Indeed, the meeting of cultures usually leads to a direct clash, rather than to recognition from afar, simply because every culture is a coherent whole, is different from others and protects itself against alien cultures.

Jürgen Habermas's analysis of communicative action rejects this approach and its multi-culturalism. He argues that the norms that are accepted as valid are those, and only those, that express a general will or, in other words and as Kant never ceased to say, that can act as a universal law. The categorical imperative can thus 'play the part of a principle of justification that discriminates between valid and invalid laws in terms of their universalizability: what every rational being must be able to will is justified in a moral sense' (Habermas 1990: 197). This principle obliges the individual to accept as ethical only those norms that are accepted by everyone concerned, and this conclusion leads to a cognitivist conception of ethics based upon reason and its universalizing principle. When it is positive, the outcome of the discussion is indeed a definition of universal norms. But what is the content of the values that are accepted by all as universal, if not the idea of universalism itself? This line of argument is close to that put forward by John Rawls. This universalism is, in accordance with the Enlightenment ideal, based upon reason. But how can this model help us to understand the possibility of communication in societies that have been fractured by social conflicts and fragmented by the existence of so many cultures? Although this is the antithesis of Lévi-Strauss's conception, it too falls back on a non-sociological solution: understanding the unconscious structures of language and social organization and invoking the universalism of reason. But both solutions leave us unable to answer the question: 'How can individuals and groups with different interests and cultures communicate with one another and, therefore, belong to the same society?'

If we base our conception of multi-culturalism on the search for similarities, make it more sociological and restrict its ambitions, we can avoid these criticisms. We cease trying to establish communication between existing communities which, although different, are all looking for the universal meaning of their accepted norms. We attempt to establish communication between collective modes of behaviour that are all striving to resolve the same basic problems: how can we reconcile order and change and, more important still, socialization and individuation? Inter-cultural dialogue is thus replaced by the similarity between cultural experiences. The dialogue between Christianity and Islam is always rather remote for most of the people who find themselves defined, usually by others rather than themselves, as Christians or Muslims. It is much more productive to investigate the comparative history of the secularization of the great religions. In still more concrete terms, we can see that the young people of both the so-called Christian world and the so-called Islamic world are torn between their desire for independence and consumer goods and their loyalty to their families and the norms they transmit.

The answer supplied by this conception is in keeping with the general hypothesis put forward in Part I of this book. In a society characterized by change rather than order, the Subject emerges at the level of personal experience and of the individual will to give a meaning to life, and not at the higher level of highly structured systems: that higher level is so high as to be unreal. Communication is established between different cultures when we realize that the immigrant mother with a sick or injured child feels the same way as we do, when we see Lévi-Strauss's photographs of young Brazilian Indians playing erotic games that look very similar to the games we play, or when the same anthropologist sees our *bricolage* as an expression of the savage mind.

This is tantamount to saying that cultures are not, at least in the modern world in which we live, separate and self-contained entities, but modes of managing change as well as systems of order. More specifically, they do not reject outsiders or see them as enemies. On the contrary, they recognize in the Other the necessary presence of an externality, of a difference, in the same way that the French society of the sixteenth or seventeenth century took an interest in the noble savage. This second approach therefore marks a departure from the idea of an overall, respectful recognition of alterity, because it does not recognize a complete alterity but, rather, more or less distant similarities between cultures.

The recomposition of the world

The weakness of this watered-down form of the second conception is that it is content with a remote and abstract level of inter-cultural dialogue and is restricted to the domain of relations between culture and the environment, or the individual and the group. Unlike the first conception of the meeting between cultures, it does not explain how cultures are constructed.

Cultures cannot be integrated if they are all regarded as particular manifestations of a universal culture which has been reduced to principles that are so general as to be incapable of establishing rules for individual behaviour. Our cultural history has been dominated by the decline of this substantive universalism. Just as real or substantive rationality has been replaced by a formal or instrumental rationality, so the idea that a universal truth can unite humanity has been replaced by the Kantian (and subsequently Weberian) idea of a divorce between the secularized world and the world of values. Modern nationalisms have reached the same conclusion at the political level, and the strength of that conviction has dominated the blood-stained history of the century that has now come to an end.

In our post- and anti-totalitarian societies, the fear of any principle that might legitimize an absolute power is, as Albert Hirschmann (1972) reminds us, so great that many have reverted to the old idea that trade has a civilizing influence and that the supermarket is the most positive expression of a multi-culturalism that has been reduced to a diversity of demands. But this answer has the same weakness as all representations that reduce society to a market. Free trade and the freedom to buy do nothing to prevent discrimination or segregation, and the starting-point for this book is the realization that mass society and cultural identities are drifting further and further apart, and that cultural identities are not being absorbed into a mass society. The problem of inter-cultural communication will not be resolved by economic globalization.

I am therefore inclined to address the problems of inter-cultural communication in the same terms as, in Part I, I addressed the more general problem of the dissociation of instrumentality and identity. The only universalism is that of a Subject defined, not by values or even by an appeal to the universality of its experience, but solely by its attempts to reconcile instrumentality and identity.

When applied to the problem of relations between cultures, the theme of the Subject becomes that of the *recomposition of the world*. The objective is to recuperate and reinterpret all that a rationalizing and voluntaristic modernity eliminated on the grounds that it offended its reason, its universalism, and then its instrumentalism. In the earliest stages of our modernization, we accumulated resources, exacerbated the struggles between the master of change and its victims, confined women within a private life which was itself controlled, colonized whole continents, and, to adopt Claude Lévi-Strauss's famous metaphor, increased the potential difference between a hot pole and a cold pole in order to create energy. The heroic and repressive stage in our modernization, which allowed the leading countries to achieve economic take-off, came to an end when the dominated rebelled and when a productive society gave way, as I have said so often, to an information society. We have learned that our primary objective must be not to master nature, but to master our mastery of nature, that our civilizations are mortal, that our planet may become uninhabitable, and that our cities burn when violence is unleashed. We have therefore undertaken a task that is much greater than economic take-off: the recomposition of a world that we have been decomposing, breaking, manipulating and technologizing for centuries.

The task consists in reuniting what has been separated, recognizing what has been repressed or suppressed, and treating as part of ourselves what we once rejected as foreign, inferior or traditional. This requires much more than a dialogue between cultures. It involves using communication between cultures to construct a human Subject whose monument will never be completed. No one (no individual, society or culture) can claim to be its spokesman or privileged representative. This recomposition of the world does not mean building a new Tower of Babel. It means, first and foremost, resisting demodernization and the dissociation of the world of instrumentality from the world of identity. Industrial society was dominated by the contradiction between two movements: namely the industrial revolution, which concentrated capital, developed technologies and uprooted populations, and a social democracy, which tried to place new social and political controls on economic activity. Similarly, we are now experiencing a constant clash between demodernization and the recomposition of the world. The theme of multi-culturalism remains too vague, and we therefore have to rethink it in the broader context of the recomposition of the world.

All parts of the world are involved in this recomposition. The dominant or central countries have elaborated the new idea of sustainable growth, which means something very different from self-sustaining growth, and have been transformed by the lowering of social barriers, the crisis in an authoritarian-rationalist educational system, and, above all, the action of women. For their part, the dependent countries are trying to reconcile modernization with the defence of their identities, and industrialization with the reduction of social inequalities. Cultural communication is being established between actors, who are like swimmers who are brought closer together and then swept apart by the waves. The wind distorts their voices, and they all speak different languages or give different meanings to the words of the trade language they are all using in an attempt to understand at least something of what is being said.

We are still so influenced by the arrogant image of colonial empires and the conquering bourgeoisie, or of men excluding women from the public space, that our greatest desire is to put an end to abusive dominations, to liberate the dominated, to make heard the voices of national, ethnic, moral, religious and other minorities. This need for pluralism is obvious, and the theme of recognizing the Other is far from having lost its power to bring about a cultural transformation. But we also require a principle of unity, and that principle must be the attempt – which never ends – to reconstruct the individuals and societies which were fragmented once material, intellectual and political resources were concentrated with a view to investment, and lines of resistance were drawn by groups that once had come under the domination of leaders. Multi-culturalism cannot be reduced to meaning an unrestricted pluralism. On the contrary, it must be defined as an attempt to establish communication between, and the partial integration of, cultural ensembles that have long been separated, as were men and women, adults and children, property-owners and dependent workers. The life of a multi-cultural society is organized around both emancipation and communication. If there is no recognition of cultural diversity, the idea of the recomposition of the world may lead us into the trap of a new universalism or the illusory dream of transparency. But without this attempt at recomposition, cultural diversity can lead only to culture wars.

As modernity spreads through very different forms of modernization, it occurs to us that we have to facilitate communication between cultures and put an end to the war between the gods. This takes us as far away as possible from cultural relativism, which rarely means more than an amateurish curiosity that can do nothing to alter the relations of domination, segregation and destruction which allow the weak to be destroyed by the strong, who believe that they are guardians of both the universal and modernity. Communication between cultures will remain impossible or limited so long as we do not accept that all cultures are involved in the same twofold task: creating the Subject and reuniting elements of human experience and thought that have been divorced and separated by the conquering but discriminatory power of Western modernization. We now have to reconcile reason with cultures, and equality with differences. And this is a task for every individual and collective life project.

We can all recompose our inner worlds thanks to the complementary mechanisms of remembrance and estrangement. Remembrance brings into our field of experience things that have been lost, driven out or debased. It is particularly important to breathe new life into what a technocratic civilization has censored because it is supposedly infantile or archaic, and what the dominated regarded as utopian or dominant. Remembrance transforms things that are far removed from us in space and time into memories. A Greek myth, a Gothic cathedral, a paddy-field or a coal mine can thus become part of my experience. This is not a matter of curiosity, or of expanding the field of our knowledge or our emotions, but of forming within each of us a Subject that never merges with our ego. It is a sort of journey punctuated by encounters which estrange the traveller from his social situation.

Remembrance and estrangement, which transform both the traveller and those he discovers, do even more than the meeting of cultures to bring about the recomposition we are discussing. As the living speak and listen, they can find parallels with what they are thinking in the lives and thoughts of the dead. Everyone who has ever lived is part of modernity, and those who live in a modern society will become Subjects only if they remember past or distant cultures and express sympathy for them. Far from being defined by its rejection of the social, political or religious figures of the Subject that came before it, the personal Subject strives to recognize its own image in those figures and even in the way they negate it. As we move further away from the positivism and evolutionism of industrial society, we search more actively for the emancipatory image of the citizen by emancipating it from the absolute power of the state. We seek for the image of the religious Subject and free it from ecclesiastical law and the customs that tradition confuses with religious belief. I hope that, when the dark shadows of Communist totalitarianism have been dispelled, we shall soon also be able to recognize the figure of the Subject that is closest to us: that of the working class and its oppressive but emancipatory labour.

The idea of the personal Subject would be too fragile to help us escape from demodernization were it not that, like all the other figures of the Subject that preceded it, it is striving to reach the point where, as Malraux put it, a historically defined experience encounters something that transcends it. This is a creative quest, but it is also a never-ending quest, as transcendence does more to destroy the personal Subject than to strengthen it. Malraux's work is itself dominated by a tension between the emancipatory appeal to an anti-destiny, to transcendence and faith, and the destruction of the Subject as it disappears into the discourse of religion, revolution, the nation or even art.

The recomposition of the world makes the personal Subject not only a historical Subject but also a tragic Subject. As Malraux said so often, the personal Subject is both actor and witness.

The recomposition of the world does supply principles that allow us to organize and transform public life, but its primary meaning is the recomposition of the individual or the creation of the Subject. The Subject is the desire and ability to reconcile instrumental action with a cultural identity which includes interpersonal relations and a sexual and affective life, as well as a collective and personal memory. Multi-cultural society is not characterized by the coexistence of different cultural practices and values; still less is it characterized by a generalized interbreeding. A multi-cultural society is one in which the greatest possible number of individual lives are constructed, and in which they succeed in reconciling, each in their own way, what makes them similar (instrumental rationality) with what makes them different (the life of the body and the mind, projects and memories). Multi-ethnic and multi-cultural empires have always been fragile, and have always collapsed. Conversely, a society that can recognize the diversity of individuals, social groups and cultures will be a strong society, provided that it can also allow them to communicate with one another by stimulating their desire to see that both they and the Other are involved in the same constructive task.

This language is applicable not only to liberal and tolerant societies; it also applies to societies in which religion is such a powerful force that it cannot be confused with customs or a law, as well as to societies in which exploited or excluded groups are struggling for recognition and to make their voices heard. Conversely, this conception of multi-cultural society opposes both communitarianist homogenization and the arrogance of the conquering reason which has so painfully torn apart the men and women who have become caught up in the Western model of modernization.

Resistance to the idea of a multi-cultural society is strongest in those European countries that identify with the universalist values of modernity, especially in France. In France, the republican idea had to struggle against an ethnic conception of the origins of the nation which, as Jean-Loup Amselle rightly notes, still exists in the discourse of those who speak of 'a hexagonal population composed of a plurality of stocks' (1996: 17). The peripheral countries, and especially those that are most actively committed to economic development, are, by contrast, making huge efforts to reconcile their cultural heritage with their involvement in the globalized economy. Mexico has long been making a conscious attempt to do this, and the work of Octavio Paz is the most highly elaborated political and intellectual expression of that country's quest. But it is in Japan that the will to reconcile the two has had the most profound effects on national and intellectual life, though that country's exceptional economic success has helped. It is not only the national and cosmopolitan élites that live in two worlds; the most oppressed populations, like the Indians of the two Americas, do so too, perhaps even more so. They refuse to be absorbed into either mass culture or a communitarianism that offers them no hope, but they are almost all bilingual, and the fusion of cultures is, for better or worse, now affecting even the most remote regions.

In a world that is changing, where no culture is really isolated, and where men and women from all continents, societies, and all forms and stages of historical development mingle on the streets of the cities, on television screens and on cassettes of world music, it is both ludicrous and dangerous to attempt to defend a timeless identity. If we wish to avoid the purely commercial exploitation of cultural diversity, and if we also wish to avoid a clash of cultures, we therefore have to assign a positive value to these fusions and encounters which allow us all to expand our own experience and to make our own culture more creative.

Europeans who see multi-culturalism as a marginal utopia or a cultural pathology are making a mistake, and they may be its main victims. This book is not outlining an ideal solution for a distant future; I am describing a real situation. And if Europeans refuse to join in the debate, they will set in motion a disastrous process of communitarianization. Universalist principles, in other words, will be confused with particular and historically specific forms of social and cultural organization to such an extent that traditions and forms of thought will be sanctified at the very moment when their particularism is becoming increasingly embarrassing. Globalization is indeed fraught with danger, but it is in many ways irreversible, and it is disturbing to see resistance to globalization hiding behind immortal principles. This transforms a culture into a graveyard for great ideas. They were indeed once a source of life, but they have been fossilized by the cult of memory. This resistance on the part of countries which were once dominant should not in fact surprise us. It is natural that the strongest defenders of multi-culturalism should be the dominated categories, those who have been deprived of their identities by the dominant discourses.

We have a choice between the clash of cultures and the work of reinterpretation and cultural expansion that every individual can bring about, and which our institutions, especially schools and the media, must encourage. The haughty vision of a European culture that identified with the universal and destroyed other cultures or kept them in a marginal or inferior position is now no more than an ideological reflection of the long-gone period when a small part of the world believed that it had a perpetual monopoly on modernity.

A critique of European ethnocentrism is not enough, however. We also have to recognize that isolated communities no longer exist, that culturally different individuals and collectivities now mingle within the open, changing spaces of technological and economic modernity. This situation may lead to the widespread destruction of cultures or to the reduction of personal and collective life to the heteronomous activities of production and consumption. Authoritarian cultural nationalisms are being mobilized to fight this regression. To prevent this disastrous solution, we have to assert our will to cultural individualization, and create a personal and collective cultural Subject that can do everything possible, but always in a particular form, to complete the great task of recomposing the world.

Women and men

The existence of the Subject is deeply involved in relations between men and women, because women's emancipatory action has put an end to the identification of the universal with one particular category of human beings. It is no longer possible to assign the human Subject one central figure; nothing transcends the man–woman duality. This further demonstrates that the Subject subscribes to both rationality and a particular cultural experience. Men and women are similar to the extent that they are thinking beings who work and act rationally, but they are different in biological and cultural terms. Their personalities are shaped in different ways, their self-images are different and they relate to the Other in different ways. Without this emancipatory action and without the abolition of the male monopoly on meaning and power, the idea of the Subject, which I am analysing here, could not have emerged and could not have been formulated. It could not have become central to modern social practices, social movements and emancipatory ideas.

Women's action can in no sense be regarded as the defence of a minority, even if we define that term as meaning a dominated category. It is better defined by the internal debate as to whether priority should be given to equality or to the assertion of difference. And it is not difficult to see that debate as a particular form of the growing divorce between instrumentality and meaning. Despite the importance of the ideas it expresses, the organized women's movement has never won the power, particularly the political power, it might have been expected to win, because it has been torn apart and enfeebled by the general process of demodernization. Demodernization has led to a truly cultural split within the women's movement. On the one hand, there is the hyper-liberal desire to eradicate gender as a factor in the distribution of social roles; on the other, there is a growing obsession with identity. The liberal call to equality was an attempt, and a very conscious attempt in the case of Simone de Beauvoir and Elisabeth Badinter, to eliminate sexual identity from as many modes of social behaviour as possible, and thereby to divorce an asexual public life from a sexualized private life. This argument was similar to that used by the liberals who wanted to ensure that all individuals had equal opportunities, regardless of their social origins. Certain women, however, emphasized their difference to the exclusion of everything else, and thus ran the risk of the confinement that threatens all differentialist movements. They dropped their more concrete demands at the very moment when the gains they had made were being threatened, mainly by religious fundamentalisms.

Just as the working-class movement either exhausted its strength by defending proletarian culture or lapsed into a narrow, market trades-unionism, because it could not elaborate an overall vision of industrial development, so women are divided and weak when they do not have a general concept of society. No general concept of society can be elaborated by contrasting feminine values with masculine values, and trying to do so can be both dangerous and a source of confusion. A general concept can be elaborated by asserting that it is both necessary and possible for all women and all men to reconcile their personal and professional lives and to lead two lives, or in other words to articulate the world of instrumentality with that of identity.

Sociological studies, particularly those carried out in Italy by Simonetta Tabboni (1996a, 1996b), have shown that it never even occurs to women, especially young women, that they might have to choose between professional life and personal life, whereas men feel restricted to their professional lives. When they do try to reconcile the two halves of their existence, they try to imitate successful women, because they have no male model of their own to turn to.

The fact that it is women rather than men who are elaborating a recomposed life model confirms the general hypothesis that it is the dominated actor, not the dominant actor, who plays the main role in the recomposition of the world. Because masculinity has been constructed by dominating femininity, men have great difficulty in finding their own way to recompose their personalities. They either imitate women or experience their inability to reconcile the two halves of their lives as a personal failure. Whilst they recognize the positive value of reconciling the two, they do not have a clear idea of how they can do it, because they are still trapped in their old dominant position. Industrial society was a man's society or was, in other words and as historians of political life have shown, based upon a male/female hierarchy. The contemporary world (and not only in the most highly industrialized societies) is, in the face of stiff resistance, constructing what might be called a feminized culture to the extent that women are more actively involved than men in articulating the divorced halves of human experience. And it is no accident that the new social movements should, for the first time, be largely organized by women, whereas the working-class movement and even national liberation struggles were, in the vast majority of cases, led by men.

Women do not want simply to abolish or minimalize the inequalities they suffer and to win the right to decide freely how to live their lives. They have also revealed to all the existence of such a new field of social and cultural behaviour that no intellectual definition of the contemporary world is possible unless we focus both our thought and our action on that field.

The reluctance of so many countries, governments, media and universities to recognize this fact, and their tendency to give women's problems a purely secondary importance, has a negative effect on society as a whole. How can we fail to draw general conclusions from the fact that it is the women's movement, or in other words a movement based upon a particular identity and not an appeal to purely universal principles, that has led to changes in the legislation that codified the discrimination that victimized women? France has learned from the experience of granting women unequal access to positions of responsibility, and particularly political responsibility, and is now beginning to learn that the call for parity is more effective than a purely universalist call for equal rights.

Just as the central debate in industrial society focused on the representation and social status of wage-earning workers, so the central debate in post-industrial society is focused on women's role in society. As the role of the Subject has always been denied them, women have to win the right to be social actresses and not the equals of men. And they can do so only by demanding both equality at work and sexual freedom, especially where their reproductive function is concerned. They can thus escape from the social order in two senses, by obliging both men and women to define themselves other than in purely social terms. Like the gay and lesbian movements, the women's movement is a reaction against a normative moralism, and it therefore reveals the Subject to be an attempt to bring about the antagonistic reconciliation of pleasure and reality.

The women's movement is trying to use economic independence and sexual freedom to escape the social order. This is difficult, and the attempt may well end in failure; but it does define a space for a female culture that is both different from, and analogous with (and equal to), men's cultural space. Those who defend customs (such as female circumcision) or legal rules that inscribe women's subordination on their bodies and in their behaviour in the name of respect for cultural differences are not defending a multi-culturalist society based upon freedom of choice. They are imprisoning women within the dominant discourse of a culture and its customs. It is even true to say that our Western culture can pride itself on having made women's liberation possible, provided that we also add that the desocialization of women has often transformed them into commodities. It is true, however, that the reign of the commodity affects men too. What is more, sexual freedom and rejection of the traditional canons of morality that restrict the management of sexuality to perpetuating the family and its heritage do facilitate the formation of a Subject that can freely manage the relationship between its sexuality and the instrumental world.

What has been termed 'women's liberation' (or, for that matter the liberation of colonized countries and exploited classes) is not simply a matter of destroying a hierarchical social order for the benefit of the laws of the market. It leads to the discovery of a women's culture, and to communication between that culture and the culture of men – hence the importance of research into the effects of this cultural gap on every domain of social organization, from education to medical care, from communication in the work-place to the practice of law. Women's freedom is a central element in the construction of a multi-cultural society, because it ensures that men and women have equal professional and economic opportunities, and that their respective cultural spaces play equal but specific roles in the implementation of basic human rights. The multi-culturalism that was based upon the separation of social categories such as lords and serfs, or clerics and laymen, is giving way to a new multi-culturalism based upon communication rather than distance. Men and women live together, often bring up and educate children together, and have sexual and affective relations. The relationship between men and women therefore illustrates, more so than any other, the fact that multi-culturalism is primarily an attempt at communication. Communication presupposes the existence not only of common languages, but also of messages with a different content and form, different expectations and, equally, different interpretations of the same message. Communication between men and women is the central element in the recomposition of the world, and I regard that recomposition as the primary form of multi-culturalism. Multi-culturalism must mean communication rather than distance, and interaction rather than a distrustful aparthood.

Whilst it is true that the gay and lesbian movement has a central role to play in the creation of erotic theories and practices that are unrelated to the social functions of sexuality, its importance must in no sense obscure the fact that an analysis of relations between men and women is an important aspect of our study of the human Subject. The women's movement has played, and still plays, a decisive role in the cultural changes we are living through. Its primary effect is to point to the need for a new analysis of the position of men and male behaviour, and above all, as Christine Castelain-Meunier (1997) has shown, for new ways of thinking about relations between men and women, and therefore the family. A recognition of the differences between the sexes will do more than any indeterminate humanism to bring about the recomposition of a world in which men and women can overcome the traditional opposition between the private and the public, and between authority and affection. In such a world, men and women will be neither completely the same nor completely different.

Identity politics

It also has to be said that the idea of a multi-cultural society is incompatible with identity politics, because it is based on an attempt to facilitate inter-cultural communications and because, like any conception of democracy, it implies the recognition of a plurality of interests, opinions and values. Talk of identity politics, by contrast, introduces a necessary link between a culture, a society and a politics, and that, I repeat, defines a community. Once a population defined (at least in part) by a culture is ruled by a political power that speaks in its name and has authority over it, we leave the domain of culture and enter that of community. This is all the more dangerous in that the cultures that have to be defended are usually minority cultures, and must therefore resort to violence in a democratic society which is subject to majority rule. Whenever one category acts solely in the name of its difference, it runs the risk of being drawn to violence and provoking its own rejection. Feminism – and particularly American feminism – has learned this to its cost. The more emphasis it placed on the theme of difference, the more it became a minority movement.

As a result, the most radical women's movements have begun to denounce identity politics. They have noticed that the assertion of feminist identity goes hand in hand with discrimination against lesbians, and that the assertion of a lesbian identity is in turn (at least in the United States, where the Queer movement is powerful) linked to discrimination against Afro-American, Hispanic-American and even butch lesbians. This has led radical lesbians to make a theoretical about-turn of great import-ance, which has been well analysed by Catharine Stimpson (in an as yet unpublished text). Rather than pursuing the assertion of an increasingly fragmented identity, they have gone back to studying the general theme of sexuality, which had been eclipsed by the stress on gender. In any analysis of the Subject, this theme must play as important a role as that of cultural identity. And this work on sexuality is the women's movement's most important contribution. It takes us beyond both liberal egalitarianism and the assertion of identity that has sustained some of the movement's most radical currents. We now know that the man–woman duality is the most general expression of the human Subject, which, far from identifying with reason, always stands at the point where rational action (which is imper-sonal) encounters the individual and collective particularity of every human being. What sometimes looks like a politically correct affectation – using 's/he' rather than 'he', for example – has major implications.

Identity politics is the antithesis of demand-based action. It is true that those who tried to reduce the struggles of women, ethnic minorities or immigrants, as well as of homosexuals, to specialist 'fronts' within a general class struggle were defeated and outflanked by the men or women they were trying to lead. The challenge to the ruling ideological, political and social order did, and does, introduce a democratic and popular dimension into the defence of the cultural rights of minorities and women. This makes them stronger, and transforms the whole of society. Identity politics, like purely universalist appeals to citizenship, works against the multi-cultural society.

The integration of immigrants

Given the rise of communitarianisms and their obsession with purity, our societies, which are subject to multiple influences, rapid changes and the fragmentation of their norms, must, said Georg Simmel, tolerate and organize a certain level of heterogeneity. The city is innovative because it makes it possible for everyone to be an outsider, and because it allows individuals from different social milieux and cultural backgrounds to meet and interact. Schools cannot help to reduce inequalities of opportun-ity unless they throw together children from different origins and accept that there are several ways of reaching the same objectives: namely a certain level of coherent rational thought and an ability to communicate and innovate.

When Simmel spoke of foreigners, he was thinking of the Jews of Berlin. We now immediately think of the situation of immigrants or the descendants of recent immigrants from non-European countries. We think of Arabs, Muslims, Turks, people from Black Africa, or of the Vietnamese and Chinese who have come from Vietnam or elsewhere. Many countries in Western Europe are asking themselves how they can integrate these foreign populations. The question is posed in particularly acute terms in Switzerland, but also in France, where the *Beurs* must, in sociological terms and at least in the short term, be regarded as the descendants of immigrants. Defining them in those terms increases the proportion of immigrants in the population at large, and makes it much higher than in Germany or Great Britain. But immigration also poses serious problems in Italy, where the number of immigrants is much lower, and even in Spain, where it is lower still.

There are two very different solutions to this problem, but they are equally far removed from the idea of a multi-cultural society. The first is assimilation, which is facilitated both by a unitary and integrative educational system and by mass consumerism. Even in periods of high unemployment, assimilation is more successful than we might believe. In the United States, many of those who are now known as African-Americans in fact live as Black Americans, even though racial prejudices and racial barriers are still particularly strong in that country. In France, the most recent studies carried out by INED under the direction of Michèle Tribalat show that many immigrants from the Maghreb rapidly make the transition from speaking Arabic or Berber to speaking French, and that a high proportion of them enter into sexual and matrimonial relations with non-Maghrebian partners (Tribalat 1996). Such assimilation occurs more easily at the local level than the national level. Young *Beurs* find it easier to describe themselves as *Marseillais* or *Lyonnais* than as French or Algerian, and often identify with a neighbourhood, a housing estate or even a gang of young people. But the experiences of America and France show that a high level of assimilation does not preclude strongly negative reactions and racist prejudices. In France, the proportion of the population that rejects immigrants is much greater than the proportion that actually votes for the National Front.

Assimilation has been the dominant solution only in those countries with a high level of immigration from countries that are culturally close to the host country. The principal melting pot was Argentina, where, thanks largely to state education, large numbers of Spanish, Italian and other immigrants were quickly integrated and granted Argentine nationality from the end of the First World War onwards. That, however, is a borderline case, and the situation is very different in Europe or North America, where immigrants came to a country that no longer had either an open internal frontier or a rapid rate of economic growth.

The alternative solution is to give the immigrant population a separate status or to organize it into homogeneous and self-governing communities. Such is the situation of the Turks in Germany, or that of the 'Chinatowns' of both the United States and France. The British or Dutch policy of recognizing ethnic communities gives rise to a situation similar to that just described. The advantage of this is that the community can act as an intermediary between the individual and the country he has entered, and this makes it possible to cushion the shocks and reactions occasioned by the French mode of integration. The disadvantage is that it makes inter-communitarian clashes much more likely.

Neither of these solutions is appropriate to a multi-cultural society. The first seeks to dissolve particular cultures into a unitary national community identified with a universal; the second respects the plurality of cultures, but does not establish any communication between them. More important still, it has no means of reacting to the relations of inequality and segregation that disadvantage minority communities or communities made up of the poorest and least qualified. We can therefore leave these extreme conceptions on one side, though we must recognize that they do attempt to deal with major problems.

The argument I am putting forward here is that the more we view multi-cultural society as an encounter between cultures and communities, the more likely we are to provoke dangerous clashes over immigration. If, on the other hand, we try to unite different cultures within the lived experience and life projects of individuals, we have a greater chance of success.

If we describe Maghrebian, African or Turkish emigration to France as an encounter between Christendom and Islam, we can predict that the majority, now redefined as Christendom or in other words as a community, will be conscious of the fragility and even the artificiality of that definition, and will react negatively to a culture which seems threatening because it is more communitarian and therefore stronger. The only way to assuage that feeling of being threatened is for the majority to make sure that this community remains marginal and apart, and to ensure that, whilst it is involved in economic activity, it makes no attempt to integrate into society. This leads to neither integration nor communication, but rather to segregation and to forms of rejection that can range from suspicious curiosity to aggression. That outcome is so obvious that the concrete policies adopted by Western countries with large numbers of immigrants have tried to reconcile social integration with cultural recognition, which is as far removed from communitarianism as it is from assimilation.

Didier Lapeyronnie (1992, 1993) has shown that the differences between British and French immigration policies are not as great as one might think. Great Britain does of course recognize communities, but it also recognizes that immigrants from Commonwealth countries have British citizenship, and its objective is to ensure that this two-tier policy integrates them into the nation. France, by contrast, does not recognize communities, and tries to integrate individuals. This can supposedly be done by granting them French nationality (in 1995 the number of individuals who gained French nationality was greater than the number of new immigrants), but social workers work with associations that often have strong ethnic identities. And we have seen demonstrators chanting the slogan 'Blacks, beurs blancs, tous unis' ('Blacks, *Beurs* and Whites, Unite'), which makes a more direct appeal to multi-culturalism than 'Vivons ensemble avec nos différences', which was the theme of the *Beur* march of 1983. The difference between a policy of insisting on integration and a policy that does more to recognize differences is, then, a matter of degree, and the two are not totally contradictory. To his great credit, Didier Lapeyronnie not only shows us how to escape from what has become a somewhat artificial dichotomy, but also demonstrates the weaknesses of the very notion of integration. That notion presupposes the idea of a national society into which immigrants are supposed to integrate. Lapeyronnie argues that the most obvious feature of Western countries like Great Britain and France is that, having created the idea of a nation-society, they are now rejecting it. Economic and social reality is becoming divorced from the cultural field; lack of involvement in professional and economic life militates against cultural integration. Integration can therefore degenerate into communitarian protests, whilst non-involvement in professional and economic life undermines the reference to cultural values and social norms.

This divorce can lead to two contrasting situations: a high level of involvement without integration or, conversely, integration without involvement. The former predominated in the post-war period, when we spoke of 'immigrant workers', a phrase which is now used only in Germany (*Gastarbeiter*), where involvement without integration is still the norm. The latter took on a greater importance with the rise in unemployment, particularly in France. It often takes the form of what Robert K. Merton's paradigm of anomic behavioural patterns terms 'deviant hyperconformity', or a consumerism that is not interested in how individuals become consumers. The first solution does not lead to a multi-cultural society, but it does allow us to arrive at a peaceful combination of economic involvement and cultural autonomy. The second solution leads to a disintegration in two senses. Becoming part of the host society implies the adoption of a way of life that presupposes skills and an income that immigrants do not possess. The problem is usually encapsulated in the critical formula: we are trying to integrate immigrants into a society that is disintegrating. This is something of an overstatement, but it does at least stress the major weakness of the idea of integration. Not only is it difficult to see how the unemployed can be integrated into society; it may actually be dangerous to speak of their integration, or of their entry into a new society and a new culture.

The one objective that is in keeping with the idea of a multi-cultural society is the reconciliation of instrumental rationality with the active defence of a cultural identity. The two can be reconciled only at the level of personal behaviour, but they must also encourage a dialogue between communities. Once it has been decommunitarianized, a traditional culture can support a personal identity that is subject to heavy pressures when immigrants begin to become involved in a society, a culture and an educational system that are very different from those associated with their background. Unless these values are internalized, there can be no multi-cultural society, as a multi-cultural society reconciles a unitary social organization with a plurality of cultural loyalties and references. That is how we should interpret the slogan 'Let us live and work together, and at the same time recognize our cultural differences'.

This conception of integration can and must be applied to all, and not to immigrants alone. Intellectuals who have been shaped by their national language and culture have to perform on a stage that is largely dominated by organizations that produce and distribute culture, and those organizations are either international or American. From that point of view, the situation of the intellectual is not, in general terms, very different from that of the Maghrebian or Turkish worker who comes to work in a car plant in Paris or Stuttgart. Far from regarding immigrants as a marginal category, we should regard them as a population living in the midst of problems that are everyone's problems. Their failures are obvious. Their successes, and their brave attempts to reconcile past and present in order to create a future, should be equally obvious, as they were in the United States in the heyday of the 'American dream', and as they were when European immigrants left 'to build America' in Argentina or Uruguay. The rejection of immigrants is an expression of a sense of insecurity, and it reveals the absence of a personal project. Recognizing the centrality of immigrants may be a more effective weapon against xenophobia and racism than an over-defensive liberalism.

Can a national society be multi-cultural? It is certainly difficult. To take a trivial example, it is impossible for a single country to make Sunday, Saturday and Friday days of rest for different groups. But this immediate objection also shows where the solution lies. Communitarian habits and customs are usually preserved by authorities, and are usually only distantly (if at all) related to the values of the community in question. They therefore cannot be preserved in a mass urban society. On the other hand, the pressures brought to bear by that urban society force the essential components to become divorced from their communitarian forms. Which brings us back to the central principle of our analysis: inter-cultural communication requires the decommunitarianization and internalization of beliefs and convictions, and therefore the separation of social space from cultural space that defines secularization and secularism. Christianity was decommunitarianized by the gradual modernization of the West. Conversely, a defensive retreat on the part of an Arab world that is in crisis or a state of collapse will sustain or strengthen a communitarian Islam.

Ethnicity

This internalization is not confined to innovators or entrepreneurs. It also occurs in dominated categories, where it may take the form of ethnicity. Ethnicity is the opposite of the communitarian ethnic consciousness that we can see spreading, with disastrous results, in so many parts of the world. Ethnicity is in fact an assertion of a culture that has been internalized by individuals living in a modern society, or in other words by individuals who recognize the importance of economic and administrative organization. Ethnicity and communitarianism often seem very similar, but the two orientations are not to be confused. Some of the girls who demand the right to wear a veil or an Islamic headscarf at school are demonstrating, either spontaneously or as a result of the pressures brought to bear by their families or some association, that they are resisting a so-called Western culture in the name of the laws of their community; but published studies of girls, both in France and in Turkey, by no means suggest that they are in the majority. On the contrary, this assertion of identity is nothing more than a reaction to the way their culture has been rejected. In the Middle East, it has been noted that the women who display their loyalty to Islam in this way are students in the faculty of science, not the faculty of humanities.

The violent rejection of the Islamic headscarf by the majority of French teachers, intellectuals and politicians shows that inter-cultural communication has come up against a consciousness and principles with a potential for intolerance. The same phenomenon has been noted in the case of the long delays in recognizing regional languages and cultures, which have been either marginalized or passively tolerated by the educational system. In this context, it is, as Michel Wieviorka has stressed, essential to note

the growing importance of the ethical dimension in a Jewish consciousness which has always spoken of the Jewish people, but which increasingly
combines an involvement in universalist activities with an awareness of
tradition, especially intellectual tradition, and loyalty to the state of
Israel.

All this leads me to conclude that a multi-cultural society can exist only
if no majority ascribes a universal value to its own way of life. French
thought still usually rejects the idea of ethnicity, and prefers, when it does
fight racism, to call for the integration of immigrants into a society
dominated by universalist values. Many French intellectuals who once
supported some very fundamentalist groups are now deserting groups
that are dominated by a consciousness of their ethnicity. They are afraid
of encouraging the existence on French soil of movements that resort to
political violence, as in the Basque Country, Corsica and Ireland. They
are also afraid that public opinion will assume that they are linked to the
Islamist forces which have on several occasions committed violent acts of
terrorism on French soil. But these arguments are scarcely convincing.

French public opinion has increasingly allowed itself to be persuaded
that there is a link between unemployment, poverty, marginality, violence,
fundamentalism and terrorism, as though some fatal chain of events led
from an economic handicap to an active and violent rejection of the
national society. The open and generous image of the Republic has been
transformed into a rejection of immigrants, and this has been exacerbated
by worries about economic insecurity and unemployment, especially
among those popular categories which have, thanks to growth, succeeded
in becoming part of the middle-class majority and which fear that they
may lose their new-found social status. To ward off that threat, they do all
they can to keep away from the social categories below them, and
especially from immigrants.

The memory of France's republican and national ideals gives the rejection of immigrants the appearance of a noble cause, but it is part of the
same trend as racism. And it is in the name of equality of opportunity that
parents take their children out of state schools and enrol them in private
schools where they are in no danger of being handicapped by the presence
of so many children of immigrants. The outcome is greater segregation.

For majority public opinion, the consciousness of ethnicity is thus
reduced to being the opposite of what it really is. Ethnicity is accused of
confining immigrants to their communities, whereas it is in fact an expression of a desire to be integrated into society. Public opinion, in France and
elsewhere, should be looking more carefully at the success of those who
combine an awareness of their ethnicity with a desire to be integrated into
society. Young immigrants living in difficult economic conditions
sometimes do better at school than young French people who live in

equally poor conditions but who experience them as a loss of status and have no personal projects for the future. Conversely, their lack of involvement in the economy, unemployment and job insecurity lead some young immigrants to try to escape anomie by turning for support to gangs or local associations, the most active of which have a religious orientation. Some of them give that religious orientation a hostile and aggressive content, and reject a society which has, they feel, rejected them. In the Lyons area and in the Nord *département* there have even been several cases in which there is a link between criminal behaviour and Islamist militancy. Here, we see rejection of a society which has itself rejected, marginalized and excluded the immigrants whom it blames for its growing difficulties.

The real choice is between an awareness of ethnicity combined with social integration and an awareness of discrimination that leads to violence. The idea that assimilation is the only solution leads to the American model, or in other words to the assimilation of a majority and the rejection and segregation of a large minority.

Cultural democracy

In a world of intense cultural exchanges, there can be no democracy unless we recognize the diversity of cultures and the relations of domination that exist between them. The two elements are equally important: we must recognize the diversity of cultures, but also the existence of cultural domination. If they become divorced, the two aspects of the multi-culturalist conception of society become distorted, and can come to mean the opposite of what they should mean. The struggle for the liberation of cultural minorities can lead to their communitarianization, or in other words their subordination to an authoritarian cultural power. Conversely, the recognition of diversity can lead to self-segregation, with each culture trapping itself within a territory and regarding any attempt at communication that comes from the outside as an act of aggression.

Cultural liberation must be combined with an attempt to promote cultural communication, and this presupposes both an acceptance of diversity and a recourse to a principle of unity. I call that principle the 'recomposition of the world'. Recomposing the world is itself a form of cultural liberation, as it offers a reinterpretation of that which has been discarded or repressed by proto-modernization. The construction of a multi-cultural society comes up against the same difficulty as any democratic undertaking: an emancipatory movement always implies the rejection of something, but must also recognize both the Other and pluralism.

Far from breaking with the democratic spirit and the individualistic universalism on which it is based, the multi-cultural society is a product of the democratic idea, because it recognizes a plurality of interests, opinions and values. That is why it is so threatened by the complementary aspects of what I call 'demodernization': mass culture, on the one hand, and the obsession with identity, on the other. Cultural globalization and cultural fundamentalisms can so easily lead to the extermination of minorities in the name of ethnic or religious cleansing.

Cultural democracy struggles, on the one hand, to allow the greatest possible number of cultures to use technologies and means of communication, and, on the other hand, to re-establish the autonomy of cultures, which can be creative only if they are the products of real collectivities. These two objectives can easily come into conflict. The use of technology can lead to the triumph of mass culture and its masters, who have the ability to reinterpret everything produced by all the cultures of the past; conversely, real collectivities can lead to an intolerant cultural nationalism. This contradiction is of the same nature as the contradiction that exists between economic liberalism and the corporatist protectionism which safeguards vested interests that can then be transformed into privileges. The fact that, in modern societies, information technologies are compatible with a great number of different experiences means, however, that they can be overcome.

In our societies, it is no longer possible to say that we are democrats if we do not accept the idea of a multi-cultural society. Many men and women do reject that idea, however, and cling to the ideal of a society based upon an individualist–universalist conception of rights. That position, and it can be an honourable one, increasingly encourages the perpetuation of practices that create inequalities. In France in particular, it is no longer possible to believe that the educational system, which refuses to take children's private lives into consideration, is the best means of promoting the equality of all or of reducing the real inequalities that exist. The school system favours the central categories which implement a system of rules, laws and technologies, and creates obstacles for both innovators and children from dominated cultures. Nor does it do anything to teach children to manage concrete changes.

France was ahead of most other countries when it came to establishing a political democracy, but it was very slow to construct a social democracy. Is France now in danger of falling even further behind in the construction of a cultural democracy, and of being trapped in a model that is too particular and too authoritarian to be understood and adopted by other countries? In a world of change, an obsession with essences, traditions and absolutes can lead only to cultural decline.

6

The Nation

The political Subject

Whilst the state has to be discussed in terms of political organization, authority and legitimacy, the nation is a different matter. If we use the term 'the French nation' to describe all those who have been granted French nationality by the state, it is a descriptive category; but it also refers to a collectivity of citizens, and that collectivity is so particular that the word 'nation' cannot be applied to the population of all states. The nation defines itself as founding the state, as though the nation acquired a state, rather than being constituted by it. The immediate objection to this statement is that nations come into being as imagined communities, as Benedict Anderson (1991) puts it, and not as political systems. According to the same author, the combination of capitalism and print culture does a lot to explain the formation of modern nations. Yet this statement too meets with strong objections, especially if we apply it to Europe, where nations emerged despite the relative isolation of local societies and cultures, or *pays* which survived for a very long time – until the end of the nineteenth century in the case of France, even though that country was supposedly unified and centralized long before then.

The idea of the nation is political rather than cultural or communitarian. The United States provides an extreme example of the truly political definition of the nation, as the cultural homogeneity of the East Coast states was rapidly swamped by the arrival of immigrants from many different countries. The communitarian definition seems, by contrast, more appropriate where the nation-state is a late phenomenon; but even in that case, the nation desired a state, and the community became a nation when it became self-reflective and conscious of being a political society.

Under what conditions can a nation establish a state? If the nation were no more than the political and administrative expression of a network of activities and exchanges that extends beyond the framework of the feudal estate or even the city-state, it would be no more than a population subordinated to an authority, and would not necessarily have any unity or national consciousness. It has been said that there are two nations in Canada, even though that country's inhabitants all have the same nationality, and it was difficult to speak of the Soviet nation. Conversely, the ethnic definition of a nation does not always coincide with the frontiers of a state, as is particularly obvious in Central Europe and in the states that have been born out of the breakup of the Soviet Union. A nation exists thanks only to a combination of economic organization and an awareness of a cultural identity. That combination presupposes the capacity to make political decisions, and that capacity is all the greater when the principle of the sovereignty of the people is recognized.

The nation is therefore a political figure of the Subject, because, like any figure of the Subject, it reconciles an instrumental activity with a cultural identity by constituting itself as a space of freedom. This ideal conception does not fully coincide, however, with either of the types of nation with which we are most familiar. Both types are ideological, and have the power to mobilize.

In one case, the association between state and nation is so close that the two are indistinguishable. The state appears to be nothing more than the power of the nation, but the nation was created by the state, its army, its administration and its educational system. In the United States and France, there is also a pronounced tendency to regard the state as the embodiment of the universal values proclaimed by the American Constitution and the motto of the French Republic. As a result, the higher interest of the state must coincide with the sum total of particular interests. This conception is very close to that of the liberal economists who, from Adam Smith to Bentham, argued that an invisible hand could reconcile particular interests with the general interest or the common good. In so far as they are political societies, neither France nor the United States fully conforms to this ideology, which can lead to a republican statism. We do, however, find this dream of a Janus-faced power – state on the one hand, nation on the other – in many countries.

In the second case, nationality from above is replaced with nationality from below. The state is the political agent of a community which is not defined as a nation in political terms, but in cultural, ethnic, religious and above all territorial terms. In multi-communitarian states, which in fact behave like empires, this conception leads every community to demand its political independence.

If we compare these images, we find that they both tend to eclipse the nation. This is more obvious in the second case, where the nation usually disappears behind the idea of the people; in the former case the nation becomes a body, and the state the head that rules it and speaks on its behalf.

Because communitarianist movements and states are now so powerful, there is a pronounced tendency, especially in European countries, but also in other continents that are resisting this development, to fall back on the position of defending the state against both the market and communities. There is therefore a danger that the great ideas of the nation and the republic will be reduced to meaning the defence of an administration and of those categories that are contractually linked to the state, as well as the status and subsidies that protect their vested interests.

Before we look at how nationalisms have destroyed the nation, we must rediscover the mediating role that the latter once played. We then have to ask ourselves if the nation can still function as a *political Subject*, or if, in other words, it can still mediate between the economic and political management of a society that is open to international competition and communitarian identities which are becoming depoliticized and fragmented.

Nation-state and citizenship

Let us now go back to the two main forms of the state–nation relationship. The two types of nation-state we have identified, and which can be respectively described as the nation-state and the nationalistic state, are very different, and we find in them a very different relationship between the individual and political society. Just as there are two forms of nation-state, so there are two conceptions of citizenship.

Citizenship implies, first of all, the idea of a collective consciousness or general will. And, from Hobbes to Rousseau, that idea has led not to a liberal democracy which respects basic human rights, but to the republican spirit and the freedom of the Ancients. According to this conception, political society is the realm of freedom and equality, whereas civil society is dominated either by tradition and privilege or by individual self-interest, and is therefore constantly threatened by violence and chaos. Order creates freedom, just as the reality principle must dominate the pleasure principle, and just as the royal courtiers' internalization of the constraints of power led, according to Norbert Elias, to the emergence of the modern Subject. The idea of the republic suggests duties, and even the sacrifices that the citizen must be willing to make to defend and make viable the community of citizens. This concept of citizenship transforms the state into a nation-state, and the personal prince into a collective prince, or in other words the people. Only the sovereignty of the people can confer legitimacy upon the state.

The other conception of citizenship, which can also be found in both types of state, is different, in that it asserts that individuals have rights not because they are members of political society but because they are human beings, as defined by the Declaration of the Rights of Man and of the Citizen. They therefore have rights over powers and institutions, and even, if need be, rights that can be used against them. This approach to citizenship gives individuals safeguards based upon natural law, and the positive law of the state cannot infringe upon those guarantees. The primacy of natural law is inscribed in the Constitution, and must determine the application of the mechanisms that ensure that laws are constitutional. The United States has always had such a system, with the Supreme Court at its pinnacle. After the end of the First World War, its example was imitated by some European countries, beginning, thanks to the influence of Hans Kelsen and Tomas Masaryk, with Austria and Czechoslovakia. In France, the 1958 Constitution's establishment of a *Conseil constitutionnel* was a much later development, but it occasioned no debate and no serious political crisis, even though the transition from a situation in which the National Assembly had absolute power to one in which laws were subject to constitutional checks marked a transition from one definition of citizenship to another.

How was it possible for a single nation to reconcile principles as different as the sovereignty of the people and human rights, when it is so obvious that the Declaration of Rights of 1789 juxtaposes them but does not integrate them? It was done by reducing the individual to a rational being and by defining society as an equally rational construct. This could be done in the West, where the model for development was based upon the divorce between the rational and the non-rational, identified respectively with modernity and tradition. The tracing of a frontier between private life and public life perpetuated the tradition of the Greek *polis*. A society was constructed on the basis of an opposition between those beings who were capable of taking part in public life and those – meaning primarily women – who had to be confined to private life. The theme of the nation as a community of free citizens was therefore, as is so often the case in egalitarian movements, associated with the rule of the *sanior pars*, or of wise and rational men who could reason, calculate, defend their interests and control their passions. In historical terms, universalist rationalism was associated with the triumph of a bourgeois oligarchy, and the founders of the American Republic, like the Whigs in

	National-liberal state	*Nationalistic state*
Rights of man and citizen	*Constitutional democratic state*	*Liberal nationalist state*
Communitarian citizenship	*Institutional state*	*National-communitarian state*

England and like Tocqueville and the French liberals, favoured the view that only adult males who were of sound mind and economically independent should exercise political rights. There was naturally a conflict between poll-tax democracy and democratic demands in all nation-states.

We find two contrasting forms of relationships between individuals and political society in nationalistic states too. In certain countries, the state was identified with modernization, and became a magnet for those who wanted to control modernization or be part of it. In other countries, the state acquired an absolute legitimacy by defining itself as the servant of a belief and a community.

These types of political participation are as different as our types of state. It is therefore possible to tabulate forms of state corresponding to the four types created by the interplay between the two binary pairs we have defined.

In the most democratic nation-states, which can draw on the strengths of a shared culture, shared experiences and a collective memory, as well as on national solidarity against enemies and obedience to the same laws, these analytic types are rarely found in a pure state.

A typology such as this contrasts the most and the least democratic types, but it also reveals the existence of two very different intermediary types. One is the institutional-republican type, which has always had great influence in France, and which can evolve either into the constitutional democratic model or, like Jacobinism itself, into Bonapartism. The other is the liberal nationalism which inspired the nationality movements of Central Europe and Hispanic America to rise up against empires that were both foreign and authoritarian.

Rather than stressing the differences between these types, we should be emphasizing the twofold duality that defines the national theme. The idea of citizenship and its universalist component inspired political liberation movements in Holland and the United Provinces, in England and, a century later, in the United States and France, where they brought about what we regard as the founding democratic revolutions. But we also find the same ideas in German thought. We find them in the thought of Herder and even Fichte, who were by no means pure nationalists, even if the latter was so rabidly anti-French as to proclaim the natural superiority of the German language (Fichte 1968). Both insisted that

those peoples who were subject to the cultural dominance of Great
Britain, and especially France, had a right of access to modern civilization. For both Fichte and Herder this meant primarily the German
people, but Herder also defended the rights of the peoples of the Baltic
and the Balkans.

To put it more simply, how can we contrast Ernest Renan, who is the
official spokesman for the French conception of the nation, with the
German *völkisch* conception, when the will to live together and the soul
that Renan describes so well are based, in both his view and that of the
German thinkers, on a shared culture and history, and on a shared destiny
as well as a democratic affirmation?

It is not the German reference to a national community that makes the
French or the American tradition superior to the strong German tradition. It is the German acceptance of social hierarchies, which, as Louis
Dumont reminds us, is still visible in Fichte, even though he defended the
French Revolution. And it is this that gives German nationalism its
authoritarian content. The American, and especially the French, idea of
the nation was, by contrast, associated with the destruction of privileges,
and therefore with the democratic spirit.

At a certain moment of modernity, the nation was the political figure of
the Subject. Like all figures of the Subject that correspond to a limited
degree of historicity, it was an unmediated expression of the Subject. At
the same time, it objectified the Subject and transformed it into the social
order's meta-social guarantor. It made it both incarnate and metaphoric.
Citizenship reduces the individual to a citizen, or in other words to someone who accepts the laws and needs of the state, and who has rights only if
he does his duty and makes a contribution to what is collectively useful or
to the general interest. At the same time, citizenship asserts that political
power's only legitimate basis is the sovereignty of the people. Within the
national idea there has never been any clear dividing line between the
republican idea of the general will, which can easily become authoritarian,
and the democratic idea of majority rule.

This is why historical nations cannot be divorced from nation-states,
even though they may found them, and why they cannot be identified with
democracy. They were not established thanks to the removal of internal
frontiers alone; the defence and conquest of international frontiers were
just as important. What national feeling could fail to be stirred by the
thought of the battles that have been fought, the sacrifices that have been
made, and the conquests that have been won? The political Subject, like
the religious Subject before it, is an agent of both emancipation and
subordination. The idea of the nation gives shape to the sovereignty of
the people, but it also gives the state that speaks in the name of the general
will an absolute power, and this implies the possibility of totalitarianism.

This makes the idea of the people, even more than the idea of the nation, a mirror image of the state, and gives the state the ability to impose its unity on the diversity of all societies. Feudalism and privileges were overthrown in the name of the nation. But regional cultures and vast expanses of the collective memory have also been destroyed in the name of the nation. It was in the name of the equality of citizens that differences and identities were condemned or destroyed, even though most personal actors cannot exist in the absence of those differences and identities. The idea of the nation inevitably inspires ambivalent reactions in us, even when we refer to the historic period of the Western revolutions, which was when it played its most positive role, especially in the United States and France (and then in Latin America and Central Europe). And that ambivalence is inescapable, because the idea of the nation comprises both the idea of the rights of citizens and that of the sovereignty of the nation-state.

Like the divine and the sacred in religious societies, the democratic spirit and the republican spirit both contradict and complement one another. The sacred founds and integrates the community, which is governed by its myths rather than its history or its projects for change, and the republican spirit is a political expression of the sacred. In both cases, the tragic intensity is at its greatest when the individual sacrifices his own life for the sake of the community's god or for the sake of the political expression of the community or the nation-state, be it republican or authoritarian. There is no difference between the martyrs who died for their faith and those who gave their lives for their country. In some cases, such as Palestine and Algeria, it is now impossible to make any clear distinction between nationalism and religion. The same is true of less tragic situations, as we can seen from the role which French Protestants played in constructing republican ideology and the republican educational system.

Religions (especially the monotheistic religions) did, on the other hand, both make it possible to challenge the social and political world in the name of God, and to separate spiritual power from temporal power. In different ways, depending upon the confession and the period in question, religions have always both advocated and opposed the sanctification of the political order, and have also challenged state power in the name of God. The medieval Christianity of the Germanic Holy Roman Empire and France's miracle-working kings sanctified the state, but the struggle between Pope and Emperor divorced God and Caesar. After 1525, the Luther who had protested in the name of faith against the transformation of the Church into a temporal power supported the German princes in their war against the peasants. In so far as it is democratic, the national idea can itself be used to appeal against the state, and its most extreme manifestation is revolution.

There is no central place in either religion, class action or the nation. Just as the personal Subject is not a fixed, stable and independent point which always succeeds in resisting both markets and communities, and just as the working class is not a historical being, so the nation is not a real character. Every figure of the Subject comes into being because it resists some form of decay. The nation can be dissolved into either the prince or the people, as well as into the false equality of rights or the false identity of a community. But despite that (or rather because of it), the nation was, and still is, at least in part, one of the Subject's historical forms. This is why, if we regard social science as the discovery of the Subject, we must recognize that the political philosophy which created and analysed the idea of the political Subject is an integral part of the history of sociology. The nation is not reducible to an early stage in a process of political modernization in which spatially restricted units evolve into nation-states, a world political state, and then supranational states like the federal Europe that inspires such official lyricism and an increasingly distrustful popular indifference as we come closer to it. The nation was the clearest political expression of the idea of society. And the idea of society was a figure of the Subject because it attempted to reconcile the subjective idea of human rights with the constitutional state that is associated with the creation of the modern economy.

The Subject was political, just as it was once religious, because it could not take a personal form while society was still dominated by reproduction and social controls, by traditions and inherited powers and privileges, by social barriers that it was impossible or difficult to cross, by the power of the families, local collectivities and norms that governed every aspect of life, as well as by the repression brought to bear on those who defied its powers and norms. The Subject inevitably took the form of the sovereignty of the people and of the proclamation of basic rights, which, whilst they were very abstract, did mobilize the nation against absolute power and gave a higher meaning to actions which would otherwise have been nothing more than riots provoked by the high price of food. It was political action, and sometimes religious action, that allowed the past's hold on the present to be loosened and then broken. The idea of citizenship, the nation or the republic allows us to relive the situation, which is still a novelty in some parts of the world, in which freedom could not but be political and where the road to freedom was inevitably the revolutionary road, because it was quite impossible to introduce freedom into either the world of production or the world of consumption, or in other words of habits and tastes. What is more, the political struggle brought the Subject closer to personal consciousness by defending freedom of conscience and opinion against the religious and communitarian foundations of power, and making the people's vote, and not the will of God, the basis of legitimation.

All the countries of Europe took part in these struggles for citizenship. They began with the establishment of free cities and with Magna Carta, which placed the first limitations on the power of the King of England, and culminated in the revolutions that founded modern democracies in Europe, North America, the former Portuguese colonies and then Brazil. But it was in France that the liberation of the political Subject was most laden with symbolic acts and became a discourse in which society spoke of itself. This was especially true of the days of 17 and 20 June 1789 (which the French should celebrate as national holidays), when the Estates General proclaimed themselves a National Assembly (17 June) and when their members took the oath of the Jeu de Paume (20 June) and swore to resist the power of bayonets in the name of the people they represented. Not surprisingly, this very forceful expression of the national idea took a republican form, and was sustained by anticlerical, and even broadly anti-religious, feelings. For the long century that lasted at least until the separation of Church and state, the struggle against reaction therefore meant the struggle of the Republic against the monarchy, and of secularism against clericalism.

To evoke, in just a few words, this long political history only serves to make us even more aware of how the ideas of the nation and the Republic have been weakened and debased. The Subject ceased to be political, and citizenship ceased to be freedom's principal form when the countries that had invented the sovereignty of the people reached the stage of industrial civilization, and when the mastery of the future became a more important source of power than the preservation of the past. In the France of the late nineteenth century, few republicans followed the example of Jaurès, who became a socialist but still remained loyal to the national idea which France had inherited from the Revolution. From that time onwards, the word 'republican' increasingly came to mean a refusal to prioritize working-class struggles and a recognition that the class relations of industrial society, and not the privileges and inequalities bequeathed by the past, were the main obstacle to freedom and equality, and that fraternity is more likely to be found amongst striking workers than amongst the notables who dine together.

The political Subject became a class subject. The people became the working class, and citizenship, especially for those who had already acquired it, became a less important objective than work, wages and working conditions. Social justice mobilized more people than civil rights. Hannah Arendt, who finds the decline of the political realm disturbing, stresses that 'the emergence of the social realm, which is neither private nor public, strictly speaking, is a relatively new phenomenon' (1958: 28).

Like the national consciousness before them, working-class struggles developed in two different directions. Some were transformed into political mobilizations that sought to establish the dictatorship of the proletariat; others into the reforms that brought industrial democracy, which can be seen as a combination of political freedom and social rights. Like citizenship before it, social justice had two different meanings. It could imply membership of a community, and therefore a willingness to exclude others, but it could also mean extending the field of freedoms.

As the rights that were being defended became more concrete, the struggles became mass-based and permanent, and there was a growing danger that they would lead to neo-communitarian policies. Communist power plunged so much of the world into totalitarianism that some people have reverted to the idea that the political realm must remain aloof from the social realm, because it is the realm of freedom and equality, whereas the social realm is, by its very nature, based upon dependence and inequality. But this republican reaction has almost as little force as the religious reaction to colonial conquests or industrialization. It is a positive factor, however, when it reminds us that limits have to be imposed on all forms of power. Yet even in that sense, it is no substitute for a positive movement that asserts rights which are increasingly concrete and increasingly defined in terms of social and cultural practices and relations.

There is nothing new about the decline of the political Subject and citizenship, or about political society's loss of its old supremacy over civil society. In the mid-nineteenth century, Marx was already denouncing the revolutionary phraseology of 1848 and the Commune, which was so blind to the emergence of the labour movement that it expelled the representatives of the International from its ranks. Other countries which, like Great Britain and then post-Bismarckian Germany, had been more deeply penetrated by the industrial economy, entered industrial democracy more rapidly. Countries like France, where industrialization was more limited and where the long war between the Church and political democracy was not completely over, were unable to establish an industrial democracy, and experienced social explosions which gave the Communist parties immense power. In both Europe and Latin America, such countries have developed an increasingly traditionalist attachment to a political model that has been transformed into a machine for defending the middle classes of the public sector, and which is as indifferent to economic efficiency as it is to meeting the demands of the most underprivileged social and cultural categories. Born on the Left, the republican spirit is completing its rightward trajectory. Those who subscribe to it do so in order to block anything that threatens the ideology and interests of those professional sectors that are most closely associated with the state.

We therefore have to abandon ideology and go back to reality. Defined as a historical reality and not as an ideology, the nation-state has not identified state with nation, and it has not dissolved all particularisms into the universalism of the law. On the contrary, it was created in countries where the central power was strictly separated from local life and where, at a later stage, public life was strictly separated from private life. The idea of secularism both proclaimed and increased their separation. The democratic idea of the nation did help to mediate between the state and local societies, sometimes to the advantage of the state and sometimes to that of the notables. When Clifford Geertz (1963) states that a state can manage a diversified society only by first recognizing and then integrating what he calls 'primordial sentiments', he is right. But when he contrasts that flexibility with the model of an all-powerful state which represses and tries to abolish all particularisms, takes France as an example, and, in an amusing paradox, describes (in French) that country as a state *manqué*, he is talking about an ideology rather than a reality. As Blandine Barret-Kriegel (1979) has pointed out, the French state, just like the British or Spanish state, has recognized or accepted particularisms, and has limited its action to a narrow domain for a long time.

Reconciling the efficient central management of the economy and the administration with a recognition of particularisms and 'localisms' was, and is, the common task of all states that wish to survive. The real problem is establishing a stable relationship between the two. The characteristic feature of countries like Great Britain, the United States and France is not that they deny the existence of particularisms, but that they have created a political system that can mediate between the centre and the particular, and which is therefore democratic. The solution that Geertz describes as the 'integrative revolution' seems, by contrast, to lead rapidly to the fusion of the state and the dominant culture. The result is what David Apter (1963) calls a system of mobilization or even a 'political religion'. Alternatively, the central state may be weakened because it has to deal with a multiplicity of communitarian demands, especially regional or religious demands. The Latin-American dualization which I have analysed elsewhere (Touraine 1988) is an intermediary case. Part of society is integrated into the state thanks to the existence of a relatively open political system, but another part is marginalized and repressed, especially when its ethnic identity differs from that of the centre, as it does in most of the Andean countries. In such countries, democracy therefore remains both limited and weak.

Neither the ideological model of the so-called republican state, whose inhabitants are supposedly citizens with no other loyalties, nor real states that are torn between the need for central management and divided loyalties have resolved the problem of reconciling managerial unity with a diversity of loyalties. Only the *democratic* conception of the nation has come up with a stable solution. It proved easier to implement this solution in countries where development was more self-sustaining, where civil society was more autonomous, open and creative, and where some form of individualism had become dominant. It was more difficult to implement where the economy and administration of the territory were poorly integrated, and when there was a high level of cultural and regional diversity. But the same problem arises in all cases, in the developed countries and in the developing countries alike: how can we reconcile unity and diversity? The only answer to this question is: 'through democracy'. David Apter has clearly demonstrated the instability of 'political religions', in which the leader or political power is sanctified.

The dream of republican ideology notwithstanding, the nation has never been a replica of the state – and both the defenders and the enemies of the French model made the mistake of believing that it could be. The nation was the birthplace of modern democracy, the place where a unitary state and a diversified society could coexist.

Nationalisms

In the earliest stages of modernity, the nation, defined as a historical Subject, was the site where the general will was reconciled with political freedom, and majority rule with a plurality of opinions and interests. It lost this central role with the emergence of an industrial society based on the ideas of progress, rationalization, positive order, class struggle and a conflict of interests. The nation was reduced to meaning national unity and the assertion thereof – or in other words nationalism – whilst the defence of freedoms became a task for class actors. Whereas political philosophy investigated the pre-conditions for the social order and the organization of political society, the national theme became detached from the theme of order and bound up with that of change. In industrial society, the nation is no longer a mediator; it provides the framework for industrialization. It is increasingly bound up with the state and the international conflicts in which is involved.

Ernest Gellner (1983) establishes a close link between nation and modernization by demonstrating that nationalism is not a desire to give a nation that already exists an independent state. Nationalism means the shaping of the nation into a political organization for a commodified and industrial society which is unable to develop in the overly narrow framework of feudal society or even of restricted principalities. Prior to economic and political modernization, peoples, or in other words ethnic groups, are the only things that exist. It is modernization that leads to the emergence of the more diversified and integrated units known as nations. I have already rejected this conception; but it does rightly underline the fact that economic exchanges and national integration converge in the process of modernization. There are even cases in which the nation is identified with the emergent modern society, as in the United States, Australia, Canada and other nation-societies that were formed by large numbers of immigrants from a wide variety of countries. In such cases, however, the national theme is, however, weaker than the idea of openness ('the land of opportunity') or the frontier that makes the conquest of the West or the interior so important. São Paolo and Medellín, for instance, were the bases for the conquest of the hinterlands of Brazil and Colombia.

Unlike the national consciousness, nationalism has for 150 years been associated with the gulf that exists between the formation or defence of the nation, and the workings of modern society. At this point, the national idea ceases altogether to be the site of a debate between unity and plurality. For better and for worse, the balance tips in favour of unification. Far from opening up a space for meetings, dialogue and negotiation, the national idea increasingly imposes a unitary image.

This first became apparent in countries that were already established nation-states, especially France, where we saw a state vigorously imposing national unity and combating particularisms. It was at this time that the republican ideology was consolidated in France. It gave a central importance to the struggle against religion, and therefore to education, and to the creation of a national ideology, which was further strengthened by the themes of revenge on the German enemy and France's colonial destiny. The new social strata which, from Gambetta to Jules Ferry and then Clemenceau, were the main support for the republican spirit did not merge into any of the social classes created by industrial society. In the United Kingdom, the imperial consciousness was even stronger, and reached its apotheosis with Queen Victoria's jubilee. In both cases, the national consciousness remained aloof from the passions of industrial society, in which capitalists and wage-earners alike were, if not internationalists, at least more concerned with their own economic interests and conflicts than with furthering the national interest.

In other situations, the gulf between national consciousness and economic society is greater still. One early form of national consciousness, which I call 'liberal nationalism', appears when a nation frees itself from an empire. In such cases, the national idea is associated with the idea of economic modernization, but tends to dominate it rather than to be dominated by it, and political debates centre on national rather than economic themes. In those countries of Central Europe that were ruled by the Austrian or Russian empires, and in the Turkish-ruled Balkans and especially Bulgaria, liberal or democratic intellectuals glorified the national idea, and took as their model Western nation-states such as France or Great Britain – and especially France, where the national idea was more independent of economic society and more closely related to what I call the 'political Subject'. The Hungarians, Czechs and Poles were fighting both for a historical community and for political freedom. We find the same combination, which is a direct continuation of the liberal French and American revolutions of the late eighteenth century, in the wars of independence waged by the Spanish colonies against the metropolis to which they were bound by the colonial pact. They freed themselves from the metropolis, often with help from England, but also thanks to the creation of nation-societies. In late nineteenth-century Brazil, where the monarchy became national when the king, having been driven out of Portugal, settled in Rio, the national consciousness took on a republican form after the abolition of slavery. It gained the support of the Freemasons and the army, and one of its first manifestations was the bloody repression of Canudos's messianic movement. The repression was bound up with economic modernization and the rise of the urban bourgeoisie, but above all with the integration of a national territory that was fragmented in geographical, economic and ethnic terms. Throughout the greater part of the twentieth century, Latin America was dominated by national-popular regimes, or in other words by states that tried to promote national integration and to struggle against dependency by redistributing resources (mainly from foreign sources, but also from national economic development) amongst a vast and predominantly urban middle class. From Cárdenas's Mexico to Perón's Argentina, from Peru's APRA to Venezuela's Trienio, from Uruguay's pioneering Battle y Ordonez to the democratic populism of Eduardo Frei and then Salvador Allende in Chile, the national idea was more important than the goal of economic development. In all cases, it was defined as a force for unification as well as for national liberation.

We find this national liberalism in late nineteenth-century Central Europe, Latin America and the renascent Egypt. Although it relies upon a mobilizing and modernizing state to overcome the obstacles of underdevelopment and dependency, the model is derived from the great Western democracies. It is, so to speak, a bridge between the political Subject of nineteenth-century Europe and the increasingly defensive nationalisms of the twentieth century.

Industrialization also leads to the rise of a *communitarian nationalism*, which is very different from this liberal nationalism. It is in conflict with a deracinated modernity, which is as desocialized and denationalized as finance capitalism and imperialism. The objective of this nationalism is not, however, the creation of a national political society, but the defence of either a historical community or a cultural, linguistic or religious being. In late nineteenth-century Vienna, anti-Semitism was widespread amongst the German population. It was directed against Jews who played an important role in a range of universalist activities, from the arts to political administration, and from science to finance. That anti-Semitism spread to both Hungary and Bohemia. It became increasingly virulent in Germany, and was terribly virulent in France during the Dreyfus Affair, when the defenders of the 'national and Catholic' tradition mobilized their forces against a Jewish officer. They reinterpreted the national tradition in fundamentalist fashion, and used it as a weapon against anything that looked foreign, even when the foreigner they were denouncing was, like Captain Dreyfus, one of the prototypical republican Jews whose history has been recorded by Pierre Birnbaum (1992). He was, in other words, a French nationalist. The upheavals created by industrialization and urbanization posed a threat to traditional sectors of society. They therefore used the language of traditionalism to denounce the obscure forces or traitors who were threatening their national identity, but the themes of anti-capitalism, populism and fundamentalist nationalism soon became more pronounced. And they did so at the very moment when the republican spirit was strengthening and imposing France's national identity.

As liberal nationalism turned into communitarian nationalism, the national idea became further and further removed from the creative and emancipatory ambiguity that had brought about the triumph of the Revolution of 1789.

In many countries, the nation-state was initially the main agent of economic modernization, and therefore of the creation of an increasingly autonomous civil society. That role was played, in very different ways, by the Bismarckian state in Germany, the Piedmontese state and the Japanese state, after it had been transformed by the Meiji Revolution of 1868. Where modernization occurred later, the internal obstacles standing in the way of secularization and the rationalization of economic and administrative life were all the greater. The state had more control over economic life and placed restrictions on democratic institutions, though the severity of those restrictions varied. Post-revolutionary Mexico, in particular, did not build a pluralist political system, and Brazilian writers rightly stress the weakness of the liberal tradition in their country, and note that the state has always played the central role in its industrialization.

There is also a third scenario in which modernization seems impossible and in which industrialization or finance capitalism appears to pose a threat to national or regional societies and cultures. The state, whose nationalism does not promote modernization, violently rejects a civil society and a commodified world which, in its view, pose a threat to the essence of the nation. Rather than acting as the guardian of civil society, the state destroys it, and speaks in the name of the people. This is not a case of society proclaiming and defending its traditions; an authoritarian power mobilizes traditions and beliefs in order to take over the state and to take complete control over the whole of society.

Ethnicity and the nation

Having looked at the rise and fall of the national idea, we now have to go back to the role it plays in our representation of political modernity. The nation has been contrasted with ethnicity, just as modernity has been contrasted with tradition, and production with reproduction. As a result, the nation has been identified with rationalization and turned into the political figure of modernity. Anthropologists suggest, however, that we should modify our conception of ethnicity, but, if we agree with them, we also have to revise our idea of the nation. Ethnicity appears to define membership of pre-state collectivities. Philippe Poutignat and Jocelyne Streiff-Fenart (1995), who are directly inspired by Fredrik Barth (1969), analyse ethnicity as 'a form of social organization based upon a system of categorical ascription which classifies people on the basis of their supposed origin, and which is validated in social interaction by the use of socially differential cultural signs'. This definition in itself marks a clear departure from essentialist and even cultural conceptions of ethnicity, in that it prioritizes ethnic identification and therefore, as Fredrik Barth stresses, the divorce between those who belong to the social unit and those who are outside it. The unusual thing about Barth – and this is why he is so influential – is that he does everything possible to minimize the importance of the cultural content of the definition of ethnicity, and promotes a more truly sociological conception of exchanges between the group and the outside world by stressing that instrumental and strategic analysis play an important role in its relations with that world.

Others, like Ugo Fabietti (1995), also stress the central importance of the strategies that are used to gain access to external resources. These strategies lead to wars and to the rejection of foreigners, and therefore give the we/them, identity/alterity dichotomy its full force. In situations where social life is organized by beliefs, myths, rules and a language, or in the situations studied by anthropologists, 'identity' can be constructed only in relation to alterity. We can therefore accept the analytic principle that anthropologists have borrowed from linguistics: the relationship with the self is governed by the relationship with the Other, and communications determine identity.

Francesco Remotti (1996) warns us against projecting our representations on to the colonized world. We once believed that the colonized world was made up of distinct ethnic groups which were rather like primitive forms of the nation. The reality is very different. 'The Banandé of Zaire', he writes, 'had no name; they used the name *bayira*, which refers to the position of farmers, as opposed to that of the pastoralists. Today, the term has taken on a pejorative meaning and this population of a million people describes itself as the Banandé.' A population defines itself not only in terms of relations of identity and alterity and with reference to common origins, but also by acquiring a political and military organization. Traditional societies function both as systems organized around values, hierarchies and beliefs and as strategic actors who establish relations of conflict, co-operation and compromise with the Other. Societies with a low level of historicity are dominated by their internal reproductive mechanisms, and their strategic action is both peripheral and partly dominated by war. But in such societies, identity derives from the binary opposition between identity and alterity, even when the Other is not the enemy.

Conversely, a society with a high level of historicity is dominated by instrumental, technical and economic action. It is open to the outside world, and this destroys its internal reproductive systems. There is therefore a danger that the identity/alterity pair will be weakened, as the Other is replaced by the impersonal forces of the market and money. Such societies do have an identity, but it is no longer defined with reference to the outside world; it is now defined with reference to the foreigner within. To put it more simply, the identity/alterity pair is replaced by the normality/difference pair. As we move from a culture of reproduction to a culture of production, we see the theme of difference replacing that of alterity. When a society is defined in terms of its trade, its output and its role in the international division of labour, pairs of oppositions such as majority/minority and centre/periphery are created within it. When it was inseparable from a hostility to the Other, identity was shaped on the frontier, and with reference to foreigners. It is now shaped within society. Things that were once considered to be part of private life now appear in public life.

The growing importance of differences is always associated with inequalities, because the majority thinks itself superior to the minority. The primary task of democratization is therefore to ensure that different individuals and categories are recognized as being equal. And democracy must be active if it is to resist the constant tendency to make those who are different inferior.

It is at first sight tempting to describe these contrasting situations as 'traditional' and 'modern' respectively, but there is also an intermediary situation. It is of considerable historical importance, and still has great influence on the way we behave. I refer to the nation-society, and we shall see that it introduces a new and important dimension. There is no nation that does not have an ethnic dimension. The French, who played such a determinant role in the birth of the modern or republican notion of the nation, recently celebrated the baptism of Clovis. That event is one of the origins of the French nation, and it is at once real and mythical. In celebrating it, they made it as clear as does any ethnic group that there is a frontier between 'them' and 'us', and clearly identified themselves as French. In so far as they are a nation, the French have all the characteristics of an ethnic group, but this does not mean that they are merely an ethnic group. Even when they point out that their nation is descended from a mixture of populations of different origins, they still refer to common physical and cultural features. Interbreeding does as much to determine origins as an assumed purity. The break between a nation and ethnicity is therefore not a complete break; both are a combination, albeit in very different proportions, of common origins and the will to construct a political organization.

Does this interdependency of cultural community and political society still obtain in the most modern situations or in the globalized economy? Yes. The open and unstable awareness of the relationships between cultural identity and political alterity that we observed in societies with a low level of historicity is replaced, after the intermediary period which sees the triumph of a state that binds together a nation and an ethnicity, by defensive action on the part of a nation which redefines itself both as an ethnicity and as a culture that can resist the forces dominating the international market. Societies with a low level of historicity can also be replaced by the ethnic consciousness of immigrants who have come into contact with modern production and consumption.

This is why I say that ethnicization is in no sense reducible to its negative aspects. It may subordinate a population to an authoritarian and truly fundamentalist power, but it can also indicate that a society is beginning to resist the omnipotence of an economy that is not regulated by any political institutions. The Japanese, the Mexicans and the French, that is, are using culture, their language, their origins and therefore their ethnic identity to defend or demand their autonomy in the face of a system of domination which is both hegemonic and internationalized. As they become more involved in the globalized economy, their political will to autonomy and self-determination will be increasingly based upon an awareness of their origins, their cultural and ethnic identity, and not, as we believed for so long, on plans to rationalize modernity.

A symbolic or synthetic ethnicity uses its original cultural identity to sustain a political will. Like Ugo Fabetti, we may well wonder, therefore, whether we are not moving from the nation to ethnicity, after having – until very recently – taken it as self-evident that historical evolution led from ethnicity to the nation.

This shift in perspective is similar to the shift I introduced in my discussion of the ideas of modernity and the Subject. Just as the personal Subject is in no sense defined by the emergence of rational behaviour, but, on the contrary, by the attempt to reconcile, within a personal life experience, instrumental rationality and a cultural and psychological identity, so the national will, if it is democratic, increasingly takes responsibility for culture and history, and not just for the economy and social exchanges. Unlike the France of the classical political philosophers, Michelet's France was largely defined in ethnic terms. And when ecologists defend cultural diversity as well as biodiversity, they combine a natural dimension with a social and cultural dimension to define an *oikonomia* which comprises the whole earth. There is of course a danger that extreme ethnicization might destroy the political system as well as economic and technological rationality. But a nation which refuses either to assert its ethnic identity or to recognize that a multiplicity of ethnic groups exists within it weakens itself by allowing the reality of the nation to come under the suffocating control of a state that claims to have a monopoly on the expression of the national consciousness.

In democratic countries, there is usually little danger of an authoritarian regime being associated with an ethno-nationalist consciousness. The association may, however, suddenly become stronger and destroy democracy, as we saw in Hitler's Germany. This is what the National Front would like to see happening in France. On the other hand, it is only logical that dominated groups, or simply minority groups, should become ethnicized. Social movements increasingly appeal to ethnicity, and sometimes to gender or age. Who can remain indifferent to the demands being put forward by Kurds living in Turkey, Iraq or other countries? Who could condemn the Chechen struggle for self-determination? Yet it would require a great deal of bad faith to say that these peoples are struggling solely for freedom and human rights. They are not simply saying that general principles of law should be respected; they are demanding independence and a recognition of their collective being. The fact that ethnic movements are often anti-democratic does not in itself prove that democracy can exist without recognizing cultural rights or, more specifically, without defining itself in ethnic terms. It is not true to say that the decline of the nation-state has led to a return to ethnicity. On the contrary, the will to collective freedom must mobilize more and more forms of identity if it is to be able to resist the dominance of the market. Such mobilizations are often led or enforced by authoritarian regimes, but democratic regimes can mobilize too. We are not citizens of the world (and we are unlikely to become citizens of the world in the foreseeable future) unless some hegemonic state forces its nationality and culture on us. We can resist the globalized economy by falling back on various forms of personal and collective identity, and democracy alone is capable of reconciling economic rationality, which is both present in, and a prisoner of, the globalized economy, and a cultural identity which is in danger of being imprisoned by cultural nationalisms.

We have to make a very clear distinction between this ethnic self-identification, which I refer to as 'ethnicization', and a very different use of the ethnic theme. Ethnic definitions of populations can be used to make one population's domination of another absolute, and to put it beyond the reach of political action or economic transformations. This was what the colonial powers in Rwanda and Burundi had in mind when they invented a Tutsi ethnicity, which was superior because its Ethiopian origins meant that it was related to the Caucasian race, and a Hutu ethnicity, which was inferior in biological, cultural and economic terms. The defenders of Greater Serbia invented a Serb ethnicity by reviving representations that were shaped in the nineteenth century. Similarly, American racism relegates all men and women with a certain amount of Black 'blood' to the inferior category of Blacks. Indeed, if more information were available, a larger proportion of the population would be Black. In general, however, racism – and especially its extreme Nazi form – cannot be identified with ethnicization. As Barth has said, ethnicization defines categories of actors in terms of their relationship with political or economic power or with other actors or social categories, whereas racism completely desocializes populations by turning them into natural species.

Anti-racism, which must make no concessions to its enemy, would be seriously weakened if it confused ethnic consciousness with racism. Ethnic consciousness is one of the component elements of social and cultural identity, and it is also one of the pre-conditions for the defence of the social autonomy and personal freedom of social actors; racism imposes the stigma of a racial definition on populations which an absolute power is trying to destroy or inferiorize. If we do not make a clear distinction between these two orders of representation and behaviour – and they are diametrically opposed to one another – we will soon end up condemning all forms of awareness of national identity in the name of anti-racism. That error of judgement could take an assertion of identity, which should be strengthening democracy, in the direction of authoritarian politics.

At the theoretical level, it is essential to stop contrasting community with society. When he examined the Jewish question at the time of the great Nazi persecutions and then the Black question in the United States, Talcott Parsons himself saw the need to bridge the gap between the two

notions. He spoke of a 'societal community' which could reconcile equal
civil, political and social rights for all with the preservation of groupings
with the lasting but diffuse solidarity provided by ethnic, religious or
family groups. I would like to make my own contribution to this broad-
ening of our representations. The crude dichotomy between universalist
civil rights and the particular cultural loyalties that some would like to
marginalize or eradicate seems to me to be a dangerous intellectual reaction inspired by a feeling of insecurity. As we move further and further
away from the republican ideology of the nation, we come into much
closer contact with the contemporary experience of the nation, which can
be a figure of the personal Subject if it reconciles instrumentality with
identity.

Totalitarianism

Like the idea of a social movement, the idea of the nation cannot be fully
understood unless we analyse its antithesis or what destroys it. A social
anti-movement is the antithesis of a social movement. When cultural
identity and political involvement cease to be complementary, and when
there is a complete overlap between a society, a culture and an authoritarian power, we witness the birth of the antithesis of the nation, or in
other words a totalitarian regime. Many people have abandoned this
notion, which was elaborated by Hannah Arendt, in the belief that they
can avoid the difficult problem of comparing the Nazi regime with the
Communist regime, or nationalisms with today's fundamentalist religious
parties. François Furet (1995) has demonstrated how the concept of
totalitarianism, which provides us with the means to understand communism, was rejected, especially in France, in favour of the anti-fascist
idea. That idea was a response to the rise of Nazism, and during the
Second World War it was strengthened by the alliance between Western
countries and the Soviet Union. It subsequently served to protect the
policies of Communist parties, thanks to the support lent them by many
intellectuals, some of whom later went so far as to sing the praises of the
Chinese Cultural Revolution. They also refused to see that, whilst Cas-
tro's overthrow of the Batista regime did have an emancipatory dimension, it also gave birth to a dictatorship that was both repressive and
modernizing. The exceptional nature of the Nazi regime, or its policy of
exterminating the Jews, was invoked to block any analysis that included
the totalitarian regimes in a more general typology of dictatorships. Is it
so difficult to acknowledge that every totalitarian regime has specific
features but is still typical of a more general category? The extermination
of the Jews is the most specific and radical aspect of the Nazi regime, and

it cannot be integrated into a broader conception of totalitarianism; similarly, fanatical forms of religious faith, be it Islamic, Christian or Hindu, lead to wars of religion. Communism did not, even though it did wage violent campaigns against religion. But over and beyond the specificities that give each totalitarian regime its identity, the common feature of all such regimes is that an absolute political power speaks in the name of the people, or in other words a particular historical, national or cultural entity which claims to enjoy an absolute superiority because it represents a reality that transcends political and economic life. A totalitarian regime is always popular, national and doctrinaire. It subordinates social practices to a power by embodying the idea that makes the people the representative and defender of a faith, a race, a class, a history or a territory. A despotic regime forces the people to obey the prince's decisions; in a totalitarian regime the prince claims to be the people and asserts that, when he speaks, it is the voice of the people that is speaking through him.

A totalitarian regime is therefore the creation not of a strong state, but that of a weak state subordinated to a party, a supreme leader and a nomenclature. It destroys the people by robbing it of its voice, and destroys the state by replacing the administration with a system of patronage. It is true that Mussolini's fascism aspired to being a strong state, that the Fascist party was a 'state party', and that Japanese militarism and Greater Serbian nationalism glorified the state, but they all rejected the liberal constitutional state in the name of what the Germans called the 'national constitutional state'. This was a cultural force – an expression that often recurs in Mussolini's speeches and Gentile's writings – in the service of the people or the race.

The same conception was also present in the Germany of 1933, when there was talk of a totalitarian state; but Franz Neumann and all subsequent analysts of Nazism have demonstrated that this conception was quickly rejected in favour of Karl Schmidt's tripartite conception of state, movement and people. Hitler's personal position was strengthened by the elimination of the SA in June 1934, and it was now the party that mobilized the people. As early as December 1933, Hitler was saying that the party was the guardian of the German idea of the state. The predominance of the party and its dynamic force made Hitler himself all-powerful. The party's dominance over the state was even more complete in the Soviet Union. The absolute power of the supreme guide and his entourage also took an extreme form in Khomeini's Iran. Khomeini was a political leader who could mobilize religious beliefs and loyalties, rather than a religious leader in the true sense of that word.

Although he is very critical of the notion of totalitarianism, Ian Kershaw, who is one of the greatest experts on Nazism, has produced a remarkable analysis of this form of dictatorial power, which is not to be confused with other types of authoritarianism. Its basic features are found in both Nazism and the Soviet regime, at least under Stalin. Kershaw (1994) emphasizes the importance of the two mechanisms of power which, in my view, provide the best definition of totalitarianism. The first is the destruction of the political system. Both regimes replaced politics – the rational pursuit of limited objectives as and when the opportunity arises – with an ideological vision and the use of an unprecedented level of state-approved violence against the society it was running. The second feature, which is the first's *raison d'être*, is that both regimes claimed to be in 'total control' of the societies they dominated; both tried, in other words, to use terror and manipulation to homogenize and mobilize the population for revolutionary purposes – which were very different – and to ensure that there was no institutional space for any alternative.

This definition of totalitarianism, which both confirms Leonard Schapiro's analysis of the destruction of the juridical order and Claude Lefort's (1981) broader analysis, allows us to reveal a basic political truth: as Kershaw rightly stresses, totalitarianism is not a stable regime. Nazism was a crisis regime established in a struggle to the death with vastly superior forces, and it was swallowed up by war and defeat. After the end of the Stalinist period, the Soviet regime and especially the People's Democracies of Eastern Europe were, to a greater or lesser extent, transformed into authoritarian regimes.

The many profound differences between the Nazi regime and the Soviet regime, which Kershaw and so many other authors rightly stress, can clearly be accommodated within a general definition of totalitarianism. The same could be said of the differences between Hitler's regime and that of Mussolini, but that undermines the idea of fascism rather than that of totalitarianism. Whilst I accept that Kershaw has produced good reasons for not seeing the GDR as a totalitarian state, he has, despite himself, produced still better reasons for defending the concept of totalitarianism.

What is more, Kershaw himself shows that the concept can be extended to include more recent regimes, such as the Khomeini regime, and it is indeed essential to do so if we are to give the idea of totalitarianism its true explanatory power. It is not enough to categorize Italian fascism, the Hitler regime, and Leninist, Stalinist and Maoist communism as 'totalitarian regimes'. The category is much broader than that. Whenever a power that speaks in the name of a community comes into being in order to fight some form of internationalized modernization or what appears to be foreign-dominated modernization, it is totalitarian. Whenever the defence of social, national or cultural interests feels itself to be threatened by an open economy and democratic institutions, totalitarianism has either taken power or is trying to take power. That is why, far from being a thing of the past, and far from having been liquidated by the defeat of Germany and Japan in 1945 and then by the collapse of the Soviet system, totalitarianism has spread to so many countries. Just as the dominance of imperialism, which was denounced by socialists at the beginning of the twentieth century, gave rise to totalitarian regimes based upon the defence of a nation or a people, so the contemporary globalization of the economy is encouraging the spread of fundamentalist resistances that are bringing totalitarian regimes to power.

After a brief initial revolutionary period, and before its transformation into a Thermidorean regime, the Khomeini regime in Iran was totalitarian. The Karadzic regime in Serbian Bosnia is totalitarian or, to be more precise, national-totalitarian. The Milosevic regime itself is largely totalitarian, as is the Khadafi regime in Libya. The failure of Westernization in Russia brought with it the threat of totalitarianism, though it did seem to disappear in 1996. In many cases, the power of an authoritarian regime is so incomplete that we cannot speak of totalitarianism. This is true of Peru, and even more so of Morocco. In Algeria there is a conflict between two equally totalitarian powers, and an alliance between the two, which some observers think possible, would create an extreme form of totalitarianism. The minority nationalist movements that have developed in France, Austria and Flanders are also totalitarian in inspiration, as was Italy's MSI, which rejoined the right-wing tradition that respects political freedoms when it became the Alleanza Nazionale. All these examples show that anyone who believes in the natural triumph of a combination of democratic institutions and the market economy is dangerously mistaken. On the contrary, we are seeing the rise of forms of cultural nationalism that can adopt liberal economic policies even though they are under the leadership of authoritarian or even totalitarian regimes.

We therefore have to take a broader view of totalitarianism, which is not reducible to a form of political regime defined by one party, the boundless power of a supreme leader, the inculcation of ideology and generalized political controls. Totalitarianism means that, during a period of secularization and market rationalization, an authoritarian power creates a model of society and culture that allows it to bend all social, economic, political, cultural and even scientific actors to its hegemonic will. Whereas despotism imposes the rule of the state on society, totalitarianism identifies society with the state, and the state with a higher being. Society therefore has to be cleansed, homogenized and integrated by the state. The notion of fundamentalism is therefore synonymous with totalitarianism. Fundamentalism is in fact a variant of totalitarianism which defines itself in cultural and religious terms rather than national or ethnic terms. In all its forms, totalitarianism destroys human beings in so far as they are Subjects, and makes society opaque to both the hopes and the fears of the human Subject.

In a totalitarian state, there are no autonomous social actors and no social demands. Neither the market nor science has any logic of its own, except in so far as the totalitarian power needs certain resources – mainly technological and scientific, but also financial – and can obtain them only by respecting in a limited way the autonomous functional norms of those sectors of activity. The Nazi regime, for example, developed some scientific and, above all technological, domains, just as Iran's totalitarian theocracy used oil specialists trained in great foreign universities, and just as the Soviet regime was able to create a space industry that could operate outside the normal administrative and military framework.

Totalitarian regimes are not based upon repression alone. They are popular. In other words, they mobilize minds, win the enthusiastic support of the masses, and especially the young, and encourage the spirit of self-sacrifice. Indeed, the sacrifice theme can be of central importance because dying for a leader, a god or a nation is the ultimate proof that society, with its multiple loyalties, feelings and interests, has become totally absorbed by the redemptive and sacred task of totalitarian power.

Totalitarianism destroys more than democracy. It also destroys social, historical and cultural movements and actors. They can exist only if relations of domination, ownership and power are contested, but also acknowledged to exist. Social movements of all kinds are inseparably bound up with the idea of historicity, or in other words with a society's ability to transform itself. It is that ability that leads to the concentration of resources and investments – and not only economic investments – and, conversely, to the desire to make the resources that have been created and accumulated available to all. A totalitarian regime, by contrast, reduces historicity to the use of economic or cultural resources to build and defend a mythical identity. Defending that identity means, in practice, legitimizing absolute power. Absolute states have always used the idea of the people as a disguise, and it is no accident that the USSR's satellites, which were totalitarian and subsequently became authoritarian, should have described themselves as 'people's democracies'. This does not mean that all forms of populism are potentially totalitarian. Populist movements and popular-national regimes such as those that dominated Latin America for so long have often overthrown ruling oligarchies, and have proved themselves to be stages on the road to democratic openness. But when populism is a response to a national, economic or political crisis, it is inspired by the need to defend a natural entity that can be represented only by a charismatic leader, and it seeks to destroy intermediate bodies and mediators, and especially political parties and intellectuals. In such cases, populism paves the way for totalitarianism, as in Austria after the

First World War, or for an authoritarian-nationalist regime, as in Hungary at the same time. Elements of populism can also sustain regimes like those of Franco, Salazar or Pétain, which were counter-revolutionary and neo-traditionalist, rather than totalitarian.

The strength of totalitarian regimes is so great that they appear to be immune to both popular rebellions and plots fomented in the name of economic interests, or religious, military or social traditions. Whereas the rule of one class has always provoked the ruled to resist and rebel, totalitarianism, and even weaker regimes that also identify individuals with a society, nation or community, weakens and destroys their ability to oppose it. The collapse of totalitarian regimes results from military defeat or their inability to resist external military or economic pressures. They are not destroyed by major struggles that begin with popular uprisings. Given that totalitarian regimes have dominated the twentieth century, we can no longer believe the old theories that described social movements as subjective expressions of the objective logic of progress, science and modernization.

It is essential to make an analysis of totalitarianism here because, unlike 'authoritarianism', the word 'totalitarianism' does not designate a type of political regime that can be compared with democratic liberal regimes. Totalitarianism is a political regime which destroys *every* figure of the Subject – personal, political and religious – because the idea of total power leaves no room for the principle of autonomy and recourse known as the Subject. Hannah Arendt is right not to reduce the authoritarian system to forms of power or even constraints, or to reject the view that it is primarily an ideology. It is only when we condemn totalitarianism in truly ethical terms that we can understand what it destroys: the dignity of human beings. Pierre Bouretz is right to say that the testimonies of Robert Antelme, Primo Levi, Jorge Semprun, Solzhenitsyn or Vassili Grossman bring us closer to the truth of totalitarianism than analyses which reduce it to a tangled web of causes and circumstances.

The national consciousness no longer has the conquering power it had at the time of the American and French revolutions. It has become a refuge for the middle categories, whose political behaviour can, in democratic societies, range from a reactionary defence of interests that are threatened by economic concentration to calls for protection from the neo-corporatist state. They may also be easily attracted to totalitarianism – hence the spread of what Seymour Martin Lipset has so aptly termed 'extremism of the centre'. He contrasts it with both left- and right-wing extremisms, and claims that it provides the best definition of fascisms. He also applies the term 'Fascist' to movements which did not take power, such as the Poujadist movement in France and, we could now add, that same country's National Front. The historical data refute all attempts to explain fascism (and especially Nazism) in terms of mass society and the social disorganization caused by the Great Crash and unemployment. It shows, rather, that, even though many of its leaders were *déclassé* city-dwellers, the Nazi movement's strongest support came from the most central categories and from those groups that were most attached to tradition, like the Catholic peasants of Bavaria, the Protestants of Schleswig-Holstein and even schoolteachers. Long after the demise of the Nazi regime and its paroxysmal racism, the contemporary world is witnessing the spread of a fundamentalist nationalism which attacks both great globalized companies that have no homeland and those political or cultural forces that pose a threat to the values of the 'moral majority'. Although it is very different from the populism of nineteenth-century Russia or even the national-popular regimes of Latin America, this fundamentalist nationalism is a reaction against the growing divorce between the globalized economy and national cultures which increasingly react to the internationalization of the economy by defining themselves in terms of traditions rather than projects.

As we move from national liberalism to fundamentalist nationalism, we see the increasingly rapid demise of the combination of nationhood and citizenship which once made French-, English- or American-style nations the Subject of freedom. The nation is becoming more and more populist and even *völkisch*, to use a word which, regardless of its original meaning, has been forever tainted by the use made of it in the Nazi regime's self-definition.

This inversion of the national idea also coincided with the growing importance of economic or international rivalries between nation-states of the European type. The history of the nation-states of Europe and of their attempts – long or short-term, long-standing or recent – to create an emancipatory form of citizenship ended with the catastrophe of the First World War. If their great intellectuals are to be believed, France, Great Britain and even Germany went to war to defend a civilization and its values. But what did those words mean in the trenches of Verdun or the Chemin des Dames? This was not a clash between nations, but one between states, peoples and soldiers who suffered and sacrificed their lives, willingly or otherwise. When the Great War ended, the emancipatory idea of the nation of 1789 and even the year II no longer existed. The multinational state of Austria-Hungary was no more. German nationalism had been punished. France's victory cost it more lives than Germany's defeat. It also resulted, although not in the same way as in Germany, in the exhaustion of a national and republican consciousness that could no longer recognize itself in the horrors and hatreds of war.

Totalitarianism was, as Dominique Schnapper (1994) puts it, the final and extreme form of the destruction of the nation as a community of

citizens. That is why it was absolutely essential to analyse this political
evil in a chapter devoted to the rise and fall of the nation as political
Subject. Totalitarianism is the central problem of the twentieth century,
just as poverty was the central problem of the nineteenth. Our century has
been dominated by politics and not economics, by states and not banks. A
long period of political mobilization and voluntaristic development is
coming to an end. In the central countries, the twenty-first century is
beginning with a return to economics, trade and consumerism. Social
movements and reformist campaigns should therefore flourish. The social
movements of the twentieth century (which began in 1914 with the First
World War, and ended in 1989, when the Berlin Wall came down) were, by
contrast, both weak and extreme, and were usually dominated by political
forces, sometimes democratic but sometimes totalitarian.

The ghost of the nation

The military destruction of Nazism did not lead to the reconstruction of
the national idea. Although its resistance and courage had made it strong,
Great Britain soon realized that its greatness was no more than a moral
greatness, and its decline drove its social classes further apart, whilst
France's lack of an adequate historical consciousness meant that it no
longer had any real sense of being a nation. It both defined citizenship in
contradictory terms and clung to its dreams of greatness. For a long time,
Germany, Italy and Japan refused to define themselves as nation-states in
an attempt to exorcise the memory of their totalitarian regimes. Even the
United States, which was the only power to resist Soviet expansionism,
combined an awareness of being a great power that could be proud of its
cultural, scientific and economic initiatives with a realization that it could
not integrate its Black population, now redefined as Afro-American, into
a unitary concept of egalitarian citizenship. The countries of Europe have
a long tradition of tolerance and of granting asylum, and take pride in
their history and freedom, but their national consciousness is now little
more than a memory of their historical role. It is increasingly torn apart
by their international economic preoccupations and a cultural fragmentation that is becoming both more obvious and more widely accepted. In a
world dominated by international markets, aggressive nationalisms and
lost identities, what room is there for the nation, national consciousness
and the citizenship that transformed a people into a nation?

It is by no means obvious that there is any room for them, and many
people now think that a national consciousness is an obstacle to the
democratic spirit. It is those who feel that they are too weak to resist
the storms of the international markets who appeal to the state rather

than the nation. It is those who are afraid of the international congresses where English has become the norm who defend the French or the Spanish language. The feeling of belonging to a nation, which is understandable and which we all share, does as much to isolate us as it does to protect us. The attachment to the past which it mobilizes is in fact the reverse side of our fear of the future. As the light moves across the face of the globe towards the new industrial countries and their emerging economies, national consciousness is becoming identified with a state nationalism that is mobilizing national or religious cultures to promote its economic development projects and, above all, its own authoritarian power.

These criticisms are well-founded, but no one finds them satisfactory. They do little to mask the dominant ideology that speaks of a globalized and self-regulating economy, or in other words of an economy that has been freed from all political and social controls, and therefore from all democratic institutions.

The prospect of nations being dissolved into a globalized economy, or of the demise of political units as they are absorbed into the global market, is out of step with reality. The one country that dominates the world economy, namely the United States, has certainly not abandoned its national consciousness. On the contrary, this is alive and well, and convinced of its legitimacy. In the new industrial countries, the alliance between economic liberalism and cultural nationalism is growing stronger, with the recent history of Japan providing the least authoritarian and most successful example. Similarly, countries which, like those of northern Europe, have been marked by social democracy have always had strong national personalities. Elie Cohen reminds us that most economic exchanges take place within nations or at a regional level.

What is in crisis is the hold of states, identified with universal values, on societies that are regarded primarily as nations. It is political categories' dominance over social categories, of unity over diversity, that is in crisis. In countries that have experienced totalitarian regimes, the crisis is obvious. In Great Britain, which has always been able to identify with a world-wide community, the crisis is latent. It is paralysing in France, which is trying desperately to be something more and other than the sum total of French people. The crisis is being well managed in Spain, which, under the enlightened leadership of Felipe Gonzalez, has both modernized and recognized the autonomy of its regions and even its nations. The open crisis in Italy reveals the weaknesses of the national unity that was created in the last century.

We can no longer take nation-states as an obvious starting-point, as they have been devoured by the internationalization of trade, on the one hand, and by a diversity of life-styles and loyalties, on the other; but we do feel the need for something that can mediate between this diversity of life-styles and the unstable unity of globalized markets. The rules that organize collective life cannot in themselves act as mediators. If they did, we would have the impression of living in a Tower of Babel where everyone obeyed the rules of coexistence without communicating with anyone else.

How are we to define this place of mediation, this public place which is something less than a civilization, much less than a community, but more than rules for co-ownership? It can establish communications between cultural identities and an economic space only if it is a political site that can transform an economic environment into a social system and, on the other hand, into inter-cultural communication. If it is to perform both these functions, the democratization of our institutions must be as thorough as possible; but there is also a need for a constant reinterpretation of what has to be called a national culture. There can be no mediation between fragmented cultural identities and a global economy unless we recognize the social and cultural personality of a political entity that is capable of being a real Subject. Such a political identity must have its own cultural identity, which must be constantly redefined, and its own economic activity. And it must reconcile the two through a democratic debate.

This political Subject asserts itself at the regional or local level, as well as at the national level. Like the personal Subject, it is defined by its will and ability to reconcile instrumental action – which in this case means primarily economic activity in an international context – with a cultural identity that is at once personal and international. In the case of the political Subject, the ability to reconcile the two does not take the form of an individual life story. It takes the form of a free, democratic decision to adopt a particular modality, either national or local, of reconciling an economy with a culture. It is important to establish a parallel between the personal Subject and the democratic Subject, so as both to avoid the idea of the personal Subject being confused with an individualism that remains indifferent to public affairs and to prevent our conception of public affairs from being identified with the strengthening of the nation-state. The main difference between the nation-state and the nation I am invoking here is that the latter is a democracy that concerns itself with the defence of the political, social and cultural rights of all, rather than a republic defined by institutions and sovereignty. Democratic action cannot reconstruct the nation-society, because nothing can be done about the contradictory and complementary forces that caused it to break up. Yet, whilst nation-societies no longer exist, there is and must be a will to live collectively. There is and must be a concrete framework within which we can reconcile a collective memory with economic activity.

Economies, defined as systems of production, redistribution and consumption, are still predominantly national, and are still influenced by national policies, even though the markets have been globalized, and even though financial flows have become largely independent of production and economic exchanges. On the other hand, no democratic action is possible if no account is taken of the historical and territorial entity it has to manage. We must therefore take into account the national culture which minorities and newcomers have to accept and transform by reconciling their particular memories with their presence in a specific place and history. This explains why Jews from Poland or Romania who have settled in France and the United States are at once similar and different from one another.

Can we still speak of the nation? The word can be a source of confusion or even misunderstandings, rather than clarity. It suggests that the idea of democracy has to be interpreted as meaning a republican nation, and this recalls the freedom of the Ancients rather than that of the Moderns. We long ago rejected the civic-republican conception of freedom, which has become more liberal in some countries and more communitarian or even repressive in others. We should be talking here of democracy in the liberal sense of respect for economic, cultural and social diversity, but we also have to be clear that such a democracy cannot survive unless it recognizes the unity and integration of a territory, and therefore a nation. Nor can a democracy survive without a collective memory and public policies.

The statist conception of the nation has to be replaced by the social and cultural conception. The nation can no longer be defined by the creation of a unitary space in which citizenship transcends social and cultural diversity. It must be defined by the quest for inter-cultural communication and social solidarity. It must be a united society that brings people closer together and tears down barriers, but in cultural terms it must also encourage a dialogue. Understanding others and integration are complementary, because we cannot recognize others solely in terms of their difference or solely on the basis of their ability to create original cultural works with a universal value. Such recognition exists only if it modifies me, only if it transforms and expands my identity and my attempts to reconcile my identity and instrumentality. What is more important, the quest for the greatest possible cultural diversity implies that we have to create the material and moral pre-conditions for the formation and defence of personal Subjects. The first pre-condition is *solidarity*, or in other words the reduction of social inequalities and exclusion. Without that, there can be no true recognition of cultural diversity. If we are to reconcile a national identity with cultural diversity, we must recognize the identity of nation-societies, as both social integration and cultural diversity presuppose that institutions which promote the democratic spirit encourage both identity and diversity.

One misunderstanding has to be avoided here. In some situations, especially in Quebec, the theme of multi-culturalism is used as an argument against the supporters of national independence. The supporters of multi-culturalism say that, rather than cutting ourselves off and retreating into a narrow identity, we should regard our diversity as a source of wealth; let us cultivate our diversity, but stay together within a political framework that encourages exchanges and encounters. This is a weak argument if relations of dominance are not taken into account. A minority that is in a dominant position does not try to secede from a political entity in which it is in such a strong position. The Alawites of Aleppo are not trying to secede from Syria, and it was not the Maronites who started the rebellion in Lebanon. Independence is a logical objective for those who feel that they are dominated and who, like French-speakers in Quebec, know from experience that if they wish to improve their social position, learning English helps, because all the big companies are English-speaking, because the immense market of the United States is a direct extension of English-speaking Canada, and because being an isolated minority is fraught with dangers. When official French spokesmen scornfully dismissed the independence of Slovenia or Croatia because it would lead to a 'Europe of tribes', they were making a serious mistake. Self-determination, and therefore independence, is a basic political right, and if we do not recognize it, we cannot speak in the name of democracy. On the other hand, the call for independence is legitimate only if it goes hand in hand with the recognition of the civil, social and cultural rights of all citizens. The people of Quebec will decide whether or not they wish to become independent, but Quebec is already a multi-cultural society in which English-speakers have important rights and safeguards, even though the Indians and the Inuit have every reason to demand the recognition of their rights, as they do throughout North America. There are no grounds for identifying the wish for national independence with the building of a society that is culturally and socially homogeneous. As I have pointed out, like so many before me, even in France, which is the classic example of a centralized country, the diversity of local cultures remained so great for such a long time that Jacques Le Goff felt justified in saying that the Middle Ages did not really end until the late nineteenth century. The ideology of a homogenized republic that was fully identified with the state and its administration was dominant only for very short periods, firstly at the time of the anticlerical and anti-religious struggle of the late nineteenth century, and then after the shock of economic globalization. The real world has always been very different, even in the domain of education, as Mona Ozouf has pointed out. The development of

Quebec and Catalonia demonstrates that a desire for real independence is compatible with the workings of democracy, provided that the independence movement is careful about how it handles relations with the state even as it tries to restrict or deny its sovereignty.

It is all the easier to defend the nation-state in that the Welfare State was created in a national context. At a more general level, democratic institutions also function in a national context. Parliaments, and contracts between social partners, the press, intellectual debates and social movements all exist in a national context. There is something disturbing about criticisms of the nation-state which promote a globalization that believes in a self-regulating economy and which takes no account of social demands and political wishes.

This reference to the nation-society can, however, be understood in two different ways. For most people, it is a matter of preserving the mechanisms of social and national integration that have been constructed since the end of the nineteenth century, and especially since the creation of the Welfare State. According to others, we also have to defend certain forms of state economic intervention and the advantages that have over the years accrued to certain social categories in both the private and the public sectors. The interventions made by a conservative state, however, have the same negative effects as the agricultural protectionism established by the Méline laws of nineteenth-century France. Conversely, the national theme can be an expression of a desire to reimpose social and political controls on economic life in response to those categories who face the greatest threats. It is because it hopes to be able to do this that Mexico's Zapatista movement declares itself to be nationalist, and explains that liberal politics pose a threat to the survival of the rural populations of the south, and especially the Indians of Chiapas. An appeal to popular social movements allows the national consciousness to combine economic efficiency with the struggle against inequality, whereas the actions of a state that protects well-organized categories have very different, negative effects in both social and economic terms.

Provided that it is oriented towards the struggle against exclusion, an awareness of national identity is essential if we are to avoid a complete break between economic globalization and cultural fragmentation. It is all the more essential in that, after 200 turbulent years dominated, especially in Europe, by society's internal struggles – civil struggles and class struggles between the ruling and the ruled, and struggles led by social movements – we are discovering that exclusion, not exploitation, is our central social problem. In other words, national unity and solidarity are once more primary objectives. The unity of society does not, however, depend upon the identification of the nation with the state. It can be based upon the defence of everyone's right to construct his or her own life project, or the particular way in which they reconcile an identity with instrumentality. This unity and this integration are as far removed from communitarian programmes or republican will to unity as they are from the complete differentialism preached by extreme liberals. They are not based upon the homogeneity of society, or even on the integrative power of citizenship, but on a recognition of the diversity of the ways and means by which citizens and collectivities can become Subjects who can produce their society and their history by reconciling their cultural memory, their individual personality, and their technological and economic projects. Unity cannot be imposed by either tradition or a globalized economy; the only possible unity is that of a democracy that strives to combine the greatest possible solidarity with respect for the civil, social and cultural rights of every individual.

7

Democracy in Decline?

In the course of the twentieth century, democracy was destroyed by authoritarian or totalitarian regimes which claimed to be popular or revolutionary; we therefore have to define democracy primarily in terms of the public and personal freedoms that place restrictions on the arbitrary use of power. To describe an authoritarian government as 'democratic' because it has improved its people's standard of education and health is unacceptable. Raising standards is a positive social achievement, but it in no sense guarantees that the regime in question is capable of responding to the population's demands or of agreeing that its actions should be overseen and evaluated by freely elected representatives of the people. At the end of the twentieth century, we tended to make the opposite mistake of reducing democracy to institutional procedures and forgetting the need for movements that can impose freedom and justice on powers. Is it impossible to reconcile negative freedom with positive freedom? In the eighteenth century and throughout most of the nineteenth, British democracy safeguarded freedoms but also stabilized the power of the oligarchy; French democracy waged a more active struggle in favour of equality, but lapsed into authoritarianism on more than one occasion. Is it impossible to conceive of a democracy which safeguards freedom of opinion and choice, but which also fights inequality? If institutional freedom disappears or if the political system is no longer capable of responding to the social demand for equality or fairness, then democracy is in crisis.

The victories of democracy are celebrated on all sides, but it seems to me that what over-optimistic observers regard as the triumph of democracy often means simply that *dirigiste* regimes are being replaced by competitive political markets. Political power's hold over social and economic life is being loosened, and sometimes shaken off. This can be conducive to democracy, but in most cases it is not. It is conducive to democracy when the all-powerful state is replaced by a variety of economic, social and cultural actors who are largely autonomous, and none of whom seeks absolute power; it is not conducive to democracy when the weakening of the state subordinates the whole of society to the interests of those with the strongest market position.

The triumph of economic liberalism is not to be confused with the victory of democracy. Of course, we should rejoice when authoritarian states collapse. We may even find marginalization and inequalities, which are growing in almost all the post-Communist countries, preferable to the massive repression implemented by the authoritarian regimes of old; but to say that the spread of the market economy is in itself democratic is to indulge in mere word-play.

The republican synthesis

It is the power of the people that provides the primary definition of democracy. In the modern world, the democratic idea is based upon the truly revolutionary assertion of the sovereignty of the people, and therefore upon the existence of a freely created political order based on universal principles that can impose limitations and rules on a social order dominated by inequality, arbitrary power and privileges. The democratic idea originally demanded that all citizens be granted the equality and freedom that society denied them. Hannah Arendt is a forceful proponent of this view. The political history of France, from Jean-Jacques Rousseau to François Mitterrand and from the Jacobins of 1789 to the democrats of 1848 and the Communards, has been the main illustration of the triumph of political society over civil society or of Jacobinism over liberalism. The United States provides the other great example of the absolute belief in the democratic will that found its expression in a Constitution based upon ethical principles, and Tocqueville underlines its foundational role.

The central principle of the sovereignty of the people linked the creative role of the social contract with the individualist–universalist vision of human beings that destroyed intermediary bodies as well as established powers and divine-right monarchies. But even when it becomes central to the political system, the power of the people does not in itself guarantee that public freedoms will be safeguarded. It tends, rather, to provide the foundations for national sovereignty, and to allow the *polis* or the king to dominate public or private life. This conception of politics is part of the general tendency to replace religious authority with political authority and to secularize the absolute foundations of power. The very idea of citizenship implies that the individual's duties to the state are sacred and take priority over individual self-interest. The replacement of God by the prince is the central moment in political modernization, but it does not found democracy, or a set of institutional guarantees that safeguard both individual and collective freedoms.

The founding principle of equality was in itself religious rather than political. When it destroyed all particularisms, it did not simply liberate a citizen who became a sovereign when the king was put to death; it subordinated that citizen to a general will embodied in the state alone. Totalitarian regimes from the Terror to Mao's Cultural Revolution have made extreme appeals to equality. The French conception of the democratic revolution was dominated by the death of the king rather than the oath of the Jeu de Paume, and it did little to protect democracy from the rise of an authoritarianism that was imposed in the name of a supposedly sacred people. Just as Marcel Gauchet (1980) regards Christianity as the religion that signals the end of religion, so direct revolutionary democracy can be seen as the last avatar of those religious societies that were based on the universal acceptance of one higher principle, and therefore as one of the most dangerous forms of the repression of social actors.

Democracy does not really exist until the ideological unity of the people explodes and is replaced by a plurality of interests, opinions and cultures. The history of Great Britain exemplifies this more than the history of either France or the United States.

The history of democracy is in fact the history of the struggle between the idea of direct democracy and that of representative democracy. Direct democracy seems to be more popular, and representative democracy more political, but in fact it is the reverse that is true. If we define democracy as people's power, we subordinate the diversity of society to the unity of a political power; the idea of 'the people' is no more than a clumsy social translation of 'political power'. The theme of representation, by contrast, implies that autonomous social actors take priority over political agents, who are to a greater or lesser extent subject to their decisions. The idea of people's power or direct democracy perpetuates the monarchical idea, and it is invoked by most authoritarian regimes. On the other hand, it is not true that representative democracy makes political parties autonomous, or that they usually use their autonomy to make themselves independent or even dominant. On the contrary, it is the existence of representative democracy that allows social movements to take shape and makes political parties subordinate to those movements. People's power, by contrast, produces demonstrations of loyalty to a political power that always transcends social interests, which are always seen as being particular and transitory.

The idea of a direct democracy that expresses the general will, the collective consciousness or the common good is in no sense radical, and representative democracy is not moderate. In countries where political life is free, the call for direct democracy tends, rather, to be an expression of a crisis of political representation. At the end of the twentieth century, that crisis was so widespread and so acute that populist discourses, nationalist campaigns, and increasingly extreme calls for 'national preference' (*préférence nationale*), cultural homogeneity and the rejection of minorities were virtually all that we heard throughout the world. And where political freedoms do not exist, revolutionary calls for direct democracy are no more than strategies on the part of very active minorities who are trying to seize power. The formation of social movements, on the other hand, is bound up with solid public freedoms, and therefore with a representative democracy that recognizes a plurality of opinions and interests.

Our political history has in fact been dominated by the gradual rise of representative democracy, as opposed to direct people's democracy. Ever since the French Revolution, there has always been a conflict between the idea of the people, which is a legacy of the monarchical state, and the idea of human rights, which soon came to mean the defence of political pluralism, human rights and cultural minorities.

The republican idea, which was associated with the national consciousness, was based upon a combination of themes that were both complementary and contradictory: the rule of law and respect for public freedoms. There can be no democracy unless the territory and its population are integrated by the same laws and by a single administration applying general and impersonal laws that make no allowances for relations of kinship, patronage or vested interests. Nor can democracy exist if the law does not recognize individual and collective rights, especially the right of freedom of expression and the right to own property. The primary objective of the early democracies was to establish the right to pay only those taxes that had been voted by representatives of the people sitting as a parliament.

In most cases, however, the rule of law and the constitutional state were established by absolute monarchies, whereas enlightened despotisms usually relied upon reason and bureaucracy to build their power and to resist democratic ideas. Conversely, freedoms were usually associated with the development of trade rather than with the formation of modern states. Those who, even today, identify democracy with the republic, or even put their faith in the republic rather than democracy, wilfully forget that there have been such things as authoritarian or oligarchic republics, and that civic republicanism was a form of nationalism. It was a force for national integration, rather than a means of establishing government for the people and by the people. The democratic spirit is based upon both the participation of all in shaping the laws and rules that govern collective life and the safeguarding of private life. It is a combination of public-spiritedness and individualism. The republican model's contemporary defenders reduce it to its universalist principles and equal rights; they ignore the fact that it derived most of its strength from the way it legitimized the nation-state. It gave greater legitimacy to Napoleon, the Convention, the supporters of Louis Napoleon Bonaparte and the Gaullistes than to the supporters of Louis Blanc or the militant supporters of anti-colonial struggles.

The oldest democracies – that is, those of Holland and Great Britain and then the United States and France – have always combined public-mindedness with individualism, and republicanism with secularism. The reason why in recent years we have seen such a powerful resurgence of the republican idea in France – and a senior Freemason has even contrasted its strength with the confusion surrounding the democratic idea – is in part that it appears to be the only idea that can still preserve the supremacy of a political order which has been freely chosen by economic or religious forces that are as alien to one another as freedom of opinion, freedom of speech and freedom of association.

Even though we have to respect the republican idea and the belief that political action can reduce social inequalities and fight injustice, we also have to admit that the republican idea is declining in importance, and, more specifically, that it is no longer self-evident that the political order takes priority over the social organization.

The history of democracy in the nineteenth century was dominated by the search for a social democracy as well as a political democracy. We can take 1848 as the symbolic date that, at least in Europe, marks the beginning of the republican conception of democracy.

At that point, the working class began to demand not only freedom and justice – which are universal principles – but also safeguards for particular categories and the right to negotiate directly with its employers. The idea of universal rights and that of particular interests soon began to converge; so too did the political and social orders. In the same way, but at a later date, women fought for equal rights, but also for the defence of their interests and personality, which were recognized as being at once different from, and subordinate to, those of men. Until the end of the nineteenth century, or in other words the start of the First World War, universalism and particularism coexisted, sometimes coming into conflict and sometimes reinforcing one another. There was an unresolved conflict between the need to build a stronger social democracy and the need to defend a common identity. Conflicts between classes and nations gave the democratic idea an extraordinary mobilizing power, but they also paved the way for the construction of homogeneous societies defined by the power of either the proletariat or a nation, and that was disastrous for democracy.

Our conception of democracy is a combination of the complementary demands for freedom and equality, the idea of the sovereignty of the people, which we more usually describe as citizenship, and the idea of human rights, which inspired the American and French revolutions and which restricts the power of the state in the name of a principle that transcends social reality. This idea accords an increasing importance to pluralism, so much so that respect for minorities has become as important to us as majority rule. The combination of these three themes – citizenship, basic human rights that place limitations on power, and a pluralistic representation of interests and opinions – found its most powerful expression in the slogan 'Freedom, Equality, Fraternity'. This was the motto of the French Republic, of the Empire between 1793 and 1814, of the Second Republic of 1848–51, and then of the Third Republic from 1875 onwards. Freedom is meaningful only because the existence of a plurality of interests has been recognized, whereas equality is a principle that transcends social realities, which are always marked by inequalities, and fraternity, which we tend to call 'solidarity', is the concrete expression of citizenship.

The republican idea was an attempt to reconcile citizenship (a principle of unity) with representation (a principle of diversity) and with the appeal to a universalist principle. It also attempted to take into account real social situations and relations by reconciling the individual, classes and all social categories within political society. Civil society was founded upon reason, which was seen both as a universal principle common to all individuals and as a principle that could reconcile conflicting interests, and upon secularism, which meant that beliefs and traditions that had nothing to do with either reason or social integration into society were relegated to private life. The republican synthesis was more than an ideology; it inspired political institutions and practices.

The crisis of this republican synthesis is a central feature of the more general crisis of the nation-state. That synthesis has in the past been threatened or destroyed by nationalist dictatorships and by regimes that described themselves as the dictatorship of the proletariat. It is now being threatened by the growing dissociation of a globalized economy from cultural identities that are becoming defensive and introverted or are being mobilized by authoritarian powers. The economy seems to be increasingly subordinate to the financial world. Individuals and nations can no longer control the flows of money, commodities and information that wash over them and have an ever-increasing effect on the way they behave. They therefore turn in upon themselves. Individuals retreat into private life, family life, sexual life and sometimes into community activities related to their leisure interests or their ethical and humanitarian convictions, whilst nations retreat into a cultural heritage which is, they feel, being threatened or dominated by some hegemonic power.

Democracy in crisis

Squeezed between the economic unification of the world and its cultural fragmentation, what was once the space of social life, and especially political life, is disappearing. Political leaders and parties are losing their representative function so rapidly that they are sinking into corruption or cynicism, or are being accused of doing so. Parties are now no more than political companies that promote candidates, rather than programmes or the social interests of those who give them a mandate. Contemporary Italy, France and Japan are obviously not living under authoritarian regimes; freedom of opinion and the freedom to vote are respected. Their citizens make what they see as meaningful choices, and one might even think that serious attempts are being made, or will be made, to reconstruct a democratic politics. Yet voters in these countries do not feel that they enjoy full citizenship. They have no faith in their political leaders, and feel that they are poorly represented, or not represented at all. In many countries, democracy means no more than the absence of absolute power and the triumph of the market economy. And whilst there can be no democracy without a market economy, a market economy is often associated with non-democratic regimes.

Three positions have emerged from the ruins of the republican synthesis. The first is a neo-republicanism which appeals to the principles that triumphed at the end of the nineteenth century, but gives them an increasingly conservative and defensive meaning. The appeal to reason, for instance, becomes a way of excluding and marginalizing social categories (especially immigrants) that come from a non-secularized culture. The invocation of the Republic becomes a demonstration of distrust of foreign influences. The distinguishing feature of this republicanism is that it does not allow dominated categories to appeal against the decisions of their masters. This school of thought is by no means confined to France, but France has such a powerful claim upon the republican idea that one is reminded of the power of the neo-Jacobinism that triumphed in the nineteenth century.

The second position is the least coherent but also the most widespread. Democracy is reduced to meaning political pluralism. The old Whig spirit of Guizot and Burke has found many new supporters. It is not up to the people to make political choices; the people has to be content with choosing between a number of policies drawn up by a social and intellectual élite whose specialist skills are called upon by a number of governmental teams. The important thing is to preserve the elective polyarchy which Robert Dahl has described as the essence of democracy. This political pluralism causes the ruling interests few problems at a time when economic power is less and less subordinate to political power. It has, however, contributed to the rise to power of judges, who seem to be the last obstacles standing in the way of the croneyism and corruption born of the collusion between political and economic leaders. In Italy, France, Spain and other countries, judges are acquiring more power at the very time that public opinion is rejecting the 'political class'.

The third position cannot but be marginal in industrialized countries enjoying self-sustaining growth, but it is important in many dependent societies: the call for communitarian, moral and religious integration. Carlo Mongardini has recently stressed that religion can once more play a regulatory role in countries where politics is in crisis (Mongardini and Maniscalco 1989). This idea has been more often expressed and applied in the United States (where the 'moral majority' brought Ronald Reagan to power) than in Europe or Latin America, but it has found a supporter in Pope John Paul II, who has both linked the world-wide defence of democracy with the crusade to defend the Christian values that must provide society with its foundations and stated that truth is more important than freedom.

In countries where states are not mobilizing all their cultural resources around a religion or an ideology, a combination of these three currents dominates the political horizon. And there is a striking contrast between their strength and the long-term decline of those currents that once called for social democracy. At a time when the socialist parties have become weak – so weak that they have ceased to exist in the case of Italy – and when trade-unionism has lost much of its strength in the United States, Spain, Great Britain and above all France, the democratic spirit is involved in the struggle against exclusion rather than the defence of categories defined by the social domination from which they suffer.

Major campaigns to sway public opinion no longer make any appeal to the democratic idea. This is as true of movements that defend identities as it is of political ecology, which is often associated with democratic currents. There are also anti-humanist tendencies at work in political ecology, however, and these may encourage the rise of anti-democratic policies. How are we to avoid the conclusion that the democratic idea no longer mobilizes hopes and demands, that it has been reduced to the defence of institutional safeguards, and that it relies on the influence of consumers rather than the will of citizens?

Democracy cannot be reduced to the organization of free elections. The measure of democracy is the political system's ability to elaborate and legitimize social demands by putting them to the popular vote, either directly or indirectly. This implies that the political system can reconcile a diversity of material and moral interests with a unitary society. And reconciling the two means that constantly shifting frontiers have to be established between legal duties and individual or collective freedoms.

If we define democracy in terms of the ability to find institutional answers to social demands, we have to recognize that we live in a period in which democracy is in retreat. Economic policies are becoming increasingly de-institutionalized, and are being decided by the market or by the boards of big companies rather than by political decisions and laws. Cultural policies appear to be evolving in the same direction, and the law does less and less to intervene in the domain of morality. Public opinion has become aware of the political system's isolation; it regards parties as political companies that handle politicians in the same way that public relations firms handle campaigns. It is now commonplace for an advertising agency to become a public relations adviser, or in other words a political adviser, to a candidate or a party leader.

Many readers will object that this picture applies mainly to that part of the world that is most deeply involved in the globalized economy, and especially to the oldest nation-states, namely Great Britain, France and the United States. And given that institutions have always been stronger than social movements in Great Britain, and that the United States, by contrast, has great faith in the open society, it is in France that the crisis in the republican model is felt most strongly.

In other parts of the world, democracy is either in just as weak a position or faces still greater threats. Economic modernization and the development of the market have reduced the level of both state intervention and social mobilization, and, whilst most of Latin America's dictators have gone, social inequality is growing. Many countries in Asia or in the Arab-Islamic world have turned to a cultural nationalism that is obsessed with homogeneity, and in some cases are even rejecting minorities and beginning the process of ethnic or religious cleansing.

The contrast between the European-style countries (including the new industrial countries) and the peripheral regions reflects that between the cultural globalization which dominates the central countries and the retreat into cultural identity that is dominant in other countries. The breakup of the republican model that is so obvious in European countries, and especially in France, is also occurring on a world scale.

The freedom of the Subject

Our negative findings mean that we must begin to think in more normative terms. How can we build a democracy, now that the republican synthesis has failed us? That synthesis presupposed that democracy's social site was a political and territorial collectivity. How can we go on speaking of democracy now that the *polis* has been replaced by the global market and by information highways and consumer highways that ignore frontiers? And how can democracy take root in countries that have been mobilized, in both political and military terms, to defend their collective identities?

Can we still speak of democracy when culture and the economy, or the world of meaning and the world of signs, have been divorced, when political power no longer dominates either an economy that has been internationalized or cultures that have been defined as heritages rather than as interpretations of new practices?

We must begin by abandoning all principles of unity, be they political or cultural, national or social. The republican model was an avatar of the religious model. This is both obvious and openly stated in the United States, where, despite the separation of church and state, society is based upon ethical or moral ideas. The same is true of France, where the Republic would not have been so passionately secular had it not wanted to replace a religious cult with a civic cult, or the Christian faith with faith in progress. The growing divorce between the economy and cultures, on the other hand, is an international phenomenon.

Increasingly, the main task of contemporary states is to defend their companies and national currencies on the international markets. At the same time, the world of consumption is being fragmented into diversified life-styles and sub-cultures. If we are to be able to tolerate this divorce, we must find new mediations between the economy and cultures, and we must therefore either re-create the political system or create a stronger one. This can be done only if the political system is increasingly divorced from what has to be called the state, though we must stop giving that word the broad meaning it has acquired in France, where it refers in a very general sense to political institutions, powers and even the nation that the state is supposed to represent. We live in a world that has been both globalized and fragmented, and in which democracy is under threat from, on the one hand, the reduction of societies to markets and, on the other, the different forms of totalitarian politics that we have experienced, from the various forms of fascism to Leninism–Maoism and then neo-communitarian regimes, be they nationalist or theocratic. The only way to avoid this danger is to separate civil society, political society and the state.

The state is increasingly associated with the economic system. Civil society is now defined in cultural terms and not, as it was in the eighteenth century, in economic terms. The primary function of political society is to restrict the power of both the market and communitarian leaders. This is not a purely negative role, as it also allows cultural actors to communicate with one another by promoting an educational policy oriented towards the recognition of the Other and a politics of solidarity that reduces the distance between social categories and fights discrimination and segregation. This solidarist society has considerable means at its disposal, especially in modern Europe, where roughly half of the national product is managed not by the market, but by political and administrative channels.

The political system that is taking shape before our very eyes rejects the state, and is based directly on public opinion. That should calm the widespread fear of the media. A hundred years ago, the same fears that are now expressed about television were being expressed about the press. There is indeed a constant danger that commercial interests or dictators might gain control of the media, but the latter are also the forum where cultural demands, economic constraints and the problems of social integration and security can be most freely expressed. It is the strengthening of cultural associations and movements, and the support the media can give them, that will do most to bring social demands into the political field, and therefore to reconstruct democracy. As we move from political democracy to social and then cultural democracy, democratic action moves from the summit to the base and is decentralized. At the same time, the distance between social actors and political agents is being reduced. Political action is now, to an excessive degree, concentrated within parties that have become centres for managing patrons and winning seats for politicians; we have no reason to fear the media unless they come under the control of an authoritarian political power or become linked to a ruling coalition of economic interests.

The exhaustion of the republican synthesis means that democracy can no longer be defined simply as a form of state, and that it is no longer possible to identify the state with the political system. The political system is a mechanism for the representation of interests and for uniting a plurality of social actors to the unity of the law. The republican synthesis occurred at the level of the state, but democratic action is now oriented towards social actors rather than the state. 'Top down' democracy is being replaced by 'bottom up' democracy, or by what the Americans call 'grass-roots democracy'.

This is not, however, simply a matter of breaking with Jacobinism or democratic centralism (and we know what the Communist parties understood that phrase to mean); it is a much more serious matter of replacing

them with a new principle of social integration: the freedom of the Subject. Our task is now to reconcile the involvement of all in the world of
exchanges and technology with the defence of everyone's cultural identity.
That synthesis can come about only if we recognize the central value of
every collective and individual actor's ability and will to construct a
personal action. And the highest form of personal action is a life story,
or in other words the ability to transform situations into elements of a
personal project.

Democracy is being displaced downwards. It is being displaced away
from the relationship between the state and the political system, and
towards the relationship between the political system and social actors.
Democracy once created a citizenship that transcended a fragmented,
hierarchical civil society; it is now defending a diversity of actors, cultures,
associations and minorities and, what is more important, a freedom
which, in a diversified and changing society, is based upon the recognition
of the other as Subject. Universalism gave human rights priority over all
interests and all powers, even the power of those who spoke in the name
of the majority. As states come to be defined as the defenders of a
majority, a class or a nation, mass mobilizations tend to bypass this
universalist and individualist conception. As we leave behind a century
that has been dominated by totalitarian or authoritarian regimes and by
so-called revolutionary or nationalistic people's democracies, we must
find a new way of expressing the idea of human rights. Human rights
must come to mean the right to concrete individuation, and not simply the
right to belong to an abstract humanity.

This really is the point at which to adopt an idea that was so dear to
Benjamin Constant, that the freedom of the Ancients and the freedom of
the Moderns diverge. So long as democracy sought its foundations in
either the interest of the *polis* or the movement of history, the freedom of
the Ancients was dominant, and was associated with an ethics of duty and
a politics of progress. When the gods of the *polis* and history grow old and
die, freedom becomes an inner freedom. The democratic idea can therefore no longer resist powers by appealing to some higher principle, but
must appeal to the resistance of the personal Subject, and to the personal
Subject's desire to be an actor and the author of its own existence. The
Subject must resist the civic or historical logic which it sees as destroying
more and more of its freedom and more and more of its identity. At this
point, the democratic idea rebels against all philosophies of history.

This reversal of perspective took place in the heart of industrial society,
when the rights of man were transformed into social rights, and the rights
of citizens into the rights of workers. From democracy's point of view,
the reversal was not always successful and sometimes led to the anti-
democratic idea of the dictatorship of the proletariat. It did succeed

with the English-style social democracy that was defended by the Fabians and analysed in sociological terms by T. H. Marshall (1964). This model for industrial relations adapted the categories of political democracy to concrete social situations. In their negotiations and conflicts, wage-earners were defending not simply their own interests, but above all the right to negotiate their working conditions, their conditions of employment and their wages. We now speak in similar terms of the cultural rights of minorities and, more important still, the rights of women.

All this marks a break with the revolutionary notion of democracy, which defined social actors as the agents of progress or, conversely, historical regression. According to the revolutionaries, we had to overcome the contradictions that existed between the growth of the productive forces and a social organization dominated either by traditions and privileges or by a quest for profit that bore no relationship to the criterion of social utility. These conflicts were not simply conflicts between actors with different interests and orientations, but conflicts between the meaning of history and the defence of private interests. Democratic action seemed all the more necessary in that the workers, the nation, or some other figure of the people, were so completely dominated, exploited or alienated. And as this idea led to voluntaristic or even authoritarian political action, there was little chance of democracy flourishing.

The end of big politics

The extension of political democracy to social democracy made the worker, rather than the citizen, central to political life, and replaced the principle of the sovereignty of the people with that of social justice; but this was no more than a stage within a transformation which, as we can now see, affects the very way we see politics and democracy. This book opened with the theme of demodernization, or in other words with the crisis affecting the political institutions that once mediated between the outside world of nature and technology and the inner world of the ethical consciousness and desire. It opened with that theme because the rise of the Subject is inseparable from the fall of the political realm, and even of what is known as society. Democracy was – and often still is – defined as the good society, as the society which makes its members citizens and protects them from the arbitrary use of power and the interests of the powerful. This presupposed that members of society had what John Rawls calls a 'first-order preference' for a fair society, and that they therefore acted as citizens rather than as individuals with interests or beliefs of their own. Society could therefore be regarded as a political collectivity. This representation was dominant in France, whereas England took an early interest in the economic actor as well as the citizen. As Judith Shklar (1969) reminds us, the political culture of the United States was closer to that of France than that of England.

It is this political conception of society that is fading away. The societies of early modernity became constitutional states. But the economy is now being internationalized, and is constantly being disrupted by technological innovations and political, administrative and juridical interventions. And the principal task of governments is not to establish order, but to encourage change.

We expect democracy to respond to these external and internal pressures by protecting the freedom of the Subject from the truly inhuman logic of economic life, trade and competition, and that is not the same thing as safeguarding a few corporatist advantages. We no longer believe that the revolution will open the gates to freedom. On the contrary, we accord more and more importance to the idea of what Charles Taylor terms the 'politics of recognition'. As SOS Racisme, which was France's anti-racist mass movement, put it, 'Touche pas à mon pote' ('Hands off my pal'). That slogan derives from the same conception of politics as the feminist slogan 'Un enfant, si je veux, quand je veux' ('I will have children if I want them, and when I want them'). This is a matter not of creating a community of citizens, but of defending personal freedom, cultural difference and solidarity, and of doing so outside the realm of a state which is increasingly preoccupied with its role as a captain of industry. This sometimes means working with the state, and sometimes means working against it.

After a quarter of a century of economic globalization, we no longer even believe that we can reconstruct national social democracies. Pierre Rosanvallon and Claus Offe, together with the philosophers of the Frankfurt school, were amongst the first to disabuse us of our nostalgia for the Welfare State, though that obviously does not mean that we have to give up our social welfare system. It simply means that we have to divorce it from the administered economy into which it has been incorporated.

The societies of early modernity were dominated by the figures of great politicians such as France's revolutionaries and the great American presidents whose faces are carved in the rock. Industrial societies accorded less importance to political leaders, except when they were acting as wartime leaders. Politics has now been secularized. We no longer expect our leaders to be charismatic. Indeed, we distrust leaders who are the embodiment of a gift for political management and also enjoy glittering social or cultural careers, but we do not necessarily agree with parties that have been reduced to electoral coalitions when they argue that the political and social realms must be completely divorced. The Latin, European and Latin-American world is finding it very difficult to accept that at the turn of the century we have no great politicians – though some leaders can obviously still accomplish great things. That they no longer exist means, above all, that there are no more political passions – hence the growing rejection of political epics, of so-called emancipatory violence and of eloquent appeals to the judgement of history. The state, the political system and civil society are separate spheres. They interpenetrate one another, but are no longer component elements of a single societal construct.

The democratic spirit is as indispensable today as it was yesterday, because the defence of the Subject is effective only if it is safeguarded by a political system that becomes more and more independent of the manager-state and more and more responsive to social movements, the voluntary sector and public opinion, or in other words the forces of civil society. Civil society's main demands are for greater tolerance and less state interference in the domain of ethics, but this does not mean that it is content to take a purely defensive attitude. It knows that tolerance can lead to indignation, and protests against all attempts to promote the social homogeneity and the ethnic or social purity which inevitably result in the repression of minorities and all those who soon come to be known as deviants, the sick or traitors. The democratic spirit is libertarian rather than socialist. It no longer believes in the necessary alliance between reason, history and the people; on the contrary, it believes in the dissociation of system and actors and of power and freedom. Our democracy no longer dreams of the ideal society; it simply demands a society we can live with. Its strength no longer derives from a political will in the true sense of that term, but from the way social actors resist the logic of power, money and globalization. And that political resistance itself presupposes the existence of social, historical and cultural movements that are both strong and independent.

The democratic principle

If it is the relationship with equality that best defines the difference between Left and Right, it is the idea of freedom that inspires the democratic spirit. Democracy is in danger whenever we feel that our personal and collective lives are dominated by necessity, irrespective of whether that necessity takes the form of the nature of things, human nature, a revealed law or reason, the international economic situation or the essence of a national culture. And conversely, whenever a collectivity asserts its right to self-determination and its ability to take its own affairs in hand – which presupposes the existence of possible choices – democracy is present and growing stronger.

This is not simply a matter of respecting and safeguarding negative freedom: democracy requires an active will to liberation and faith in a collective capacity for action. Freedom and responsibility are inseparable. There can be no democracy if leaders are not accountable to the people and if they do not submit to both the voters' decision and the judgement of the law. More important still, the democratic spirit can exist only when we cease to believe in the need to surrender to some necessity, and only when the spirit of responsibility asserts itself. The republican struggle for political freedom, battles for social rights, the recognition of the cultural rights of all, and an awareness of our responsibilities to the past and the future, to our environment and to our own physical and psychological integrity, are all so many figures of democracy. That is why democracy is synonymous with the politics of the Subject, of a Subject that is always involved in collective emancipatory actions.

Jürgen Habermas defines democracy as a discursive and argumentative process that shapes a common will. That is why he wishes to place institutions and the law under the surveillance of citizens, who must all have equal access to that process and be involved in taking decisions that will lead to general agreement. This is a broader and more dynamic conception than Norberto Bobbio's more institutional conception of democracy and, as Alain Renaut (1989) rightly points out, it is not entirely different from John Rawls's conception. But can we agree with Habermas when he argues that individual rights and democratic institutions must be regarded as being coeval, and even that the institutions that allow the democratic process to take place are more important than the recognition of individual rights? We can agree with him if we take the view that individual rights exist prior to the political process and are truly natural, whereas it is only in concrete political and social situations that the Subject can be defended against economic or communitarian power. More specifically, we no longer believe that the right to defend one's property must be regarded as a basic individual right, as it often involves an element of domination. This is of central importance, because it means that we cannot identify democracy with Habermas's discursive and argumentative process. This is primarily because that process is never dominant; in most cases, it is unlikely to be anything more than a setting or an environment, and therefore it cannot succeed, as Luhmann stresses, in penetrating the internal logic of the systems of domination or the systems that reproduce that domination. The Subject never triumphs, and democracy is always an effort, a protest and a will to reform that never succeeds in establishing a community of citizens. This is why the liberation of the Subject must take priority over the political process – which means that the real objective of democratic action is not to build a fair society, but to create more room for freedom and responsibility in a society that is always unfair. Social movements always take priority over institutions. All references to participatory democracy are dangerous, because they imply an attempt to legitimize state power, and state power has never been separated from economic or communitarian power. This is the meaning of the distinction I make between the state and the political system, which cannot be divorced from social movements.

Whilst the importance that Jürgen Habermas accords to the process of discussion does make democratic action more dynamic, there are no grounds for agreeing with Apel's (1990) claim that, being based upon the inevitable universal presuppositions of argumentation, the discussion process inevitably and ideally encourages the parties involved to adopt a role. The debate is usually blocked by the defence of vested interests, the construction of ideological systems and defensive tactics. As John Rawls notes, a dialogue between individuals does not lead to decisions that everyone regards as having a universal import. It leads at best to a universal recognition of what is being unconditionally defended by all. Jean-Marc Ferry expresses this central idea in striking terms when he criticizes the golden Kantian rule of not doing unto others what you would not like to be done to you, 'as though that meant that Ego did not have to worry about what Alter would not like to be done to *him*' (1994: 74).

The debate must lead to the recognition of the Other and, more importantly, to the recognition of the basis of the Other's subjectivation: the ability to reconcile instrumental action and cultural identity by himself and for himself. A democratic process results not in the formation of a general will, but in the recognition that everyone has a space in which he or she is free to act. What stands in the way of that recognition is the resistance of self-interest, and the constant temptation to thwart it by appealing to shared communitarian values. If we do that, we reintroduce the forms of power that the Subject must resist in order to exist, and they may swallow up the Subject. These resistances and obstacles are not really taken into account by Habermas, and especially not by Rawls. Halbrecht Wellmer remarks of the latter that 'The concept of an "original position", which is a conceptual fiction, is the means whereby Rawls guarantees that the strategic calculations made by individuals will be made under the constraints of a universalist morality' (cited by J.-M. Ferry 1994: 82). Defining forms of social safeguards that can defend personal freedom is democracy's primary task. Democracy is an absolute assertion, not of the sovereignty of the people – which is indistinguishable from the absolute power of the state – but of the universal right to individuation, and therefore subjectivation. Institutions and models of the ideal society are not ends in themselves; they are means of promoting a non-social principle.

Democracy and social movements

Social movements and democracy are closely linked; one cannot exist without the other. Democracy is both the instrument and the outcome of the institutionalization of social conflicts. Without democracy, social movements could not take shape. They would either be reduced to explosions of anger, or would be used by political forces trying to seize control of the state. Without social movements, democracy would be both weakened and restricted to meaning a contest between political coalitions.

The link between social movements and democracy does, however, take very different forms in proto-modern or industrial societies and in the contemporary world, which is dominated by the autonomy of a globalized economy.

For a long time democracy was experienced as a liberation from both economic exploitation and a social domination which prioritized inherited wealth at the expense of labour and preserved the privileges of ruling classes with private means. At this time, the democratic idea was fairly close to the revolutionary idea, but that ceased to be the case when it succeeded in having social rights recognized, and thus in restricting social domination. It could do so because, although they were in conflict, the social adversaries concerned recognized the same values – namely labour, progress, science and technology.

Social democracy, which developed in European countries, was always threatened on the one hand by revolutionary uprisings and on the other by the power of parties which were often unrepresentative of those social categories that were most directly involved in class relations. From its beginnings in Great Britain and Germany at the end of the nineteenth century to the great development of the Welfare State after the Second World War, social democracy spread constantly. Indeed, it was seen for generations as a *true democracy* which could be contrasted with both *formal democracy* and the authoritarian regimes born of revolutions. Our industrial democracy derived its strength from social conflicts, and it resolved them in legal or contractual ways. Those industrial countries that, like the United States and France, were slow to establish this industrial democracy could not, despite what they said about themselves, be regarded as profoundly democratic until the era of the New Deal and the Popular Front. Conversely, and even though class differences remained greater than in other countries, Great Britain could be regarded as the democratic country *par excellence* because labour disputes were handled institutionally at a very early stage. Although the Tocquevillean tradition defines equality, and therefore democracy, in terms of the destruction of social barriers, it is the legal and contractual limitation of social, economic and national domination that now best defines the struggle for equality, and therefore democracy.

If, however, we take the view that social democracy is a way of handling conflicts that are bound up with the forms of domination specific to modern societies, our definition is more applicable to industrial and commercial societies than to our own society. As economic power becomes more impersonal and comes to be based on profits rather than privileges, and on commerce rather than production, the primary contradiction, as we have seen, is not between property-owner and dependent wage-earner, but between the technical, commercial or financial apparatus and the dependent consumer. Domination becomes impersonal, whilst dependency becomes personal. It is the individual, defined as a personality rather than a particular social role, who is affected by the logic of the international financial system, or of the structures of medical care, the educational system or the media.

Whereas social adversaries once came into conflict over the social use of the cultural values they all shared, we now have a conflict between, on the one hand, a system which imposes its meaning and, on the other hand, individuals, categories and collectivities that have been denied the ability to create meaning, and have been either marginalized or excluded. In this new situation, there is a great danger that there will no longer be any possible basis for negotiations between the dominant system and its victims, and that the latter will either suffer a personal or collective crisis or will retreat into a counter-culture because they cannot build a social movement. What, in these circumstances, might the objective of a democratic politics be? In a world dominated by markets which intervene more and more in the domain of culture and personalities, and not simply in that of material goods and services, democratic politics has more to do with the defence of personal and collective identities than with appeals to universal rights.

This democracy, which we can describe as a cultural democracy, therefore differs from earlier forms of democracy, in that it does not appeal to a philosophy of history but to a moral philosophy, not to a vision of the future or of the end of humanity's prehistory but to a conception of human rights that founds a whole series of rights. These rights are as universal as the rights of the citizen, but they must be defended in concrete situations, or in other words in opposition to a system of domination. There are three such situations. First, the domination of the global economic and financial system leads to growing inequalities and more exclusion. Second, this impersonal domination forces social actors to fall back on their personal or communitarian identity, and therefore encourages the rejection of minorities. Because they live in the heart of the information society, consumers must, finally, rely on organized health care, education and information, and are therefore subject to the instrumental logic of systems of production and management.

Democracy therefore has three main objectives. First, it must reduce class differences, and that means strengthening the social and political controls on the economy. Second, it must ensure that cultural diversity is respected, and guarantee equal social and cultural rights for all. Third, it must take into consideration the demands of those who must not be reduced to being mere consumers of health care, education and information.

The freedom of the Subject is the central principle on which democracy is based. Democracy cannot be reduced to a cultural *laissez-faire* policy or to a generalized tolerance, as a purely negative politics would lead to the complete fragmentation of society, or in other words to exacerbated inequalities and segregation. Freedom must be actively defended by ensuring equal opportunities for all, creating the pre-conditions for mutual recognition, and stimulating an awareness of being part of a free society.

Nothing, therefore, could be more dangerous, for social movements and democracy alike, than the idea of a free and fair society. The dream of a society and a culture that have been completely transformed by the socialist idea, or by some political force closely associated with a social movement, inevitably leads to authoritarian solutions. Democracy and social movements can be reconciled only if they remain separate, and only if both terms are defined within certain limits. The work of Norberto Bobbio represents an attempt to give a definition of democracy that goes beyond the domain of the state and extends to all aspects of social life – and, as he writes in *The Future of Democracy* (Bobbio 1987), to business and the public administration in particular. At the same time, Bobbio retains a truly institutional definition of democracy. The institutional definition becomes more pronounced as we move from *Which Socialism?* (first published in 1976) to *The Future of Democracy*. The analysis he makes, especially in his earliest book, is quite similar to the analysis I subsequently made in *What is Democracy?* (Touraine 1997), where I defined the three essential elements of any democracy as limitations on power, socially representative political leaders and citizenship. No matter whether we use these terms or those employed by Bobbio (wider participation, controls from below and freedom of opposition), we are defining the political pre-conditions for the existence and activity of social movements, which are the main agents of reforms. And this is a far cry from trying to bring about a revolutionary mutation in society by seizing power. This definition of democracy is at once broad and restricted, and it calls for an equally open definition of social movements. This is why it has to be stressed that the conflict around which a social movement is organized is not a fight to the death or a confrontation with an enemy, as both adversaries share the same cultural orientations.

We now have the overwhelming impression that part of the world's population and part of every country will be excluded from a globalized civilization. In Western countries in particular, where average wages are high and the social welfare system is generous, there is a marked tendency to support the competitive sector, which has a high rate of value added, and to accept the marginalization of sectors with low productivity and low wages, as they are more exposed to competition from the new industrial countries. This dualization is familiar in the Third World, where the economy is divided into two sectors: the formal and the informal. The formal sector guarantees higher productivity, higher wages and better social welfare, but in a number of countries the informal sector is much larger. This is the case, for example, in Peru, where, thanks to the pioneering work of José Matos Mar and Hernán De Soto, this phenomenon has long been the object of serious study. Can we speak of democracy when this type of duality is dominant, and was there any cause for surprise when Alberto Fujimori came to power in Peru both because the poor voted for him *en masse* and because he had the support of economic leaders? Can we speak of democracy when the dominant feature of the economy is the structural heterogeneity described by Latin-American economists like Celso Furtado and Anibal Pinto? These marginalized categories, which are largely made up of unemployed youth, are part of a mass culture to the extent that they are consumers, but they do not have the means to become Subjects; they are influenced by mass consumerism and the media, but they are also trapped in local territories that tend to become ghettoes.

In such a situation, the decline of democracy is serious, because the political system has no control over either mass consumerism or communitarian identities. Solidarity cannot be limited to providing welfare for those who have lost their jobs, or for the sick, the victims of accidents, the unemployed and the retired. Personal social security must be supplemented by a collective social security which fights growing social inequalities, the isolation of underprivileged neighbourhoods, segregation and the rejection of minorities. Solidarity is as essential an aspect of democracy as the recognition of diversity. Without it, democracy means no more than the organization of political competition.

The politics of the Subject

The expression 'the politics of the Subject' appears to me to provide a better definition of democracy today than any other formula. The new forms that are now taken by the general principles of 'Freedom, Equality, Fraternity' are the recognition of cultural diversity, the rejection of exclusion, and the right of every individual to have a life story in which he or she can realize, at least to some extent, a personal and collective project.

Such ideas encounter resistance, and it centres on two main objections. It is claimed that they ignore social struggles and encourage a hedonistic or utilitarian individualism rather than the classical conception of democracy, which stressed the importance of civic duties and regarded every individual as a citizen.

The former objection is the stronger of the two. In all eras, democracy has been contrasted with oligarchy or monarchy because it represents government by all, as opposed to government by the few or by one person. How can it be denied that there is a conflictual and militant dimension to democracy? How can we take the risk of denying that the liberation movements or the wars of independence that gave rise to the democracies of Holland and the United States were democratic actions? The answer to these doubts is that democracy is possible only if conflicts are social before they become political, and therefore only if the political plays a subordinate role. The best definition of the goal of contemporary cultural movements is the idea of empowerment or autonomy, which demands that groups and individuals should have the power to act on their environment, and to become the actors in their personal and collective histories. Democracy cannot really exist, or exist actively, unless political institutions can absorb or reduce the pressures brought to bear by markets or communities and thus give actors a greater autonomy. This presupposes that the political system actively intervenes on behalf of the most dependent so as to guarantee their safety, freedom and capacity to take the initiative. The future of democracy, today as in the past, depends both on the safeguarding of free institutions and on the strength of the movements that oppose all forms of domination, be they economic, national or religious.

The liberal or institutional conception of democracy must be defended against dictatorships that speak in the name of the nation or the proletariat, but that does not mean that political negotiations should defuse social conflicts. A democracy that is not based upon autonomous social struggles and the defence of the truly cultural issues that are at stake is a democracy built on sand. The Western democracies of the past were strong when they were based upon an open class struggle, as in northern Europe, but they were weak in southern Europe, where the working-class movement became subordinated to either republican, Communist or anarchist political struggles, and where there was only a marginal role for direct action syndicalism. In France, a country in which political categories have always dominated social categories, Jacobinism and republicanism were mainly responsible for the weakness of the labour movement. When the class struggle becomes political, social movement ceases to be democratic. Those who, especially in Italy, thought that the skilled working class that created the labour movement could be replaced by mass-workers and state monopoly capitalism, and that priority should therefore be given to political struggles against the state, soon became involved in anti-democratic actions and even terrorism. Similarly, those who, in Latin America and elsewhere, defended the 'focista' thesis, or the idea that class struggles had no autonomous field in countries characterized by extreme dependency, were drawn into guerrilla actions which had no real links with the populations in whose name they mobilized, or they supported authoritarian regimes. The people's wars instigated by the Khmer Rouge in Cambodia and Sendero Luminoso in Peru were even more destructive, because they plunged their countries into violence. Their use of violence unleashed even greater violence against them. The idea of class struggle lost most of its mobilizing power when it came to mean that a political vanguard controlled a social movement that was both weak and dominated by that very vanguard. It is difficult to win recognition for the democratic ideal in countries which have become accustomed to revolutionary action, which is usually identified with a form of vanguardism. Its most disastrous effect is to replace social actors with militant revolutionaries from a radicalized middle class. They speak in the name of the people, but their motives are much more political than social. For such revolutionaries, the combination of a desire for self-sacrifice, a taste for power and the will to destroy the past was much more important than any project for the future – which was usually defined solely in terms of the seizure of power. They gave birth to a world of war and death in which there was a clear distinction between good and evil. And the militants themselves were its prisoners.

The other set of objections is put forward in a less tragic context. These objections tend to be voiced in societies that enjoy sustained development, or so-called developed societies. Does not the call for diversity necessarily destroy equality? On the contrary. It can be argued that affirmative action programmes or positive discrimination and the quest for fairness do more to promote the democratic idea than general principles of equality which do not challenge real inequalities precisely because some people can use abstract equality to their own advantage. The taxes paid by the population as a whole, for instance, are used to pay for the education of the children of the middle and upper classes. It is a long time since PREALC, which was the ILO's Latin-American research centre (it no longer exists), launched its manifesto *Desarrollo con equidad* ('Development and Fairness'). This called for the repayment of the 'social debt' owed to the popular categories which had borne the full burden of the economic and financial crisis of the 1980s, and for a struggle to be waged against an inequality that was, and is, growing. Giving to everyone in accordance with their needs means encouraging social categories to negotiate, but it also means taking political decisions that benefit the most underprivileged categories. When women demand equal political representation, their demands shock the defenders of a pure equality of opportunity, who point to the dangers of introducing proportional representation for all social categories. We have to support women's demands, because it was in the name of the rationalist bourgeoisie's dichotomy between rational and non-rational beings that the right to vote was for so long restricted to men, or certain categories of men. The law therefore has to impose equal representation for men and women, or in other words recognize that women are political Subjects too. Equality is a right, but in the real world it must take the form of a search for a negotiated fairness and of measures that favour the weakest. In democratic countries, social inequalities must not be allowed to develop or to persist because they may be hidden behind the general principles of freedom and equality.

The excesses of political correctness in the United States must not obscure the essential point that that country's cultural movements are engaged in a struggle against all forms of cultural domination and the illusion that history has a single or integrated meaning. The women, Blacks, Indians and white male Americans who live in the United States obviously do not have separate histories, but the categories employed by historians are broadly identified with the vision of the dominant group. Shedding light on what Nathan Wachtel calls 'the vision of the defeated' is a matter of urgency.

It would once have been argued that these themes have nothing to do with a discussion of democracy. But we now see them as central to that discussion, as democracy means freeing ourselves from the effects of domination and encouraging a dialogue between cultures which are not, I repeat, completely separate worlds, but so many attempts to give a general meaning to different combinations of cultural identity and instrumental rational action.

The democratic spirit is not reducible to a demand for equal rights that ignores real inequalities. If, in industrial society, the democratic spirit had not led to the safeguarding of workers' rights and, more specifically, to the signing of collective labour contracts, it would have become an ideology promoting the interests of the new bourgeoisie, which hid behind the struggle against clericalism and religion in order to defend its own material interests. In the same way, the democratic spirit is now weakened whenever it fails to take into consideration cultural rights, and therefore the dignity of all, or in other words the right to live in accordance with one's own values. It is weakened when it does not strive to establish the rule of fairness, which is defined by relationships between social and political actors. Fairness means the application of equality in concrete situations, but equality implies a reference to a principle that exists outside real social relations.

There is certainly a danger that this principle of fairness will be used by interest groups which do not want to reduce inequality. But there is no destiny that forces our societies to reduce their political management to a market in particular interests. Fairness and respect for the dignity of all are principles of social organization that promote the freedom of the greatest possible number.

When we speak of equality, we introduce the principle of a correspondence between personal rights and social organization by eliminating all reference to concrete social situations or by accepting 'the veil of ignorance'. This makes it possible to conceive of an ideal society, and thus to justify the absolute power of any expression of the general will. The idea of fairness, by contrast, not only asserts the role of negotiations and contracts; it also admits that it is impossible to define an ideal situation, to enter the realm of the universal, or to ensure that rational thought and rational institutions recognize universals. This displacement is analogous to the shift from rational to reasonable made by John Rawls in his *Political Liberalism* (1996). He was later obliged to accept that where questions of morality or religion are concerned, a public consensus as to basic philosophical questions cannot be reached unless the state infringes upon basic liberties. In so far as it is a search for a truth defined as an independent ethical and metaphysical order, philosophy cannot provide a common or practical basis for a political conception of justice in a democracy. Which brings us back to the idea of secularism, not in the sense of an artificial divorce between private life and public life, but in the sense of the subordination of public life to the Subject's demands for freedom.

Whatever the outcome of democratic processes (which must be set free from all juridical reification, as we are reminded by Jürgen Habermas, who, like Horkheimer and Adorno before him, does not trust the social state), the gulf between the Subject and society can never be bridged. We therefore have to reconcile fair compromises with the ethics of conviction that places limits on state interventions. The call for fairness does not favour the most powerful. On the contrary, it makes it possible for all to become involved in a democratic debate in every domain of social life.

Many ideologues continue to resist these ideas. Yet they do correspond to practices that can be seen everywhere. This is especially true of the social work field, which is in such direct contact with reality that it has no time for ideas that do not enhance the capacity of the weakest for action and freedom. And that capacity cannot be enhanced unless we reconcile, in the life of everyone, a cultural and psychological identity with involvement in the activities and decision-making processes of society.

Two pre-conditions for democracy

How are we to bring about this reconciliation? Democracy must be seen as a set of institutional political mechanisms that safeguard and facilitate the process of reconciliation. If such mechanisms are to come into being, a communitarian culture must first be transformed into an inner conviction or an ethics. That transformation did occur to some extent in the West, though not without some serious distortions, thanks to the Protestant Reformation and certain aspects of the Catholic Reformation. It must now take place in the Islamic world thanks to the new interest in the mystical tradition and thanks to an active critique of the way a social organization has become confused with religious beliefs. There is a name for this dissociation: secularism. Secularism is not simply an ideology associated with the struggle against the temporal power of a church. It is an essential element in democracy, because, by separating temporal power from spiritual power, it limits both. It opposes both theocracy and civil religions. The principle of secularism condemns both clericalism and the civil-clerical Constitution introduced by revolutionary France and the way in which some liberation theologians have become identified with a political power in Central America.

The second function of democracy is to ensure that there are social controls on economic activity, and to prevent a system of means from being transformed into a system of ends. The democratic spirit prioritizes politics, not economics. In Western Europe, it is Germany that has done most to develop the capacity for social negotiations, initially between employers and unions. Federalism, the Greens' partly successful transition to political action and *Bürgerinitiativen* have all played an important role here. France, by contrast, is exhausting itself in an attempt to defend an increasingly ideological republican model. In a period of accelerated economic upheavals characterized by huge losses of jobs in industry, the need for reskilling on a mass scale, the threat of growing dualization and an urban crisis, France must find a political way of managing the social changes brought about by technological and economic developments. The only explanation for the persistent distrust of state intervention is that interventionism is still associated with the old image of the centralizing and mobilizing state. Interventionism must become less statist and more political, and must be based on direct negotiations between the social partners involved.

Liberal thinkers have often reacted to the permanent danger that more forms of domination (or, conversely, forms of dependency) will emerge by proposing that what Michael Walzer calls 'spheres of justice' should be kept separate. Their separation, it is argued, will ensure that a dominant position in one sector of social life does not give privileged access to decision-making powers in others, will stop us from being governed by the rich, and will ensure that politicians no longer control what is taught in schools. This appears to be a truism: it is essential that religious authority should be separated from political power, and that the economy should depend on the market rather than the political will. Some even go so far as to define modernity in terms of the growing differentiation of particular social systems which require specific evaluative criteria and modes of government, rather than general managerial principles. We have to look at this more closely. First of all, it is artificial to regard religion, politics, economics, education and family life as sets of equivalents, and to say that whether they should be interlinked or separated is up to us. In modern societies at least, no one would dream of giving school-teachers full powers, or of taking the family as a model for the workings of society. There are, on the other hand, political or economic (and sometimes religious) models for the management of society as a whole. A society is not made up of relations between institutional domains; it is defined by the relations that exist between institutions and, on the one hand, political power and, on the other, private goals that can range from the accumulation of wealth to security and interpersonal relationships. Our freedom requires *raison d'état* to be separated from private interests; our servitude is complete when an all-powerful state is in the hands of private interests. When that happens, we speak of corruption, and it is a disease that can kill democracy.

Institutions such as the economy, the educational system, the family and even religion are all forms that mediate between the state and individuals, and they must be able to communicate with one another if they are not to be trapped in a one-way, unbalanced relationship with the state. If the law had no effect on the economy, it would be as meaningless as an educational system that ignored the needs of industry, or a religious life which had no effect on the family or the law.

The democratic spirit cannot be confined to the political domain alone. It must spread to every aspect of social life, to the work-place, schools and hospitals, the city and the voluntary sector, the courts and political meetings. The one thing that binds institutions together is the fact that they all have to answer the same question in their respective domains: how can we reconcile the unity of a social entity with the diversity of its component elements, and the different interests, values and opinions of its members? The ability to handle this problem does much more to determine the degree to which a society is democratic than the separation of – or the overlap between – various institutional spheres. The primary definition of democracy is that private demands, both individual and collective, take priority over the principles and objectives of political power. This downward displacement is a perfect expression of the democratic spirit. The separation of various intermediary institutional domains is not in itself an essential feature of democracy; nor does it pose a threat to democracy. Rather than wavering between Jacobinism and liberalism, let us choose representative democracy. But we have to understand that term as meaning the subordination of political agents to social actors, and not as the antithesis of direct democracy. Democracy must become representative once more. If it is not closely bound up with popular social movements and does not represent the demands and protests of those who are dominated by élites hiding behind the impersonal principles of rationality and order, democracy loses its strength and is used by the powerful as an instrument of political management.

Modalities of democratic action

The defence of the personal Subject always requires both institutional safeguards and a collective mobilization. But which element plays the main role varies, depending upon the historical situation. Hence the justification, or the need, for comparative analyses. We do need these synthetic studies, but we also need to adopt a more analytic approach and to construct types of regime or types of democratic action by looking at the relative importance of what might be regarded as the basic elements of, or tendencies within, democracy. The analysis proposed by Mary Douglas (1995) is sufficiently abstract to have great explanatory power. Similarly, the analyses made in this chapter can be used to construct a typology of the forms taken by the democratic spirit and democratic action, provided that we also define the most significant variables.

The first variable concerns the relative roles of the assertion of the Subject and the creation of the institutional pre-conditions for the freedom of the Subject. This is the most important dimension, as it defines the relationship between civil society and political society, and that between societal movements and institutional interventions. Democratic action cannot take place unless a social actor demands it. Democratic action cannot take place unless political agents take political decisions in response to democratizing demands, even though they respond at the level of institutional means and not at the level of social and cultural ends, which is where societal movements operate.

The second dimension, which is always present, is the nature of the obstacle standing in the way of democratization. Demands for justice always begin as protests against injustice; there can be no democracy without social conflict. Our analysis of social movements has shown, however, that, whilst they are conflictual, they always appeal to values that rise above the social conflict. It is because they defend those values that social movements come into conflict with what can be variously described as tradition, egoism or disorder. Democratic action therefore encounters both social obstacles and cultural obstacles. These two variables can combine in very different ways, depending on their relative weight in different historical situations. For the moment, we will content ourselves with defining the simple types generated by their interplay.

	Personal freedom	*Collective freedom*
Cultural obstacles	*Freedom*	*Emancipation*
Social obstacles	*Social movements*	*Equality*

The table reveals the existence of two extreme types of democratic action and two intermediary types. The combination of a collective action, or in other words a mobilization to obtain institutional safeguards, and a direct social conflict gives rise to truly political action, defined in the maximalist sense. That is why, as Norberto Bobbio's analysis demonstrates, the theme of equality plays the central role here. If, conversely, democratic action centres on the assertion of personal rights, and if the obstacles it encounters are not social, but cultural, and have more to do with the resistance offered by privileges or traditions than with relations of domination, its primary role is to defend freedom.

Defining the intermediary cases is the most important thing of all, as they are not reducible to the dichotomy between liberalism and socialism. A call for institutional measures, combined with a struggle against cultural obstacles, provides a good definition of interventionist politics, and the Welfare State was, and is, the primary example. Interventionist policies have been stimulated by emancipatory campaigns such as feminist campaigns to legalize contraception and then abortion. We can describe actions that are clearly centred on voluntaristic legal interventions as 'emancipatory'. The combination of a direct appeal to the Subject and a social conflict defines, finally, the nature of societal movements in societies which have reached an advanced stage of modernization, and which have the highest degree of historicity or the greatest capacity to act upon themselves. It is in such cases that democratic action comes closest to social action, whereas the themes of equality and emancipation are more political than social.

The contemporary importance of cultural movements and of resistance to the political system, which is still dominated by the institutionalization of past social conflicts, confers a particular importance on those radical demands and protests that exist on the fringes of political institutions and juridical mechanisms. In many cases, there is a great distance, and even great hostility, between political or union organizations, and grass-roots social movements which, in order to achieve their goals, rely upon the power of protest and the support of public opinion rather than the institutional mechanisms of reform. The social movements of industrial society are on the wane; those of the societies of late modernity are still being shaped, and political life is therefore developing in a social void. This helps to weaken democracy still further.

We can agree with Mary Douglas (1995) and Michel Albert (1991) that Reagan-style capitalism was associated with liberal movements, whilst Rhenish capitalism encouraged collective actions – and especially what I call 'emancipatory campaigns'. The dimensions identified by Mary Douglas – 'the degree to which the group makes demands on its members' and 'quantitative structural limits that restrict the right or individuals to negotiate freely amongst themselves' (Douglas 1995: 145) – are, however, very similar, whilst the nature of the conflict in which a democratic actor is involved is a dimension that simply must be included in the analysis, as no democratic action is free of conflict.

This typology does not define types of political regimes, or even types of conceptions of justice, but forms of democratic action. This is a direct result of the above analyses, which showed the need to situate democratic action in relation to the functional models of the social systems it is fighting, not in relation to an image of the ideal society.

Two ways out of the liberal transition

We have come a long way from our starting-point, which was the search for a principle that could limit the power of the state. After a century of totalitarianism, it was essential to ward off the most immediate threat and to ensure the recognition of a public space. So long as freedom, defined in that immediate sense, has not been guaranteed, there can be no meaningful discourse about democracy. In most of the world, that threat has receded and we now have to respond to the opposite threat of institutional formalism. This is less brutal, and can even be made to look attractive, but it too debases both freedom and democracy, and reduces them to the impersonal logic of the market. The fact that the logic of the market was an essential element in resistance and emancipation at the time when we were ruled by authoritarian regimes, and sometimes personality cults, does not legitimize the reduction of democracy to a competitive, or rather oligopolistic, political market. Without ever losing sight of the pressing need to defend freedoms, we must therefore give democracy a social and cultural content, and define it as the defence of those who are prevented by social relations of domination from living as Subjects.

The hopes we placed in the liberation of the proletariat and colonized people turned into a twentieth-century nightmare as social and historical movements turned into oppressive regimes. That explains the triumph of liberal thought in the last half of the century. That period is now coming to an end, and it is becoming apparent that reducing the management of the economy to the free play of market forces, and especially the free movement of capital, has its limitations and is dangerous. We have to begin to reconstruct a social conception of democracy. To take an example: if Algeria is to escape being crushed by the twin authoritarian threats of a military dictatorship and religious totalitarianism, movements that defend personal freedoms must emerge. The most important is the women's movement, as the status of women lies at the heart of the conflict. Is there any hope of a solution, other than a call for an uprising for freedom? No one knows if such an uprising is possible, or if it could transform the situation and lead to a peaceful solution. But the least we can say is that Algerian women are the living embodiment of democracy, as democracy cannot live without convictions and commitments.

So-called republican discourse no longer has this power to mobilize. Economic liberalism, which in practice meant policies of structural adjustment, played a major role in liquidating voluntaristic regimes and discourses that had become exhausted, paralysed or perverted. Are we therefore condemned to relive Europe's nineteenth century, to accept a new proletarianization, growing social inequalities and the triumph of the commodity? And does political choice have to be limited to a contest between two or more governmental teams? If we take that road, and those who belong to the upper middle class of the rich countries certainly find it tempting to do so, we will soon see the rise of new authoritarian or totalitarian regimes, and they will declare holy wars or mount attacks on the dominant countries in the name of nationalism.

Looking to the past will not provide us with a way out of this ambiguous liberalism either. Invoking socialism and the labour movement will not resurrect the democratic spirit or inspire democratic protests in our post-industrial societies. Appealing to the republican synthesis of the nineteenth century will have even less effect. We have to understand that the democracy which once fought inequality and social fragmentation by appealing to the unity of citizenship, and which then defended workers' social rights, must now defend cultural rights, or in other words the dialogue and mutual recognition between all those life projects that reconcile instrumental rationality and a cultural identity. There can be no democracy if personal and collective freedoms do not have institutional safeguards; but nor can there be any freedom if cultural movements do not promote both cultural diversity and personal freedom. This conclusion is not utopian; nor is it simply a critique of the dominant male culture. It merely reveals the significance of the real cultural movements that are making an important contribution to the construction of a new political culture: the women's movement, the defence of minorities, the struggle against fundamentalisms and the rejection of social exclusion.

The politics of the Subject is not reducible to the defence of the individual. Indeed, it would be an illusory politics if it allowed social determinisms to operate blindly. To speak of democracy does not mean safeguarding private life and leaving consumerism to develop unchecked. It means allowing both individuals and groups to become actors in their own histories, rather than being blindly influenced by the quest for profits, an exclusive belief in rationalization, the will to power or the worship of communitarian values. Democracy is the political form of the recomposition of the world. And the recomposition of the world is central to my argument, because I reject the dissociation of a globalized economy from fragmented cultural identities. Politics is the art of reconciling unity with diversity.

Social integration

Every society relates to violence in a specific way. The classic sociocentric society contained violence by strengthening institutionalized and internalized constraints, and by subordinating the pleasure principle to the reality principle, and private justice to public justice. This system is becoming exhausted, as is the nation-society of which it is one attribute. It is not being replaced by a consumerist individualism which holds that everything should be permitted and whose only solution to violence is the illusory solution of the attractions of consumerism. It may, however, be replaced by a new emphasis on the individual as Subject. Angelina Peralva follows François Dubet (1991) in stressing that many adolescents display what he calls 'anger', and what she calls the 'fear of death' or even 'anxiety about death'. The threat which makes them behave violently is not a threat to the social order, but one which affects the individual as Subject. The analysis has to be displaced away from a search for the economic or social causes of violence. We have to investigate the mechanisms that shape the violent individual. This approach presupposes a drastic change in the way we make sociological interventions. The analysis must not begin at the top, or with the law, but with the interpersonal relationships in which individuals, and especially young people, feel valued or devalued. It must recognize the dignity of the individual in concrete terms, and this presupposes that we recognize the territorial, ethnic, familial and religious identity of every individual, rather than defining and treating the individual as a desocialized or wild being.

In our societies, integration cannot be achieved by introducing stricter rules and greater conformism. It can only be achieved by displacing the goal of integration from the system to the actor, and from society to the individual. The important thing is not to stress that the integration of all (and not only immigrants) presupposes both that they have jobs, or in other words an organized social activity, and that they can assert their cultural and social identity, but to stress the need for the self-assertion of the Subject. When the unemployed youth of the suburbs say that they want someone to listen to them and understand them, or in other words that they want to be involved in political decision making – especially when it affects them – they are expressing an idea that is as important as the workers' old demands for social rights, or, at an earlier stage, the assertion that the people was sovereign and that all were equal in the eyes of the law. The words and the life of every individual must be central to collective life; before he or she becomes a citizen who takes part in the life of the state or a worker who plays an economic role, the individual must be a personal Subject who can construct an individuated life. This is the road we have to take if society is to rediscover the integration it has lost, and it will not do so by calling for stricter discipline or appealing to the general interest.

As we try to re-establish this bond of representation, we move further and further away from the rationalist-élitist conception of politics that brought liberals to power in the nineteenth century. Herbert Gans is right to wish that the democratic spirit would take more account of 'middle American individualism' (1988: 123): if citizens cannot or will not go to political institutions and play a part in them, those institutions must go to the citizens. This means that political parties and institutions must be more open to the influence of organized social demands and forces, and show a greater interest in enabling the underprivileged to take part in political life. And it will not be possible for them to do so without improvements in the social welfare system.

A long tradition has accustomed us to regarding individualism as the major threat to social integration. Yet it is the crisis in individualism, or the way the individual is torn between the world of objects or technologies and the world of culture, that provides the most profound definition of the crisis affecting our societies. We must stop believing that we are moving from integration to disintegration, that violence turns order into chaos, and that individuals whose lives have no social and cultural framework revert to being savages. Such arguments merely fuel nostalgia, and offer no solutions to the problems that they themselves define as the inevitable result of modernization.

We are emerging from a world in which violence was highly institutionalized, and are entering a world in which it is individualized. Our Western-style societies are at once relatively tolerant at the institutional level and harsh and violent at the level of individual behaviour. This has always been the case in the United States, which is a land of equality and respect for the Constitution. But it is also a land where the West was won by violence, a land which segregates Blacks, and a land with a brutally repressive police force and legal system.

Individual violence is as central to our societies as collective violence was to the societies of early and mid-modernity. Rather than strengthening norms and repressing deviance, the answer to individual violence may be to transform individuals' anger or fear into forces that can transform institutions, or at least create more social space for personal projects. It seems to me that the most serious forms of disintegration are those that prevent individuals from acting as Subjects, that destroy their personalities, prevent them from establishing links between their past and their future, between their personal histories and their collective situations, and which chain them to an addiction. Once again, analyses that concentrated on systems are giving way to different analyses which give pride of place to the ability of all individuals and all social categories to be the actors in their own existence, and to manage the changes which would otherwise be experienced as an incoherent series of accidents.

The crisis affecting our political institutions would not be felt so strongly if they were not the object of social and cultural demands to which parties and institutions have no adequate answer. Just as, 100 years ago, traditional political parties seemed to be blind to the social problems of industrialization and thus encouraged the formation of revolutionary vanguards, so the new demands at the end of the twentieth century, which are cultural rather than social, cannot find any political expression. In other words, social demand is once more outstripping political supply. And the democratic spirit is being reborn, not in the rivalry between parties, but in the way in which public opinion reacts when it opposes the negation of the Other, ethnic cleansing, wars to the death between ethnic, religious, political or social groups, and the perpetuation of the inferior position of women. The overall orientation of today's social and cultural movements is democratic, because they call upon us to live together with our differences.

8

A School for the Subject

The clearest manifestations of a society's spirit and organization are its juridical rules and its educational programme. The central themes of this book are the Subject, inter-cultural communication and democracy. If we are to be able to answer the question 'Can we live together?', or in other words, 'How can we reconcile the freedom of the personal Subject, the recognition of cultural differences and the institutional guarantees that safeguard that freedom and those differences?', we have to discuss education.

Although this may seem a self-evident truism, and although it is a favourite theme with politicians, education is in fact rarely discussed. This is not simply because of the scale of the problems posed by the massification of secondary and higher education, the difficult issue of the relationship between general education and vocational training, or the rise of violence in schools. Industrial society itself did not pay great attention to education, because it was so centred on production and labour relations. There appears to be an even greater lack of interest in contemporary society, where our schools often feel that they have been overtaken by what has been called 'alternative education', or in other words the media, especially television. It is as though our schools were on the defensive. It is as though we were witnessing the collapse of academic culture and were having to renounce the old conception of public education. It is as though our schools had been invaded by a youth culture which teachers find alien, especially when, given that most of them are from a middle-class background, they are faced with young people belonging to a sub-proletariat from a non-French background. Many politicians and managers find it so difficult to make secondary schools and universities function on a regular basis that they see almost no contemporary relevance in debates about education itself, and such debates are quickly dismissed as theoretical.

It was the triumph of political institutions, defined as agencies for the integration of rationalization and ethical individualism, that made education so vitally important from the sixteenth to the eighteenth century. In France, which was still thinking in terms of pre-industrial categories, or in political and institutional terms rather than economic and social ones, it remained of central importance until the development of the republican school of the late nineteenth century. In a society which made no distinction between citizenship and education, the school was seen as an agency for socialization. When individuals ceased to be defined as members or citizens of a political society and began to be seen primarily as workers, education became less important, because it had to be subordinated to productive activity and to the development of science, technology and well-being. Some people are still tempted to see education simply as a preparation for what they call the 'active life'. They argue that it should be controlled from below, or in other words that it should be adapted to meet the needs and capacities of the job market. Can we in fact describe that argument as being about education? Surely not, as it takes no account of the demands of those who are in education, and who are preoccupied with their personalities, their personal lives and projects, and their relationships with their parents and their friends. It is impossible to speak of education when individuals are reduced to the social functions they have to take on. What is more, the future of work is unpredictable, and most of those who are now at school will experience such great discontinuities that we should be asking schools to prepare them for change rather than teaching them skills that will soon be outdated or useless. To strike a more negative chord, we might add that it is dangerous to try to make young people adapt to an economy in which there is a high probability that they will be unemployed or will experience years of job insecurity. There is therefore no excuse for not thinking about what kind of education will help to remedy the effects of the demodernization that we are experiencing and to improve individuals' chances of becoming the Subjects of their existence.

From one educational system to another

Classical education was based upon three basic principles, and they were highly integrated.

The first was the will to liberate children (or newcomers to society) from their particularisms and to introduce them, through their own work and the formative disciplines they were obliged to study, to the higher realm of reason and knowledge. Children were also taught how to express themselves and to construct an argument. This principle was in keeping with the particular nature of Western modernization, which was based upon the dichotomy between the traditional and the modern, and on the revolutionary will to sweep away the past in order to promote progress. In France, we still use the expressions 'faire ses devoirs' (meaning both 'to do one's homework' and 'to perform one's duties') and 'étudier une discipline' ('to study a discipline'), even though they no longer imply any reference to a particularly authoritarian educational system. Corporal punishment was used for a long time, especially to prevent children from speaking their own language or dialect.

The second principle was the assertion of the universal value of the culture or even the society in which the child or young adult lived. What we used to call *paideia* (which has come down to us from the Greek) or *Bildung* (a product of German thought) meant much more than the acquisition of positive knowledge, socialization or learning to play social roles. The objective was, on the contrary, to give children a sense of truth, beauty and goodness, and to provide them with models of science, wisdom, heroism or sainthood. Education was moral as well as intellectual; but this culture of universal values was also closely associated with the glorification of a society that was considered to be the cradle of modern civilization and modern values. The history that was taught was that of the shaping of modern European civilization, beginning with the Greeks and Romans, and sometimes the Jewish world, and then moving on to Christendom (even though it was sometimes criticized), the Renaissance and the birth of modern democracy. If culture can be defined as a way of using particular practices to construct a universal meaning, this was indeed a cultural education, not simply an instrumental or utilitarian education. For a very long time, great importance was attached to the study of the classics and of national literatures, which formed the central core of the humanities. Classical education was clearly not reducible, that is, to socialization. This tradition's defenders were right to criticize attempts to reduce education to technical or vocational training. Whilst the old model of education did correspond to a figure of the Subject which, as I have already said, had long been in decline, it is still true to say that it was based on a concept of education. The same cannot be said of ideas which reduce education to learning to play social roles and internalizing the norms that govern them. Classical education did not reduce individuals to their social roles, even when, as was usually the case, it conformed closely to the ruling ideas and ruling political forces.

The third principle was that this twofold attempt to free children from tradition and to teach them higher values was closely related to the social hierarchy. As the higher categories were those which came closest to universalism and which had done most to free themselves from particular traditions and beliefs, schools tried to select the most hard-working individuals, or those who were most capable of abstract thought and of devoting themselves to values that were at once universal and national. This is what France called republican 'élitism'.

This conception was also modern, in that it was a challenge to the aristocratic and élitist model perfected by the Jesuits. Simonetta Tabboni gives a particularly good description of how that model was applied in the Collegio Moncalieri, which trained much of the social élite of Piedmont. This was a college which trained its pupils to assume positions of command, power and responsibility. As in the English public schools (which are in fact private), educational methods were harsh, and were designed to be character building rather than intellectual. Its young pupils (all boys) learned to be very self-disciplined because they would have to be able to impose discipline on others. They also acquired what their teachers called a consciousness of their responsibilities, or in other words a class consciousness. This was not the goal of 'modern' education (whose three main principles were described above). Germany's *Gymnasien* and France's *lycées* were its best representatives. The modern idea of education triumphed in higher education when the University of Berlin was established at the beginning of the nineteenth century. Its example was followed by Oxford and Cambridge at mid-century and then by American universities, beginning with Johns Hopkins and then Harvard in the second half of the nineteenth century. Modern education was intended to establish a new social hierarchy based on merit, not social origins, and it introduced a hierarchy of knowledge based upon levels of abstraction or formalization. As the eminent geophysicist Claude Allègre has pointed out, France still clings to the idea that mathematics is a higher form of knowledge than the experimental sciences, which are themselves superior to the observational sciences. On the 'arts' side, philosophy is at the top of an imaginary hierarchy, with the humanities occupying the intermediary levels, and the social sciences the lowest level.

This classical conception was quite in keeping with the nation-society, which at that time played a central role and identified particular nations with universal values, such as economic freedom and democracy in Great Britain; freedom, equality and fraternity in France; theoretical thought in Germany; political philosophy in Italy; or constitutional principles and equality of opportunity in the United States. More important still, it is based upon the idea that access to values and personal freedom is conditional upon involvement in social life, and that the nation is the expression of either the sovereignty of the people or a cultural and historical community. It can thus be demonstrated that there is a profound continuity between the three basic civilizational achievements: individual reason controls the passions; the state has a monopoly on legitimate violence; and scientific knowledge masters nature.

This conception of education is centred not on the individual, but on society, on what are known as values and on rational knowledge in particular. It departs from the Greek idea of the *kalos kagathos*, or the ideal, handsome and good individual, or in other words an individual who conforms to canons of excellence that are established by society but which also define an individual type. The individual of classical modernity learns to serve progress, the nation and knowledge.

This overview brings out the difference between classical education and a *school for the Subject*. A school for the Subject is oriented towards the freedom of the personal Subject, inter-cultural communication, and the democratic management of society and the changes that occur within it.

(1)   The first principle of a school for the Subject marks the most obvious mutation: education must shape and enhance the *freedom of the personal Subject*. We must, at least at this stage and if only to make a clean break with the theme of socialization, demand a shift from a supply-based educational system to a demand-led system, even though the expression might be dangerous. It does not mean that the school is a market where supply meets demand. Such a representation is obviously false, as a pupil has little ability to modify a supply which is defined, not as such, but in terms of the values to which a child has to conform in order to become a civilized social being. But it does strongly emphasize the fact that a school for the Subject cannot simply impose norms on its pupils, and that the powers it delegates to its teachers cannot be limited by political power alone. Rather than believing that individuals are savages until they have been socialized, schools must recognize the existence of individual and collective demands. A child who comes to school is not a blank sheet of paper on which a teacher can write knowledge, feelings and values. At every point in its life, a child has a personal and collective history, and that history always has particular features. Rather than freeing the universal from the particular, as in the classical model, education must make motives and objectives converge; a cultural memory must converge with the operations that allow individuals to play a part in a world of technologies and commodities. The individualization of education means that we have to put an end to the old divorce between the private sphere and public life, and therefore that between home and school. This has in fact already happened. The declining importance of the family means that schools now have to teach children things that, traditionally, they learned at home (in some cases, this can include teaching them about nutrition and personal hygiene). In many countries, on the other hand, children's

parents have already won the right to be involved in the life of their
schools.

(2)   The second principle is also the direct antithesis of its equivalent in
classical education. A form of education centred on the culture and values
of the society that provides the education in question is replaced by a form
of education that gives a central importance to diversity (both historical
and cultural) and to recognition of the Other. It begins by establishing
communications between boys and girls or young people of different ages,
and then encourages every possible form of inter-cultural communication.
A national form of education is an obstacle to what Edgar Morin calls the
'dialogical dimension' of contemporary culture. The dialogical dimension
implies a need for a school which is socially and culturally heterogeneous
and as far removed as possible from a communitarian school defined by
the fact that all its pupils have the same social, cultural or national
background. This orientation is essential in a world where time and
space have been 'compressed', where things that are far away and very
different become closer to us, either physically or in the form of images.
Things that we considered to be successive become simultaneous. Patterns
of migration develop. At the same time, we are all trying to defend what
makes us different in a world where the unifying forces of mass culture
and economic globalization seem to have gained the upper hand. Recognition of the Other is inseparable from the self-knowledge of a free
Subject that both has roots in one or more particular cultural traditions
and uses the same instruments as everyone else.

(3)   The third principle is the will to compensate for unequal situations
and inequality of opportunity. Whereas the classical model started out
with a general and abstract conception of equality that was very similar to
the idea of citizenship, and used it to construct a hierarchy based upon
merit, not birth, this new model takes real and observable inequalities as
its starting-point, and makes an active attempt to compensate for them.
This introduces a realistic vision of collective and personal situations
rather than an idealized vision, and makes it possible to relocate knowledge (and so-called values) in concrete social and historical situations by
relating science and society to ethics. We already do this in the domain of
the physical sciences, and especially the biological sciences, and we must
do the same in the domain of economics, the social sciences and history.
This conception of education is therefore not specific to democratic
society alone. It gives the school an active role in the process of democratization by taking into account the particular conditions under which
different children have to deal with both the same instruments and the
same problems.

Brief as they may be, these formulations are sufficient to show that our objective here is to outline a conception of education which differs from that promoted in the classical era. The old conception has been on the decline for the last half-century, mainly because most young people in a given age cohort now pursue longer courses of study, and because a significant proportion of them go on to post-secondary education.

I am not suggesting that we have to find better ways of adapting education to what society expects of it. We have to find ways of defining an educational policy that is part of what I term the 'politics of the Subject', or in other words democratic action. This approach may seem inappropriate at a time when schools are on the defensive, and when it seems more important to struggle against academic failure or an inadequate understanding of our national language (written and oral). This is a valid objection, and it is to be hoped that the efforts that are being made to solve those specific problems will gradually lead to a more general, critical and innovative approach. It would, however, be artificial to contrast the two approaches. Given that we live in societies characterized not only by change and communications, but also by desocialization and isolation, we must enhance everyone's ability to play an active part in the changes that are occurring. If we simply rely on principles of order, we will merely widen the social gulf between those who belong to the central categories and those who live in peripheral zones dominated by lawlessness and dependency.

A school for the Subject

In so far as it means that the state must be separated from the church and that the judiciary must respect all religious practices and beliefs that conform to the principles of the law, the idea of secularism is part of the very definition of modernity. If the call for secularism is a way of challenging the intolerance of states that do not permit the existence of minority religions or opinions, then I proclaim myself to be a militant and unconditional supporter of secularism. I can even understand why the secular spirit is still associated with anticlericalism or the active rejection of all religions in countries where a church has long been associated with an authoritarian power that uses the dominant religion to repress those who do not subscribe to it. And I would like to see state schools playing a greater role precisely because they are secular, or in other words because they promote heterogeneity and diversity rather than a communitarian-style unity.

The fact that the idea of secularism is indispensable should not, however, be an excuse for perpetuating the old divorce between public life and private life or between the educational roles of schools and families. To divorce the two has a negative effect in two respects. It has a negative social effect because it favours children from a highly structured social background, whose families do more to educate them and to help them formulate their projects. It also has a negative cultural effect because it destroys our ability to create the Subject. The Subject is not reducible to the rational thought and the sense of social responsibility that are inculcated into children by an educational system that is both national and scientific.

We have to abandon the notion of education-for-society. Rather than brutally ignoring the most intimate aspects of children's lives in order to transform them into 'civilized' beings, or in other words beings who have been reconstructed in accordance with the categories that dominate society, we have to reconstruct their personalities, which tend to be divided between two separate worlds: the world defined by the material opportunities (and especially career opportunities) offered by society and, in more concrete terms, the labour market and the world that is constructed by the youth culture spread by the media and transmitted by peer groups. Neither of the worlds in which young people are involved tends in itself to enhance their ability to elaborate personal projects. In both worlds, young people are consumers who respond to stimuli and prohibitions. Both educational and familial institutions must, by contrast, do all they can to reconcile personal expectations with the opportunities offered by the techno-economic environment. These expectations are no longer determined only by a cultural and social heritage; they are individualized, because we live in a changing society which attaches greater importance to individual life histories, and institutions can do less and less to predict their trajectory. More and more university students have moved from one country to another, or from one area to another. They may have experienced economic hardship, and may come from broken homes. Their lives may have taken an erratic course, but they have also been determined by choices. In a world of rapid change, where norms are more relaxed and where accidents are more and more common, individuals have to be able to be self-reliant. Rather than forgetting about their 'private' lives when they go through the school gate, they have to be fully committed to their studies.

When it no longer has to fight a combination of church and authoritarian power, the noble idea of secularism is all too often reduced to meaning that the educational system falls back on its task of transmitting knowledge and refuses to take on board the problems – and they are admittedly difficult to handle – of vulnerable young people who are reluctant to accept rules and who are therefore stigmatized by the educational system on the grounds that they perform badly or come from a bad area. Schools must concern themselves with the most intimate aspects of their pupils' lives. Lessons that look at both religious beliefs and the history of religion surely do not offend the principle of secularism. The refusal to talk about the realities of religion is, on the other hand, an unacceptable affront to the spirit of objectivity and truth that state schools claim to respect. The same spirit should prevail in so-called church schools, and more should be done to protect them from communitarian closure.

We must also be wary of divorcing general education from vocational training, even though separating the two has produced positive results in Germany, where the apprenticeship system is well organized and where there is, at the level of post-secondary education, a divide between technical institutes and universities. Great Britain had a similar system, but has now abolished it. It would indeed be dangerous for young people from lowly social backgrounds to be encouraged to follow vocational courses and for general education to become the preserve of the children of the middle and upper classes. Our objective must be to arrive at the most elaborate possible combination of vocational projects and personal and cultural motivations – which implies recognizing that schools have more than one function. The function of a school is not restricted to the provision of training; it also has an educational function. Schools must both encourage cultural diversity amongst their pupils and promote activities that allow them to develop and assert their individual personalities. Do we have to make a distinction between teachers and instructors, with the former taking children in the morning and the latter taking them in the afternoon? There can no more be a general answer to that question than to the question 'How should hospitals treat both the patient and the illness?' Functions do have to be differentiated to some extent, but everyone involved must make an effort to ensure that he or she is working towards the same goal. Many teachers do so spontaneously, but they are neither trained nor encouraged to do so by the school–university system.

A school for the Subject will move further and further away from the model that sees education as an agency for socialization. Schools are obviously part of a particular society. They teach that society's language, and history and geography lessons concentrate mainly on national or regional realities. Having such roots is essential, but schools are not there for society's benefit. Their primary mission must not be to train citizens or workers, but to enhance individuals' ability to become Subjects. Schools must concentrate less on transmitting a body of knowledge, norms and representations, and more on teaching children to handle instruments and on personal development and self-expression.

Seymour Papert has demonstrated that the development of rational thought can and must be associated with self-expression through, for example, play. Paris's Cité des Sciences has learned this lesson well. It welcomes hundreds of thousands of children every year, and allows them to handle instruments, take measurements and set up experiments. The observational and experimental sciences, both natural and human, that allow pupils and students to take the initiative and to demonstrate that different methods can produce the same results are obviously important, but encouraging self-expression is also important.

A school that both offers technical training and promotes self-awareness is far from being an agency for communitarian integration or for the inculcation of group values and norms. It is also far removed from those tendencies that reduce academic life to a juxtaposition of a utilitarian culture, defined in the most mediocre of senses as preparing for exams, and a group culture that simply consumes the products of mass culture.

The classical model is falling apart before our very eyes, and outlining a new conception of education is therefore a matter of urgency. Teachers feel threatened by the decline of an academic culture which is being invaded by utilitarian preoccupations on the one hand and mass culture and pupils' affective problems on the other. We must both establish a new institutional unity in our schools and safeguard the autonomy of academic space and time. And those goals can no longer be achieved by a sociocentric conception of education. The appeal to the duties of the citizen, the worker and the child can no longer be heard in a society which has become both massified and individualized. To be more specific, it cannot be heard by young people who are involved in mass culture and mass consumerism but who are kept on the sidelines of production because either they or their parents are unemployed or have little job security. The crisis in the prevailing educational model means that schools, especially in the context of contemporary economic difficulties, tend to increase rather than reduce social inequalities, because children from a difficult social or home background get poorer marks. If, on the other hand, we prioritize the formation of the personal Subject, schools will be more independent of their pupils' social background, and will therefore be able to pay a more active role in the fight against inequality of opportunity.

The discussion cannot be confined to schools. Individuals do not become Subjects only during the years they spend at school; they do so throughout their lives. We need vocational retraining, but, no matter how old or young we may be, we also need the time and space to regain control over our lives, to reflect on our past experiences, and to prepare our choices for the future. Secondary schools, vocational schools and universities should all accept pupils of all ages and from all backgrounds.

A school that communicates

All too often, schools define themselves in terms of the curriculum, the knowledge they transmit to their pupils or students, and the exams they use to evaluate the acquisition of knowledge. For a long time, this definition was rejected by only a small number of educationalists, most of whom were marginalized by the school system.

The example of television helps to reveal the strange nature of our educational practices. Umberto Eco makes a distinction between 'paleo-television', which concentrates on the messages and information it broadcasts, and 'neo-television', which gives more importance to the medium itself and to the viewer. Priority shifts from the message to communication, and it is a mistake to see this change of orientation as having a purely negative effect. Schools are still strongly defined by messages rather than communication, because they focus not on their audience, but on society, or in other words the set of values, norms and hierarchies that make up the social order, and because they think that educating children means transforming them into social beings. Conversely, it is impossible to speak of a school for the Subject unless we defend schools that communicate, and it is at this point that we encounter the greatest resistance. Whenever this topic comes up, both parents and teachers refuse to talk about it. They are afraid that if the uncontrollable disorder of affective relations is allowed into schools, they will be unable to carry out their primary mission, which is to teach children and to prepare them for the examinations that open the door to employment. Some even think that the theme of communication is a hypocritical way of reintroducing and justifying social inequalities at school. They argue that those children who are most integrated into their families and their backgrounds and who are most confident about the future are more likely to benefit from educational activities that prioritize communication over the acquisition of knowledge. This argument, which is a mixture of truths and falsehoods, of observations and prejudices, was satisfactory only as long as schools kept children from different social classes apart. In France, for example, the republican school kept the children of the people apart from those of the bourgeoisie. It could then devote its energies to transmitting knowledge and pretend to ignore the social segregation in which it was colluding. The children of the lower classes were taught practical subjects, and the children of the bourgeoisie more abstract subjects which symbolized their higher social status. Divorcing academic culture from private problems is a factor that increases inequality, because it is those children who live in the most difficult situations who need most help from school. François Dubet has demonstrated that the classical system of French

secondary education survives only in the élite *lycées* whose pupils come
from higher social categories. If we then look at the lower social categories
and the *lycées professionels* (secondary schools for vocational training),
most of whose pupils come from those categories, we find that the
classical system is in an advanced state of decay (Dubet 1991). The
primary historical purpose of reducing education to a form of public
instruction based upon the transmission of knowledge and the acquisition
of disciplines was to make it the ideology of a new bourgeoisie and, more
specifically, of a state bourgeoisie.

In most European countries, the introduction of mass education, the
creation of the *collège unique* or comprehensive school, and the introduction of a standardized higher education system (despite the existence of
élite universities and the classes that prepare pupils for France's *grandes
écoles*) have brought about the collapse of a system which worked only
when it was associated with a high degree of social differentiation. Given
that its function was to socialize children, or in other words to prepare
them for life in what was already a hierarchical society, this was only
logical. And it is precisely when the school-as-socialization system breaks
down that we have to demand a school for the Subject, or schools that
communicate. What schools do should not be defined solely by the end-
destination of their pupils. They should be more like school complexes,
defined by the fact that the teachers and the taught communicate with one
another, and that teachers and educational administrators also communicate. Although it has traditionally been evaluated in terms of its drop-out
rate, the number of pupils it holds back for a year and its average
examination results, a school's performance is largely determined by
its ability to communicate. When teachers insist on defining themselves
solely in terms of the subjects they teach, and do not collectively discuss
the problems of their individual classes and of the school as a whole, their
pupils' achievements are lower than when teachers communicate actively
with one another, their pupils and the administration.

All too often, schools resemble factories run on Taylorist lines: teachers
believe that they know that 'the one best way' to teach is to impart
objective truths. That there is more to their pupils' lives than this is
obvious from the way they play, cause mayhem in the classroom, day-
dream, fail their exams or even commit suicide. Children defy their
teachers because they represent both authority and society. In the
early years, they usually accept the pupil–teacher relationship because
the family still provides their primary frame of reference. When they
reach adolescence, they challenge it. When they go to university, it
no longer exists. The fact that it no longer exists seems to students to
be a sign that they have entered the adult world, whereas, in fact, it
simply reveals the educational system's inability to organize a type of

communication other than the family model which still prevails in primary schools.

The need to make the transition to a school that communicates is, I repeat, most urgent for schools attended by children from poor social backgrounds; when a school does not function as a communications network, violence breaks out and destroys the institution. A school can resist acts of violence, which can originate in either external or internal circumstances, if it has a good communications network; it will collapse if everyone, and especially every teacher, retreats into their own professional sphere. And the situation is at its worst when the social distance between teachers and taught is so great that violence breaks out between the two groups, as has happened in schools in Brooklyn, where Black students have violently attacked their liberal Jewish teachers.

Teachers usually respond to comments like this by saying that they are not trained to be instructors, social workers or psychologists, and that their decision to teach a particular domain of knowledge was a matter of personal choice. They liked history or mathematics, and thought that teaching those subjects was either desirable or acceptable. The sincerity of their reactions cannot be ignored, because it reveals only too crudely that one model of education is now exhausted and that the new model that should be replacing it does not yet exist. To make matters worse, in many countries the educational system is largely under the joint management of administrators and teachers, or at least their elected representatives, and they are usually more interested in defending the professional status, careers and rights of teachers than in thinking about education. This is an obstacle to the creation of a new educational model, and attempts to create such a model come up against the conservatism of intermediate decision-making bodies, both administrative and corporatist.

The situation in our schools is deteriorating so rapidly, especially in those that serve the most underprivileged social categories and areas, that acting in self-defence has become the norm. The most common reaction is to exclude difficult pupils and to reinforce the school's social homogeneity. The measures taken to isolate difficult cases – and such measures are not to be rejected out of hand – are accepted with a disturbingly good will by teachers and parents alike, even though the parents are well aware of the dangers involved in marginalizing children who are going through a crisis, and even though most of them are from backgrounds blighted by poverty, unemployment and cultural isolation. Pleas in favour of the social and cultural heterogeneity of schools are therefore widely regarded as inappropriate. Yet, just as a city comes to life only when different populations rub shoulders and communicate with one another, so a school must be a place that encourages inter-cultural communications. This is all the more important in that children or young adults do not categorize their partners as strictly as most adults, and find that individual attributes are at least as important, or even more important, as the signs indicating which culture or society they belong to.

In those countries where social distances are very great and where the dominant liberal ideology views the market as a model that can be applied to all social activities, private schools educate the children of the middle and upper classes, and the social hierarchy that is established between them finds its concrete expression in the fees they charge. As a result, the state schools which often achieve brilliant results, especially in Latin America and in Chile, Argentina and Uruguay in particular, tend increasingly to become schools for the poor, where poor teachers teach children from the lower social categories. The children's poor performance quickly confirms middle-class families or upwardly mobile working-class families in their belief that they have to send their children to the private schools that will help them to better themselves rather than the state schools that will drag them down.

The same trend is observable even in countries like France, where state schools once had a reputation for being better, and where private schools seemed to be answerable only to the Catholic Church. It is true that the idea that both are part of a public education service has brought them closer together. It is also true to say that some private schools have proved to be better than state schools in showing an interest in their pupils' private problems. The danger is that standards in state education have fallen so much that we have to be reminded of the need to defend state schools. Even though they have never really been open to all, and did keep apart children from different classes, state schools can, more so than private schools and much more so than communitarian schools, become sites of social integration and inter-cultural communication, provided they abandon the sociocentric conception of education and agree to individualize the way they relate to their pupils.

When schools attempt at all costs to adapt to the dominant tendencies within society, which, in the industrialized countries, mean the world of office-workers, technicians and civil servants, who are now in the majority, they tend to exclude pupils who come from a different background, and particularly those who come from poorer backgrounds and who do not take kindly to being educated for a type of work and a life-style they are unlikely to achieve – hence the paradox whereby raising the school-leaving age can lead to greater social inequality. Schools should be more child-centred and less concerned with the needs of society, which are usually described in ideological terms, or with helping their pupils to adapt to them.

A school that communicates must give special priority to both the capacity for self-expression, oral and written, and the ability to understand written and oral messages. We do not perceive and understand the Other thanks to some act of empathy; we do so by understanding what the Other is saying, thinking and feeling, and through our ability to converse with the Other. There is no communication without language, and public opinion is quite right to insist that schools must give priority to teaching the language which children will use in their most important exchanges. Above all, schools must involve their pupils in a dialogue, and teach them to argue amongst themselves by analysing the discourse of the Other, both in order to learn to handle the national language and to be able to perceive the Other, as that is a pre-condition for living together. We usually assume that communication requires us to divorce the message that is to be transmitted from its particular historical, geographical or individual context, and to formalize it as much as possible. We should in fact be taking quite the opposite view and learning from linguistic pragmatics: the message should be combined with a willingness to act, just as a historian looks for intentions in documents and then puts them in a context that clarifies their meaning.

None of these ideas represents a challenge to the school's role as a place where children acquire knowledge and learn how to reason. There are two reasons why scientific knowledge, in particular, must have an important role in schools. The first is that it allows pupils to find the truth by themselves, to distinguish between true and false, and to ensure that what they are saying is coherent. The second is that scientific method is the best defence against arbitrary power or communitarian traditions, and that, as Jean-Claude Milner has pointed out, it allows us to communicate in a world that is retreating into private experience.

Positive knowledge safeguards the freedom of teachers and pupils alike. This is a powerful idea, but it must obscure schools' other problems, or detract from the need to do more to defend the freedom and creativity of those they are educating. Schools and universities must, first of all, investigate the social role of science, and at the same time fully mobilize the motivation and imagination of students, so as to allow them to carry out scientific or technological experiments. The scientific knowledge that discovers the laws of nature is important, but so too is the interpretive knowledge of the human sciences that deal with intentional behaviour. We must also recognize the existence of the natural human sciences, which are highly developed, particularly in the domain of the cognitive sciences. We therefore have to agree to offer pupils a wide range of subjects and to ensure that they all combine scientific method with an analysis of social and cultural practices. More important still, no one subject should be identified with the recruitment of an élite, as that would devalue other subjects and oblige many young people to study a subject that is not to their taste. Schools must teach their pupils to decipher all social languages, from those of town planning and administrative action to those of scientific research and technology.

Above all, schools must teach pupils to read the media, and especially television, whose main weakness is its tendency to decontextualize messages. Rather than contrasting textual commentary with watching television, should we not be treating certain texts and images from television, the radio or the cinema as documents we can discuss so as to evaluate their content? The film critic André Bazin liked to point out that we are usually unable to describe the content of a cinematic shot or sequence, whereas we can analyse or summarize a text. And the quality of Bazin's own commentaries on cinematographic texts, which I have never forgotten, proves that it is possible to apply techniques of textual analysis to very different types of messages.

The main emphasis, however, must be on inter-cultural communication in the strict sense of that term. This is not a matter of expressing surprise that there are differences between individuals from different cultural backgrounds – 'How can anyone be Persian?', as Montesquieu (1993) put it – but of noticing the similarities and discrepancies between the interpretations that people from different cultures give of the same documents or events. According to UNESCO's Commission on Education, which was chaired by Jacques Delors, the most important of what it defines as the 'pillars' of education (learning to live together, to understand, to do and to be) is the first:

> We have to learn to live together by developing our understanding of others, and of their history, traditions and spirituality. By doing so, we can create a new spirit which, thanks to our perception that we are increasingly dependent upon one another, can make a joint analysis of the dangers and challenges of the future, encourage the realization of joint projects or the intelligent and peaceful handling of the inevitable conflicts. (UNESCO 1996: 18)

A school for the Subject will allow us to understand the Other in terms of the Other's culture, or in other words in terms of his or her attempt to reconcile identity and instrumentality within a conception of the Subject. In order to establish communication, we have to understand the actors themselves and study their speech-acts. And, as Jürgen Habermas insists, the most important thing of all is to learn to argue in such a way that every message contains something which can be universalized.

A school that communicates might, it is true, succumb to the facile attractions of commentary and the search for hidden meanings, rather than the rigours of proof, just as schools that are oriented towards the transmission of knowledge can lapse into formalism and a narrowly conformist academicism. But such deviations do not provide grounds for condemning either form of teaching; they simply point to the dangers we have to avoid.

Thirty years ago, I would have begun this section of this chapter by stressing the need for mixed classes, so as to allow boys and girls to learn to understand one another. Mixed classes do now exist, although they are a very recent innovation in some cases, and are so widely accepted that we condemn others for practising the sexual segregation we ourselves practised in a none too distant past. But can we say that our schools are doing enough to help their pupils or students understand that there are differences between boys and girls, given that our scientific findings in this domain are still so poor, despite the pioneering efforts of Carol Gilligan (1982) in particular? AIDS prevention campaigns have forced schools to talk about sexual relationships. It is shocking, however, that the huge question of affective and sexual relationships between young people of different genders, or even the same gender, and the still broader question of sexuality, as it is practised and represented in the individual and collective imaginary, should have been reduced to bits of advice about using condoms, essential as that advice may be. It is rather as though sexuality concerned schools only to the extent that it can be a source of medical or social problems.

We might also ask whether our schools are doing enough to teach young people to understand and analyse relationships between parents and children, or the shaping of the personality. Internationally (but not in France), girls still spend fewer years at school than boys, and women receive a poorer education than men. Why, as the recent Beijing conference asked, are schools not intervening more actively to do away with this inequality?

As we can see, it is easy to raise, within the space of only a few lines, immense questions relating to the family, sexuality, inter-cultural relations, historical knowledge, interpersonal communication and even the act of communication itself. Why is it so difficult to accept that all these topics should be covered at every level of the educational system? The existing curriculum should be expanded to include the motivations, social situation, projects and cultural origins of those who are not only pupils or apprentices but above all individuals. As they begin their lives, their greatest desire is to behave as Subjects, to act in accordance with projects, and to establish links between their personalities and the social and economic field in which they will later intervene.

For a long time, the training of teachers was reduced to the acquisition of knowledge within a single academic field. It has recently been extended to include the study of how particular disciplines should be taught. In some cases, so much time is spent on this that there is not enough time to stress both the importance of knowledge and the need to listen to the children. It is not enough to introduce new courses on child psychology or a vaguely defined philosophy of education. It is much more important to expand a curriculum-based system and to transform it into a school that communicates.

Many teachers – and they are often the best – are suspicious of talk of pedagogy or, more generally, communication because they are convinced that the individual effort to learn must play the central role. They even argue that emphasizing teacher–pupil relationships is a way of subjecting pupils or students to social controls, or of emphasizing the social and non-intellectual content of the school's message at the expense of its cultural content. This is a meaningless debate. Do we also have to oppose vocational training and contrast it with general culture, so as to prevent young people from coming under the influence of economic powers? These accusations are as superficial as those made by the people who, at the opposite extreme, are demanding closer links between schools and the economic world so as to do away with a supposedly archaic academic culture, or those who claim that, given that the acquisition of knowledge is a game, pupils and students should be motivated by the pursuit of pleasure.

Do we have to contrast the message with the way it is communicated? And is it possible to take an interest in education, or in other words communication, without concerning ourselves with the personal and social characteristics of the receiver? If we accept that the important thing is to enhance a pupil's capacity for free action, we have to draw two equally important conclusions from that principle. The first is that we must be at least as much concerned with those we are teaching, whatever their age, as with 'what' we are teaching; the second is that learning is impossible without work and effort on the part of the learner. That gives him or her a capacity for taking the initiative that can later be applied in other domains. Let us therefore close this false debate and invite both sides to make a joint effort to counter the educational clericalism that confuses knowledge with traditional forms of organization in schools, or with what some describe as its economic goals. Let us learn from the idea of *Bildung* that education must not be a form of socialization, but above all a way of developing the capacity to act and think in the name of a creative personal freedom that cannot be developed without coming into direct contact with the intellectual, technological and ethical constructs of both the past and the present. Subjectivation is so far removed from individualistic 'consumerism' that it is better sustained by cultural creation than by keeping to the curriculum or accepting an economic or administrative definition of the professions.

If we are to avoid growing social inequalities in our schools and a worsening academic crisis in underprivileged areas, we must help teachers not to hide behind the prestige of their disciplines so as to protect themselves from pupils from what they perceive as an inferior or dangerous background. Teachers have to recognize – and many already do recognize – that a school's results depend primarily on the quality of teacher–pupil relationships, and that their quality will certainly not be improved by lowering the standard of knowledge that is transmitted. The whole of the educational establishment has a lot to learn from what certain teachers have achieved in difficult situations, and in some of France's ZEPs (Educational Priority Zones).

For that to be possible, schools must be self-governing, rather than being governed by an administrative service or the labour market. It is primarily up to the teachers to establish the communications system we need. So long as schools are defined by their socializing function, it is obvious that their organization and norms will be defined by 'society', which actually means the administration. If, however, schools are centred not upon society, but upon individual Subjects, it becomes clear that the way they work must be decided by those who teach and learn in them – that is, by those who spend most of their lives in schools or who are preparing for their personal futures there. Parents can represent their children only to a limited extent, and I do not accept the argument that pupils should not be responsibly involved in how their school lives are organized, and therefore in how they are taught. And how can a communications network be established if a school's teachers have been brought together by the same random administrative decisions that put the most experienced teachers in easily managed schools, and leave the least experienced to deal with the most difficult situations? A school must be a team of teachers who come together at the suggestion of a team leader, and by mutual agreement. The team must draw up a contract with the authorities that takes account of the concrete conditions in which it will be working. Such proposals will meet with resistance, but a laudable desire to protect teachers from the political authorities does not mean that we have to deny that their role is to teach.

Such far-reaching cultural transformations cannot be introduced suddenly by reforms and acts of parliament. They must be launched by limited initiatives and innovations. Perhaps they are more acceptable now than they were in the past, simply because we are experiencing so many failures and difficulties.

A school that democratizes

An educational system that defines its mission as enhancing the capacity and will of individuals to become actors and to learn to recognize that the

Other enjoys the same freedom, the same right to individuation and the same right to defend social interests and cultural values that he or she enjoys is a democratizing system, provided that it recognizes that the rights of the personal Subject and inter-cultural relations require institutional safeguards that only a democratic process can supply.

Its role in democratization must, however, be more active than this. When democracy was primarily political, and meant calling for the sovereignty of the people to be respected or calling for the destruction of the power of the monarchy and the privileges of the aristocracy, it was forged in the street, on the barricades and in parliaments. Democracy was therefore present whenever the people rebelled against the ruling minorities that dominated them. Industrial society saw workers' struggles against their exploitation or for their social rights as manifestations of democracy. The fate of modern democracy, defined as a politics of the Subject, will be decided mainly in our schools and cities. In educational terms, we have to construct a school for the Subject and for inter-cultural communication, or in other words recognize that the goal of education is not to train and prepare young people for society, still less to train them for their future economic roles. Its goal is to train and educate them to be themselves, to enable them to become free individuals who can discover and preserve the unity of their experience throughout the upheavals of life and despite the pressures that are brought to bear on them. The same is true of our cities, because whilst they are, *par excellence*, places for encounters and exchanges, they are also places that can be segregated.

If they are to play a democratizing role, schools must do more than treat all children equally. They must provide more than compulsory, secular and free education. If that is all we require of them, we are actually doing little to promote equality. How can we give equal treatment to a child living in a family with a high standard of education and a child whose parents do not speak French, simply on the grounds that they both attend the same school? How can we teach one child the history of the other's ancestors? It is difficult to achieve the goal of equality, and we can approach it only if we compensate for real inequalities. The idea is so obvious that many attempts have been made to make greater efforts on behalf of those pupils who, for either personal or collective reasons, are most seriously handicapped. This is difficult, and those who attempt to change things come up against many objections, some of them well founded. That lesson was learned to their cost by the supporters of bussing in the United States, who tried to destroy racial segregation by transporting children from one neighbourhood to a school in another neighbourhood so as to produce a mix of children from different cultures and different origins. Just as we must be suspicious of irresponsible calls for a generalized mixing or interbreeding, because they make people

worry about losing their identity, so we must have the courage to take
direct action against inequality, discrimination and segregation. The call
for equality has all too often been monopolized by a state apparatus that
is afraid of civil society, and that finds it all the easier to pass itself off as
the representative of great principles in that it is incapable of giving those
principles the concrete, active form without which they are no more than
a hypocritical tribute to the victories of the past.

It is difficult, finally, to understand how a democratizing educational
system could be run on authoritarian lines. A school is obviously not a
political institution; nor is it a factory, a hospital or an administration.
The fact that the pupils and students who are elected to staff–student
committees are not truly representative may give too much power to a few
representatives and the organizations to which they belong. It is, on the
other hand, essential for the educational system to take the initiative in
public debates about how schools are run, about society's major problems, and then to take decisions as to how the life of our schools should
be organized. In Chile, a country which has a great tradition of education,
the Liceo Manuel de Salas, which is the University of Chile's experimental
school, initiated such debates before the Second World War. It is no
coincidence that its teachers and pupils were able to resist the dictatorship.

Does the critical consciousness that I would like to see developing in
our schools mean that the professional status of teachers has to change?
Teachers employed by central government tend, at best, to defend the
independence of their knowledge and their profession from that government, rather than to grant their pupils more autonomy; and at worst, they
help their pupils to adapt to the established order in a conservative way. If
the educational system is to be democratic, perhaps it should come under
a directly elected authority.

The question has to be asked, and the answer to it has to be negative.
The independence of teachers, like the independence of the judiciary, is an
essential pre-condition for the existence of a democracy, whose primary
task is to restrict the power of the state and social powers of all kinds. If
we wish teachers to defend the freedom of the Subject and inter-cultural
communication, the possibility that security of employment might have
negative effects and might encourage conformism or corporatism is surely
less important than the primordial need to guarantee teachers' independence. If, on the other hand, we recognize that education is a public service,
then teachers' working conditions must be the subject of a democratic
debate. If it is a local collectivity that mobilizes the resources needed to
run this public service properly, then the debate must take place as close
as possible to the problems that have to be dealt with. Just as the
independence of teachers' careers and jobs must be safeguarded, so the

way they teach and the way schools are run must be the subject of democratic debate, or in other words be determined at the local level in so far as that is possible. Every aspect of the educational system itself should be centrally managed in accordance with the provisions of the law and the agreements reached by representatives of the administration and the unions. The professional status of teachers should be defined and safeguarded by law, either at the national level in the case of centralized countries or at the local level in the case of federal countries. If they are to be independent of both local authorities and teachers themselves, assessment systems must also be controlled by the centre. The objectives of individual schools and the way they are run must, on the other hand, be defined at the local level and be open to public scrutiny.

Similarly, whilst it is necessary to protect teachers and pupils from acts of violence, it is still more necessary to help schools think about how they are run and about how they can limit or prevent the effects of that violence, which is largely the result of a deteriorating economic and social situation. It would be tragic for a society to believe that its schools are incapable of taking the initiative and have become so weak that they have no alternative but to turn to the police for protection. And it would be all the more tragic in that an appreciable number of teachers are taking on a more ambitious role which is both more creative and more dangerous.

Trust in the school system, especially in France and the Latin-American countries where state schools have succeeded in rapidly integrating many immigrants into society, has survived many a crisis. And whilst we have to accept that certain of the institutions which played a key role in democratization now have to hand on the torch (as do both parties and unions), we cannot conclude that the same is true of our schools, especially at a time when disillusionment leads to sterility and paralysis. We must make our schools central to the life of our society, and this goal can be achieved only by encouraging teams of teachers to take the initiative.

Societies in crisis do not dare to elaborate projects. If they have inherited a high-quality educational system, they are happy with its general principles and stop thinking about how to adapt its content and way of teaching. This defensive strategy postpones the fall, but cannot prevent it. Although echoes of paeans to the republican school can still be heard in France, sociologists have been demonstrating for decades that the educational system does not reduce inequality, and sometimes makes it worse, that teachers have become trapped into an academic culture that no longer means anything to their pupils, that the sytem has not succeeded in transforming massification into democratization and shows little interest in inter-cultural communication. And many teachers find that the system no longer supports their educational projects.

In the most important book on education to have been published in France for a long time, François Dubet and Danilo Martuccelli (1996) have demonstrated that the crisis in academic culture becomes all the more obvious as we move down the social ladder, and that teachers and pupils have become more alien (and even more hostile in many cases) to one another than we dared think. How can we fail to understand that, quite apart from the problems of school organization and the position of teachers, it is essential for any society to have a conception of education and to ask itself how its schools can be democratized?

I refuse to be an extreme pessimist, and I maintain that if we think about the world in which we live, and if, more specifically, we try to build bridges between the continent of the economy and the continent of cultures, which are drifting further and further apart, then we must develop a new conception of education. I have devoted this chapter to education in order to assure the reader that the ideas expressed throughout the greater part of this book are intended to be a theory of practices and of ways of transforming those practices, not simply a set of observations about society and the crisis it is experiencing. But it is the teachers who have to intervene. If you do not wish to see the teacher's vocation being reduced to the defence of a profession (though it is legitimate to defend it), a curriculum or a discipline, I beg you to speak out. If your voices are not heard inside the system, there is a danger that defensive caution and corporatism will become unshakeable.

Our society is too ready to accept that it has run out of ideas about education, to ask schools to do no more than supply knowledge and hand out certificates, to rely on the home environment to ensure our children's future, and on their Walkmans to give them pleasure. Why can't towns, local or regional authorities or universities respond to teachers' initiatives, or recruit their active support to establish experimental schools? Why do they not force the state to provide funds to run them, or encourage people to think innovatively? A school that is no more than an administrative service is unacceptable.

Conclusion: Ethics and Politics

A world divided

As the globalization of the economy, the technological revolution and the appearance of new industrial countries all continue to speed up, economic reality seems to rule the world and its transformations. At the same time, ideologies have collapsed, and politics has become more pragmatic. Authoritarian or totalitarian regimes have fallen, but almost never as a result of pressure from below. Countries have been hit by sudden falls in their standard of living, but that catastrophe has not provoked revolutionary uprisings. Political parties have been transformed into electoral agencies, and they no more represent social movements than they defend social projects. Whilst political life is dominated by economic programmes for structural adjustment and their side-effects, private life takes up more and more space. In many countries, it is an ethnic or religious consciousness, rather than economic self-interest or class consciousness, that inspires the most impassioned movements and even some political regimes. Social and political space is either empty or shrinking, because it is dominated by technological and economic realities on the one hand and by the rise of nationalisms, religious fundamentalisms or the problems of private life on the other hand.

Political and social thought are in a state of decay. The collapse of the Soviet empire has not led simply to the demise of the ideas it transformed into ideologies in the service of power; it has also led to the collapse of the various Third Worldisms which based their attempts to defend a national or cultural identity on their rejection of an imperialist domination that could be overthrown only by the Soviet empire. This presupposed that the East and the South formed an alliance against the American and

European West. The Western 'progressivism' that linked the social demands of Western countries, and especially those of the labour movement, with support for the Soviet Union and the Communist parties, has collapsed in the same way, and for the same reasons. Revolutionary ideologies are in a state of decay. At the same time, the great conservative constructs of the economic and social policies of the post-war period have been abandoned, because their belief in rationalization, modernization and free trade has become stultifying. Social thought is bankrupt in almost every country. On the Right, it has been swallowed up by liberal economic policies; on the Left, it has been swept away by the collapse of revolutionary movements.

In the circumstances, discussing social movements, the nation and democracy may seem to be something of a paradox. Might it not be wiser to reconstruct a representation of social life based upon limited practices, demands and worries that are directly related to the economic situations or to the concrete political choices which might, in the event of parliamentary or presidential elections, give rise to a new public debate? Any theoretical analysis must certainly begin by looking at these new practices. If it ignores them, it will look like an artificial construct. Conversely, if we have no general representation of society, there is a danger that the issues at stake in political choices and the practices of actors will disappear into a confused welter of sectorial demands and ideologies that are either too extremist or too directly influenced by the heritage of a past that has gone for ever. We have to begin by looking for something that can resist both the omnipotence of the markets and authoritarian communitarian politics, and then make a general analysis on the basis of the social facts we have uncovered.

The starting-point for this book was the idea that modernity was in crisis. It argued that, whereas modernity had always been defined by the divorce between the world of technological action and the world of human self-consciousness, the idea of rationality, which was itself based upon an individualist–universalist conception of human beings, could no longer hold the two together. Once economic activity – production, mass consumption and mass communications – became immune to political power's interventions, the globalized, or in other words desocialized, economy was inexorably divorced from a self-consciousness which sometimes used sexuality or individual desire as a support, but was more often displaced into a neo-communitarian project. The starting-point for my analysis was therefore the question, 'How can we prevent this dissociation from becoming complete and irreversible?' It is essential to prevent that happening, because it debases two things: the economy is reduced to financial flows and strategies, and cultures are reduced to being authoritarian powers which enforce their laws in the name of a community or a divine message.

Two threats to the Subject

In order to answer our question, we must first reject the answer that triggered the very crisis we have to resolve, or in other words the argument that any society must submit to the rule of law, the pursuit of the general interest and the principles of reason. This elevated the political realm above the social realm, and the state above civil society. This political model – and I pay tribute to it – provided nation-societies with a principle of unity for a long time. Without it, they would not have been able to reconcile rationalization with ethical individualism; but it belongs to a past that is now long gone. We tried to revive it after the Second World War, notably by giving it the shape of the modernizing nation-state, but both the state and economic leaders are increasingly in competition with a growing number of countries and companies. The entrepreneurial state is replacing the juridical state, and the primary objective of those who wield power is efficiency rather than stability. As a result, every general model – economic, social and political – of the nation-society has collapsed.

The central idea expressed in this book is that the only way to overcome both the absolute power of markets and the dictatorship of communities is to enlist in the service of the personal Subject and its freedom by fighting on two fronts, against both the desocialized flows of the financial economy and the closure of neo-communitarian regimes. The two struggles complement one another. The optimistic evolutionism of the defenders of progress crushes social movements and freedom on the pretext that progress will create a rationalized world; at the opposite extreme, nationalist or communitarianist voluntarism produces a culturally homogeneous society, and recognizes individuals only in so far as they are members of a collectivity.

Economic liberalism does as much as cultural nationalism to destroy the individual. What is individual about a consumer whose demands are predetermined? What is individual about a man or a woman who submits completely to the law of a community? *Laissez-faire* economics and cultural nationalism are both enemies of the personal Subject. Both try to force the Subject to obey their laws. One defines them as impersonal laws; the other defines them as the assertion of a particular identity or even a historical vocation.

We must therefore rid the debate between liberals and communitarians of the confusions that obscure it, as both camps are divided. Those we call liberals may well defend the way free trade is globalizing the world, but many liberal thinkers take the opposite view and want to see restrictions on all powers and to promote the autonomy of individual and collective cultural projects. Conversely, some communitarians wish to force cultural unity on the people, whilst others want to recognize the Other's cultural project. Although they have their differences, Enlightenment philosophers like Jürgen Habermas and communitarians like Charles Taylor both respect alterity. Many liberals are quite happy to let money do the work of normalization, and many communitarians appeal, at the international level, to a national or religious ethnic identity, and deny minorities their rights in the name of an indispensable cultural homogeneity.

Rather than choosing between the two camps, we therefore have to state that there exists a deeper contradiction. I refer to the contradiction between the assertion of the need to defend the personal Subject and its freedom and the logic of systems, be it the logic of the market or that of a national or cultural identity. My goal in writing this book was to explore the possibility that the personal Subject could exist, and to look at how we could promote its existence and give it greater strength. It was to explore the reasons why the personal Subject is asserting its rights, and to look at the battles that allow it to defend and extend the territory in which it can act autonomously. We must refuse to choose between a globalization that is controlled by the industrial countries and dictatorships that are established in the name of the rights of communities. The planet is now dominated by the conflict between these two forces, and they both pose serious threats to the freedom of the Subject.

When we place our trust in the desire of individuals to become the actors in their lives, or to become Subjects, we displease those who swear only by the rationality of the market, and whose greatest fear is the negative economic effects of relying upon a non-economic principle to manage society. We also displease those who take the opposite view and refuse to moderate their radical critique of the existing social order by introducing a positive principle which might, they fear, pave the way for a reformist compromise.

The answer to our first critics is that they are pursuing a mirage. There has never been such a thing as a society regulated solely by a market, and the adoption of that model in the countries of Western Europe would cause such upheavals that they would be left paralysed. Economic liberalism is no more than a temporary remedy to be applied when the social controls on the economy are inappropriate, when they paralyse the economy, or when they work to the advantage of private interests. If we look back at Europe's historical experience, we can see that liberalism was an effective remedy, in that it allowed Europe to gain a decisive lead over the rest of the world at a time when capitalist development had destroyed the earlier order; but it also led to sharp social divisions, and it would have the same effect today. We therefore have to find a way out of the liberal transition as rapidly as we embarked upon it, and this presupposes that reforming parliaments and governments respond to pressure from below.

The difficulty is that both backward-looking ideologues and the most highly organized and most influential categories resist this action logic, and that, as they are neither the poorest nor the most vulnerable members of society, liberals denounce the resistance of vested interests, corporatism and privilege at every possible opportunity.

Because they are faced with a possible breakdown of law and order, our societies do have a tendency to sacrifice both innovators and the excluded, in order to defend the middle classes of both the private and the public sectors. Those classes are in the majority, and they are well organized, which means that we have no option but to choose between a brutal liberalism with high social costs and a policy of state intervention which, rather than strengthening the economy or reducing social inequalities, works to the advantage of vested interests. We do require new political controls on the economy, but we also have to find new ways of managing both an economy that is open to international competition and personal life stories that are becoming more and more individualized. This means turning our backs on communitarian powers as they use their economic resources only to further the defensive integration of societies which, because they cannot play an active role in it, see the modernization they are undergoing as a threat. The freedom of the Subject therefore fights on two fronts to reconcile cultural identities with an involvement in systems of instrumental action. Rather than relying on the state to get society out of the crisis it is experiencing, we must restore every individual's capacity to reconcile, within their personal lives, forces that appear to have come into conflict at the international level. This does not mean defending an individualism that is indifferent to public affairs; on the contrary, it means enhancing the ability of social actors to intervene in public life.

But is not the weakness or the absence of social actors the most characteristic feature of the contemporary world, in which there are so many crises and so few social movements, so much poverty and no revolutions? We already saw the same constellation taking shape at the beginning of the industrial revolution: widespread poverty, attempted *putsches*, the formation of revolutionary minorities, and the triumph of an industrial capitalism which was (apart from a few humanitarian campaigns) as indifferent to social problems as is today's globalized economic system. But in at least some countries, the rapid development of a working-class consciousness did lead to industrial democracy. In the same way, we are now seeing the emergence of movements that defend cultural rights and social solidarity. Only they can bring about the reconstruction of political life and a transformation of society. Neither a good liberal conscience nor communitarian radicalism will encourage the emergence of the social movements without which no major political reforms are possible. A good liberal conscience will ensure the triumph of the privileged, whilst communitarian radicalism serves only to hasten the rise to power of authoritarian states. No matter whether they applaud it or condemn it, those who think solely in terms of the logic of the social system cannot do anything to help new social actors to emerge. The only thing that can help to produce stronger actors is an analysis that gives central importance to the freedom of social actors and their capacity both to take the initiative and to survive.

Desiring the Subject

Where, today, are the forces that can generate new social movements, the forces that have as their objectives solidarity and diversity, and that can, in other words, inspire a politics of the Subject? The demand for subjectivation is present everywhere, and it is active, but it is kept at the infra-political level by the effects of the globalization of the economy, and because it is blocked by political-style organizations such as parties and unions. Those movements are heirs to social movements that no longer exist but which still have considerable political and ideological influence. To say so is to give intellectuals a major responsibility: their role is to shake up our ideas and to translate what public opinion is trying to say into organized action and political decision making.

I say that the demands of public opinion are everywhere, but just where are they to be found? They are not being expressed in either political society or productive society. The principal political actors of the near future will be neither citizens, as was the case in our early modernity, nor workers, as in industrial society. They will be those individuals or groups who strive to reconcile private cultural experience with involvement in the world of instrumental action, and they are already present everywhere. The historical actors of the future will not be the most objectively determined categories, as was the case in the past, and they will not be the most fragile categories. They will be those categories that are most directly defined by the need and the will to make compatible the two worlds that have been separated by demodernization. That is why young people, women, immigrants, members of minorities and the defenders of the environment have, for at least twenty years, been the most obvious historical actors, at least in industrialized societies. It is they who are striving most consciously to act and to be recognized as Subjects.

The most visible actors are those young people who, having been largely excluded from work, fall back on their personal lives and on their self-assertion as Subjects. Poor job prospects and the absence of political militancy have not trapped them into hedonism. Their attitudes are influenced by music, television and films, but they are also apparent in their involvement in humanitarian action and ecological campaigns. They are inspired by a desire to be Subjects, and this desire finds direct expression in their desire for life and their defence of a self-identity that is threatened by the shattering of their professional and social existence. The defence of civil society is being replaced by the defence of personal life, and most young people's lives have not been reduced to a craving for consumer goods and demands for welfare.

Women are playing an equally important role, because they have learned, in the course of their victorious struggles, to reconcile their professional and personal lives in their projects, and to reconcile the instrumental universe and the symbolic universe. They have learned, that is, to act as Subjects. The fact that organized women's movements have been weakened has not prevented women's consciousness from growing stronger or from defining itself in terms that go far beyond mere demands for equality or identity politics. And this has allowed women, far more than men, to define themselves as Subjects who can reconcile their professional and affective lives, and who can thus overcome the contradictions of the modern world.

From politics to ethics

The Subject is present in every expression of the will to be both memory and project, both culture and activity. It is absent whenever emotion is repressed, whenever the past is covered up, and whenever the discipline of either reason or the law becomes more harsh. And above all, it is absent when Western societies choose their leaders by destroying their ability to become Subjects in their own right and turn them into bosses who are at once competent and incapable of recognizing the Other, including the Other within themselves.

The fact that the international political stage is empty must not prevent us from seeing that the wings of history are full of life, aspirations and, above all, individuals who are capable of self-reflexivity. Many people are striving to tear themselves away from an existence that reduces them to being passive consumers or passive participants. They are beginning to challenge the assumptions of social life, sometimes by remaining aloof from it, but in most cases by preparing to defend their awareness of their identity in a world that is changing.

We increasingly use the term 'civil society' to describe the space that permits the emergence of actors who want to be recognized as Subjects. In the early stages of industrial society, the term was used to describe an economic society that was trying to break free of the political order. Economic society has, however, become the dominant order at both the national and the international level, and the idea of civil society gradually merged into that of class struggle as the structural conflicts of industrial society became institutionalized. The idea of civil society is now reappearing, and it is coming to mean opposition to both the imperatives of the globalized economy and the order enforced by communitarianisms. In the name of an absolute principle such as freedom or justice, civil society is challenging the constraints that those who speak in the name of economic rationality or a cultural identity would like to introduce. Rather than negotiating, it is acting in self-defence. More important, it is ethical rather than political, because, rather than making conquests, it is resisting invasions and manipulations. Today, few actions are undertaken with a view to seizing power; in Mexico, Marcos and the Zapatistas have explicitly rejected that vanguardist ideology. Actions inspired by a vision of history and attempts to build a new society and a new humanity are giving way to protests in the name of diversity and solidarity. They are attempts to make democracy stronger and to extend it, rather than to make revolutions.

Freedom once meant that a majority overthrew a minority. The freedom that we defend today means recognition of the social and cultural rights of minorities, and therefore defending diversity, and the right of every individual to be themselves and to reconcile their values and their forms of action with the instruments of historical action. Justice once meant that all were equal in the eyes of the law, and that privilege must be destroyed; it was subsequently defended because it meant fairness. It meant that everyone should receive what was due to them, that a balance could be achieved only through democratic debate or by legal and contractual means. Increasingly, the defence of justice takes the specifically ethical form of the defence of basic human rights. Justice now means the institutionalized defence of freedom and the condemnation of abuses, violence and corruption, and this brings us closer to the struggle against privilege that led to the overthrow of the *ancien régime*. But the crimes that we condemn most severely are crimes against the dignity of the individual, or the right of every individual to be a Subject and to be recognized as such – hence the increasingly severe condemnation of rape and the scandal provoked by the sexual abuse of children. Hence too the rejection of the racism that turns individuals into natural species and rejects any universalizing reference to the Subject.

The era of political passions is over. The period to come will be dominated by ethical passions in which the idea of democracy, which has for so long been lukewarm or even a safeguard for the bourgeoisie and the rising middle class, will acquire the rousing power that the idea of revolution lost when it was tarnished by totalitarian regimes that imposed their arbitrary power in its name. This change in the ethical and political world is as important as the change that took us from the building of nation-states to the globalization of the world economy. The decline of political ideologies and the population's loss of confidence in their leaders mask an upheaval in experience and collective action that is as far-reaching as the emergence of industrial society and the formation of nation-states before it. The old forms of collective action are in decline because they are no longer social liberation movements, and because they have become locked into the corporatist defence of vested interests or exhausted ideologies. At the same time, new voices are making themselves heard. They speak with emotion and passion of the crimes that have been committed against humanity, of the diversity that is being threatened by cultural homogenization, and of the social exclusion that is being exacerbated by an economic system that rejects all political controls.

The democracy that dreamed first of all of direct participation and then of the fair representation of social interests is now being supplemented by a democracy that provides safeguards to protect the freedoms, diversity and dignity of human beings who are much more than citizens or workers; they are individuals who are defending their right to be Subjects.

The need for the economic mutations we have to bring about is so urgent that we are often tempted to reduce public life and political action to the conflicts and negotiations that will lead to either their success or their failure. Yet the political and ethical mutations analysed in this book are at least as important, and are just as difficult to understand and to carry through to a successful conclusion. Our ideas are behind the times, and that poses more serious problems than resistance on the part of vested economic interests or outdated forms of administrative organization.

In this context, political ecology becomes very important. Even though it all too often degenerates into an anti-humanist nature cult, it is an important element in the cultural mutation we are living through, because it induces an awareness that there are limits to organized and technical human action. It reminds us that human beings are no longer the conquerors of a nature where there were almost no clearings. Having acquired the ability to transform or even destroy their planet, they have become responsible for it. Their actions can no longer be inspired by a faith in boundless progress; they must be inspired by an awareness of the threats to humanity's survival, and particularly of the need to preserve a diversity of species and cultures. We are now aware that our survival is bound up with that of all the elements that make up our environment, and with the need to defend cultural diversity rather than replace it with the unity of a globalized economy. The consciousness of the Subject and a consciousness of the concrete totality to which we belong will provide the basis for a new cultural politics on a world scale.

Social actors behind the times

The emergence of organized social actors who are capable both of holding social convictions and of undertaking collective actions is usually blocked because they have no definition of their adversary. The adversary can no longer be a will, a prince or a ruling class that proclaims its superiority, speaks in the name of a god, of history or of a nation, gives orders and and has forces at its disposal. Class struggle was a historical truism only for so long as the popular classes encountered the barriers of inherited wealth or the ruling class's claim to rule by divine right. When conflicts are no longer economic, the mechanisms of the market take over, and there is no longer any absolute difference between the labour market and the market where material goods are exchanged. Conflicts between companies or the state and the trade unions may lead to violence, but they no longer generate social movements. When power is no longer in the hands of the employers, and is controlled by financial, technological and information networks, it becomes elusive, and provokes withdrawal or rebellion rather than conflict.

When social problems arise, the modern world encourages loyalty or exit rather than voice, to borrow Albert Hirschmann's (1972) categories. We are emerging from a period in which social movements were defined primarily by what they were fighting. They were anti-capitalist, anti-colonial or anti-machines. Social movements now have to be constructed on the basis of positive assertions of freedom and the will to live a responsible and happy life. We find it difficult to identify the groups who rule the world, but we can see the exclusion, the famines and the poverty. That is why collective actions are now armed with moral convictions rather than economic analyses. It is now more difficult than it used to be to mobilize armies of protesters, or to define fronts and the objectives of struggles. Such military metaphors, which were so essential to the idea of class struggle, now inspire fear rather than enthusiasm, because we know that social wars, like all wars, lead to authoritarian regimes and not to democratic participation. Collective action is becoming both more reflexive, and more oriented towards what might be termed an attempt at collective subjectivation rather than trench warfare or the final assault on the fortress of the ruling class and the state.

The social stage is empty. The world seems to have fallen silent in our time. The rich countries seem to be almost totally preoccupied with

economic calculation, technological innovations, political spectacles and
mass entertainment. This is not because there are no more social actors.
On the contrary, social actors are impatient to assert themselves and to
demand recognition of their freedom as Subjects – so much so that we are
being inundated by a moralism which can find no outlet in political
action. There are two main reasons for this. The first is that we are
experiencing the problems not so much of a new society like post-
industrial society or the information society, as of globalization, or in
other words the problems of a mode of development rather than of a type
of society or a mode of production. It is the current mode of development
that gives rise to the conflicts I have mentioned so often: namely those
between a globalized economy and the defence of a threatened community of identities. In this conflict, as in the conflicts caused by the imperialism of the nineteenth century, resisting the dominant forces often works
to the advantage of authoritarian powers. There is therefore a considerable difference between these cultural nationalisms, which in some cases
can be described as fundamentalist, and the appeal to the Subject. The
defenders of the Subject have been caught in a pincer movement. Social
action has been reduced to commerce and consumerism, and neo-
communitarian powers reject freedom, and resort to terrorism and other
forms of repression. Autonomous social actors can emerge only when
conflicts internal to a type of society are more important than conflicts
bound up with a mode of development. For the latter do not generate
grass-roots movements either; they lead to mobilizations from above, or
to truly political mobilizations. Their objective is the seizure of power,
and their action is of the military type, whereas societal movements
seek freedom and justice, rather than power or the dictatorship of the
proletariat.

The other reason why no collective action has been organized and why
the desire for subjectivation has not been transformed into a social movement and political action is that the political field is still occupied by
representations of old social movements that are now passing away. The
parties and unions of both the Left and the Right that were once bound
up with the great conflicts of industrial society should long ago have
become agents for managing the changes brought about by the transformations in the world economy and in life-styles. That mutation has occurred
in countries such as Germany, but in others such as Great Britain and
France the persistence of the old conflicts has led either to the defeat of
the unions and the disorientation of the parties of the Left or to the
triumph of liberal orthodoxy. All that remains of the political life of the
past are groups of activists and, more important, modes of thought and
action that have become major obstacles to the revival of collective movements. This is particularly obvious in France. After the explosion of

May 1968, which threw up so many new social and cultural themes and revitalized so many aspects of French society, fragments of Bolshevism and even Blanquism permeated the whole of political and intellectual life, and blocked the formation of new demands and new strategies.

If new social actors are to emerge, we must first recognize the existence of a new type of society. Today's dominant ideology represents the world as a set of uncontrollable flows that exist in a state of permanent transformation. As a result, it is assumed that the development of new social movements, or even reformist action, is impossible. Collective action, by contrast, is based upon the will of every individual, group or nation to influence economic realities, to construct and transform their identity and integration, and to defend an ideal of solidarity. This positional inversion may seem surprising. The leading forces are no longer defined by the attempt to maintain order, but by movement, openness, change and the fastest possible circulation of goods, services and information; whereas the dominated categories are demanding security, safeguards and what Jacques Delors has termed a 'reconstruction of the social bond'. It is no longer a matter of preserving a social order, but of creating social conditions that can safeguard both personal freedom and cultural diversity, and at the same time resist the utopia of a world in a state of perpetual motion that is swept towards an increasingly rapid rise in consumption and communications.

Intellectuals and actors

Although the partisan and ideological cadres of political life are out of step with the new political culture that is emerging, the gap between the two is no greater than the gulf which, throughout most of the nineteenth century, existed between, on the one hand, a parliamentary life dominated by conflicts between liberals and conservatives, clerics and free thinkers, or monarchists and republicans and, on the other hand, a capitalist industrialization that crushed millions of workers. Reducing the gap between the two should be a task for intellectuals, but they often tend to widen it, because so many of them still cling to categories of action and thought characteristic of a society that no longer exists.

Left-wing intellectuals often speak in the name of an impersonal principle such as reason or history, or make such a radical critique of society that the existence of social actors and social change becomes unthinkable. As for right-wing intellectuals, they usually rely upon the idea of rational choice to ward off the thing that frightens them most: the appeal to cultural identity, which seems to them as great a threat as the appeal to the working class was to their ancestors.

The many social initiatives that are being taken all over the world to defend cultural identity or solidarity are too rarely supported or analysed by intellectuals. The latter are therefore in danger of missing what should be their vocation: playing a part in the recomposition of the world and preventing the widening of the gulf between a technological world that has become too open and cultural nationalisms that have become too closed. In more positive terms, they should be reuniting that which has been torn apart by Western modernization and its insistence on divorcing modernity from tradition, reason from sentiment, men from women, and the rulers from the ruled. If intellectuals do not choose to heal the wound in the world which was opened up centuries ago, and which is growing wider, they themselves are in danger of being contaminated by the decay of the social and political mediations that can no longer reconcile the instrumental world with the symbolic world. If that happens, the symbolic world will come under the sway of communitarian dictatorships, whilst mass society needs only those intellectuals who agree to become the servants of consumerism and profit. Intellectuals must therefore, as a matter of urgency, provide us with a representation of the world, of the changes occurring in it, and of the actors who can transform the spontaneous tendency to defend and assert the existence of the Subject into conscious actions and movements which can, in their turn, make political action meaningful once more. Our most urgent need is the need for ideas, rather than political or economic programmes. Practices are always ahead of theories.

For too long, or ever since classical sociology's faith in institutions was shaken, social thought has been dominated by two ideologies, and the conflict between the two has done more to reveal the crisis in sociology than to shed light on the contradictory facets of observable reality. One reduces social life to what Louis Althusser called 'Ideological State Apparatuses', or the mechanisms that reproduce inequalities and power; whilst the other reduces social action to a search for rational choices, and takes utilitarian thought to extremes. Neither discourse can perceive (and neither has perceived) the way in which public opinion and demands have been transformed, the rise of new social movements (organized or otherwise), the forms of the modernization that is now penetrating every part of the world, the increasingly widespread unease about rationalization and industrial civilization, or women's assertion that the human Subject is always gendered.

Philosophical thought, fortunately, has found a new vigour that compensates for the enfeeblement of sociological thought. Today's intellectual renewal will come from political and moral philosophy, rather than from descriptions of the new forms of production, exchange and redistribution. After a period of eclipse, sociological thought itself is beginning to undergo a renaissance and a transformation. It has stopped studying social systems, and now concentrates on action. Whereas it once analysed order's conditions of existence and its transformations, it is now trying to understand how actors are shaped, how men and women can create a new society, how private life and public life can be reconciled, how democracy can be made more representative, and how social unity can be reconciled with cultural diversity. This will breathe new life into a social and cultural sociology which was marginalized by a sociology of modernization obsessed with its belief in progress. What is more important still, it will keep sociology well away from the terroristic ideological discourses which tried to impose the idea of a history without a Subject, and to reduce social life to either the march of progress or the absolute power of a hidden god, state or bourgeoisie.

The new innovatory practices are not developing at the international level, or even at the national level for that matter. They are developing at the local level, and centre on concrete issues involving or relating to direct interpersonal relations. Just as the labour movement was born of informal organizations and of demands put forward on the shop-floor, so today's revival of social action is taking place at the grass-roots level. The creative and emancipatory initiatives are coming from the base. This obviously does not mean that everything that comes from the base is innovatory, but it does mean that the emancipatory spirit consists in defending and enhancing the freedom and dignity of every individual.

The guiding theme of this book is that the personal Subject is our starting-point, and that democracy is our goal. Inter-cultural communication is the path that leads from one to the other. Without the freedom of the Subject and the Subject's attempts to bring about the recomposition of the world and to reunite elements that have been divorced and that have come into conflict, interpersonal and inter-cultural communication are impossible. Pure tolerance and the acceptance of differences do not in themselves make inter-cultural communication possible. And democracy would be meaningless if it ignored social and cultural differences, or meant only that we are all citizens who are equal in the eyes of the law. Democracy is real only when it permits social and cultural rights to be defended because they are concrete forms of the right to be a Subject, or in other words to reconcile a particular lived experience and rational action in such a way as to give individuals their creative freedom. The three themes of the Subject, communication and solidarity are inseparable, just as freedom, equality and fraternity were inseparable during the republican phase of democracy. Their interdependence delineates a field of social and political mediations that can re-establish the link between the instrumental world and the symbolic world, and thus prevent civil society from being reduced to a market or an enclosed community.

To accept the divorce between the world of instrumentality and the world of identity is extremely dangerous. Just as we have to do away with evolutionist thought and the dangerous utopia of the necessary and imminent reign of reason and progress, so we have to ward off the danger that the world will decompose. If we fail to understand the need to recompose the world, or if we fail to bring about its recomposition, we will soon experience shocks similar to those which, in the first half of the twentieth century, led to the conflict between a so-called democratic world sick from its economic crises and its lack of social justice, and totalitarian regimes which, in the name of the struggle against a capitalism that had no home land, brought to power destructive dictators who won over enthusiastic or servile crowds. Trapped between an unbridled capitalism and parties with totalitarian projects, we did not do enough to build a social democracy, and we did so in too few countries.

No social movement and no anti-establishment school of thought is content to denounce a power or an ideology; they always have some idea of what a fair society might mean, but that idea can take two very different forms. It may invoke a radical principle of equality in order to do away with man's power over other men, or assert that all human beings are equal because they are the children of God, beings endowed with reason, citizens or workers. If, however, this equality is to be forced upon a society that is always unequal, an absolute power based upon the sovereignty of the people is required. That sovereignty must be either expressed directly or entrusted to a charismatic leader or a dictator who has been elected, either democratically or by acclamation.

The idea of justice, by contrast, results in a struggle to place limitations on all forms of power by demanding the recognition of both social rights, which can be defined in terms of justice and fairness, and cultural rights, which can be formulated in terms of identity and difference. This book subscribes to that conception, which is equally far removed from authoritarian egalitarianism and from the reduction of democracy to a competitive political market. The same conception of democracy, which is based upon respect for basic human rights, also provides the framework for a debate between various conceptions of basic human rights. One conception recognizes that all cultures aspire to be universal; the second, by contrast, stresses the specificity of all cultures; whilst the conception I am defending here defines human rights as the right of the Subject to come into being by reconciling a specific cultural experience with the universalism of instrumental reason.

In my view, this conception is not simply the most intellectually satisfactory of the three; it seems to me that democratic thought cannot do without it. Extreme communitarianism, which is the direct antithesis of the inter-cultural communication that I see as essential, represents the

triumph of cultural and political diversity over social unity, and it inevitably leads to violence and social deregulation, especially when the market
has lost its integrative function. Conversely, the dream of a rational
society has the effect of transforming social integration into the defence
of the most central categories at the expense of innovators, marginals and
minorities alike. The negative effects of communitarian differentialism are
obvious, and often spectacularly obvious. The negative effects of republican unitarianism are less obvious, because it does not permit the public
existence of anything that fails to conform to the central model. It does,
however, frustrate a great number of initiatives. It hinders the construction of the personal Subject, and leads to the formation of repressive
social and political forces on the pretext that the unitary model is in
danger.

From ethics to politics

Are these conclusions to be understood as a farewell to politics? Do
we have to concede that, after a long historical period dominated by the
social relations of production, class struggles and revolutionary movements, we now live in a consumer society or a market where collective
problems have, at least in the industrialized countries, given way to
individual projects or individual crises, whilst the new industrial countries
are mobilizing for economic growth rather than social redistribution?

No. Absolutely not. Whilst it is true that we are leaving behind industrial society, with its belief in progress and its conflicts over work, it is not
true that society has been reduced to a set of markets, rational strategic
actions and the pursuit of individual pleasure. This book has attempted to
define the new issues at stake and the new actors of social life who can
reconstruct a political life that can build a bridge between the world of
instrumentality and the world of identity, or find a point where the two
can meet and be reconciled. Political and social institutions can no longer
be the servants of a supposedly rational order or a progress that is
supposedly inscribed in the laws of historical evolution; they must be
made to serve the Subject, which is the one principle that can build the
bridge we need between our two worlds. Politics has become subordinate
to ethics, whereas it tried for a long time to establish itself as an ethics or a
civic morality, and to defend the radiant future from the past.

This is a complete reversal of perspective, and it affects both our
conception of society and our ideas about justice, freedom and happiness.
I have therefore attempted to show not only that it is possible to define
human rights, social movements and repesentative democracy in new
ways, but also that the new modes of behaviour, the ideas and the shifts

in public opinion that are appearing all over the world, are already part of the historical field whose relief and contours I have been trying to map.

Our new battles will be battles for diversity rather than unity, for freedom rather than participation. Our greatest passions will be aroused by the domain of culture rather than that of economics. In our post-industrial era, our information society and our globalized economy, projects and debates pertaining to collective life will, however, be as central to all our lives as they were in industrial society or, going still further back in time, in the era when nation-states were founded. The political world, on the other hand, is still dominated by the interests and representations of industrial society, even though that society is in decline. If politics continues to lag behind, there is a possibility that political life will be increasingly ignored by public opinion, and this could be very dangerous. It is to be hoped that those who have chosen to become the people's elected representatives will make their own contribution to the necessary revival of social thought and social action.

Modernity has become problematic. And if we do not succeed in lashing together the two worlds it has separated, perhaps demoderniza-tion will triumph. Our task is no longer to study the social effects of modernization, but to study the conditions and the forms of technological and economic change that will allow a new modernity to be based upon communications between individuals and collectivities that are at once similar and different. Some think that the problem is insoluble. They say that we should work together, use the same technologies and calculations, and be involved in an increasingly complex division of labour; as for the rest, they think that we should keep our private lives, our beliefs, our feelings and our dreams to ourselves, respect the privacy of others, and support those laws that do most to safeguard the freedom of all. My ambition has been to show that, on the contrary, the juxtaposition of an economy reduced to flows and identity politics will debase economic rationality and cultures alike.

Because the religion of progress is, like communitarian religions, fraught with danger, and because the separation between private and public life is no more than an illusion, our only solution, if we wish to avoid demodernization, is to install the personal Subject in the place left empty by the death of the political Subject, and the religious Subject before it. The personal Subject means every individual's desire to be the actor in his or her existence, the master of a time and a space, of memories and projects that are constantly traversed by external forces that come from afar. The latter may be either seductive or threatening, but the personal Subject tries to turn them into a lived experience and a personal history. The success or failure of these personal projects depends mainly upon the collective recognition of subjective rights, and of the right of every individual to reconcile a cultural identity with instrumental activities; but such recognition is possible only if political life is animated by a collective demand for creative freedom. Politics has now been reduced either to adapting every national economy to the system of world trade, or to resisting globalization in the name of self-interest. Is a new representative politics possible? Only if it is dominated by the struggle that is being waged against both those who want to speed up the movement of capital, information and commodities, and the defenders of threatened communities. And this struggle is being led by those who are calling upon individuals and collectivities to assert themselves as free Subjects who can unite and transform both the world of the economy and the world of cultures.

Making political choices does not simply mean applying economic or sociological analyses. If, however, political choices are not based upon a general vision of change, or if they are reduced to mere defensive actions, they cannot predict their own consequences. When a society shies away from what it sees as purely destructive transformations, it denies itself the means to overcome or use them. A society which believes that it can overcome its own blockages and weaknesses by going with the flow is in serious danger of being torn apart. In various parts of the world, we are in danger of surrendering to one or other of these temptations, and of becoming incapable of understanding the new world we are entering, of being incapable of acting upon it, of struggling against its dangers and of taking advantage of the possibilities it offers.

In the mid-nineteenth century, Europe's thinkers and politicians had to make a great effort to understand that what they were experiencing was not the aftermath of the French Revolution, but the birth of industrial society and its conflicts. If we wish to be actors in a world that is mutating, we too must successfully undergo a difficult mutation.

References

Abelove, Henri, Barale, Michèle Anna and Halperin, David M. (eds) 1993: *The Gay and Lesbian Studies Reader*. New York: Routledge.

Affichard, Joëlle and Foucauld, Jean-Baptiste de (eds) 1995: *Pluralisme et équité: la justice sociale dans les démocraties*. Paris: Commissariat du Plan/Esprit.

Albert, Michel 1991: *Capitalisme contre capitalisme*. Paris: Seuil.

Albrow, Martin and King, Elizabeth (eds) 1990: *Globalization, Knowledge and Society*. London: Sage.

Amselle, Jean-Loup 1996: *Vers un multiculturalisme français: l'empire et la coutume*. Paris: Aubier.

Anderson, Benedict 1991: *Imagined Communities: Reflections on the Origin and Spread of Nationalism*, 2nd rev. edn. London: Verso.

Apel, Karl Otto 1988: *Diskus und Verantwortung*. Frankfurt-am-Main: Suhrkamp.

Apter, David 1963: Political religion in the new nations. In Clifford Geertz (ed.), *Old Nations and New States*. New York: Free Press, 57–104.

Arendt, Hannah 1951: *The Origins of Totalitarianism*. New York: Harcourt, Brace & Co.

—— 1958: *The Human Condition*. Chicago: University of Chicago Press, 2nd edn, 1998.

—— 1961: *Between Past and Future: Six Exercises in Political Thought*. New York: Viking Press.

Aron, Raymond 1970: *Democracy and Totalitarianism*, trans. Valence Ionescu. London: Weidenfeld and Nicolson. Original French edn, 1965.

Balibar, Étienne and Wallerstein, Immanuel 1988: *Race, Nation, Class: Ambiguous Identities*, trans. Chris Turner. London: Verso.

Barret-Kriegel, Blandine 1979: *L'État et les esclaves*. Paris: Calmann-Lévy.

Barth, Fredrik (ed.) 1969: *Ethnic Groups and Boundaries*. London: Allen and Unwin.

Bauman, Zygmunt 1993: *Post-modern Ethics*. Oxford: Blackwell.

Bayart, Jean-François 1996: *L'illusion identitaire*. Paris: Fayard.

Beck, Ulrich 1986: *Risk Society: Towards a New Modernity*, trans. Mark Ritter. London: Sage.

Beck, Ulrich, Giddens, Anthony and Lash, Scott 1994: *Reflexive Modernization: Politics, Tradition and Aesthetics in the Modern Social Order*. Cambridge: Polity Press.

Bell, Daniel 1980: *The Winding Passage: Essays and Sociological Journeys, 1960–1980*. New York: Basic Books.

Bernham, Marshall 1982: *All that is Solid Melts into Air: The Experience of Modernity*. New York: Simon and Schuster.

Birdsall, Nancy 1993: *Social Development is Economic Development*, World Bank Policy Research Working Paper 123. Washington: World Bank.

Birnbaum, Pierre 1992: *Les Fous de la République: histoire politique des Juifs d'état de Gambetta à Vichy*. Paris: Fayard.

Bobbio, Norberto 1980: *Democracy and Dictatorship: The Nature and Limits of State Power*, trans. Peter Keneally. Cambridge: Polity Press. Original Italian edn, 1980.

—— 1987: *Which Socialism? Marxism, Socialism and Democracy*, trans. Roger Griffin. Cambridge: Polity Press. Original Italian edn, 1976.

—— 1987: *The Future of Democracy: A Defence of the Rules of the Game*, trans. Roger Griffin. Cambridge: Polity Press. Original Italian edn, 1984.

—— 1990: *Liberalism and Democracy*, trans. Martin Ryle and Kate Soper. London: Verso. Original Italian edn, 1988.

—— 1994: *Destra e sinistra*. Rome: Donzelli.

Caldéron, Fernando, Hopenhayn, Martin and Ottone, Ernesto 1996: *Esa esqiva modernidad. Desarrollo, ciudadania u cultura en América Latine y Caribe*. Caracas: UNESCO/Nueva Sociedad.

Castelain-Meunier, Christine 1997: *Mémoire d'habilitation*. Paris: EHESS.

Cohen, Jean and Arato, Andrew 1992: *Civil Society and Political Theory*. Cambridge, MA: MIT Press.

Cohn-Bendit, Daniel and Schmidt, Thomas 1993: *Heimat Babylon: Das Wagnis der multikulturellen Demokratie*. Hamburg: Haufmann und Lampe Verlag.

Connor, Walker 1994: *Ethno-Nationalism: The Quest for Understanding*. Princeton, NJ: Princeton University Press.

Crespi, Franco and Segatori, Roberto (eds) 1996: *Multiculturalismo e democrazia*. Rome: Donzelli/Centauri.

Danielsen, Don and Engle, Karen (eds) 1995: *After Identity*. London: Sage.

De Finis, Georgio and Scartezzini, Riccardo (eds) 1996: *Universalità e differenza: cosmopolitismo e relativismo nelle relazioni tra identità sociale e cultura*. Milan: Franco Angeli.

De Lauretis, Teresa 1994: *The Practice of Love: Lesbian Sexuality and Perverse Desire*. Bloomington: Indiana University Press.

Del Lago, Alessandro 1996: *Il Conflitto delle modernità*. Bologna: Il Mulino.

Delanoix, Georges and Taguieff, Pierre-André (eds) 1991: *Théorie du nationalisme*. Paris: Kimé.

Democrazie e Diritto 1995: nos 2–3: *Nazione*.

Descombes, Vincent 1994: Philosophie du jugement politique. *La Pensée politique*, 2.

—— 1995: Universalisme, égalité, singularité: réponse aux objections. *La Pensée politique*, 4.

Desroche, Henri 1973: *Sociologie de l'espérance*. Paris: Calmann-Lévy.

Diderot, Denis 1964: *Supplément au voyage de Bougainville*. In *Oeuvres philosophiques*, ed. P. Vernière. Paris: Garnier, 1964. Originally published in 1772.

Douglas, Mary 1970: *Purity and Danger*. Harmondsworth: Penguin.

—— 1995: Justice sociale et sentiment de justice. In Affichard and Foucauld, 23–149.

Dubet, François 1991: *Les Lycéens*. Paris: Seuil.

—— 1995: *Sociologie de l'expérience*. Paris: Seuil.

Dubet, François and Martuccelli, Danilo 1996: *À l'école*. Paris: Seuil.

Dumont, Louis 1983: *Essais sur l'individualisme: une perspective anthropologique sur l'idéologie moderne*. Paris: Seuil.

Elster, John (ed.) 1985: *The Multiple Self*. Cambridge: Cambridge University Press.

EPHESIA 1995: *La Place des femmes: les enjeux de l'identité et de l'égalité au regard des sciences sociales*. Paris: La Découverte.

Esprit 1992: *L'Universel au risque du multiculturalisme*. December.

—— 1996: *Le Totalitarianisme*, January–February.

Fabietti, Ugo 1995: *L'Identità etnica. Storia e critica de un concetto equivoco*. Rome: NIS.

Featherstone, Mike (ed.) 1990: *Global Culture: Nationalism, Globalization and Modernity*. London: Sage.

Featherstone, Mike, Lash, Scott and Robertson, Roland (eds) 1995: *Global Modernity*. London: Sage.

Ferrara, Alessandro (ed.) 1992: *Communitarismo e liberalismo*. Rome: Editori Riuniti.

—— 1994: *Intendersi a Babele: autenticità, phronesis, progetto della modernità*. Messina: Rubettino.

Ferry, Jean-Marc 1994: *Philosophie de la communication. II. Justice, politique et démocratie procédurale*. Paris: Cerf.

Ferry, Luc 1992: *Le Nouvel Ordre écologique: l'arbre, l'animal et l'homme*. Paris: Grasset.

—— 1996: *L'Homme-dieu ou le sens de la vie*. Paris: Grasset.

Fichte, Johann Gottlieb 1968: *Addresses to the German Nation*, ed. with an introduction by George Armstrong Kelly. New York: Harper and Row. Originally pub. 1807–8.

Finkielkraut, Alain 1984: *La Défaite de la pensée*. Paris: Gallimard.

—— 1996: *L'Humanité perdue: essai sur le XXe siècle*. Paris: Gallimard.

Friedman, Jonathan 1994: *Cultural Identity and Global Process*. London: Sage.

Fukuyama, Francis 1992: *The End of History and the Last Man*. London: Hamish Hamilton.

Furet, François 1995: *Le Passé d'une illusion: essai sur l'idée communiste au XX siècle*. Paris: Robert Laffont/Calmann-Lévy.

Gans, Herbert J. 1988: *Middle American Individualism: The Future of Liberal Democracy*. New York: Free Press.

Garcia Delgardo, Daniel R. 1994: *Estado y sociedad: la nueva relacion a partir del cambio estructural*. Buenos Aires: Flacso Norma.

Gaspard, Françoise and Khosrokhavar, Farhad 1994: *Le Foulard et la république*. Paris: La Découverte.

Gauchet, Marcel 1980: Les Droits de l'homme ne sont pas une politique. *Le Débat*, 3.

Gaulejac, Vincent de 1996: *Les Sources de la honte*. Paris: Desclée de Brouwer.
Geertz, Clifford 1963: The integrative revolution: primordial sentiments and civil politics in the United States. In *Old Societies and New States*. New York: Free Press.
Gellner, Ernest 1983: *Nations and Nationalism*. Oxford: Blackwell.
Giddens, Anthony 1991: *Modernity and Self-Identity: Self and Society in the Late Modern Age*. Cambridge: Polity Press.
—— 1992: *The Transformation of Intimacy*. Cambridge: Polity Press.
Gilligan, Carol 1982: *In a Different Voice*. Cambridge, MA: Harvard University Press.
Glazer, Nathan and Moynihan, Daniel 1963: *Beyond the Melting Pot*. Cambridge, MA: Harvard University Press and MIT Press.
—— (eds) 1975: *Ethnicity, Theory and Experience*. Cambridge, MA: Harvard University Press.
Gorz, André 1980: *Adieu au prolétariat*. Paris: Galilée.
Habermas, Jürgen 1975: *Legitimation Crisis*, trans. Thomas McCarthy. London and Boston: Beacon Press. Original German edn, 1973.
—— 1990: *Moral Consciousness and Communicative Action*, trans. Christian Lenhardt and Shierry Weber Nicholsen. Cambridge: Polity Press. Original German edn, 1983.
—— 1995: Reconciliation through the public use of reason: remarks on John Rawls's *Political Liberalism*. *Journal of Philosophy*, 92.
Hassner, Pierre 1992: Vers un universalisme pluriel? *Esprit*. December.
Haut Conseil de l'Intégration 1995: *Liens culturels et intégration*. Paris: La Documentation française.
Heller, Agnes 1985: *The Power of Shame: A Rational Perspective*. London: Routledge.
—— Heller, Agnes and Feher, Ferenc 1991: *The Grandeur and Twilight of Radical Universalism*. New Brunswick, NJ: Transactions Press.
Hirschmann, Albert 1972: *The Passions and the Interests: Political Arguments for Capitalism before its Triumph*. Princeton, NJ: Princeton University Press.
Hobsbawm, Eric 1962: *The Age of Revolution 1789–1848*. London: Weidenfeld and Nicolson.
—— 1990: *Nations and Nationalisms since 1780: Programme, Myth, Reality*. London: Weidenfeld and Nicolson.
Horowitz, Donald and Noiriel, Gérard (eds) 1992: *Immigrants in Two Democracies: French and American Experiences*. New York: New York University Press.
Huntington, Samuel P. 1996: *The Clash of Civilizations and the Remaking of World Order*. New York: Simon and Schuster.
International Review of Sociology 1996: Special issue 1613 on *Gender, Space, Perception and Construction of Social Reality*, ed. Lorella Cedron.
Jonas, Hans 1979: *Das Prinzip Verantwortung*. Frankfurt-am-Main: Insel Verlag.
Kershaw, Ian 1994: Totalitarianism revisited: Nazism and Stalinism in a comparative perspective. *Tel Aviv Jahrbuch für deutsche Geschichte*, 23.
Kis, Janos 1989: *L'Égale dignité: essais sur les fondements des droits de l'homme*. Paris: Seuil.
Kristeva, Julia 1991: *Strangers to Ourselves*, trans. Léon S. Roudiez. Hemel Hempstead: Harvester Wheatsheaf, 1991.
Laing, R. D. 1965: *The Divided Self*. Harmondsworth: Penguin.

Lapeyronnie, Didier 1992: *Les Immigrés en Europe: politiques locales d'intégration*. Paris: La Documentation française.
——1993: *L'Individu et les minorités: la France et la Grande-Bretagne face à leurs immigrés*. Paris: PUF.
Lash, Scott and Friedmann, Jonathan (eds) 1992: *Modernity and Identity*. Oxford: Blackwell.
Lefort, Claude 1976: *Un Homme en trop*. Paris: Seuil.
——1981: *L'Invention démocratique: les limites de la domination totalitaire*. Paris: Fayard.
Lévi-Strauss, Claude 1952: *Race and History*. Paris: UNESCO.
——1977: *L'Identité*, ed. J.-M. Benoit. Paris: OIST.
——1985: *The View from Afar*, trans. Joachim Neugroschel and Phoebe Ross. Oxford: Blackwell. Original French edn, 1983.
Levy, Bernard-Henri 1994: *La Pureté dangereuse*. Paris: Grasset.
Lipovetsky, Gilles 1983: *L'Ère du vide: essais sur l'individualisme contemporain*. Paris: Gallimard.
——1987: *L'Empire de l'éphémère: la mode et son destin dans les sociétés modernes*. Paris: Gallimard.
——1992: *Le Crépuscule du devoir: l'éthique indolore des nouveaux temps démocratiques*. Paris: Gallimard.
Marshall, T. H. 1964: *Class, Citizenship and Social Development*. New York: Doubleday.
McIntyre, Alistair 1981: *After Virtue*. London: Duckworth.
Melucci, Alberto 1996a: *Challenging Codes: Collective Action in the Information Age*. Cambridge: Cambridge University Press.
——1996b: *The Playing Self: Person and Meaning in a Planetary Society*. New English edn. Cambridge: Cambridge University Press.
Meschonnic, Henri 1988: *Modernité, modernité*. Paris: Gallimard. New edn, 1993.
Meyer-Bisch, Patrice (ed.) 1993: *Les Droits culturels: une catégorie sous-développée des droits de l'homme*. Fribourg: Éditions Universitaires.
Mongardini, Carlo and Maniscalco, Maria-Luisa (eds) 1989: *Moderno e postmoderno: crisi di identità di una cultura erulo della sociologia*. Rome: Pulzani.
Montesquieu 1993: *Persian Letters*, trans. C. J. Betts. Harmondsworth: Penguin. Originally published 1721.
Noiriel, Gérard 1988: *Le Creuset français: histoire de l'immigration, XIX–XXe siècle*. Paris: Seuil.
Peyrefitte, Alain 1995: *La Société de confiance*. Paris: Odile Jacob.
Polanyi, Karl 1944: *The Great Transformation*. New York: Rinehart.
Poutignat, Philippe and Streiff-Fenart, Jocelyne 1995: *Théorie de l'ethnicité*. Paris: PUF.
Rawls, John 1996: *Political Liberalism*. New York: Columbia University Press.
Remotti, Francesco 1996: *Contra l'identità*. Rome: Laterza.
Renaut, Alain 1989: *L'Ère de l'individu*. Paris: Gallimard.
Revue international de politique comparée 1994: *L'État et la nation* (1/3).
Rosanvallon, Pierre and Viveret, Patrick 1977: *Pour une nouvelle culture politique*. Paris: Seuil.
Roy, Olivier 1992: *L'Échec de l'islamisme politique*. *Esprit*. August–September.
Rubert de Ventos, Xavier 1994: *Nacionalismos: el laberinto de la identitada*. Madrid: Espasa Calpe.

Sandel, Michael 1984: *Liberalism and its Critics.* New York: New York University Press.
—— 1995: *Democracy's Discontent: America in Search of a Public Philosophy.* Cambridge, MA: Belknap Press and Harvard University Press.
Schnapper, Dominique 1992: *La France de l'intégration: sociologie de la nation en 1990.* Paris: Gallimard.
—— 1994: *La Communauté des citoyens: sur l'idée moderne de nation.* Paris: Gallimard.
Segalen, Martine (ed.) 1989: *L'Autre et le semblable.* Paris: CNRS.
Semprun, Jorge 1997: *Literature or Life,* trans. Linda Coverdale. New York: Viking Press. Original Trench edn, 1997.
Sen, Amartya, K. 1984: *Resources, Values and Development.* Oxford: Blackwell and Cambridge, MA: Harvard University Press.
—— 1996: Development Thinking at the Beginning of the XXIst Century, paper delivered to the Development Thinking and Practice Conference organized by International Development Bank, Washington DC, September 1996.
Shklar, Judith 1969: *Men and Citizens: The Study of Rousseau's Social Theory.* Cambridge: Cambridge University Press.
Smith, Anthony and Williams, Bernard (eds) 1981: *The Ethnic Revival in the Modern World.* Cambridge: Cambridge University Press.
Tabboni, Simonetta 1996a: Lo Straniero e il dibattito contemporanea sulla democrazia. In Crespi and Segatori 1996, 121–34.
—— 1996b: Sociologia dello straniero, sociologia del razismo e dell'etnicità essenzialista. In De Finis and Scartezzini 1996, 235–54.
Taguieff, Pierre-André 1990: *La Force du préjugé,* new edn. Paris: Gallimard.
Taylor, Charles 1992: *Le Malaise de la modernité.* Montréal: Bellarmin.
Taylor, Charles et al. 1994: *Multiculturalism: Examining the Politics of Recognition,* ed. Amy Gutman. Princeton, NJ: Princeton University Press.
Todd, Emmanuel 1994: *Le Destin des immigrés.* Paris: Seuil.
Todorov, Tzvetan 1981: *On Human Diversity: Nationalism, Racism and Exoticism in French Thought,* trans. Catherine Porter. Cambridge, MA: Harvard University Press.
—— 1991: *Face à l'extrême.* Paris: Seuil.
Touraine, Alain 1971: *The Post-Industrial Society: Tomorrow's History: Class, Conflict and Culture in the Programmed Society,* trans. Leonard Fox Mayhew. New York: Random House. Original French edn, 1969.
—— 1988: *La Parole et le sang.* Paris: Odile Jacob.
—— 1995: *Critique of Modernity,* trans. David Macey. Oxford: Blackwell. Original French edn, 1992.
—— 1997: *What is Democracy?,* trans. David Macey. Boulder, CO: Westview Press. Original French edn, 1994.
Tribalat, Michèle 1996: *De l'immigration à l'assimilation: enquête sur les populations d'origine étrangère en France.* Paris: La Découverte/INED.
Turnaturi, Gabriella 1994: *Flirt, seduzione, amore: Simmel e le emozione.* Milan: Anabasi.
UNESCO 1996: *L'Education: un trésor est caché dedans,* ed. Jacques Delors. Paris: UNESCO.
United Nations Development Programme 1990, 1995: *Report on Human Development.* New York: UNDP.

Veca, Salvatore 1989: *Etica e politica*. Milan: Garzanti.
——1990: *Cittadinanza*. Milan: Feltrinelli.
Vernant, Jean-Pierre 1989: *L'Individu, la mort, l'amour: soi-même et l'autre en Grèce ancienne*. Paris: Gallimard.
Viard, Jacques 1996: *La Société d'archipel*. La Tour d'Aigues: Éditions de l'Aube.
Walzer, Michael 1992: Les Deux Universalismes. *Esprit*, December.
Wieviorka, Michel 1991: *L'Espace du racisme*. Paris: Seuil.
——1993a: *La Démocratie à l'epreuve: nationalisme, populisme, ethnicité*. Paris: La Découverte.
——(ed.) 1993b: *Racisme et modernité*. Paris: La Découverte.
——(ed.) 1996: *Une Société fragmentée? Le Multiculturalisme en débat*. Paris: La Découverte.
Young, Iris M. 1990: *Justice and the Politics of Difference*. Princeton, NJ: Princeton University Press.

Index